U.S. DIPLOMACY
SINCE 1900

U.S. DIPLOMACY SINCE 1900

Sixth Edition

ROBERT D. SCHULZINGER
University of Colorado

New York   Oxford
OXFORD UNIVERSITY PRESS
2008

Oxford University Press, Inc., publishes works that further Oxford University's
objective of excellence in research, scholarship, and education.

Oxford   New York
Auckland   Cape Town   Dar es Salaam   Hong Kong   Karachi
Kuala Lumpur   Madrid   Melbourne   Mexico City   Nairobi
New Delhi   Shanghai   Taipei   Tokyo   Toronto

With offices in
Argentina   Austria   Brazil   Chile   Czech Republic   France   Greece
Guatemala   Hungary   Italy   Japan   Poland   Portugal   Singapore
South Korea   Switzerland   Thailand   Turkey   Ukraine   Vietnam

Copyright © 1984, 1990, 1994, 1998, 2002, 2008 by Oxford University Press, Inc.

Published by Oxford University Press, Inc.
198 Madison Avenue, New York, New York 10016
http://www.oup.com

Oxford is a registered trademark of Oxford University Press

Library of Congress Cataloging-in-Publication Data

Schulzinger, Robert D., 1945–
U.S. diplomacy since 1900 / by Robert D. Schulzinger. — 6th ed.
p. cm.
Includes bibliographical references (p.) and index.
ISBN 978–0–19–532049–7 (pbk.: alk. paper) 1. United States—
Foreign relations—20th century. 2. United States—Foreign relations—
2001- I. Title. II. Title: United States diplomacy since 1900.
E744.S399 2008
327.73009'04—dc22

Printing number: 9   8   7   6   5   4

Printed in the United States of America
on acid-free paper

For my niece and nephews
Sara, Ari, Jonathan, and Joshua

Contents

Preface to the Sixth Edition

Interest in U.S. foreign relations has never been higher than it is in the early twenty-first century. It has increased dramatically since the terrorist attacks of September 11, 2001, and the wars the United States has fought in Afghanistan and Iraq. Students have a deep thirst for understanding the roots of contemporary U.S. foreign policy. They want to know what has changed and what has remained constant in the more than a century since the Spanish-American-Philippine War of 1898.

The sixth edition of *U.S. Diplomacy Since 1900* addresses this demand for an understanding of the historical antecedents of contemporary foreign relations. I have revised the book more extensively than at any time since its original publication in 1984. Specifically, I have consolidated the three chapters in earlier editions that dealt with the United States in World War I and its aftermath into a single chapter entitled The United States in the Great War. Shortening the account of the years before 1914 has enabled me to devoted two full chapters at the end of the book to events after the end of the Cold War.

The sixth edition incorporates the latest scholarship in the history of international affairs. Much of this new work uses the insights of work on gender, race, ethnicity, and intellectual history. There has also been a vast increase in the documentary record of the history of the U.S. government in foreign relations. I have updated the historiographical parts of each chapter to reflect recent works and to omit accounts that are no longer as useful to students and scholars as they were when earlier editions of this book were published.

The revisions in the sixth edition have been informed by my work since 2001 as editor in chief of *Diplomatic History: The Journal of the Society for Historians of American Foreign Relations*. As editor in chief, I have been privileged to read and arrange for the publication of some of the newest and most intellectually stimulating work on the history of American foreign relations. The insights of dozens of historians whose work has appeared in *Diplomatic History* have deepened my understanding of the field, and I have incorporated their findings in many places in the sixth edition of *U.S. Diplomacy Since 1900*. In addition, I have served on the State Department's Historical Advisory Committee and the Central Intelligence Agency's Historical Review Panel while revising this book. Both of these groups work hard to make the historical documentary record of U.S. diplomacy accessible to the public. This greater access has made the recent scholarship on the field more sophisticated and detailed than it has ever been.

Every year I teach this history of U.S. foreign relations to more than 100 undergraduate students at the University of Colorado, Boulder. Their questions, concerns, and insights constantly revitalize my enthusiasm for the subject. Their curiosity about the direction of U.S. foreign relations has encouraged me to revise this book to help answer their many question.

Boulder, Colorado   R.D.S.

Preface to the First Edition

Whenever I answer the all-purpose icebreaker "And what do *you* do," with "I'm a professor of American diplomatic history," a sure, swift sneer comes back: "I didn't know the United States had a foreign policy." *American Diplomacy in the Twentieth Century* is my effort to show that it does. It traces the record of the foreign relations of the United States from their modern beginnings in the 1890s to the present.

This book tells what has happened, who has made decisions, how they have done it, what their critics and supporters have said, how Americans remember what their leaders have done, and what difference those recollections made for current actions. It begins with an explanation titled "The Setting of American Foreign Policy," a chapter devoted to the international environment in which diplomats have operated, the types of people who have been in charge, their relations with nongovernmental supporters and detractors, and the ideas which have moved officials, commentators, and critics. Thirteen narrative chapters follow. Each can be read in its own right, but the coherence of foreign policy becomes most clear if readers keep in mind the framework laid out at the beginning.

Readers will notice the extra attention paid to historiography—analysis of the controversies among writers over the causes, significance, and consequences of events. These capsule evaluations of the writings of professors, diplomats, politicians, reporters, and columnists demonstrate the ongoing conversation between present and past. They appear throughout the narrative rather than being packaged discreetly at the back of the book because memory, whether accurate or flawed, always affects current actions. To understand American foreign relations at any time in the century requires unraveling the way contemporaries recalled earlier diplomatic episodes. More than anything, historiography suggests that what happens today affects our interpretation of a living past which, in turn, alters our perception of the morning's headlines.

Many people and institutions helped make this book possible. Four close friends, all scholars of recent American history, read the manuscript and made it better with their suggestions. Leonard Dinnerstein, Bruce Kuklick, Leo Ribuffo, and Michael Schaller all provided unstinting encouragement with their comprehensive comments on early drafts. Useful details, interpretations, and approaches also came from the following fellow researchers, friends, and students: Robert Blum, Robert Dallek, Alton Frye, Lloyd Gardner, Daniel Guttman, Walter Hixson, Richard Immerman, James Jankowski, Melvyn Leffler, John McCamant, James Nugent, William Olson, Bradford Perkins, Robert Pois, Barry Rubin, Lee Scamehorn, Ronald Steel, Peter Van Ness, and William Wei. During the summer of 1981, I directed a National Endowment for the Humanities Summer Seminar on "The War in Vietnam and Its Legacy." I was privileged to try out my ideas on recent foreign policy on the participants, many of whom helped me sharpen my concepts. I am most grateful to five seminar participants for their perceptive comments: Frank Burdick, Dorothy Donnelly, John Hellmann, Milton Katz, and Marianna Sullivan.

Nancy Lane, my editor at Oxford, deserves special praise. She has been enthusiastic about this project from the beginning, always has had the right word to say, and kept the book moving along. No author could want more. Abby Levine, Oxford's copy editor, also made this book better.

Generous financial support came from the University of Colorado's Council on Research and Creative Work, the Council on Foreign Relations, and the National Endowment for the Humanities. My thanks to all.

The manuscript was typed, retyped, and typed again by Tina Ament, Holly Hammond, Sandy Marsh, Carol Watson, and Dolores Young.

Marie Manes, good friend and gifted writer, has been a never-ending source of inspiration. As always, my parents have been a great strength with their reassurance, extra bedroom, and indispensable editorial help. My sisters Ellen Adler and Jane Fox and their husbands Bill and Michael can always be counted on for good food, good talk, and good perspective. I've dedicated this book to their children, a happy quartet whom I like very much. I expect them to read it and promote it.

Boulder, Colorado   R.D.S.
April 1983

The Setting of U.S. Foreign Policy

AN AGE OF INTERDEPENDENCE AND GLOBALIZATION

United States foreign policy since the Spanish-American-Cuban-Philippine War of 1898 has sought to ensure U.S. supremacy in the Western Hemisphere while at the same time asserting American influence widely around the globe. Until 1945 U.S. foreign policy makers sought to fashion the United States into a great power, the equal of the major European nations. During the Cold War era, the United States surpassed the Europeans and contended with the Soviet Union, the other so-called superpower, for mastery of world politics. In the decade after the Cold War, it stood at the apex of an international hierarchy. The men and women in charge of U.S. foreign policy have usually based their statecraft on the idea that the United States is in a unique position to provide balance and stability to world politics. In an era of increasing economic and cultural interdependence, or globalization, the wealth, military power, and cultural diversity of the United States has helped officials promote the idea that the United States was bound to lead. This very preeminence has enjoyed considerable support at home and internationally from people who have benefitted from the United States. The preponderance of American power has also provoked criticism and doubts that the United States has used its political, economic, and military might in the world's best interests.

Since 1900 most officials in charge of setting American foreign policy have consistently sought to engage the United States deeply in political and economic affairs beyond the water's edge. Outside the executive branch, members of Congress, the press, and well-spoken and influential private citizens have all sought to set the direction of the United States in foreign affairs.

The power of many nations has waxed and waned, but much of the international environment remained familiar after 1900. Nations competed and cooperated during a century of rapid technological change and improved communications. These developments seemed to shrink the size of the world: a process often called interdependence or globalization. Americans welcomed the challenges of a shrinking world. In the Bicentennial Year of 1976, one-fifth of the members of Congress expressed their willingness to sign a Declaration of Interdependence with the rest of the world. Twenty years later, after the end of the Cold War, Deputy Secretary of State Strobe Talbott explained how globalization demanded even greater involvement of the United States in international affairs. He noted that "in an increasingly interdependent world, Americans have a stake in how other countries govern, or misgovern themselves. The larger and more close-knit the community of nations that choose democratic forms of government, the safer and more prosperous Americans will be."

Identical arguments about the knitting together of the world's regions and resources and similar suspicions of "rabid nationalism" filled the air earlier in the century. In 1910 Norman Angell, a British peace reformer, surveyed the world economy in the generation after 1880 and decided that foreign conquest no longer made sense. "The cause of this profound change," he assured skittish citizens, "is due mainly to the complex financial interdependence of the capitals of the world."

The last decades of the nineteenth century have aptly been called an "age of imperialism," an epoch which has continued, with some modifications, until the present. The major powers of Western Europe, joined by Russia, Japan, and the United States, alternately combined with and opposed one another for preeminence throughout the world. Earlier in the nineteenth century, the United States had maintained a pose of bored indifference to Old World quarrels outside the Western Hemisphere. This aloof neutrality derived from preoccupation with the creation of a Yankee empire on the North American continent. English-speaking settlers, mostly Protestant and white but many taking black slaves with them, moved west to subjugate, displace, and kill native American Indians and Spanish-language Mexicans. Officials in Washington responded to calls for continental "manifest destiny" with wars against Great Britain (1812–1815), Mexico (1846–1848), native American Indians (1783–1890), and Spain (1898), and threats against and purchases from France (1791–1799, 1803, 1867), Spain (1783–1898), Britain (1818–1848), Russia (1821–1867), and Mexico (1825–1853). These expansionist thrusts provided vast territory and an enormous internal market. The triumph of American arms and the submission of nonwhite, non-Protestant peoples left a legacy of cultural supremacy for the twentieth century.

Having completed the conquest of North America, the United States by the 1890s participated fully in the struggle of the great powers around the world. To observers in Europe and even to some Americans who wanted to see their country become a great power, the conduct of American diplomacy imitated Europe's outward thrust. In the 1890s the United States grandly expanded the scope of the Monroe Doctrine in the midst of a dispute between Venezuela and Great Britain (1893), added the Hawaiian Islands to its possessions (1897), and fought what U.S. ambassador to Great Britain John Hay told his friend Theodore Roosevelt was "a splendid little war" with Spain (1898). That brief passage of arms left the United States in possession of the islands of Puerto Rico, Cuba, and the Philippines. The expansion into the Pacific provided "vast and varied opportunities for further increases of American exports" into China, the diplomat W. W. Rockhill asserted. Cushman Davis, chairman of the Senate Committee on Foreign Relations, thought that the newly acquired Pacific islands meant that "we can commercially [do] what we please" in Asia.

While some Americans, such as Assistant Secretary of the Navy Theodore Roosevelt, his friend Massachusetts senator Henry Cabot Lodge, and his teacher Adm. Alfred Thayer Mahan, comfortably acknowledged that they were "imperialists," others did not like this label. For some, such as the industrialist Andrew Carnegie, the seizure of territory by the United States marked a departure from the traditions of republican rule. Carnegie's brand of antiimperialism led him to combine with men such as the other senator from Massachusetts, George Frisbee Hoar, to block the annexation of the Philippines. Americans who supported administering the islands found a champion in President William McKinley, who assured a group of visiting Methodist ministers that a night on his knees left him with God's clear instruction "that there was nothing left for us to do but to take them all, and to educate the Filipinos, and uplift and civilize and Christianize them." Such moralizers were not as proud of the imperialist identification as Roosevelt and his circle.

Americans who resisted the tag of imperialism recalled how previous diplomats had sought to distinguish their conduct from that of the Europeans. After all, that premise underlay the Monroe Doctrine proclaimed in 1823. President James Monroe then declared in his message to Congress that the United States would remain aloof from European quarrels because its democratic social system differed from the autocracies of Europe. Smugness like that often made Americans seem overbearing to nineteenth-century Europeans. Some of them, such as Britain's prime minister at the time of the American Civil War, Lord Palmerston, ridiculed a nation of slaveholders claiming to be democrats. Nevertheless, many Americans liked to believe that their country conducted a "democratic" foreign policy. And advocates of a more active American role in world affairs were loath to acknowledge similarities between their actions and those of other great powers.

Even Theodore Roosevelt, who happily called himself an imperialist, stressed the altruistic aims of his forward foreign policy. While Europeans spoke of bringing the benefits of "civilization" to benighted races of the world, they seldom lost sight of the competitive nature of the race for preeminence. Americans, on the other hand, often implied they differed from the Europeans in having the best interests of the world at heart. Americans proclaimed that the United States had entered the race to prevent the bad Europeans from conquering the world. Instead, the United States, richer and more republican than everyone else, could do more to mediate disputes among other countries than any other imperial state. This conviction gave a missionary flavor to American diplomacy that often irritated and sometimes bewildered people in the rest of the world.

HOW AMERICANS MAKE FOREIGN POLICY

Government Officials

Who has been in charge of American foreign policy? How have they created it? At the top, of course, stands the president. At times, notably under the two Roosevelts, Woodrow Wilson, Herbert Hoover, John F. Kennedy, Richard M. Nixon, and George H. W. Bush, the president himself has been someone who has thought deeply about foreign affairs. Other occupants of the White House have also conducted foreign policy, and some have presided over crises, over successes and failures of magnificent proportions. Nonetheless, the remainder of twentieth-century presidents did not put an individual stamp on the conduct of America's foreign relations.

While several presidents have had distinctive notions of what to do in foreign affairs, most of the elections in which they ran for the highest office turned on domestic issues. Exceptions prove the rule. When foreign affairs received attention during presidential contests, voters had trouble distinguishing the views of Democrats and Republicans. Two presidential campaigns, 1916 and 1940, occurred while the United States stood neutral in world wars. Both times the rivals expressed interest in the outcome while assuring the voters that the United States would not fight. Foreign affairs questions have arisen in other presidential elections, especially those after World War II, but rarely, if ever, has foreign policy been the decisive issue.

In office, the chief executive divides his attention between foreign and domestic concerns. Many presidents, including those who claimed no special diplomatic expertise, enjoyed the drama of meeting other rulers. Foreign travel gave them a sense of accomplishment, the image of activity, and relief from carping critics. Woodrow Wilson conducted a campaignlike swing through Europe after World War I. Herbert Hoover went to Latin America to show that the United States no longer sought domination in the hemisphere. Franklin D. Roosevelt served longer than any president and traveled more than his predecessors. Before the Second World War, he cruised the Caribbean and South America. During the war the navy and air force took him to conferences in the North Atlantic, North Africa, Iran, and the Soviet Crimea. With the arrival of airplanes, presidents became even more peripatetic. Truman followed FDR in traveling to summit conferences. Dwight D. Eisenhower, a popular figure to Americans with his wide grin and upraised arms, aroused audiences around the globe. John F. Kennedy started the practice of sending his wife to mend fences. Lyndon B. Johnson, Richard M. Nixon, Gerald Ford, Jimmy Carter, George H. W. Bush, and Bill Clinton all seemed to cheer up when they departed from Washington and traveled to other countries.

Since a president cannot spend all of his time dealing with foreign affairs, he assembles a staff of subordinates who do that. The principal aide entrusted with foreign affairs has been the secretary of state. In the twentieth century, several of them—John Hay (1898–1905), Robert Lansing (1915–1919), Charles Evans Hughes (1921–1925), Dean Acheson (1949–1953), John Foster Dulles (1953–1959), Henry Kissinger (1973–1977), and, possibly, although it is too early to have proper perspective, James Baker (1989–1992) and Madeleine Albright (1997–2001)—have left records of achievement. Others have been remembered primarily because they occupied the premier position in a president's cabinet.

All secretaries of state want to be the government's foremost initiator of foreign policies, but they have shared their authority with other functionaries. In the process, secretaries have sometimes become jealous of competitors— the heads of the Treasury, Commerce, Agriculture, and War and Navy (later Defense) Departments. Since no one can draw a clear line separating foreign and domestic policies of the government, remaining cabinet secretaries reason that they have the right to pursue their own goals overseas. Hence, the Commerce or Treasury secretaries have handled questions of international economics. Military leaders, who realize that diplomacy rests on the forces under their command, believe that their voices should reach the president's ear.

Sometimes the president mediates disputes among his cabinet departments through his personal staff. In the post–World War II era, originators of numerous schemes for reform of the apparatus of foreign policy noticed that the president himself had a set of personal and private advisers who whispered foreign policy instructions in his ear. The process began early in the twentieth century. Theodore Roosevelt had what he called a *kitchen cabinet*, made up of personal friends who went outside the traditional channels of the executive departments to advise him on what to do abroad. In the two world wars, special presidential envoys and advisers—men such as Edward M. House, who advised Woodrow Wilson, and Harry Hopkins, who worked with Franklin D. Roosevelt—achieved positions of dominance in the conduct of foreign policy. Their easy access to the president caused tremors of envy in the corridors of the Department of State, whose professional staff found themselves shunted aside by presidents who wanted to control foreign policy.

As the United States came to adopt an ever more active role in world politics, whereby every move made had effects on every other state in the world, the president's special adviser took on even more tasks. The National Security Act, passed in 1947 to make some sense out of the confused lines of authority in foreign affairs, established a National Security Council headed by an official who was to be the president's chief of staff in foreign affairs. The national security adviser made few waves until the 1960s, but in the administration of John F. Kennedy he became a dominant figure. From McGeorge Bundy (1961–1965), to Walt Whitman Rostow (1965–1969), to Henry Kissinger (1969–1975), to Zbigniew Brzezinski (1977–1981), to Condoleezza Rice (2001–2005), the modern national security adviser was often a former college professor with geopolitical inclinations who wanted the United States to pursue an activist role. From his or her original duties as housekeeper of foreign affairs, the national security adviser became the official who maintained direction in American foreign policy.

If the executive branch of the government speaks with several voices on foreign affairs, the problem becomes still more complicated when Congress gets involved. All modern presidents have wanted to use Congress to ratify their foreign policies, but none has wanted to share power with the lawmakers. Legislators have been permitted to lead cheers for a president's conduct, and sometimes the Senate and House have acted as mediators between the chief executive and the public at large. But members of Congress do not always passively accept their role as the meek upholders of the president's undertakings. Sometimes members of Congress have their own projects in foreign affairs. Issues which involve foreign and domestic affairs together, such as immigration and trade, always have attracted congressional scrutiny. Usually the interests of the representatives have diverged from those of the executive because Congress members bend to constituents' wishes while presidents often look to the effects of immigration restriction or trade barriers on events overseas. Occasionally, when Congress has tried to conduct trade or immigration policy, the president and his advisers have sighed and said, in effect, "Well, what can you expect from a parochial group who care only about 'low policy'? We in the foreign affairs department look to a greater question of 'high policy.'" Distinctions between "high" and "low" policy were imports from Europe, where the aristocratic diplomats of the eighteenth and nineteenth centuries claimed that they paid attention to the "high" questions of war and peace. "Low" issues of trade and the movement of individuals were subjects fit only for the money-conscious middle class.

Unfortunately for the self-esteem of American diplomats, Congress refused to keep to "low" questions. During and after the First World War, in the period before the Second World War, in the early Cold War, and during the war in Vietnam, lawmakers became interested in the "higher" questions of whether and how the United States should get involved in foreign conflicts. Sometimes legislators accused the president and his secretaries of state of aping the Europeans by getting the country involved in foreign wars. At other times, senators and representatives did not think that the president had been militant enough. Now and then Congress went on investigatory binges, calling officials to testify why they "lost" China, why they thought it a good idea to slip Fidel Castro a poisoned cigar, or why they overthrew the government of Chile. In each episode of congressional attempt to control foreign policy, the president and his advisers responded with a combination of disdain and fear, vowing all the while to quiet Congress.

Outsiders

Much as officials might like it to be the case, foreign policy is by no means the exclusive realm of the government. Some critics of American diplomacy even suggest that the government really is not the prime mover in diplomacy. Instead, a group of dissenters, often called *revisionists*, pointed to the domination of the foreign policy of the United States by businesses, which long for markets. These charges, first raised by antiimperialists in the 1890s, gained currency through revisionist writers such as Charles Beard and Harry Elmer Barnes in the twenties and thirties and were revived in the post–World War II years by an enthusiastic group of diplomatic historians influenced by William Appleman Williams. In an important work, *The Tragedy of American Diplomacy*, first published in 1959, Williams argues that twentieth-century American diplomacy has sadly been characterized by continuing attempts to find markets for goods that could not be sold at home. Business leaders and farmers, who also wanted to export their products, persuaded Washington to adopt an "Open Door" policy which called upon all of the nations of the world to offer a "fair field and no favor" to the goods produced by all industrialized nations. According to this view, the Open Door policy that resulted was made up of equal measures of avarice, hypocrisy, and a stubborn refusal to acknowledge what actually went on in the rest of the world.

While revisionists occasionally overlooked any foreign policy impulses *other* than the urge to expand exports, they did open eyes to the role played by nongovernmental spokesmen in setting diplomatic goals. Government has never been a simple puppet of great interests, dancing to a tune set by the Rockefeller family, as some critics claim, but neither has it ignored the needs of powerful interests. Sometimes officials hope outsiders will be quiet and accept policies set by their "betters." But on other occasions, people in Washington have eagerly followed the lines set down by planners who did not hold public office. In fact, no one can untangle officeholders and private citizens. A "foreign policy establishment" arose, made up of men (and much later women) who alternated tours of government service with stints in private institutions—law firms, banking houses, universities, research foundations and institutions, or industrial corporations. Several secretaries of state—Elihu Root (1905–1909), Philander C. Knox (1909–1913), Robert Lansing (1915–1920), Charles Evans Hughes (1921–1925), Henry L. Stimson (1929–1933), Dean Acheson (1949–1953), John Foster Dulles (1953–1959), William P. Rogers (1969–1973), Cyrus Vance (1977–1980), and Warren Christopher (1993–1997)—came from prominent law firms. Edward Stettinius (1944–1945) had been president of United States Steel; Dean Rusk (1961–1968) came from the Rockefeller Foundation; Alexander Haig (1981–1982) had headed United Technologies, a major supplier of modern weaponry; and George P. Shultz (1982–1989) was president of the Bechtel Corporation, a multinational construction firm, before returning to Washington. Important officials of the Commerce, Defense, and Treasury departments, which had major roles in setting foreign policy, came from heavy industry (Secretary of Commerce Herbert Hoover [mining] and Secretaries of Defense Charles Wilson, Robert McNamara [automobiles], and Caspar Weinberger [international construction]). Investment banking supplied Secretary of Defense James Forrestal. Secretary of the Treasury Andrew Mellon (1921–1929) made his fortune in aluminum and banking.

Much of the theorizing about foreign affairs originates in the minds of journalists, academics (in universities and private research organizations such as the Council on Foreign Relations, the Brookings Institution, and the American Enterprise Institute), international lawyers, political activists, or religious leaders who did not take jobs in the government. The daily business of conducting foreign affairs demands so much attention that officeholders rely on the ideas of outsiders with the leisure to create plans for the future. Some of these figures, men such as the columnist Walter Lippmann, editor of *Foreign*

Affairs, Hamilton Fish Armstrong, and Columbia professor James T. Shotwell, exercised influence while taking only minor government positions for short times. Others—*Time* publisher Henry Luce and Reinhold Niebuhr, the neo-orthodox theologian—never joined the government but made their views known. Still other professors—Henry Kissinger, Zbigniew Brzezinski, and James Schlesinger—established solid academic reputations before turning full time to public affairs.

FUNDAMENTAL INTERESTS

Regardless of their positions in private life, opinion molders have served the function of setting limits of acceptable or responsible debate on foreign policy. Their theories have given foreign policy a sense of consistency, undisturbed by changes in presidential administrations and sometimes impervious to alterations in the world as a whole. Not that there has been unanimity in views among the establishment over the course of the century. Some thinkers, such as Andrew Carnegie, advocated "internationalism"—a belief in international cooperation to solve world difficulties—while others, such as Henry Cabot Lodge, favored "nationalism"—an approach that paid less attention to the desires of other nations. Adm. Alfred Thayer Mahan and civilian strategists Nicholas John Spyckman and Bernard Brodie emphasized the role of force in international relations, while Brooks Adams stressed economic power and Elihu Root praised the gently soothing effects of international organization. Woodrow Wilson paid attention to moral appeals to others. George W. Bush revived Wilsonian themes in the aftermath of the September 11, 2001, terrorist attacks. In his second inaugural address he proclaimed, "There is only one force of history that can break the reign of hatred and resentment, and expose the pretensions of tyrants, and reward the hopes of the decent and tolerant, and that is the force of human freedom." Some "realists" of the 1950s such as Hans Morgenthau urged diplomats to concentrate attention on influencing the conduct of other governments. "Idealists" such as Franklin Roosevelt's undersecretary of state, Sumner Welles, thought it was shortsighted to neglect the attitudes and activities of foreign citizens in favor of what their governments did. Many more differences in the advice of foreign policy experts occurred over the century, and they will be discussed later, but no one should overlook the near unanimity of opinion among foreign policy advisers on certain fundamentals. First, they believed that foreign affairs matter to mature minds. Next, they felt that America was superior to other nations. Third, they feared that other countries presented dangers. And finally, they shared an optimistic faith that American military strength, wealth, and political values could be artfully applied to improve the lot of the world's peoples.

A belief in the importance of foreign policy has not always been as obvious as it seems today. During the eighteenth century, Americans took comfort in Tom Paine's 1776 call in *Common Sense* for North American colonies to separate themselves from a Europe constantly embroiled in stupid quarrels and wars. One of the mainstays of American diplomacy in the nineteenth century, the Monroe Doctrine, rested on a belief that the United States should have as little as possible to do with the great power game of nations.

By the twentieth century, few Americans believed their country could ignore the rest of the world. Even "isolationists" such as the America First Committee in 1940 or conservative Republican senator Robert A. Taft of Ohio in 1950 thought the rest of the world affected the United States; they simply had less enthusiasm than did their counterparts among internationalists for the way the United States affected the rest of the world.

A widespread faith in the superiority of the United States moved diplomats. Historians have stressed the missionary and moralistic flourishes of American diplomacy. A former diplomat turned scholar, George Kennan, traced this urge to make the rest of the world over into the American image to the deep strains of Puritanism running through American culture. While Puritan self-righteousness undoubtedly has characterized American history, it is a mistake to think that such ideas as Manifest Destiny or "defending the free world" derived from seventeenth-century theologians such as Cotton Mather or Jonathan Edwards. Instead, it makes more sense to consider American messianism a form of the nationalistic exuberance which afflicted all of the great powers at the end of the nineteenth century.

Whatever the sources of the sense of mission—an urge to mask insecurities, a carry-over from a Puritan past, the natural inclination of powerful nations to force others to conform to their will—Americans imposed their views on others. Despite recognition of the need for cooperation, consultation, and partnership, American diplomacy has been bedeviled by an urge to lead. When Americans speak of international consensus or compromise, as they did in negotiations establishing a League of Nations in 1919, the United Nations in 1945, or the General Agreement on Tariffs and Trade in 1948, they hope to bring other nations round to their way of viewing problems.

Of course, it is the essence of diplomacy to yield on the form of one's demands while retaining the substance of one's claims, and shrewd negotiators try to make other nations see things their way. American diplomats followed this pattern, and their missionary style added spice to their approach. Customarily, Americans believed that their country stood above others' quarrels. This aloofness is both moral and economic, but whatever its origin, its consequences are clear. American diplomats like to see their country as the balance wheel of the international system, mediating disputes among other nations.

Sometimes the sense of moral superiority has made Americans want to withdraw in disgust from the world's woes. The neutrality laws of the thirties, the America First Committee preceding entry into the Second World War, and suspicion of members of the United Nations in the seventies and eighties arose, in part, from a fear that other countries carried corruption. More often than not, though, American disappointments with international events led to a redoubling of reform efforts. The creation of the League, the UN, or alliance commitments to international monetary reform after 1945 and the beginning of economic assistance for poor countries represented ways of painting the international environment in American hues.

At the turn of the century, Americans such as Theodore Roosevelt and his secretaries of state, John Hay and Elihu Root, who advocated making their country a preeminent world power, did so from two contrary sources. They reckoned that America's strength made it equal to European great powers. But they also knew that the United States differed from Europe. In the words of some theorists, the country was "unique." Woodrow Wilson and his secretaries of state, William Jennings Bryan and Robert Lansing, held this view. Since the United States had been blessed with two oceans separating it from Europe, it had not developed the traditional animosities of the Old World. Lacking a warrior class, the United States also escaped Europe's militarism. Finally, the blessings of prosperity appeared more widespread in the United States than in Europe. No great class cleavages rent American society, so there were fewer impulses to engage in foreign adventures.

We know that this view of American society overlooked many details. While separated from Europe, Americans had their share of local animosities, directed toward neighbors to the south. The lack of a hereditary warrior class did not make the United States any less bloodthirsty in its call for the humbling of its enemies. Few reputable historians speak nowadays about the absence of class divisions in the United States, and even at the end of the nineteenth century, when a business leader looked to an aggressive overseas policy, he did so precisely because he hoped it would diminish class tensions at home.

Whether correct or not, the grip of this idealized portrait of the United States and its foreign policy had its effects on diplomacy. Americans went abroad serenely sure of the harmony of their society. They offered economic aid, political guidance, and diplomatic mediation to anyone who requested them and many who did not. The Republic of China, Korea, the Philippines, Japan, Greece, Italy, Morocco, Jordan, Israel, and Liberia—different countries around the world have, at various times, requested, received, and gratefully acknowledged American financial assistance and diplomatic protection. But the United States arrived without invitation or soon wore out its welcome in the Dominican Republic, Iran, Lebanon, Zaire, and Angola, to name a few.

Time and time again Americans found that other nations resented their preachings. The British, an ally during the Second World War, came to dread American lectures on the shape of the postwar world. Charles de Gaulle, president of France from 1958 to 1969, looked forward to a "Europe from the Atlantic to the Urals" which excluded the United States. During the Cold War, neutralists such as India and Egypt, which opted out of the struggle between the United States and the Soviet Union, resisted Washington's blandishments to join an anti-Communist alignment.

Americans found themselves especially ill-equipped to respond effectively to revolutionary nationalism. These upheavals often followed the lead of men and women who wanted nothing more than to be left alone. Americans, who distinguished between themselves and other foreigners, could understand why Cubans, Chinese, or Russians might want *other* nationals to go away. But Americans could never comprehend why overseas revolutionaries wanted *Americans* to steer clear. Having only recently convinced themselves that the rest of the world needed the attention of the United States lest it fall into barbarism, Americans were shocked to learn that parts of the world did not want to listen to them. Whenever nationalist revolutions occurred in the twentieth century, Americans responded that the people in charge had temporarily lost their good judgment. Eventually, Americans hoped revolutionaries would come to see things as the United States did. In the meantime, Washington did what it could to make life difficult for those who took power—in Mexico in 1913, in Russia in 1917, in China in 1949, in Guatemala in 1954, in Cuba in 1959, in Iran in 1979, and in Nicaragua after 1980.

In its relations with other great powers that did not undergo revolutionary upheavals, American diplomacy followed a traditional mode. Anyone familiar with the behavior of the European states in their struggles for mastery of the continent would have no difficulty in following America's relations with the great powers in the twentieth century. The United States used its wealth and military might to gain influence. It entered two world wars, revived the economies of Europe with the Marshall Plan, created the North Atlantic Treaty Organization, and looked with approval on the formation of the European Economic Community as a sort of embryonic United States of Europe.

American diplomacy in the twentieth century resembled Britain's in the nineteenth. Just as Britain sought to ensure that no single power was strong enough to dominate Europe, so did the United States in the twentieth century try to make sure that no other nation was strong enough to unite other countries against the United States. The Atlantic Ocean provided a sense of security that enabled Americans to tell Europeans how to conduct their affairs, acting all the while like a sort of honest broker. American attitudes toward Europe were filtered through the prism of the "special relationship" with Great Britain. Throughout the twentieth century, the United States and Great Britain, despite a good deal of bickering, were aligned together on most international questions. By the Second World War, however, it no longer was a relationship of equals. Instead, the United States became the leader of the English-speaking peoples.

As the United States became more involved in European politics after the Second World War, its attention encompassed the whole world. The Cold War—the competition between the Soviet Union and the United States and between the alternative economic systems of capitalism and communism—framed foreign relations. Americans imbued the Soviets with awesome powers and detected evil intentions toward world domination. World politics became a "great game" for preeminence, just as it had been at the turn of the century. The stakes, however, rose steeply after the development of atomic weapons. When, around 1960, both the United States and the Soviet Union acquired the capacity to destroy life in each other's countries, the rivalry took on a grisly aspect.

American diplomats tended to see the remainder of the world as subsidiary theaters of the Cold War. Communism became the enemy, and Americans thought that Marxist governments and movements everywhere took orders from the Kremlin in Moscow. In the 1970s a subtler view emerged, and some experts, diplomats, and politicians awoke to the fissures of communism. China, for many years a place where Americans hoped to find friends, wounded American pride when it turned to Marxism in 1949. In the seventies, however, the United States "normalized" relations with Beijing to "play the China card" against the Soviets.

In the 1980s U.S. foreign policy often continued to paint revolutionary movements around the globe as pawns of the Soviet Union. Many traditional allies of the United States and experts on conditions in the underdeveloped world complained that Washington too often asserted that all the disorder in the world emanated from Moscow.

The end of the Cold War and the disintegration of the Soviet Union in the years 1989 to 1991 held enormous potential for a more harmonious, democratic, and prosperous world. In the immediate post–Cold War years, many thoughtful people inside and outside of government believed that an irreversible process of globalization would ensure the triumph of the old American ideal that ordinary people would make war and bloodshed obsolete by going about their daily affairs. The end of the Cold War did eliminate the real danger of nuclear annihilation. Democratic institutions, free markets, and Western prosperity did expand after 1990, but progress was much slower and more uneven than many optimists anticipated. Communism left a bitter legacy in Eastern Europe, Russia, and the other states of the former Soviet Union. These lands sometimes sank into interethnic tension, national rivalry, and even despair. The noncommunist regions of the world also continued to experience a mixture of progress and decline after the Cold War. Globalization brought prosperity to millions; it left others behind, envious and angry. Revolution, war, and famine persisted in many areas of the globe after 1990. Without the organizing principle of anticommunism, Americans had difficulty defining a coherent and consistent post–Cold War foreign policy. Most Americans thought it necessary for the United States to remain deeply involved in foreign affairs, although a significant minority wanted to turn inward. Most thought it important for the United States to promote human rights, democratic governments, the rule of law, and free markets in other countries. Many believed that globalization held out significant promise for human improvement, but many others feared that globalization gave too much power to unregulated corporate interests.

Outside government, the rise of America to world power since 1945 drew a mixed reaction. For the first twenty years of the Cold War, broad consensus existed that the United States had to counter the Soviet Union and its allies everywhere in the world. That consensus collapsed during the tragic war in Vietnam, and Americans then engaged in a heated debate over their country's proper role in world politics. These controversies did not restore a consensus about the aims and means of U.S. foreign policy. After the United States left Vietnam, each successive administration drew a different lesson from that engagement. Jimmy Carter, president from 1977 to 1981, acknowledged that the American involvement in Vietnam had been a mistake, a misadventure, and an arrogant misapplication of American military power. Many Americans welcomed Carter's restraint, but by the end of his term, they felt vulnerable. They responded to the muscular nationalism of Republican Ronald Reagan, who followed in 1981. Reagan preferred to characterize the American effort in Vietnam as a "noble cause," which failed only because the United States failed to commit itself fully to victory. The Reagan administration promised an assertive America able to take the initiative in the Cold War. Reagan's confrontational style won an almost equal number of backers and detractors.

The end of the Cold War came with a suddenness that surprised but also deeply satisfied most Americans. They welcomed the triumph of Western-style ideals of self-government, human rights, and the abundance promised by free markets. As the United States entered the twenty-first century, most Americans believed that their own prosperity and physical safety depended on continuous engagement in foreign affairs. The terrorists attacks of September 11, 2001, dramaically raised the stakes of U.S. engagement in foreign affairs. The Bush doctrine of preemptive war led the United States to a long, bloody, and inconclusive war in Iraq that proved to be increasingly unpopular at home and

around the globe. People in many other countries continued to look to the
United States for leadership and admired its political institutions, its diverse
culture, and its robust economy. But with the United States embarked on a
war in Iraq that many people around the world considered unnecessary and
unjustfied, international opinion of the United States dropped. Many people in other countries looked with anguish at a United States that seemed
to have abandoned its century-long traditon of international cooperation
and collective security in favor of unilateral military actions. Friends, competitors, rivals, and foes all acknowledged, however—as Americans had done
since 1900—that the United States exercised great influence over the shape
of international relations.

CHAPTER TWO

The United States as a World Power, 1898–1908

THE WAR WITH SPAIN AND ITS AFTERMATH

Modern American diplomacy dates from the war with Spain in 1898. The brief, four-month passage of arms between a major new imperial power and a decrepit empire left the United States in possession of Cuba and Puerto Rico in the Caribbean and the Philippines and Guam in the Pacific. More important than the specific territorial acquisitions, the war permitted the United States to compete equally with the Europeans in the race for pre-eminence in world politics.

The war with Spain did not occur accidentally. Both the immediate aim of the war—the eviction of the Spanish from Cuba—and its long-term implications—catapulting the United States into the first rank of world powers—had roots of more than half a century. Southern slaveholders in the United States had coveted Cuba before the Civil War. Cuba remained an island of desire even after slavery was eliminated. Ulysses S. Grant's secretary of state, Hamilton Fish, cast longing glances in that direction. Grant even tried to buy outright the country of Santo Domingo in 1869. Yet the reasons for insular expansion changed in the late nineteenth century.

Before the Civil War, the justification for seizing the islands of the Caribbean was the need for more slave territory. In the years after the Civil War, Americans looked outward in order to trade more effectively abroad. Much argument has gone on over whether Americans wanted to trade with the islands they eventually acquired from Spain. After all, some critics of the idea of a foreign policy based upon trade expansion have argued, there really was very little the Cubans or Puerto Ricans could buy from the United

States. Even the overseas investment by Americans went to other places than Cuba.

But the islands of the Caribbean were important for the navy, the protection of a proposed canal across the Isthmus of Panama, and to show that the United States was a power to be reckoned with. The modern American navy, the forerunner of the military establishment of the twentieth century, came to life in the 1880s. From then until the end of the century, the United States built capital ships while naval officers developed the theories of modern warfare. Admirals Alfred Thayer Mahan and Stephen C. Luce became the two most notable advocates of a strong navy. Mahan developed the idea that whichever nation controlled the seas controlled the course of world politics. He saw strong links between the navy and overseas trade. Each required the other: a flourishing trade made a large navy necessary, while the larger the fleet, the more trade was possible.

Advocates of a grand navy found allies among traders who wanted ships to carry goods abroad. Joseph C. Hendrix, president of the American Bankers' Association, expressed the view of many businessmen when he observed that "we have the Anglo-Saxon thirst for wide markets growing upon us." Demands to rid the United States of surplus production grew in the aftermath of the Panic of 1893. A strike at the Pullman Sleeping Car Company near Chicago, a march by veterans demanding payment of a Civil War bonus, and mass demonstrations by unemployed workers sent shivers down the spines of the business community. The *New York Tribune* anguished over "social restlessness...arraying class against class and filling the land with a nondescript socialism as dangerous and revolutionary as it is imbecile and grotesque." As Brooks Adams, a disillusioned scion of a distinguished family, mourned, there was a "law of civilization and decay": societies either expanded or they died. Josiah Strong, a popular commentator on current events, pointed the way out: "Overproduction compels a quest for ultimate supremacy in the markets of the world....The United States is to become the mighty workshop of the world and our people the hands of mankind."

An expansionist desire to look outward coincided with urges to convert others to what came to be known as "the American way of life." The most numerous groups of Americans who wanted to spread the word about the United States overseas were, of course, missionaries. By 1900, some 7,000 Americans were teaching the gospel and, incidentally, the benefits of American republicanism, in more than thirty countries around the world.

Missionaries helped get the message across in the Far East, especially China. Americans had been trading with the Chinese since the *Empress of China* had sailed into Guangzhou (Canton) in 1784. Since the Treaty of Wangxia of 1844, the United States had been one of the non-Chinese powers permitted to open trade with ports on the mainland. Over the remainder of the nineteenth century, American missionaries accompanied American traders in China. Together they sent home word of developments abroad, and they encouraged the American government to take a greater interest in the competition for advantage in China.

Closer to home, in the Western Hemisphere, Americans had less to worry about from the competition of the European powers. By the end of the nineteenth century, the Europeans had all quit the New World at the prodding of the United States and because the Latins themselves had evicted them. While the United States was engaged in the Civil War, the French under Napoleon III had a brief fling at establishing a New World empire in Mexico. In 1867, however, the Mexicans expelled the French and executed an ineffectual Hapsburg prince, Maximilian, whom the French had made emperor.

In the late 1890s it was Spain's turn to lose its final foothold in the New World. The Spanish Empire was the first to be established in the Western Hemisphere. It was outlived by the British, French, Dutch, and even Danish Empires, but the demise of New Spain was far more spectacular than the fall of other European colonial societies. The end came quickly in a 123-day land and sea fight that ended with American ownership of the Philippine Islands, taken because President McKinley thought he heard God's voice. The revolution in Cuba, which had gone on intermittently since 1868, was the proximate cause of the American decision to fight. For people alive in 1898 as well as for historians, the question of why President McKinley asked Congress to declare war against Spain on April 11, 1898, provoked argument. On one side were those who saw the burst of imperialism of the war as nearly accidental. According to this view, the president favored a peaceful resolution of the dispute with Spain, but he could not resist the incessant public demand for war. He opted for war only to preserve the unity of his party in the face of a clamor for a strong policy on the part of the sensational yellow press led by Joseph Pulitzer of the *New York World* and William Randolph Hearst of the *New York Journal.* The *World* denounced the cruelties of Spanish commander Valeriano Weyler, who had left "blood on the doorsteps, blood, blood blood! The old, the young, the weak, the crippled—all butchered without mercy." Hearst's *Journal* assailed "Weyler the brute, the devastator of haciendas, the destroyer of families, and the outrager of women." McKinley also listened to the voices raised by American businessmen who dreaded the prospect of the Cuban revolution endangering their belongings in the islands.

At the end of the twentieth century, historians became more alert to cultural and gender influences on foreign policy decisions. The historian Kristin Hoganson's book *Fighting for American Manhood* explains "how gender politics provoked the Spanish American and Philippine American Wars."

She quotes extensively from critics who complained that McKinley was weak, indecisive, lacking in backbone, and unmanly for resisting war with Spain. The *Atlanta Constitution* derided McKinley as a "goody goody man." Later it said that the public wanted a "declaration of American virility," and "the people need a man—an American—at the helm."

A more sinister view of the origins of the war with Spain, expressed by such historians as Julius W. Pratt and Walter Millis in the 1920s and 1930s and by leftists such as Philip Foner in the 1960s, holds that the war with Spain marked the culmination of the traditional American policy of expansion. To these writers it mattered little that McKinley was a weak and vacillating leader without a clearly thought-out foreign policy. Even if he responded only to the pressure brought to bear by elements within the Republican Party and the business community, that was enough to set the United States on a course devoted to imperial expansion.

Another interpretation is that the imperialism of the late 1890s was conscious but temporary. In a phrase made famous by the historian Samuel Flagg Bemis, who taught at Yale University for more than thirty years in the mid-twentieth century, the three years after the Spanish-American War were a "great aberration" in American history. Bemis suggested that the excursion into rivalry with the Europeans was short-lived, and by 1902, when the Philippine-American War ended, the country had abandoned the attempt to compete with the Europeans as a colonial master over the poorer, nonwhite regions of the world. The notion of a great aberration has few adherents nowadays, but the idea that the United States had a gentler, more humanitarian foreign policy than Europeans has had a powerful pull on the imagination of American foreign policy makers over the years.

In Europe and in America, then, at the end of the nineteenth century, there was a growing awareness that the pace of international relations had quickened recently. Another, more ominous sense also gripped diplomats. Thoughtful observers of international politics such as Elihu Root, a lawyer who became secretary of state in 1905, believed that if things were left to take their course, war might erupt. This fear even penetrated the mind of the czar of Russia, Nicholas II. He called a meeting of the diplomats of Europe and America at The Hague on his birthday, May 18, 1899, to discuss ways to make the world a more peaceable place.

The Hague Conference of 1899 attracted delegates from twenty-six countries, all of the "civilized" world at the time. Along with its successor conference in the Dutch city eight years later, the meeting at The Hague set the pattern for schemes of reform of international politics in the twentieth century. At The Hague delegates sipped tea and wrote plans to make modern warfare less horrible. They wrote rules for the use of such weapons as balloons, explained how prisoners should be treated, and provided some limited protection for civilians during times of war. The conference did nothing at all to prevent the outbreak of war, its ostensible purpose. This pattern remained for the rest of the twentieth century—international meetings that began with high hopes for a revolutionary change in the way in which diplomacy was done ended in acrimony with few of their original goals achieved.

This, then, was the world of international relations at the turn of the century. At least seven rapidly industrializing nations (the United States, Great Britain, France, Germany, Italy, Russia, and Japan) whose governments were in the hands of newly enriched elites confronted one another. They depended to one degree or another upon the support of their newly franchised populations. These governments competed far from home in nonindustrial lands inhabited by nonwhite peoples.

EXPANDING THE PACIFIC EMPIRE: THE OPEN DOOR POLICY

After the United States crushed Spain, Americans and foreigners saw American power rivaling Europe's. New Yorkers recalled the glories of Rome and Napoleon by erecting a triumphal arch in Central Park through which passed Adm. George Dewey, the hero of Manila Bay. Across the country, editorials praised the "new empire." Englishmen discovered some new virtues in an America they once had scorned. Colonial Secretary Joseph Chamberlain proposed an alliance between the United States and Great Britain in terms that would have brought calls for his examination by a psychiatrist ten years before. "Even war itself would be cheaply purchased," he said, "if in a great and noble cause the Stars and Stripes and the Union Jack were to wave together over an Anglo-Saxon Alliance." In Latin America, newspapers voiced concern over the "colossus of the North," while across the Pacific, too, Chinese and Japanese diplomats acknowledged that the United States had become a "world power."

What did it mean to be a world power in 1900? For European nations such as Britain, France, Russia, and Germany, the answer was easy. World powers had empires around the globe, and they demanded to be consulted wherever boundaries changed. Their merchants and bankers could be found in the remotest regions, and citizens of less fortunate lands paid them timid respect.

Having taken the Philippines, Guam, Puerto Rico, and Cuba from Spain, the United States too possessed a fledgling empire. Its merchants were just as active as those of Europe. While debate raged in Congress and the country at large over whether the United States should keep its new acquisitions, Massachusetts Republican Henry Cabot Lodge put the case for empire and world power to his colleagues in the Senate. He likened a nation to an athlete who "does not win a race by habitually sitting in an armchair." To anti-imperialists such as Andrew Carnegie or Democratic presidential candidate William Jennings Bryan, who wondered why enter the race in the first place, Lodge replied that it built masculine character: "This necessity for watching over the welfare of another people will improve our civil service, raise the tone of public life, and make broader and better our politics."

Across the Pacific in China was one place where the athletic American empire joined the race. "We believe our interests in the Pacific Ocean are as great as those of any power," Secretary of State John Hay observed. In 1844, Americans gained the right to trade in the Treaty of Wangxia, which Caleb Cushing of Massachusetts negotiated with the Chinese government. China opened to the Americans the same ports it had allowed the British to enter two years before at the end of the Opium War. Americans and Britishers also won the right of "extraterritoriality," or exemption from Chinese law. The Chinese had not wanted to trade with Britain, but having lost the war they had no choice. Nor did the Chinese consider the Americans to be any more "civilized" than the "barbarous" British, who had forced opium upon China. Cushing's demand to receive equal treatment with the British was scorned as "jackal diplomacy" by the Chinese, who taunted the Americans for arriving after the fight to demand the spoils of war. For the remainder of the nineteenth century, Americans managed to ignore the jibe. Out of the natural tendency of people to think well of themselves, American merchants, missionaries, and diplomats in China thought that they had come there to protect the Chinese from the designs of greedy Europeans. Charles Denby, the American minister in China, predicted to Ohio Republican senator John Sherman in 1897 that "the statesmen of China will understand that in our case foreign control does not mean territorial absorption nor governmental interference, while both these results are possible, or even probable, in dealing with European powers."

Chaos ruled China in the 1890s. The Chinese shocked everyone, including themselves, by losing a war with Japan in 1895. Europeans and Americans who watched the speedy collapse of the Chinese armed forces felt "nothing but disgust…for the weakness and incompetence by the Chinese." One English expert on China, Lord Charles Beresford, crisscrossed America in early 1899 promoting his book, *The Break-Up of China*, which predicted that the Asian nation would soon fall to the European empires the way Africa had done in the last two decades. If China were to be "sliced like a watermelon," he informed his audiences, Americans must be prepared to take their share. They should be especially wary of the designs of the Russians.

Surprisingly, Americans did not rush to carve China. Ambassador Edwin Conger and railroad promoters James Hill and Edward H. Harriman remembered the bitter debate in 1898 before taking the Philippines. Although they longed for the riches of the East, they recalled how President William McKinley had been forced to promise that the United States eventually would offer independence to the Philippines. If the American public had to be fooled in this way into accepting the "responsibilities of empire," then the future of imperial America seemed dim. There was one way, however, that the United States matched the other world powers. Economically, the United States held its own with anyone, and the ports on the West Coast placed it closer to China than was Europe. If taking colonies held political risks in the United States, an "informal empire" based on the principles of free trade gave Americans a leg up on their rivals.

In September 1899 the American government moved to establish a "fair field and no favor" for foreign merchants and investors in China. Without consulting the Chinese government, Secretary of State John Hay sent notes to all other imperial powers asking them to maintain an "Open Door" for traders of all nations inside their Chinese spheres of influence. Hay had been persuaded by an American diplomat in China, W. W. Rockhill, that since American goods could be sold more cheaply in China than those of any other power, the Open Door policy would work to the advantage of the United States. Receiving no answer from Europe and Japan, Hay took silence for assent and proclaimed China open to trade.

The next year, 1900, Hay again wrote notes to the major European powers when China erupted in the Boxer Rebellion. This popular rising against foreign domination of China initially won the support of China's empress dowager, Cixi, who hoped the Boxers (the Society of the Righteous Fists) could rid her country of the humiliating presence of the Europeans, Japanese, and Americans. When the rebels laid siege in June to the German embassy, capturing the foreign diplomats, the empress dowager distanced herself from the Boxers. For fifty-five days the diplomats were prisoners of angry nationalists while a joint expedition of Japanese, Russian, British, and American marines marched from the coast to rescue them. As the diplomats and their families languished under house arrest, the secretary of state sent his second Open Door notes to the powers on July 2, asking them not to dismantle China in their anger over the envoys' capture. The recipients coolly acknowledged his notes and made vague promises to respect China's territorial integrity if the others followed suit. That was enough for the American secretary of state, who publicly proclaimed China's safety. Privately, he approved a contingency plan to seize a Chinese port for the United States in case the other powers broke their word.

Hay has been called "naive," "moralistic," and "easily gulled" by historians. His cavalier assurance that the other powers had accepted the Open Door policy when, in fact, they had made polite murmurings was seen by scholars who advocated what they called realism in foreign affairs as a flagrant example of American misunderstanding of the workings of power. Yet Hay's subsequent critics underestimated him. The secretary had a weak diplomatic hand since he knew that the United States would not use force in China. Still, he wanted an informal empire. Making the most of a bad situation, he maneuvered the other imperial states into taking account of what Americans had to say.

For Europeans his demands for equality of treatment seemed hypocritical and self-serving. The British liked the Open Door policy, but for different reasons than did the Americans. For British merchants, the new policy meant that they, the world's premier traders, would sweep the field. For the Russians, Germans, and Japanese there was no such saving feature to America's attempt at moral suasion. The Open Door notes suggested to them that the United States had in charge of its foreign affairs a man who did not fully appreciate the vast changes that were occurring in China. The powers might agree to humor him, but they would pursue their own ends in China without taking orders from the United States.

The Europeans knew that the United States was engaged in the bloody suppression of a nationalist movement in its newly conquered Asian territory of the Philippines. This was one explanation for their failure to take seriously American demands that they forgo territorial ambitions in China. From 1899 until his capture in 1901, Emilio Aguinaldo led 200,000 independence fighters against the American occupiers of the islands. Aguinaldo's forces had fought the Spanish before the American arrival, and he was puzzled that the new colonial masters did not seem to want immediately to offer national freedom.

The United States sent 126,000 troops, who engaged in a fierce guerrilla war against the nationalists. Some 4,000 American soldiers and about five times that many Filipinos lost their lives in battle. Filipino *insurrectos* were subjected to a slow, painful water torture in which American soldiers and marines forced water down captive Filipinos' throats. Interrogators then jumped on their distended bellies until they talked or died. One American officer who served in the war told a reporter, "We must bury all qualms ... and have no scruples about exterminating this other race standing in the way of progress and enlightenment, if it is necessary." Racism grew among the American troops, who began calling Filipinos "niggers" or "gugus" (a term later changed to "gooks" and used derisively by American forces in Vietnam more than sixty years later). Two commissions, headed respectively by Jacob Gould Schurman, president of Cornell University, and William Howard Taft, an Ohio Republican politician, investigated conditions in the Philippines in 1900 and 1901. They heard an American anthropologist assert that "the great mass of the people here are ignorant. They have a very vague idea of either independence or liberty

U.S. troops firing on Philippine nationalists
(National Archives)

as such." Taft privately complained to his boss, President Theodore Roosevelt, that stories of atrocities ruined the morale of the American soldiers.

THE RISE OF THEODORE ROOSEVELT

Theodore Roosevelt, who took office in September 1901 when an assassin shot President McKinley, had a clearer idea than many presidents about what he wanted to accomplish in foreign affairs. He advocated "Progressivism," a mixture of nationalism, moralism, racism, social Darwinism (the competition of the fittest peoples), uplift, and social planning. Suspicious of businessmen, he sometimes advanced their interests because he thought that might project American power. He divided the world according to race and culture. He considered the projection of American power abroad to be part of "the essential manliness of the American character." He likened involvement in foreign affairs to the necessity for men to go to work. Just as "each man, while doing his first duty and the children within his home, must yet... strive mightily outside the home, so our nation...must not shrink from playing its part among the great nations without."

As a Progressive, Roosevelt believed in the power of government to regulate at home and abroad. As a nationalist, he thought the United States superior to its rivals. In the 1890s, he had joined Henry Cabot Lodge and Adm. Alfred Thayer Mahan, the architect of the modern American navy, in demanding a large American fleet, a war with Spain, and a canal across the Isthmus of Panama. As the historian Howard Beale writes, "Though he valued the blessings of peace, he craved the excitement of war." The prospect of leading troops against Spain made him leave his comfortable job as assistant secretary of the navy to join the army in 1898. He had more fun charging up San Juan Hill at the head of his Rough Riders than he had at any time in his life since he left his ranch in North Dakota in his twenties. Blood was part of the thrill. "Did I tell you," he wrote Lodge, "that I killed a Spaniard with my own hands?"

How to assess such a man? A typical view was expressed by Beale in the most thorough examination of Roosevelt's diplomacy, *Theodore Roosevelt and the Rise of America to World Power* (1956). Beale acknowledges Roosevelt's grasp, energy, and intelligence but admits that "the trouble lay not in his abilities but in his values." He was a bombastic nationalist who influenced America's course "that by mid-century was to bring her face to face with grave dangers." H. W. Brands, a recent biographer, calls Roosevelt the "last romantic" who set the standard for what became "[a] signature of twentieth–century America; an assumption of responsibility for international order."

Along with his swagger, Roosevelt had a strategy. He wanted the United States to act as a great power, fully the equal of the imperial states of Europe. Consequently, he created the Panama Canal, policed the Western Hemisphere, built up the navy, mediated the war between Russia and Japan in 1905, called for the Second Peace Conference at The Hague in 1907, and took a seat at the 1906 Algeciras Conference, which decided the fate of Morocco. While maintaining that the United States was fully the equal of the other great powers of the world, he sought to maintain good personal relationships with all the European diplomats in Washington. He referred to the British ambassador, Cecil Spring-Rice, as "Springy" and the ambassador from Germany, Speck von Sternberg, as "Specky." The French ambassador, Jules Jusserand, had a forbidding presence that rebuffed nicknames, but Roosevelt included him on his rambles through Rock Creek Park.

Roosevelt, a racist and social Darwinist, thought it obvious that the fiercest competition in the modern world took place between different races. He spoke of an English-speaking "race," comparing it favorably to "backward" Chinese, Latins, whose "day is over," and blacks, kept down by their own "vice and criminality" and their "shiftlessness and laziness." Shortly before he became president, he thrilled a crowd in Minnesota with,

"It is our duty to people living in barbarism to see that they are freed from their chains, and we can free them only by destroying barbarism itself.... Exactly as it is the duty of a civilized power scrupulously to respect the rights of weaker civilized powers...so it is its duty to put down savagery and barbarism."

The Trans-Isthmian Canal

Roosevelt showed how he would put down savagery and barbarism in the Western Hemisphere. Consider his maneuverings to have the United States build and fortify a canal across the Isthmus of Panama. In 1850 the United States and Great Britain had agreed that neither power would build such a canal on its own. Ever since that Clayton-Bulwer Treaty, American diplomats and politicians had kicked themselves for having yielded such an important right to the British government. Not that it mattered very much before the technology of digging a lock-type canal of some thirty miles in length had been developed. But in the post–Civil War era, it became possible for the first time to create a canal with locks across the isthmus.

The first group to try to do so was the French company that had completed the sea-level Suez Canal in 1869. Ferdinand de Lesseps, the creator of the Suez Canal, lost his money and his sanity in the effort to dig across the northern Colombian province of Panama. The bankruptcy of the Panama Canal Company became a major scandal in France in 1889, and it also provided the United States with an opportunity to annul the Clayton-Bulwer agreement and cut its own canal.

After the war with Spain, the United States was firmly committed to a canal, but the question was whether the ditch would be dug across Panama, where it would be shorter but would require locks, or across Nicaragua, where it would be longer but use a sea-level path. For the reorganized French company, which had been digging for fifteen years in Panama, the only way to recover at least part of its investment was for the Americans to select a route through Panama. If the Americans chose Panama, then they would buy the equipment left by the French.

While a special commission under Adm. J. C. Walker studied the preferred route, Secretary Hay negotiated with the British to allow the United States a free hand in digging a ditch between the Atlantic and Pacific oceans. Hay worked out two treaties with the British ambassador in Washington, Julian Pauncefote. In the first Hay-Pauncefote agreement, initialed in February 1900, the British agreed to an American canal but insisted that the waterway be neutral and unfortified. When Roosevelt became president, he refused to submit this treaty to the Senate and sent Hay back to Pauncefote with instructions to get a treaty that allowed the Americans to construct a canal and protect it with its own navies. Faced with the obvious determination on the part of Roosevelt to have a canal with or without British agreement, Pauncefote capitulated in 1901. The second Hay-Pauncefote agreement gave Americans everything they had asked for, although the British did insist that the tolls levied against them be the same as the ones levied on American ships.

Now that the United States had a free hand, the French company went to work making certain that the canal would be built across the territory where its equipment lay rusting. A French mining engineer, Philippe Bunau-Varilla, who had not seen Panama for the previous fifteen years, became the company's chief representative in the United States. Bunau-Varilla hired a Wall Street lawyer, William Nelson Cromwell, to lobby for the Panama route. As the Senate debated, the House passed the Hepburn bill, which recommended the route across Nicaragua. Bunau-Varilla and Cromwell placed on the desk of each senator a Nicaraguan postage stamp showing the volcano Momotombo in full eruption in the middle of the lake through which the canal would pass. On June 28, 1902, Congress approved the Panama route and the purchase of the French company for $40 million.

The question changed to how the United States would come to terms with the government of Colombia, which was sovereign in Panama. In January 1903, John Hay signed an agreement with Thomas Herrán, the Colombian minister to the United States. In return for a payment of $10 million and an annual rent of $250,000, the United States would have the right to lease for ninety-nine years a canal zone six miles wide across the Isthmus of Panama.

The Senate of Colombia rejected this treaty unanimously, hoping for more money from the United States. When Theodore Roosevelt learned that Colombia had turned down the treaty, he was outraged. He lashed the Colombians as "inefficient bandits" and "a corrupt pithecoid community." Cromwell, who visited the president, emerged to report, "President Roosevelt is determined to have the Panama Canal route." If necessary, he would help Panama secede from Colombia.

Some businessmen in the province of Panama also were alarmed at their Colombian Senate's decision to reject the treaty. These men had holdings in the French canal company, and they saw that a rejection of the treaty would ruin them. What if the Roosevelt administration decided after all on the Nicaraguan route? In order to prevent the loss of their investment, a junta in Panama City conspired with Philippe Bunau-Varilla to detach the province of Panama from Colombia. Once an independent Panama came into being, it could sign its own treaty, letting the United States build the canal. Legitimate nationalists who had long chafed under Colombian rule also joined the revolution. The successful secession of 1903 capped a sixty-year drive for independence that had seen at least four previous uprisings. A Panamanian diplomat remarked years later that his country became independent through "the interests and sentiments of the people of Panama, not the arbitrariness of Roosevelt." But Roosevelt played a major, dishonorable role.

While the junta in Panama City organized a revolt, Cromwell and Bunau-Varilla pressured the U.S. government to recognize revolutionary Panama. Bunau-Varilla went to the White House on October 10, 1903, to ask Roosevelt's help. Roosevelt later told a cheering crowd of students at Berkeley, "I took the isthmus," and in a way he did. When the revolutionaries proclaimed their independence on November 1, 1903, Roosevelt made certain that the American ship *Nashville* stood off the coast to prevent a Colombian landing. Two days later, a fleet of six American ships menaced the coast.

Events moved fast in Washington after the junta declared independence. Bunau-Varilla, although a French citizen and never having resided in Panama, named himself the foreign minister of the new government. The nationalists in Panama City wired him the news in New York that their rebellion had succeeded and told him that a delegation was on its way to Washington to negotiate a treaty with the United States. Bunau-Varilla had no intention, however, of waiting until the Panamanians, some of whom might be nationalists, arrived. They might try to get a treaty more favorable to their nation than the one Colombia had rejected. The Frenchman feared that Roosevelt would spurn the Panamanians if they upped the ante, leaving his company stranded. Bunau-Varilla scurried to Washington on the night of November 8 and met with Hay the next morning. He carried with him a draft of a treaty that he got Hay to sign before the Panamanians arrived. When they showed up at Washington's Union Station on November 18, they were shocked. One of them was so angry at Bunau-Varilla that he punched him in the nose; another fainted when he learned what the United States had gained from Panama.

Later, Panamanians denounced the Hay-Bunau-Varilla agreement as "the treaty no Panamanian signed." Under its terms, the United States received a permanent lease upon a canal-zone territory ten miles wide. The United States would pay the same $10 million and $250,000 per year promised Colombia. Bunau-Varilla, wishing to sweeten the deal, included language allowing the United States to act "as if it were sovereign" in the zone. This grant of quasi-sovereignty bedeviled relations between the United States and Panama for seventy-five years until a treaty restored control of the canal to Panama in 1978. In the United States at the time, a few opposing Democrats denounced Roosevelt and the treaty. William Randolph Hearst's Democratic *Chicago American* called it "a rough-riding assault upon another republic over the shattered wreckage of international law and diplomatic usage." But such voices were few. Most Americans, *Public Opinion* asserted, wanted "an Isthmian canal above all things." The Senate ratified the treaty on February 23, 1904. Roosevelt knew the popularity of this accomplishment. He wrote a campaign manager in the 1904 election, "Can you tell our speakers to dwell more on the Panama Canal? We have not a stronger card."

The Army Corps of Engineers spent the next ten years in the mud, contracting yellow fever and supervising construction. While the army boasted of its campaign to eradicate the disease, it also hired some 30,000 black laborers from the West Indies to perform the truly backbreaking work of digging the canal at ten cents an hour, ten hours a day, six days a week. "Segregation by color...became established policy." Thousands died from fatigue, overwork, and bad food. Those who survived suffered the contempt of their army

Theodore Roosevelt personally digging the Panama Canal, 1906
(Library of Congress)

foremen who complained that West Indians were "wasteful...stupid...pos-
sessed with unutterable hatred of exertion other than conversation." In 1906
Roosevelt became the first American president to leave the country while in
office, sailing to Panama in November to look at the canal. He climbed into
a giant ninety-five-ton Bucyrus steam shovel to have his picture taken watching "the dirt fly."

Expanding the Monroe Doctrine

Once the United States had purchased the rights to the isthmus, the protection of the area took on importance. James Monroe had announced
that the United States would block any new European colonies in the Western Hemisphere in 1823. No American statesman had made much of the
doctrine during the first fifty years of its existence, but in the 1890s it had
become a major principle of American foreign policy. During a border
dispute between the government of Venezuela and British Guiana over the
headwaters of the Orinoco River, the American secretary of state Richard
Olney interjected himself as mediator in the controversy without having
been asked for his opinion by either side. In one of the most famous comments ever made on U.S. dominance of the Western Hemisphere, Olney
bluntly informed the British government that "the United States is practically sovereign in this hemisphere and its fiat is law upon the subjects to
which it confines its interposition."

Ten years later, Roosevelt showed how many hemisphere subjects the
United States considered relevant. After the war with Spain, Roosevelt did
not fear direct rule from Europe, but economic ties between Europe and
Latin America gave him pause. On one hand, European lending and investment in the Western Hemisphere made business more difficult for American firms. Therefore, the U.S. government might support governments in
the Caribbean and South America that wanted to evict European bankers
and replace their funds with dollars from New York. On the other hand, lenders in Europe and the United States had to stick together in a common
front against borrowers. Should the Latin American nations default on their
European loans the investments of Americans might be next.

In 1902 the government of Venezuela stopped payment on some $12.5
million in loans from European, mostly German, bankers. The dictator of
Venezuela, Cipriano Castro, who had long denounced Europeans and the
United States in equally harsh terms, became embroiled with the German
kaiser, William II. At first the United States paid no attention, as Roosevelt
personally liked the kaiser and detested Castro. He told his friend German
ambassador "Specky" von Sternberg, "If any South American state misbe-
haves toward any European country, let the European country spank it."

The chastisement began in December when the Germans and British sent a fleet to Venezuela, shelled the coast, and imposed a blockade. Roosevelt was pleased, but the *Literary Digest* reported that many American newspapers "think that the allies have gone too far." Roosevelt also worried that a Venezuelan capitulation in the face of European armed force would give an excessive boost to German prestige in the Western Hemisphere. Accordingly, he urged arbitration upon Venezuela and the Europeans. The two sides took their case to the International Tribunal at The Hague, which ruled in February 1904, upholding the claims of Germany and Britain against hapless Venezuela. In 1916 in the midst of his campaign to have the United States declare war against Germany, Roosevelt added a twist to the story of the Venezuelan dispute when he claimed that the Germans had actually intended to seize a port on the coast. "I took action accordingly," he said. "I assembled our battle fleet...for maneuvers, with instructions that the fleet...should be ready to sail at an hour's notice."

Two years after the Venezuelan affair, in December 1904, the president formally appointed the United States "the policeman of the west." The occasion was another financial row in the Caribbean. The Dominican Republic had placed its finances in the hands of an American financial concern optimistically calling itself the "Santo Domingo Improvement Company." In 1901 the government of the Dominican Republic threw out the American financiers, who appealed to the State Department for help in recovering $4.5 million. Belgian bankers also pressed suits, and the American minister in Santo Domingo, "an eager friend of intervention," reported that the government was considering inviting the Germans to establish a naval base on the island. Roosevelt himself warned in the spring of 1904 that he might have "to do what a policeman has to do."

The president waited until his resounding electoral victory in November. When Congress convened in December, he used the situation in Santo Domingo to announce his corollary to the Monroe Doctrine. He decried the "chronic wrongdoing, or...impotence which results in a general loosening of ties of civilized society." He told Congress that "in the western hemisphere the adherence of the United States to the Monroe Doctrine may force the United States, however reluctantly, in flagrant cases of such wrongdoing or impotence, to the exercise of an international police power." In these words, Roosevelt had transformed the Monroe Doctrine from a warning to the Europeans not to intervene in the Western Hemisphere into an American commitment to intervene whenever the United States saw "chronic wrongdoing" among its neighbors.

Three weeks after he spoke, the State Department opened discussions with the government of the Dominican Republic designed to establish American control over Dominican customs and tax receipts. A compliant

Dominican government agreed and readily signed a treaty in February 1905, but Democrats in the Senate prevented its ratification. Roosevelt then acted informally, appointing an American as controller of Dominican customs and stationing the navy off the coast just to make sure. On February 25, 1907, the two nations signed and ratified the treaty. While testifying for the agreement, the new secretary of state, Elihu Root, explained how the Panama Canal required the United States to "police the surrounding premises."

Roosevelt on Asia and Russia

But Roosevelt himself never clearly distinguished between economic and strategic motives in his foreign policy. He thought that many businessmen had far too narrow a view of the national interest: they were "lazy [and] preferred ease to the strenuous life." At the same time, he believed that American businessmen were superior to those of other nations. Sometimes he sought to stiffen the spines of American businessmen and have them aggressively seek markets they might otherwise ignore. In China he thought that American business could be the stalking horse for the government. He encouraged a reluctant J. P. Morgan in 1905 to back a railroad in China even though it was a bad investment. The president fulminated against businessmen who took only a short view. Even if the American-China Development Corporation lost money, U.S. businessmen could maintain an American presence in a country where the United States could not use force.

Roosevelt was especially concerned that the United States was losing influence in China to Russia, which had moved into Manchuria after 1900. In the war between Russia and Japan of 1904 and 1905, the rest of the world watched as those two nations fought to determine the major imperial power in China. When the war broke, the United States sided with the Japanese. Russia had enjoyed good relations with the United States in the eighteenth and nineteenth centuries, when it had supported the American definition of neutral rights. The United States had also supported the call of Czar Nicholas II for the peace conference at The Hague in 1899. But in the Roosevelt administration, relations deteriorated badly. A pogrom against Jews in the south Russian city of Kishinev in 1903 sent shock waves across the Atlantic Ocean. Jewish immigration from Russia had risen throughout the decade of the 1890s, and it shot up dramatically after the attack, which killed forty-nine people. From 1890 to 1910, some 1.5 million Jews left Russia for the United States. President Roosevelt denounced the pogrom and with it the entire government of Russia as a "barbarous despotism."

When Japan attacked the Russian fleet at Port Arthur without warning on February 8, 1904, the American public reacted gleefully. Elihu Root asked the president, "Was not the way the Jap began the fight bully?" He admired their "perfect preparation and willingness to take action," and newspapers chimed in with high praise for Japanese cleverness. Just as the reputation of Russia had sunk in the United States at the end of the nineteenth century, that of the Japanese had risen over the years. Some Americans felt flattered by the Japanese imitation of the habits of the West. Hundreds of Japanese had attended universities in the United States, going home full of enthusiasm for American science, business methods, and political structure. But not all Japanese were so loved by Americans. While hundreds of students came to American universities to learn techniques they could apply back home, 30,000 more Japanese came to America as laborers, where they encountered nativist demands for their exclusion, segregation, and repatriation. When the Japanese vanquished the Russians, American feelings toward them were thus mixed. On one hand, Americans admired the Japanese capacity to learn from the West and improve themselves. On the other hand, deep strains of racism turned the Japanese into a threatening people who might overtake the West.

The war with Japan helped create a revolution in Russia that threatened to topple the czar's despotism in early 1905. It also had immediate and long–term effects upon American thinking about Russia. The initial American reaction to the "democratic" uprising in St. Petersburg in 1905 was enthusiasm for the reformers, who seemed to want to imitate the democratic form of government favored in the United States. Roosevelt himself thought the revolution was an encouraging sign, and it made him more favorably disposed toward the Russian side in the war. Americans quickly discovered, however, that the revolution was not the "liberal" movement they hoped would become the standard for the world. The ambassador in St. Petersburg reported the alarming presence of socialists, Communists, and communitarians in the leadership of the revolutionary forces. The czar might have been "stupid, cruel, despotic," but the radicals who longed to replace him were worse. The government's shakiness made Roosevelt want to mediate an end to the war with Japan, while his alarm at the radicals foreshadowed later American uneasiness with a new generation of Russian revolutionaries twelve years later.

Roosevelt's attitudes toward the war typified the views of others. Along with his countrymen, the president detested Russian despotism and felt flattered by the Japanese imitation of American habits, but at the same time he feared the Japanese. Neither complete Japanese nor Russian victories pleased him. He injected himself as a mediator in the war in order to make sure that the United States had a say in the future of China. Roosevelt worried that no matter what the outcome, it would leave China at the mercy of either Japan or Russia. In either case, the United States and the Western European powers would find themselves frozen out of deciding what the future of China would look like. He tried, therefore, to stop the two powers from completing their conquest of China. Roosevelt hoped that his mediation would cause the combatants to draw back from dismembering China, but even if he did not succeed, he wanted to demonstrate to the Chinese that the United States had their best interest at heart. He would be an honest broker to the belligerents; to the Chinese, he would be a protector.

In June 1905 Roosevelt asked representatives of Russia and Japan to meet with him at Portsmouth, New Hampshire, to end the conflict. Exhausted by war, both powers accepted, and the peace conference assembled on August 9 in the midst of the hottest summer in New England history. The Japanese wanted the Russians to pay a huge indemnity, yield a free hand in north China and Manchuria, and hand over their lease on the Liaodong (Liaotung) Peninsula, the base at Port Arthur, and Sakhalin Island. Roosevelt felt the Japanese had a right to expect an indemnity from the Russians, but he did not want the Japanese to take over the Russian port. Under the terms of the Open Door policy, Roosevelt also was worried about the Japanese desire for a free hand in the north of China. Russia refused to provide an indemnity or all territory demanded.

The conversations at Portsmouth therefore did not go smoothly. The United States was contemptuous of the Russians and a little afraid of the Japanese. Russia had lost the war and was convulsed by revolution at home. For their part, the financially spent Japanese could no longer press their advantage. Both sides sullenly accepted a compromise Roosevelt presented on August 28. Japan dropped demands for an indemnity and agreed to accept only half of Sakhalin in return for virtual control of north China and Manchuria. In 1906 Roosevelt won the Nobel Peace Prize for his work. The next year, however, Russia and Japan quietly buried the hatchet and agreed jointly to dismember north China and Manchuria. The United States found itself out in the cold.

Japanese nationalists thought that Roosevelt had deprived them of their just gains, and an ugly riot broke out in Tokyo. Protesters demanded that the government reject American mediation and take every inch demanded of the czar. The crowd denounced Roosevelt and hanged an effigy of the American president in front of the U.S. embassy. The Japanese government had helped organize the rally against the United States, but once the people had blown off steam, officials dropped opposition to the treaty.

Racial disagreements between the United States and Japan continued after the Russo-Japanese War. In October 1906 the school board of San Francisco sent Japanese children to segregated schools in that city. There happened to be fewer than 200 Japanese students in the district, but the board decided anyway that these children were a disrupting influence upon the lives of the rest of the scholars. Japan angrily protested to the Department of State in Washington about the segregation order. Elihu Root, the conservative New York lawyer who had succeeded John Hay as secretary of state upon Hay's death in 1905, thought the school board had gone too far. He had no special concern for the feelings of Japanese in America, but Root believed that the United States could not afford to offend the government of Japan. Roosevelt as well was furious with the San Franciscans, denouncing the segregation order as a "wicked absurdity." He summoned the California congressional delegation to the White House on January 3, 1907, to reveal his plan to have San Francisco drop segregation while he stopped further immigration from Japan. He let the Japanese ambassador know that he personally disapproved of the segregation order, believed that the Californians were bigots, and wanted the Japanese to continue to have good relations with the United States.

Eventually, in the winter of 1906–1907, Roosevelt worked out a gentlemen's agreement with the San Francisco school board and the government of Japan. The Californians would return the Japanese school children to their regular classrooms, and the Japanese government would finally ban emigration to the United States. The Japanese would not have to suffer the indignity of being singled out, as had the Chinese, as members of a race that could not enter the United States. Under the gentlemen's agreement, no Japanese came directly to the United States for the next two decades.

A Great Power Everywhere

Theodore Roosevelt also involved the United States in European conflicts, which traditionally had not interested the American government. One of these involved Morocco. By the early twentieth century, this sand dune in North Africa, officially part of the Ottoman Empire, had fallen under the control of France. The German emperor, William II, thought that France should yield a share of the direction of Moroccan affairs to Germany. In March 1905 the kaiser showed up in Tangier and offered a toast to the bey of Morocco which pledged support to him in resisting the French. France complained that the Germans were fishing in troubled waters, and William II replied by asking President Roosevelt to intervene on his side. Roosevelt, eager to see the United States assume a prominent role in world affairs, readily agreed to invite the great powers to a conference at Algeciras on the Spanish coast.

No one could say that the United States had a direct interest in what happened in Morocco, but Theodore Roosevelt insisted that the American government receive an invitation to the conference, which assembled at the Spanish port city in January 1906. He reasoned that if the United States truly was a world power with interests everywhere around the globe, then America should be included in the conferences that drew up the boundaries. Brushing aside the objection that the Monroe Doctrine had formerly prevented the United States from involvement in European politics, Roosevelt asserted he participated "to keep matters on an even keel in Europe."

On another occasion in the Roosevelt administration, the United States led the way in calling a general conference of the major nations. In the summer of 1906, Americans joined forty-three other countries at The Hague to complete the work of the First Hague Peace Conference of 1899. The Second Hague Conference continued the work of the first in setting the rules of war. New weapons developed over the previous decade made the work of the conference all the harder. What would the diplomats, admirals, and generals have to say about the new battleships, poison gas, and war from balloons in the air? All the participants worried that these new techniques of destruction might ruin them in a coming war. They also hoped, however, that the new weaponry would be exactly what they needed to overcome their opponents. The American delegation, led by John W. Foster, a former secretary of state and a grandfather of a future one, John Foster Dulles, led the way in establishing some new rules. Poison gas was outlawed, but the powers could not agree on other new frightening weapons—the submarine, the aerial balloon, the airplane, or the battleship. The admirals and generals refused to ban these modern instruments of destruction. They thought that the advantages they could gain from using these weapons would outweigh any dangers that might ensue.

The Hague Conference made a start in creating a predictable world through the codification of international law. Reformers expected the court to grow into what Andrew Carnegie called a League of Peace or a League of Nations. Some reformers anticipated the birth of an international congress to enforce the judgments of the Hague court. Richard Bartholdt, one of the organizers of the American Society of International Law in 1906, confidently predicted that in due time an international congress would grow and become "more perfect in form and accomplish for nations what a Federal union like ours accomplished for the constituent states."

Secretary of State Elihu Root, who lent his name to the creation of the American Society of International Law, had more modest hopes. At the beginning of the twentieth century, international law was nothing more than the treaties previously drawn up between states. Nations might agree to regulate their affairs with one another according to treaties, and the courts of two nations might rule that the treaties had the force of law. Root proposed to make the treaties conducted by individual states available to every nation. He suggested that a central organization record all treaties nations had drafted with one another. Registration of treaties would fulfill several functions: it would set standards for other nations to uphold in their treaties, permit the Hague court to make judgments, and eliminate the practice of "secret treaties," agreements with clauses known only to the nations signing them. Reformers believed that this kind of treaty created discord and resentment among states since nations could only fear that secret clauses contained threats. The reformers of international law acknowledged that strong states would still rule the world once treaties were codified. Still, the growing body of international law could make the world more predictable for the weak as well as the strong. Lesser nations would have to respect the mighty, but they had less to fear from their caprice.

As secretary of state, Root began a campaign of arbitration treaties for the United States. Under terms of these agreements signed with twenty-four states throughout the world, each party agreed to bring outstanding disputes between them to the world court at The Hague. In this way, Root sought to offer some respect to the world court.

Root's career as a jurist was a curious one. Early in the Roosevelt administration, he had served as one of the president's hand-picked panelists on an arbitration board deciding the boundary between Alaska and Canada. Seated alongside Root for the Americans were Henry Cabot Lodge and a former senator from the state of Washington, two intense nationalists. The dispute arose over control of the Lynn Canal and the port city of Sitka. Once gold had been discovered in the Klondike River basin of Alaska in 1899, it became important to Alaskans and Canadians alike that they have access to the sea.

The Canadians insisted to both the British government in London and the American State Department in Washington that the ports on the coast belonged to Canada. Otherwise, there would be no way that Canadian gold could be shipped out without going through Alaska. The British government did not favor the Canadian claims, as the Foreign Office in London thought good relations with the United States mattered more than did satisfying the demands of their lower dominion. The British agreed to bring the case before a mock arbitration panel in order to quiet the Canadians. Roosevelt could appoint men to the panel who were bound to support the Alaskan claims. The British side of the delegation consisted of two Canadians and an English judge, Richard C. E. Alverstone. Since the Americans would hold for their side and the Canadians for the claims of the Yukon, Alverstone had the final say. He held for the United States, outraging the Canadians. London supported the Americans in the controversy since it did not wish the growing entente between the two countries to be jeopardized to satisfy Ottawa's parochial interests. Canadians grumbled that the defection of the British meant that Canada had no choice but to seek control of its own affairs. Eventually, in 1921, Canada gained such independence.

The British capitulation to the United States in 1903, however, indicated that they had decided that the Western Hemisphere belonged to the Americans. Britain's period of "splendid isolation" had left it threatened by other powers. It needed friends, and America seemed a good candidate. Insofar as the British had ambitions in world politics, they would be satisfied in Europe first, then in the Middle East, and then in Africa and Asia. The United States and the British would become good friends, but only at the cost of a division of the world into spheres.

In 1907 Roosevelt decided literally to show the flag. He had the American navy, which he happily called the "Great White Fleet," travel to Europe, Africa, and Asia to impress world leaders with American might. When the fleet was halfway around the world, the American Congress, in a cost-cutting mood, threatened to stop payment for such imperial pomp. Undaunted, Roosevelt informed Congress that the fleet could stay abroad, demonstrating that the United States was indeed a premier nation, if the money did not arrive to bring it back to the United States. Of course, Congress relented, and the Great White Fleet sailed home triumphantly.

When Roosevelt turned over his office to William Howard Taft, his hand-picked successor, on March 4, 1909, he had laid the foundations for subsequent progressive diplomacy. He bequeathed an enthusiastic American nationalism that distrusted the flag-waving of other countries. Valuing stability and the capacity to influence the future above all else, the makers of foreign policy saw other peoples' nationalism, revolutionary fervor, and great power rivalry as threats to a predictable world order.

CHAPTER THREE

The Diplomacy of the Dollar, 1909–1920

In the 1920s the term *dollar diplomacy* became a curse mouthed by liberals, radicals, and muckrakers who damned the foreign policies of William Howard Taft and Woodrow Wilson. One reform-minded author, Scott Nearing, wrote a book called *Dollar Diplomacy* to prove how Taft and Wilson had boosted the fortunes of selfish Wall Street bankers at the expense of the people of China, Central America, Mexico, and the Caribbean. Critics even discovered forgotten virtues in the nationalism of Theodore Roosevelt. If the flamboyant Rough Rider had been loud and abrasive, at least he was fun to watch. Taft, with his countinghouse mentality, appeared dull, and Wilson, with his sermons to foreigners who resented his moralizing interference, seemed a hypocrite.

Self-satisfied and good-natured, William Howard Taft never seemed bothered by the criticism. He thought his quieter, less martial, more realistic conduct of foreign relations surpassed that of his predecessor. His secretary of state, Philander C. Knox, a former corporation lawyer, proudly spoke of dollar diplomacy, thinking it represented an advance in the way the United States conducted its foreign affairs. Instead of dwelling on conflicts among nations and preparing for war, Knox urged support for international traders and investors who knit the world together. Any government tries to shield its citizens working abroad, yet dollar diplomacy went far beyond protesting harassment by foreigners of Americans. Instead, Knox elevated international businessmen to a position in which they, rather than diplomats, represented the best interests of the United States overseas. In contrast to Theodore Roosevelt, who tolerated businessmen but thought them too timid and unmasculine to do much good for the American cause overseas, Knox believed that business leaders actually were morally superior to military men. Their sober calculations of risk and profit made them better advocates for the United States. "True stability," he informed Congress, "is best established not by military but by economic and social forces... [F]inancial stability contributes perhaps more than any other one factor to political stability."

Under Taft the government tried to make certain that U.S. traders would be welcomed alongside those of every other nation and that American bankers got their share of the booming market for foreign loans. As European and American railroad promoters and mining companies sought investment opportunities in underdeveloped regions of the world, Knox believed that the rest of the world had finally caught up with the American way of diplomacy.

Taft operated at a time when the expansion of European and American capital abroad helped ignite nationalistic resentments against the imperial powers. Revolutions erupted in Asia and Central America, the two regions most attractive to American investors. The pace picked up under Woodrow Wilson, who clung to a belief that the United States was somehow more moral than the imperial powers of Europe. "In Wilson's completely liberal ideology, imperialism and militarism were seen as essentially European phenomena associated with a past America had escaped," writes historian N. Gordon Levin in *Woodrow Wilson and World Politics* (1968). This notion of "American exceptionalism" served U.S. interests, for it enabled Wilson to claim "a mission to lead mankind." His first secretary of state, three-time Democratic presidential candidate William Jennings Bryan, did not fit the mold of a worldly eastern lawyer as chief diplomat. He was an advocate for the rural poor, was a fervent evangelical Christian, favored prohibition of alcohol, and was an opponent of militarism and war. Wilson's appointment of the Nebraska-born "Great Commoner" raised eyebrows among more sophisticated easterners. Six weeks after taking over the State Department, Bryan served White Rock water and grape juice, but no wine or liquor, at a farewell reception for Britain's ambassador. *Grape juice diplomacy* became a derisive phrase among Bryan's detractors. One of his friends remarked that he provoked "wholehearted, comprehensive, constitutional, fundamental, temperamental, special, religious, anatomical, gastronomic, and sartorial disagreement."

For all of his apparent lack of sophistication, Bryan as much as Wilson believed that the United States occupied a special place in God's favor. When it came to explaining their duties to foreigners, he obediently followed his chief's instructions. After he resigned in 1915 in protest over Wilson's increasingly hostile attitude toward Germany in the First World War, his place was taken by a more traditional diplomat, Robert Lansing, a well-connected but nonpolitical lawyer. Lansing did not enjoy Bryan's base within the Democratic Party, and by the time he became secretary, Wilson had acquired enough confidence in his own diplomatic skills that he wanted only a clerk as his principal foreign policy adviser. Lansing performed this secondary role with some misgivings as Wilson grappled with the changes nationalism and revolution brought to world politics.

AMERICA, CHINA, AND THE PROBLEM OF REVOLUTION, 1909–1915

One place the Taft administration sought to practice dollar diplomacy was China, where Knox moved quickly to distinguish his policy from Roosevelt's. The Rough Rider had quietly dropped the Open Door policy in the wake of the Russo-Japanese War, acknowledging that Japan's and Russia's proximity to China gave them the power to do what they wanted in Manchuria. While the American consul general in Mukden, Willard Straight, complained that the Russo-Japanese rapprochement of 1908 effectively froze the United States out of north China, Roosevelt thought there was little the United States could do about it. The principal American interest in the Far East was the protection of the Philippines, which could be done by mollifying Japan.

Taft and Knox paid more attention than had Roosevelt to Straight, who returned to Washington to become chief of the Division of Far Eastern Affairs, and Huntington Wilson, the first assistant secretary of state. Both men detested Japan and promoted China. They encouraged Knox to urge American investment in China to counter the influence of Japan and Russia. The Chinese government in Beijing also hoped that investment from the United States and perhaps Great Britain would check Japanese expansion.

The American effort to enter the investment market of north China began in the summer of 1909. Taft cabled Prince Chun, the Chinese regent, asking him to grant American investors an equal share of a loan being floated in Europe to construct a railroad in southern China. In 1910 the Europeans reluctantly acceded to Chinese and American importunities and allowed Americans to invest. About the same time, Willard Straight left the State Department to represent the American bankers who wanted to build railroads in Manchuria. He went to Europe and China to obtain agreement for his sponsors to join a consortium building a trans-Manchurian railroad from Chinchow to Aigun. In October Chinese representatives in Manchuria authorized Straight's group to finance the road.

While Straight worked the private sector, Knox proceeded along a diplomatic front to establish an open door for investment and make the United States the savior of China. The State Department proposed the "neutralization" or "internationalization" of all railroads in Manchuria and north China. Japan was the obvious target of this scheme, which would force the island empire to yield its exclusive control of the south Manchurian railroad. Knox hoped that Russia and Great Britain would welcome the chance to block Japan. Unfortunately for his plan, their fears of Japanese military power exceeded their greed. Britain had been allied with Japan since 1902, when London felt the need for friends in remote places. British support for the neutralization plan would jeopardize the alliance. Knox had no better luck with Russia, which drew closer to Japan in the face of the neutralization plan. The Russians feared Japanese retaliation while expecting that their agreement with Japan over the exploitation of north China offered more protection than agreeing to American proposals.

Having been rebuffed by the British and Russians, the Taft administration kept at it. The next area in which it sought to have American businessmen participate was in direct loans to the government of China to meet its operating expenses and stabilize its currency. The finances of China, like those of so many dying empires, were in disarray at the turn of the century. As the government lost control of outlying districts and as its expenses mounted, it found itself deeply in debt. As had been the case for the Ottoman Empire, Egypt, and Morocco in the late nineteenth century, the Chinese discovered that the only readily available source of funds was the bankers of the outside powers.

Chinese government officials knew what had happened in North Africa in the previous decades when the local governments had borrowed in Europe. In some cases the debts had led to seizures of the customs houses. In others European powers had established protectorates over the debtor. Chinese diplomats feared the same fate, so they actively encouraged the Americans to join the consortium making loans for their currency. The more participants in the consortium, the Chinese reasoned, the easier to play one against another. Tang Shao, a leader of the Manchurian railroad, also detected a more impartial attitude on the part of the United States. He complained that "the great powers of Europe, aside from Germany, openly give to Japan the advantage over us and conclude with her agreements to our detriment, but the United States continues to have in the Far East a national policy independent of all foreign alliances."

The American government wanted New York bankers to join in loans to China, with Knox insisting that participation would preserve the Open Door. He encouraged Straight to alert bankers to their patriotic obligations to join the loan consortium organized in support of China's government. The secretary of state passed the word that "when we support the open door in China that is not so-called dollar diplomacy, but the recognition of a high moral duty."

Duty, perhaps, but bankers saw no reason to bear the major burden of morality. They scorned the meager promise of 5 percent interest, doubted the

Chinese would pay even that modest amount, and wondered if Washington used them as a "wedge" to gain preeminence in China. Nonetheless, Knox carried the day in persuading them that if the United States did not participate in the loans, then the empire would fall apart. In 1911 the American firms of J. P. Morgan and Kuhn Loeb and Company made more than $2 million available for the Chinese government.

The government tried, but the transfusion of money could not revive the Manchu Empire. In April 1911 China underwent one of the revolutions that convulsed it in the twentieth century. Under the leadership of Sun Yat-sen, an American-educated doctor, Chinese revolutionaries overthrew the monarchy and created a republic. For Americans, the initial success of the revolutionaries represented a vast improvement over the empire. Knox thought revolution in China a far better thing for American interests than the Boxer Rebellion of 1900. The earlier uprising had been a nationalistic, antiforeign movement. While the earlier Boxers opposed the government of China, their animosity toward the authorities derived from the government's having turned the country over to the foreigners. The republicans of 1911 opposed the corruption of the court itself, arguing that China should use the West as a model. Sun's government would resemble the American system in outward form. American officials were flattered by the Chinese mimicry.

The pride Americans felt when the Chinese emulated them clouded the American judgment about their revolution. Unwilling or unable to recognize that Chinese republicans took only those elements from the American experience that they believed to be most relevant to their own, the Americans thought instead that the Chinese wanted to become like the United States. When it later became clear that the republicans remained proud of their own heritage and resented the West as much as had the Boxers, lovers of China felt betrayed. How dare the Chinese try to find their own way of organizing their society?

The response to the Chinese revolution followed the pattern set by the Russian revolution of 1905. For the remainder of the century, Americans maintained ambivalent feelings toward nationalist upheavals. During these eruptions the reaction often became a short-lived initial burst of enthusiasm as Americans heard echoes of their own eighteenth-century revolution. Americans longed to see themselves as a model, and they considered Europe a source of reaction and autocracy. But this sympathy soon collapsed under the weight of revolutionary nationalism. When revolutionaries turned against the United States, Americans reacted with anger. They came to believe that the revolutions had been captured by "fanatics" who lacked the sense of balance and perspective needed to run a modern state.

In the aftermath of the Chinese revolution of 1911, Secretary of State Knox redoubled his efforts to have Wall Street bankers loan money to the new republic, hoping to influence it in favor of "moderation" and the United States. For his part, Sun Yat-sen would have the Western consortium continue to loan money so long as the terms of the loan could be revised in China's favor. The European powers, on the other hand, demurred, suspecting the independence of the new republican government. They resisted according diplomatic recognition to the republic for a year after the revolution, while negotiations to refinance the loan bogged down.

By the time a new agreement was reached in early 1913, the Taft administration was a lame duck, having been defeated in November 1912 in a three-way race with former president Roosevelt, running as a Progressive, and the winner, the Democrats' Woodrow Wilson. During the election campaign foreign affairs had not been an issue. Instead, the more progressive candidates, Roosevelt and Wilson, had complained about the probusiness attitude of the leader they both called "lazy." Wilson, the former governor of New Jersey and president of Princeton University before that, had campaigned for the "New Freedom," a vague promise of government intervention to protect middle-class Americans from the grip of large, heartless business interests. As a professor of political science, Wilson had written extensively on the structure of American government but little about foreign affairs. His views were the standard opinions of Democratic politicians of the day: a commitment to low tariffs and free trade, rejection of Theodore Roosevelt's strident nationalism, and a reluctance to hold formal colonies.

A week after he took office on March 4, 1913, Wilson reversed Taft's support of the American bankers' participation in the China loan consortium. After March 13, he told the press, J. P. Morgan's bank, and the American minister in Beijing, American financiers would be on their own in China. For Wilson's admirers, this abrupt reversal cancelled dollar diplomacy and made him, in the words of Arthur Link, "the first effective anti-imperialist statesman of the twentieth century." Link, the comprehensive biographer of Wilson, argues that he broke up the consortium because he "utterly detested the exploitative imperialist system" and because the consortium "threatened the political independence of China." Few others have expressed quite so rosy a view of Wilson's China policy. Emily Rosenberg writes in *Financial Missionaries to the World* (1999) that although Wilson's policy "was announced as an anti–big business policy and portrayed as a repudiation of Taft's dollar diplomacy, in fact the bankers themselves had had hope for termination of the stalled project and were relieved to be rid of government pressure to continue their fruitless and time-consuming venture."

For all of Wilson's scorn for Theodore Roosevelt's juvenile enthusiasm, the new president's Asian policy followed Roosevelt's attempt to reach an accommodation with Japan. Joint ventures with Japan cast a spell over

American financiers for the next year. When, however, Europe erupted into war in August 1914, the Japanese saw their opportunity to exploit China without the help of any other power, including the United States. Wilson himself became preoccupied with events in Mexico and Europe in 1914 and 1915, as we shall see shortly, and the United States found itself without influence in China. In 1915 Japan presented China "Twenty-One Demands," which required that China become a virtual protectorate of Japan. Despite Lansing's protests, Japan got its way from 1915 to 1919.

INTERVENTION AND DOLLAR DIPLOMACY IN CENTRAL AMERICA AND THE CARIBBEAN

The U.S. government had an easier time getting its way through dollar diplomacy closer to home where it had less competition from imperial rivals. Taft and Knox sent the American marines to occupy Nicaragua and the Dominican Republic, took over the customs receipts of Guatemala and Honduras, and meddled in Mexico. The Wilson administration occupied the Dominican Republic and Haiti and nearly fought a war with America's southern neighbor, Mexico. In each case the United States intervened to prevent what was called "anarchy." Often intervention made things worse, as the government assisted private traders and investors who hoped to steal a march on competition from Europe. Taft and Wilson went beyond the Roosevelt Corollary to the Monroe Doctrine by intervening in Central America before there was a hint of the "chronic wrongdoing" that Roosevelt had insisted called for the United States to wield its policeman's stick.

The case of Nicaragua provided one of the longest-running episodes of American interventions in the hemisphere. In 1909 American businessmen helped a local junta overthrow the dictatorship of José Zaleya, who had led the country since 1893. A nationalist, Zaleya had been a thorn in the side of the United States, waging wars with his neighbors Honduras, El Salvador, and Guatemala. Worse, from the American point of view, he financed his country's national debt through European banks in May 1909. Under the terms of this agreement, Europeans had control over the customs revenues, and their governments could intervene directly should the Central American country default on its debt.

American landholders and miners in Nicaragua accordingly sought ways to rid the country of Zaleya, and in 1909 they financed a revolution against him. The rebels, led by Juan Estrada, conducted a guerrilla campaign, and during one of the military engagements, Zaleya's troops captured and executed two U.S. citizens fighting with the insurgents. In Washington Knox responded by denouncing Zaleya to Nicaragua's chargé d'affaires as a "blot on

UNITED STATES INTERVENTION IN THE CARIBBEAN

UNITED STATES

GULF OF
MEXICO

MEXICO
(U.S. Invasion, 1916–17)

● Mexico City

Vera Cruz
(U.S. Occupation, 1914)

PACIFIC OCEAN

GUATEMALA

BRITISH
HONDURAS

HONDURAS
(U.S. Troops, 1924–25)

EL SALVADOR

NICARAGUA
(U.S. Protectorate, 1911–24;
Troops, 1912–25, 1926–33)

COSTA RICA

PANAMA
(U.S. Protectorate, 1903)

PANAMA CANAL ZONE
(Leased to U.S., 1903)

COLOMBIA

VENEZUELA

ATLANTIC OCEAN

BAHAMA
ISLANDS (Br.)

CUBA
(U.S. Protectorate, 1903–34)

Guántanamo
(U.S. Naval Base)

JAMAICA (Br.)

HAITI
(U.S. Protectorate,
1915–34)

DOMINICAN
REPUBLIC
(U.S. Protectorate, 1905;
Troops, 1916–24)

PUERTO RICO
(Annexed, 1898)

U.S. VIRGIN
ISLANDS
(Purchased from
Denmark, 1916)

CARIBBEAN SEA

United States intervention in Cuba

the history of Nicaragua." The secretary then broke diplomatic relations and announced the United States would welcome a victory of the insurrection. Faced with American support of his opponents, Zaleya resigned and fled to Mexico.

By August 1910 the guerrillas had triumphed and installed as president Adolfo Díaz, who once had worked as a bookkeeper for an American mining firm in the country. American businessmen there welcomed Díaz's assumption of power, but they let him know that if he was to maintain the nation's finances, he must look to the United States for help. Knox thought that an American loan would end the residual British interests in that country. In June 1911 Knox signed an accord with the Nicaraguan minister to Washington, Salvador Castrillo, that would turn the latter's country into a protectorate of the United States.

Under the terms of the Knox-Castrillo Convention, the United States refunded the Nicaraguan debt with an American loan. As collateral, the Central American nation pledged its customs receipts, and the commissioner of customs became an official approved by the American government. Knox had no respect for the self-restraint of any of these "banana-republic" politicians and claimed that placing the customs house under control of the United States would remove an incentive to oust the new government by eliminating the prize of the tariff revenues.

Less than a month after signing the convention, the Managua government defaulted on the debts contracted with the Europeans in 1909. The Department of State unofficially encouraged American bankers to step into the breach. They did so by providing a short-term credit of $1 million and a promise to negotiate a settlement with the European creditors. Americans also took over control of the Nicaraguan customs house. In December 1911 Knox appointed an American army officer to take charge of the collection of customs duties in Nicaragua. Knox explained "We are...because of the Monroe Doctrine, held responsible for the order of Central America, and because of its proximity to the Canal makes the preservation of peace in that neighborhood particularly necessary."

While all of these activities occurred in Central America, the Senate considered the Knox-Castrillo agreement, which would make them formal. Democrats objected, accusing Knox of wishing to extend the power of the United States too broadly. In May 1912 senators turned back the Knox-Castrillo pact. American bankers, however, continued their supervision of the customs houses of Nicaragua. With the connivance of Taft and Knox, the Americans maintained a sort of informal protectorate over the finances.

In Nicaragua itself American domination aroused resentment from nationalists led by former president Zaleya. In July 1912 they attacked the government in Managua, and Díaz wired Washington for assistance to put

U.S. marines on the move in Nicaragua
(National Archives)

down the revolt. American bankers also desperately wanted assistance because they feared that their own holdings in the country might be appropriated. Taft sent a flotilla of eight American warships bearing a force of 2,500 marines, and sailors landed to crush the revolt. After Díaz was saved, 100 marines remained to guard the American legation, and an American warship remained stationed off the coast as a warning to the revolutionaries. Díaz's control had been restored, but he could never be safe so long as his treasury was insecure. Furthermore, American lenders wanted greater assurance than their supervision of the country's customs houses that they would receive repayment. In early 1913 they encouraged Díaz to negotiate a new treaty with the United States to underwrite their loans. In February the two countries signed a treaty under which the United States received naval bases and the right to build and operate a canal across the country. In return for these favors, the United States would pay, not loan, Nicaragua $3 million. Wilson became president in March, and he submitted the treaty to the Senate with an additional guarantee of Washington's right to intervene. This new Bryan-Chamorro Treaty was not ratified until 1916, when the Senate dropped the intervention clause. Wilson sent American warships to patrol Nicaraguan waters during the 1916 presidential election.

While the affair was the most spectacular extension of American power in the Caribbean during the Taft administration, the United States also took over tax collection of the other nations of Central America. All of the

Central American countries except El Salvador had defaulted on their debts to Europeans. Knox reasoned that these creditors might seize control of the customs houses unless some arrangements were made to refund debts. At the same time Knox was negotiating American control over Nicaragua's tariff revenues, he also offered to reorganize Honduras's finances. The American minister in Honduras took a hand in negotiating an agreement between the government and its creditors. Most lenders were European bankers who knew that their governments never would support an intervention in Central America if it meant coming into conflict with the United States. So in return for a payment of a few cents on the dollar, the creditors agreed to refund the debt. Even this token payment exceeded the means of the Hondurans, but the American minister promised that the United States would provide the money to pay the European debts. In return the customs houses would come under U.S. control. In January 1911 Knox signed a treaty establishing American control over the customs houses, but the United States Senate as well as the Honduran Congress rejected it. In the case of the Senate, Democrats objected to the idea of the U.S. dollar diplomacy, while in Honduras the congress thought that the government had turned the country over to the Yankees.

Knox tried again in Costa Rica and Guatemala to extend U.S. control over customs receipts. In both cases, however, the countries refused his offer. In 1911 the prospect of an American attempt to take over the customs houses forced Costa Rica to conclude an agreement with European creditors to repay part of the debt. Guatemala's president also felt pressure from the State Department to negotiate an agreement with his foreign creditors. The State Department wanted American bankers to refund the debt of Guatemala. Despite their best efforts, the Americans never could get Guatemala to agree to a refunding program, and the scheme died.

The United States also took over the island of Hispaniola, shared by the Dominican Republic and Haiti. In 1912 Taft sent marines to the Dominican Republic, the country where Roosevelt had invoked his corollary and seized the customs. A revolution broke out, forcing the closure of seven customs houses operated by the Americans under the terms of the 1907 treaty. In September Taft sent a contingent of 750 marines to force the resignation of a corrupt Dominican president and supervise a new election. The troops came home to the United States in December, but the Wilson administration kept a close watch on politics in the Dominican Republic. In September 1913 a threat of another revolution brought an American squadron to the coast. Things calmed down until May 1916, when the next insurrection occurred. The American navy landed sailors, while the commanding admiral threatened to bombard the capital, Santo Domingo, unless the insurgents surrendered. At the same time the State Department worked out a treaty giving the United States effective control over Santo Domingo's tax collections and spending. Even this was not enough for a worried President Wilson, who feared German intervention in the country. At the end of 1916, when it appeared likely that the United States would soon enter the European war against Germany, Wilson proclaimed the military occupation of the Dominican Republic. The American navy remained to govern there until 1922.

Political unrest and financial instability also brought the U.S. navy and marines to Haiti. Political murder and revolutionary upheaval had tormented that nation ever since the slave rebellion of Touissant L'Ouverture had thrown out the French at the beginning of the nineteenth century. A depressed economy had not encouraged Americans to invest, and such commerce as existed was in the hands of a few French and German expatriates. Chronic instability often spilled over to the Dominican Republic, where Americans were deeply involved. Once war broke out in Europe, the Wilson administration feared that European control could lead to a German fleet in Haiti threatening the approaches to the Panama Canal. Wilson therefore opened negotiations for an American receivership of Haitian customs. The response in Haiti was another bloody revolution, which toppled the government of Guillaume Sam in July 1915. Wilson, who had once described nonwhite countries as living in the "childhood of political development" and dismissed democracy for them as a "curse," dispatched 2,000 marines to impose martial law on Haiti. At the same time Secretary of State Lansing drafted a treaty with a compliant Haitian government granting the United States control of the country's finances. The United States occupied Haiti and trained its military until 1934.

If Knox's attempts to get Americans included in the financial arrangements of other nations represented one side of American diplomacy, an even stranger episode occurred when Massachusetts Republican Henry Cabot Lodge, the chairman of the Senate Foreign Relations Committee, injected himself into the debate. The so-called Lodge Corollary to the Monroe Doctrine went beyond Roosevelt's gloss, excluding private foreign companies as well as foreign governments from the Western Hemisphere. Under Lodge's prescription the New World was to become a commercial as well as a strategic sphere of influence for the United States.

The issue arose over a Japanese attempt to purchase an American tract of land and a fishing concession off the coast of Mexico's Baja California in 1912. In one sense Lodge raised an issue that had been settled the previous year. In 1911 a group of Japanese in San Francisco had opened negotiations with Mexico to purchase the rights off Baja. The State Department had blocked the sale, fearing that it would result in the establishment of a Japanese colony in the Western Hemisphere. The matter seemed a dead issue until 1912, when Lodge revived it by pointing out that outsiders could appear at any time. Lodge's speech denouncing the threat of "some great eastern power" taking possession of Baja got picked up by one of William Randolph Hearst's papers. Soon the *Los Angeles Examiner* announced that the Japanese government was ready to set up a naval base in Magdalena Bay on the Baja Peninsula. The very next day the Japanese government denied such plans. Knox, at the State Department, said he did not think the Japanese were moving to Mexico, either, and he privately asked Lodge to stop making provocative anti-Japanese comments. The Massachusetts senator refused to be silenced, and he convened the Senate Foreign Relations Committee to warn Japan. The committee drafted a resolution opposing the transfer of strategic sites in the Western Hemisphere to private companies outside the New World. The Senate passed Lodge's thinly veiled attack on Japan by an overwhelming margin.

CONFRONTING REVOLUTIONARY NATIONALISM IN MEXICO

The Mexican Revolution of 1910–1917 caused an earthquake in U.S. foreign policy. Taft and Wilson both meddled in Mexican affairs to outflank Europeans and maintain a favorable climate for U.S. investors. Neither reckoned the depths of nationalism among the Mexicans, nor did American presidents seem to realize the damage they could do to the United States by attempting to dominate Mexico's politics and economy. The story deserves detailed explanation, for it later recurred in different forms in other lands.

As a weak neighbor inhabited by a largely nonwhite and Catholic population, Mexico had drawn the scorn and attracted the greed of expansionists north of the border in the nineteenth century. In a war waged against Mexico from 1846 to 1848, the United States had stripped its southern neighbor of nearly one-third of its total land area. Later, after the Civil War, the United States helped Mexican revolutionaries, led by Benito Juárez, depose and execute the Austrian duke Maximilian, whom the French had installed as emperor of the country. Juárez had little luck with his own rule, losing the support of the United States and abdicating his presidency to Porfirio Díaz in 1877.

Díaz was one of those "modernizers" of recent history who have sought to drag their countries into the global economy by selling or giving away rights to extract their nations' natural resources to international investors. Díaz looked to North Americans to dig the mines, build the railroads, and create plantations in Mexico. Over the next twenty years the Guggenheim family sank millions into Mexican mines, E. H. Harriman purchased most of the railroads of Mexico, and scores of American landlords took over control of the countryside, owning more than half of the available land. All the while, Díaz borrowed money to construct government buildings and stabilize the nation's currency in the credit markets of the United States and Europe. English investors also actively participated in the exploitation of the natural resources of Mexico, and by 1910 a British company had begun exploring for oil.

While Díaz had encumbered nearly two-thirds of Mexico's wealth with debts and concessions to foreigners, he had also engaged in a ruthless campaign of suppression of the nation's Indian population. In addition, his government was exceedingly corrupt, with ministers demanding kickbacks from foreign investors before allowing them to bid on government projects or permitting them to look for minerals in the country. Still, outside businessmen accepted these restraints upon their actions with good humor and grace because they rightly believed that they would eventually recoup all of the money they had invested in the country.

For the American government Díaz was exactly the kind of leader they hoped to see in a neighbor. While he might suppress his own people and demand payoffs from the foreigners who invested in his country, he kept his word. The concessions eventually were granted, and best of all, he paid his debts to foreign bankers. This reputation for probity meant that Mexico was not likely to become an arena for intervention by the Europeans.

By the twentieth century, however, Díaz was losing control. Some members of the Mexican middle class thought that they had been overlooked in the boom. Only the president's friends and relatives profited by the expansion of overseas investment in the country, and urban merchants and professionals lacking close connections with him felt cheated. In 1910 a revolution broke out among the mostly mestizo (mixed Indian and white) population of south central Mexico. In the following year the middle class joined the opposition, and in 1911 the president had to flee the country for Paris.

The revolutionaries called themselves Constitutionalists, since they promised a republican form of government based on a written constitution. They installed an ineffectual scholarly lawyer, Francisco Madero, as president and set about dismantling the state established by Díaz. Very quickly Madero ran into difficulties as he was whipsawed between radicals who wished to see an immediate end to all vestiges of Díaz's rule and members of the old regime. Army officers mocked the Constitutionalists as timid reformers, while common soldiers worried about losing their jobs.

The foreign community in Mexico also feared that the new rulers would be less sympathetic to their exploitation of resources than Díaz had been. These fears proved well founded, for if Madero himself favored compromise with the international investors, his party contained more radical elements who thought that Díaz had plundered the country with concessions to foreigners. For these more nationalistic members of the Constitutionalist party, the aim of the revolution was to return Mexico's wealth to Mexico. They would renege on the concessions for the mineral and oil companies. Those claims that were not actually being explored and mined by the foreigners would revert to the government of Mexico. Where the concessionaires were actually at work extracting minerals and petroleum from the soil, the tax would go up. Some radicals also wanted to redistribute the land of the large plantation holders. North Americans and the Catholic Church, the largest holders of land in Mexico, faced expropriation of their property.

Naturally, expatriates in Mexico worried their privileged position would vanish if Madero stayed in power. Led by Lord Cowdray, a local representative of a British oil firm, British minister Sir Francis Strong, and Henry Lane Wilson, the U.S. minister to Mexico, they plotted with disgruntled officers to oust the government of Francisco Madero. The man they selected to lead the assault on the Constitutionalist government was Victoriano Huerta, one of Díaz's trusted generals who had grown disgusted with the government's hostility to the armed forces. In late 1912 the plotters met, and in early 1913 they moved. In February troops loyal to Huerta surrounded the presidential palace in Mexico City and arrested and murdered Madero. Huerta became president of Mexico and quickly applied for diplomatic recognition of his country by the European powers and by the United States. Great Britain recognized the government, but the United States demurred. The coup occurred only three weeks before Woodrow Wilson took office as president, and the Taft administration left the recognition question to its successor.

When Woodrow Wilson took office he refused diplomatic recognition of Huerta's government, reversing the traditional practice of accrediting the diplomats of any regime that seemed strong enough to establish effective control over a country. There was no question that Huerta had effective control over Mexico, but Wilson detested his coup d'état. Less than a week into his presidency, Wilson condemned Huerta as being one of "those [men] who seek to seize the power of government to advance their personal interests or ambition." The president believed that the rise of a Constitutionalist party in Mexico represented the best hope that country ever had of establishing a tradition of democratic rule on U.S. lines. He became incensed when he learned of the part that Henry Lane Wilson, the American minister, had played in the sordid murder of Madero. Woodrow Wilson recalled Ambassador Wilson as his minister in August 1913 and replaced him with John Lind.

Sending Lind to Mexico City by itself did not mean that the United States recognized Huerta's authority. Instead, Lind carried a proposal to settle the civil war in Mexico on terms drawn up by officials of the Southern Pacific

Railroad and the Phelps Dodge Mining Company. The proposal they drafted would have the American embassy in Mexico City arrange a nationwide election to decide between the Huerta government and the Constitutionalist opposition. Neither side in the Mexican civil war had sought mediation, neither wanted it, but Woodrow Wilson believed that a militant policy would force both to accept his proposal.

Lind also had authority to offer a loan to the Mexican government if it would accept supervision of its election. Lind arrived in Mexico City on August 11 and went to the foreign minister, Federico Gamboa, with the proposal for American-supervised elections and a loan, or bribe, to Huerta to effect the plan. The foreign minister repudiated the right of an American president to interfere in Mexican elections because it would "compromise for an indefinite future, our destinies as a sovereign entity and all the future elections for president would be submitted to the veto of any President of the United States of America." Gamboa also turned down the offer of a loan: "When the dignity of the nation is at stake, I believe that there are not loans enough to induce those charged by law to maintain it to permit it to be lessened."

Indignant though Gamboa might have been, he did concede an important point, because he noted that President Huerta would not succeed himself when an election occurred. Lind told Wilson that the ban on Huerta's seeking a second term represented a substantial victory for the United States. The ambassador's dispatch did not reach Washington until the evening of August 27, and on that afternoon Wilson had taken the nearly unprecedented step of personally addressing Congress on the state of United States–Mexican relations. He unveiled the proposal that Lind had taken to Huerta, and he denounced the Mexican president for having rejected all of it. The United States now should change course with the Mexicans and follow a policy of "watchful waiting" until the Mexican government paid respectful attention to what the Americans had to say. He pledged that the United States would "follow the best practice of nations in the matter of neutrality" and not export arms to either side of the civil war. (Wilson was to regret he ever mentioned the "best practice of nations" because his interpretation was demonstrably wrong. Two years later during World War I, Americans exported arms to Britain and France, and supporters of Germany flung Wilson's words back at him.)

Over the next five weeks the crisis between the United States and Mexico eased. Then, in October, Huerta reversed his conciliatory course and sent his gendarmes into the Mexican Chamber of Deputies, arresting 110 Maderista members and proclaiming a military dictatorship. Wilson considered Huerta's move a slap in the face and accused the Mexican of breaking faith with him personally. Beyond that, Wilson told Bryan to take a hard line with the Europeans, who the president believed had encouraged Huerta to seize the parliament.

The State Department never sent Wilson's note to the European powers, but he delivered it himself to the world in a famous speech at Mobile, Alabama, on October 27. He said that one day soon Latin Americans would be freed from the thralldom of "foreign interests." These remarks were a veiled reference to Wilson's opposition to the British concessionaires and a warning that the United States was about to take action to oust them from Mexico. He also attempted to assure the Mexicans that his opposition to the British did not mean that the United States coveted the territory.

The British found Wilson's attitude hypocritical. Foreign Secretary Sir Edward Grey wanted assurances from the United States that if the government of Huerta were overthrown, the United States would undertake to protect British property. Wilson calmed Grey's representative by explaining that any government that the United States approved would surely protect the rights of property holders. He then affirmed that his policy in the Western Hemisphere would be to "teach the South American republics to elect good men."

The Mexicans proved to be very slow learners in electing what the United States considered to be good men, and they resented American instruction. The American president was baffled that the Constitutionalist "first chief," Venustiano Carranza, rebuffed an offer for joint cooperation against the Huerta government. Carranza thought Mexican elections were no business of the United States, and he told William Bayard Hale, Wilson's personal representative, that all he wanted from the Americans was recognition of his status as a belligerent and the right to buy arms. Carranza demanded recognition as the only legitimate government. Hale denounced Carranza's government as "the gentlemen across the border who are with such admirable skill preventing their friends from helping them."

By the beginning of 1914 the president realized that he either must let Carranza purchase weapons in the United States or else carry out his threat to depose Huerta. The United States finally lifted the arms embargo against Mexico in February. Carranza could now receive weapons, and the Wilson administration had become identified with the revolution. In both Washington and Mexico City foes of the Huerta government confidently expected that the dictator would soon pass into oblivion. It did not happen that way, partly because support for Carranza provided Huerta with a means of rallying nationalists to his cause. The church, landed interests, and businesses, which formerly had been lukewarm toward Huerta, now changed their tune and actively offered their support.

In April Wilson found an excuse to send troops. The incident that sparked the American intervention has been called "an affair of honor," but it more resembled a bad opera. On April 10 the paymaster and crew of the U.S.S.

Dolphin, visiting the port of Tampico, were arrested by a colonel when they landed their small boat without permission from the federal troops. When the officer in charge of the Huertista forces learned of the Americans' arrest, he immediately ordered their release and personally apologized to Adm. Henry T. Mayo, the commander of the American squadron stationed off Vera Cruz. The matter would have been settled had not Adm. Mayo demanded a twenty-one gun salute from the Mexicans to salve the honor of the United States. In Washington Wilson backed Mayo, and a preposterous exchange ensued between Lind in Vera Cruz and Huerta in Mexico City. The Mexican president noted the absurdity of the American demand for a salute from a government it did not recognize. He would agree to his forces saluting the Americans only if the Yankees would respond to each volley with a shot of their own. An insulted Wilson decided finally to rid Mexico of Huerta by force of arms.

Wilson went before a joint session of Congress on the afternoon of April 20 and recounted the Tampico incident. Two days later he ordered the American navy to land at Vera Cruz and occupy the city. Mexican forces made up of naval cadets and civilians resisted. By April 23 the Americans had gained control of the port of Vera Cruz. The Mexicans had suffered 126 killed and 195 wounded, while the Americans had lost 19 dead and 71 wounded.

Reaction came swiftly at home and abroad, with most people who took a stand on the issue believing that Wilson had behaved badly. Wilson received protests of his action from the American peace movement. The Federal Council of Churches, the Socialist Party, and the Antiimperialist League all denounced the move into Mexico. Andrew Carnegie wrote Wilson an angry letter, as did the liberal editor of the *Nation*, Oswald Garrison Villard, and the president of Harvard, Charles W. Eliot. Even conservative Republicans who usually took a nationalistic position on international affairs, men such as former president William Howard Taft and former secretary of state Elihu Root, opposed the occupation of Mexican territory.

Latin Americans expressed outrage. Street demonstrations broke out in Uruguay, Chile, Costa Rica, and Guatemala. In Mexico itself Wilson's intervention accomplished the almost impossible feat of unifying the Constitutionalists and the Huertistas. Carranza, the Constitutionalist leader, condemned the American invasion and announced that his troops would fight and expel the invaders.

Secretary of War Lindley M. Garrison urged Wilson to send the army from the coast to Mexico City immediately. Then the ambassadors of Argentina, Brazil, and Chile offered mediation between the United States and Mexico. Wilson believed that accepting the proposition from the so-called ABC powers would hasten the downfall of the Huerta government. Talks convened at Niagara Falls, Canada, from May to July. While the conversations continued, the civil war in Mexico proceeded, with the Constitutionalist forces driving closer to Mexico City. Huerta frantically informed the conference that unless something were done to stop Carranza in his tracks, the Constitutionalists would triumph.

Carranza took the capital on July 20, five days after Huerta resigned the presidency and fled. With a Constitutionalist provisional government, it might have seemed as if the aims of Wilson's diplomacy had been accomplished. Yet so personally insulted was Wilson and so angry that the first chief would not accept American guidance that immediately upon Carranza's installation as president the United States began looking around for a more malleable replacement. Such a man was found in a Constitutionalist general, Francisco "Pancho" Villa, who had been feuding with the first chief.

Gen. John J. "Black Jack" Pershing in futile pursuit of Pancho Villa
(National Archives)

In Washington Wilson and Secretary of State Bryan welcomed Villa's breach with the Constitutionalist leadership because they believed that Villa could assume the presidency of Mexico and be friendly to the United States. Villa gave the outward appearance of accepting a new constitutional convention, but on September 23, three weeks before the assembly was scheduled to open, he declared war. The convention attempted to install Villa as president. All Constitutionalist generals were forced to choose sides, and most decided to throw in their lot with Carranza. Villa was left to form an alliance with Emiliano Zapata, a peasant leader who had been waging his own war south of Mexico City for several years.

The United States backed the Villa-Zapata forces on the grounds that they would be easier for North Americans to control. But the open support given to Carranza's enemies inflamed the first chief's hostility to the United States. In the first nine months of 1915, Carranza's regrouped armed forces successfully pushed Villa's army out of central Mexico and northward toward the U.S. border. Wilson's government fell into confusion. Early in February Wilson finally proclaimed that now the United States was strictly neutral in the civil war and that the Mexicans should settle their own differences. This pledge found little support in Mexico, for now Villa was unhappy that the Americans had abandoned him, while Carranza thought that he deserved support. On June 2 Wilson said that unless the Carranzista and Villista factions concluded a cease-fire, the Americans would intervene.

Thus, in June 1915 it seemed as if Wilson had finally adopted the advice of the interventionists. Over the summer, however, American foreign policy took another turn. The United States now became embroiled in conflict with Germany over neutral rights in the North Atlantic. If, as seemed possible during the summer of 1915, the United States and Germany were to fight each other, the Americans could not fight Mexico at the same time. In August Wilson decided that the United States must recognize the Carranza government. After two months of further negotiation with the South American republics, most of whom were reactionary regimes that opposed Carranza, the United States as well as these Latin American republics extended recognition. On October 19 the United States finally extended formal recognition to Carranza, thereby ensuring the enmity of the Villa forces as well as of American Catholics alarmed by Constitutionalist anticlericalism.

Villa now felt betrayed. Driven northward by the federal troops, on March 9, 1916, he crossed the border into the United States and attacked the town of Columbus, New Mexico. His forces killed nineteen Americans, and the pressure on Wilson to invade Mexico finally achieved fruition. On March 15 an American punitive expedition led by Gen. John J. "Black Jack" Pershing drove into Mexico to begin a ridiculous three-month scramble to find and capture Villa. Carranza had been willing enough to let the Americans into

Mexico when he thought they would send a small force that would quickly rid him of his main rival. Instead of a quick expedition, however, the Americans sent more than 11,000 officers and men. They marched 300 miles into Mexico and still could not find their tormentor. By the middle of April Mexico's president had had enough of North Americans on his soil. Carranza demanded that the Americans leave. Then Villa struck again in the United States, crossing into Texas and attacking some soldiers at Glen Spring.

Wilson federalized the National Guard, dispatched 100,000 of them to patrol the border, and sent American warships to Mexican ports on the east and west coasts. On June 21 a battle erupted near Carrizál, Mexico. The Americans attacked a force of 250 federal troops, fully expecting the Mexicans to turn and run. Instead, they resisted, killing twelve Americans and capturing twenty-three. In Washington news of this encounter was treated as an ambush of the Americans, although Pershing's troops had, in fact, been the aggressors. On July 4 Carranza offered to open negotiations, and Washington agreed to appoint a Joint High Commission.

The United States would withdraw its troops only if American economic interests, petroleum, and mining were protected and if the taxes on U.S. citizens in Mexico were lowered. Unable to reach an agreement on these points, the Joint High Commission disbanded on January 15, 1917. The commission had not ended the dispute, but it had kept Mexican affairs quiet during the presidential election campaign of 1916. In early 1917 the United States faced the prospect of war with Germany, which made another war against Mexico less likely. In January Wilson decided that Carranza would have his way and the American forces would withdraw on the 27th. The first chief had won his victory over a stubborn American president. The Mexicans had not been deterred from writing their own constitution while the invasion went forward. This progressive document phased out foreign control of Mexico's mineral wealth, curtailed absentee ownership of land, and reduced church control over education. The Mexicans had elected a constitutional assembly in October, and it had drafted a new fundamental law in December and January. Mexico chose a new congress and confirmed Carranza as president on March 11. Two days later the United States extended formal recognition.

Relations between the United States and Mexico continued to be bad for a generation after Wilson's misguided tampering in that country's revolution. American interference in Mexico typified an attitude toward nationalist revolution around the globe. While the United States sometimes opposed reactionary governments and demanded that European nations stay out of the internal affairs of revolutionary states, Washington insisted that revolutionaries follow a model of "development" based on that of the United States.

CHAPTER FOUR

The United States in the Great War, 1914–1920

The First World War was the worst thing that had ever happened to Europe. By the time it ended in November 1918, 8 to 10 million people had been killed, and millions of soldiers had been maimed by machine guns and paralyzed by deadly poisoned gas. Veterans never wanted to repeat the horror of months in muddy trenches battling more against lice, rats, and gangrene than the enemy. Combat changed the shape of European society. Millions of homeless civilians wandered forlornly around the countryside looking for sanctuary. *Refugee*, a new word describing their plight, slipped into the language and was heard often after the Great War. Revolution swept away the old German, Austrian, and Russian empires. Governments that survived intact feared that they might collapse next. Both winners and losers emerged weaker, poorer, and more fearful of their neighbors. One of the most shocking things about the conflagration was that few people on either side of the Atlantic expected it to break out, and almost no one thought it would last as long and cost as much as it did.

President Woodrow Wilson and the American public seemed as bewildered as were Europeans when war came in August 1914. They believed that the world had grown interdependent in the past fifty years, with increased trade and modern communication making war unlikely, but on June 28 the heir to the throne of the Austro-Hungarian Empire, Archduke Franz Ferdinand, was murdered in the Bosnian town of Sarajevo by Slavic nationalists lurking in the crowd. The government of Serbia, one of the states created from the wreckage of the Ottoman Turkish Empire, supported

60

the killers, thereby suffering the wrath of the Austrians, who sent an ultimatum demanding an apology. The summer crisis of 1914 seemed to resemble earlier crises in the Balkans and North Africa, which, while dangerous, had not led to a major war.

In the July 1914 crisis European nations seemed bent upon ending their
insecurities and fears for the future. The alliances that had developed since
the 1870s went into force. Once Austria presented the Serbians with an
ultimatum on July 24, Germany backed its partner with a so-called blank
check. Berlin told Vienna that whatever it did against the Serbs would receive full support. Germany even promised Austria aid in a war against Russia. First the Russians, then the Germans, and then the French mobilized
their troops. On August 1 Austria and Russia declared war on each other,
with their two allies, Germany and France, respectively, quickly following.
After German armed forces swept through Belgium on August 1, the British
government declared war on Germany. The ostensible reason for Britain's
action was Germany's violation of Belgium's neutrality, established in 1831.
More important, however, was Britain's commitment to France. Since 1904
the British and the French had engaged in an informal entente. Though no
formal alliance bound the countries, British and French generals had coordinated their policies over the previous years. When hostilities erupted
British leaders concluded it would be dishonest and unfriendly to the French
not to join their fight. On August 4 Parliament voted for war.

NEUTRALITY

The first official American reaction to combat was President Woodrow Wilson's
declaration of neutrality. When Wilson issued the customary order keeping
the United States out of battle, he exceeded the traditional declaration and
asked the American public to stay neutral "in thought as well as in deed."
From August to December Wilson developed his notions of why war had
occurred. He concluded that all the powers were more or less equally responsible for it and that this fight was a recent example of conflicts that had
marred European politics for centuries. In the fall Wilson remarked that
bloodshed resulted from "the competing alliances" leading Europeans into
a quarrel.

By insisting on the right of Americans to trade with all belligerents, Wilson
thought he followed a traditional approach to neutrality. He did, but old
principles did not recognize changes in military technology.

This large conception of the rights of neutrals led to a rift with his own
secretary of state, William Jennings Bryan, who never accepted his superior's
insistence on the protection of American citizens wanting to travel to the war

zone. The secretary of state knew that modern conditions and weapons had changed the way nations fought. The distinction between civilian and soldier vanished in the twentieth century, and the European conflagration allowed no sanctuary to neutrals. This might be regrettable, but if Americans wanted safety, Bryan urged them to steer clear of the fight.

Bryan concluded that Germany's use of submarines meant that the United States would have to adopt a new policy toward searches and seizures on the seas. Once an underwater warship was developed, the possibility of boarding neutral ships evaporated. In order for a submarine to do its deadly work, it had to stay submerged, because if it surfaced, it could not defend itself.

In early 1915 the German navy banned all ships from a war zone around the British Isles. If any neutral vessels sailed into the forbidden area, German U-boats would sink them without warning. Wilson considered this practice a violation of the rights of neutrals, and he vowed to make Germany change its policy. For Bryan Germany's declaration may have been an insult, but it represented a natural and realistic consequence of the changes in military hardware. Bryan believed that if Americans wanted to travel to Europe, they should do so at their own risk.

The secretary resigned over his disagreement with Wilson's advocacy of strict neutrality. His departure from government came after Germany sank the British liner *Lusitania* on May 7, 1915. This passenger ship carried a cargo of weapons bound for Britain, which is one reason it exploded and sank immediately in the Irish Sea twenty miles from the British coast. The loss of 128 American lives infuriated the public.

"It was as if one of two pugilists had suddenly lashed out at a ringside spectator," writes Patrick Devlin, who provided an exhaustive account of Woodrow Wilson's neutrality in *Too Proud to Fight* (1975). Three days later Wilson calmed the nerves of Americans shouting for vengeance when he assured an assembly of 4,000 recently naturalized citizens in Philadelphia that "there is such a thing as a man being too proud to fight. There is such a thing as a nation being so right that it does not need to convince others by force that it is right." Then, on May 13 Wilson banged out a brutal protest to Germany on his own typewriter without consulting Bryan. He demanded a German "disavowal" of submarine warfare, reparations for the *Lusitania* sinking, and a promise not to do it again. He sent an even stiffer note in early June, again without paying attention to Bryan's worries that he was moving the United States toward war. Bryan resigned on June 9, 1915. The president replaced him with Robert Lansing, a conventional lawyer who was a counselor, or second in command, at the State Department.

Wilson's protest over the sinking of the *Lusitania* began a series of diplomatic protests to Germany over submarine warfare. On August 19, 1915, a

German submarine sank without warning the *Arabic*, a large British liner, killing two American citizens. Wilson implied that he would break off diplomatic relations with Germany unless it stopped torpedoing passenger ships. This complaint brought forth the "*Arabic* pledge": the German government promised that "liners will not be sunk by our submarines without warning." Some "mistakes" occurred over the next few months, and on March 24, 1916, a German submarine torpedoed the *Sussex*, a British channel steamer, killing four Americans. Wilson issued an ultimatum: unless Germany stopped "its present practice of submarine warfare," the United States would break relations with Germany. On May 5 Germany provided the "*Sussex* pledge," offering to suspend unrestricted submarine warfare if the United States could compel the British to lift their blockade.

submarine propellant (margin annotation)

Public Opinion and the World War

As the war intensified in Europe, some Americans found fault with Wilson's neutrality. Theodore Roosevelt led Americans who sympathized with Britian and France. The nationalists also thought that the United States, as a great power, needed to have a say in the outcome of the war. Army general Leonard Wood, the Navy League, and the Army League for American Armament joined Roosevelt in calling for "preparedness" for war. In early 1915 hundreds of wealthy men pledged thousands of dollars to bring a group of undergraduates from the most prestigious universities on the East Coast to the Plattsburgh army camp on the shores of New York's Lake Champlain to receive training as officers.

wanting to enter the war (margin annotation)

The president responded with a preparedness movement of his own. In December 1915 he asked Congress for $500 million for the navy to add ten battleships and 100 submarines over the next ten years. In June 1916, after Wilson had crisscrossed the country speaking in favor of preparedness, Congress passed the National Defense Act, doubling the size of the army to 200,000 men and 10,000 officers. In August it followed with a navy bill and a shipping act enlarging the merchant marine.

American ethnic groups also tugged the president in different directions. On one side were supporters of the British position, descendants of settlers from the British Isles. New York banks, many of which were controlled by Anglo-Saxons, arranged loans of $2.25 billion to the Allies in the first two and a half years of the war, giving the house of Morgan, the National City Bank, and others a stake in the success of the Allied cause.

Arrayed against the supporters of the British and French were other ethnic groups, Irish, Germans, and Jews, each of which had its own reasons for wishing the Allies ill. Throughout the years before the United States entered the war, the Irish warned against tying American policy to the British. Ethnic

Germans in the United States opposed a foreign policy that seemed to lean toward the British, and many Jewish Americans dissented from the bias shown by the Wilson administration toward the Allied side. The major concern of the Jewish Americans, however, was with the czarist government of Russia. Until the revolution of March 1917, they had dismissed the claims of British supporters that the war would be fought for democracy and in opposition to authoritarianism. The government of the czar seemed to be excessively authoritarian as well as anti-Semitic. American Jews thus saw no reason to support any policy that might align the United States with the Russians.

American Mediation Efforts

In early 1916 Woodrow Wilson tried to mediate an end to the fighting. By the winter of 1915–1916, armies had dug into cold, damp, muddy trenches in the earth. Soldiers got infected feet, dysentery, and trench mouth when they stayed put, and when they reluctantly followed their officers' orders to climb over the top and expose themselves to the enemy, things got worse. As many as 30,000 men could die in one day of combat in northeastern France, and at the end of eight hours of slaughter, the front lines might have moved only 400 yards.

Wilson sent his confidential agent, Edward M. House, to Europe in the first months of 1916. He met with British Foreign Secretary Edward Grey, who expressed the fear that Britain and France might not be able to withstand Germany for another year. House and Grey developed a plan, presented as the House-Grey Memorandum, under which the United States would preside over a peace conference after the belligerents withdrew to the positions they held before the war. Wilson believed that Germany would reject a plan calling for it to withdraw before a peace conference. He modified the House-Grey Memorandum into a vague American offer of mediation that neither side took seriously.

THE ELECTION OF 1916

Over the next six months Wilson sought support for reelection in November 1916. The Republicans nominated U.S. Supreme Court Justice Charles Evans Hughes. During the campaign Hughes sought to embarrass Wilson by portraying him as not responding to the threat posed by the war. The Republican ran on a platform of increasing American preparedness. The president's campaign stressed what he had done over the past year to boost the nation's military. At the same time, he argued that the campaign for preparedness meant that the United States would not have to use its soldiers. Now that the United States was prepared to fight, it would never have to do so. One of his campaign managers coined the slogan "He kept us out of war." The president was not happy that his supporters would make such a blatant appeal to noninterventionist voters, because he thought that someday the United States might actually have to fight.

Most perceptive observers of American politics seemed certain that Hughes would win in November. Insofar as voters thought about events in Europe, Hughes also seemed to have the more consistent position. He argued more forthrightly for preparedness, and he could take the offensive against Wilson. Wilson, on the other hand, occupied a confused middle position, favoring preparedness while preserving neutrality. He would have the United States both in the war and aloof from it. Expecting victory, Hughes went to sleep on the night of Tuesday, November 6, thinking that voters had given him the prize. Not until midday on Wednesday, when the late tallies arrived from California and Ohio, had Wilson eked out a victory.

MOVING TOWARD WAR

The carnage of the Great War worsened in the winter of 1916–1917, and the conflict became for the first time a "total war." For the first time since the Napoleonic conflicts, the British government had to establish a conscription law. The British cabinet, led by the Liberal Party's prime minister, Henry Asquith, fell, replaced by a coalition of Liberals and Conservatives with a radical member of the Liberals, David Lloyd George, as its head. Lloyd George turned the British domestic economy over to the Ministry of Supply. All production in the country was directed by the government. All able-bodied men had to register for work in either the military or in weapons plants.

The same process went on in all the belligerent countries, reaching its peak in Germany. There the military itself took charge of organizing the domestic economy. World War I was the first conflict during which petroleum became important, and Germany lost access to sources of fuel in Russia and the United States.

By December 1916 the German military commanders worried about surviving another year of fighting. Even if the government continued to expropriate the bulk of production, Germany would die of the effects of the British blockade by late 1917. The generals hoped, however, to win the war by committing the reserves and overwhelming the British and French in a final offensive in 1917. Submarines would impose a counterblockade against Great Britain, sinking every ship bound for British ports. Since the British had not lifted their blockade, a condition of the *Sussex* pledge of May 1916, the Germans could resume unrestricted submarine warfare.

For Generals Erich Ludendorff and Paul von Hindenburg, the choice was clear: either declare unrestricted submarine warfare and antagonize the United States, or face slow starvation. To do so required the assent of the kaiser, William II.

The kaiser resented hearing bad news from anyone, and Chancellor Theodore von Bethmann-Hollweg had little success in explaining that the war must end. Ludendorff and Hindenburg outargued the chancellor over the Christmas holidays of 1916. The generals pointed out that the Allies had rebuffed a German peace initiative in early December. The kaiser accepted the generals' logic, and on January 31, 1917, the German foreign ministry let the United States know that Germany was no longer bound by the *Sussex* pledge. Germany proclaimed Great Britain under blockade and said that all neutral ships traveled there at the risk of being sunk without warning. Only a British agreement to lift the stranglehold on Germany's food imports would stay the order.

THE FINAL DECISION TO FIGHT

Germany's announcement that it would soon resume attacks on American shipping forced Wilson to do something. Wilson thought that if the public would not stand for attacks by Germany on American shipping, then it might be better to ask Congress for a declaration of war before the inevitable war whoops forced his hand. Besides, Wilson lost what little patience he had for the opponents of a strong anti-German policy as he surveyed the reaction to his plan to arm American merchant ships. When he recommended a law for that armament to the Senate on February 26, he blew up in disgust at the reaction of Progressive antiwar senators. Led by Senator Robert LaFollette of Wisconsin, some ten senators filibustered against the bill, preventing it from coming to a vote. Wilson denounced the Progressives as a "little group of willful men who have rendered the great government of the United States helpless and contemptible," and he decided to arm the American merchant fleet on his own without waiting for congressional approval.

Another episode that led Wilson finally to ask for a declaration of war from Congress was Germany's grand mistake in promising Mexico a share of the spoils if it would fight the United States. Berlin's reasoning for inviting Mexico into an alliance made military sense. The kaiser expected the Americans to join the war eventually anyway. When the United States did fight, the important thing was to make certain that the United States did not have enough forces to turn the tide in Europe. Arthur Zimmermann, the German undersecretary of foreign affairs, cabled his ambassador in Mexico City, telling him to offer the Mexicans portions of the United States ceded from Mexico in 1848 if they would declare war on the United States once the Yankees joined the Allies.

(Zimmermann).

The Mexican government probably never would have accepted the offer in the first place, but it never had the chance to reject it. British intelligence intercepted the telegram and sent a copy to American ambassador Walter Hines Page, a supporter of the Allied cause, who immediately forwarded it to Lansing as proof of German duplicity.

Wilson realized that the evidence of German attempts at persuasion of the Mexicans would whip up patriotic frenzy, and he changed his mind on why the war should be fought. By March, Wilson believed that Germany's government was more immoral than that of the other belligerents. The fact that Germany was an autocratic monarchy offended the president, an Anglophile, who admired English liberals who advocated a democratic foreign policy. Wilson also finally accepted the suggestion of Lansing and House that Germany represented a threat to the physical and economic security of the United States. If Germany defeated the British and the French, it would be in a position to organize the economies of Europe as it pleased. The Germans might also take over the colonies of the Allies, ending American hopes to see the Open Door policy applied around the world.

Sometime during the last week of March, Wilson made up his mind that the United States had to fight Germany, and he went to Congress on April 3, 1917. Promising a battle "for democracy, for the right of those who submit to authority to have a voice in their own governments, for the rights and liberties, for a universal dominion of right by such a concert of free peoples as shall bring peace and safety to all nations and make the world itself at last free," the president received a prolonged ovation by both houses, which quickly voted on the declaration. Such dissent as was heard came from a few Progressives, led by Wisconsin senator Robert LaFollette, who feared what might happen at home. He reminded colleagues of the sorry history of conscription in the United States; riots and inequities had besmirched the draft during the Civil War. He recalled traditional American intolerance for pacifists; critics of the Mexican War and Northern dissenters during the Civil War had gone to jail for their unpopular opinions. Worst of all, LaFollette predicted that joining the Allies would kill Progressive reform at home and turn the government over to the richest and most reactionary men in the country. Outside Congress another Progressive, Randolph Bourne, warned his fellow liberals that "the American intellectuals...seem to have forgotten that the real enemy is War rather than Imperial Germany."

On April 2, 1917, the United States joined the enemies of Germany, but President Wilson carefully pointed out that America fought as an "associate," not an "ally," of Britain, France, and Russia. For the president the United States fought for nobler aims than the Europeans, and he wanted to make certain that it stood aside from the deals struck by Europeans before the war. "Secret diplomacy" had caused the war, he proclaimed, and his country would have no part of it. Gen. Tasker Bliss, the U.S. representative at the Supreme War Council in London, had the authority to discuss American military particpation in the war, but he could not discuss political or diplomatic issues.

RELATIONS WITH JAPAN AND CHINA

While the United States wanted to avoid the messy compromises of diplomatic deals with Britain and France, Wilson and Lansing tried to placate Japan in July 1917. Japan had declared war on Germany in the fall of 1914 even though the Japanese-British alliance did not require either power to join its ally's fight unless attacked in Asia. Japan saw the European war, though, as a splendid opportunity to complete its dominance of China. In the fall of 1914, Japan quickly seized the German leasehold on Kiaowchow. Early in 1915, Japan went further and issued what became known as the Twenty-One Demands. Japan insisted that China recognize Japanese preeminence in the lands. Germany had yielded and, more ominously, required agreement to accept only Japanese bankers as sources of capital. China was even required to clear all its overseas diplomatic business with the Japanese ambassador.

China temporized as best it could, refusing to put all its foreign affairs in the hands of Japan but acknowledging Japanese dominance of Shandong (Shantung). It also agreed to follow Japan's lead and declare war on Germany. American experts on Asia feared that Japan might have ambitions on the American possessions in the Philippines. The United States wanted assurances from Baron Kikujiro Ishii that Japan did not intend to supplant the United States in the Philippines. Secretary of State Lansing and Ishii reached an agreement under which Japan acknowledged American control of the Phillipines and the United States acknowledged Japanese preeminence in parts of China. Lansing included language concerning the Open Door policy in China. How could the United States continue to support the notion of an Open Door in China while at the same time agreeing to Japan's conquest of the German leaseholds? The contradiction bedeviled American policy toward Japan and China during the war and in the peace conference that followed.

REVOLUTION IN RUSSIA

While Americans assembled an army to send to Europe, a revolution grew in Russia. In March, before the declaration of war, the czar lost his crown, *renew wy abrolie power.*

helping Wilson present the war as a fight of democrats against autocrats. The overthrow of the czar by an apparently liberal government headed by a lawyer, Alexander Kerensky, seemed to answer Wilson's hopes for a more democratic Russia. Kerensky's announcement that his forces would wage war more vigorously soothed the nerves of Western generals. But their leader's eagerness to fight the Germans disappointed many war-weary Russian peasants and workers, who, over the spring and summer of 1917, threw down their weapons and, in the words of Vladimir Lenin, head of the most radical faction of the Social Democratic Party, the Bolsheviks, "voted with their feet" against war. By August, thousands of disgruntled, hungry veterans flooded the major cities of Russia, where they listened attentively to the Bolsheviks' call for "all power to the Soviets" (worker-peasant councils dominated by the radicals that were set up in the spring of 1917). Kerensky's government became a hollow shell bereft of an army, unable to fight the Germans, and incapable of meeting the peasants' calls for land and citizens' cries for food.

Lenin comes to power

The success of the Bolshevik Revolution in November 1917 shook optimistic assumptions about the future of Russia. Lenin took power vowing to change world politics and end imperial rivalries and war in terms that challenged Woodrow Wilson. Lenin proclaimed that the war signaled "the death throes" of capitalism and that a world revolution would sweep aside "the imperialist order."

Bolshevik leader Vladimir Lenin addresses a crowd during the Russian revolution.
(Library of Congress)

From the triumph of Lenin's Bolshevik Party on November 7, 1917, to the present, the United States has opposed communist movements and governments throughout the world. From 1945 to 1989, Washington's confrontation with the Soviet Union stood at the center of U.S. foreign policy.

THE FOURTEEN POINTS AND INTERVENTION IN RUSSIA

Bolshevik insistence that the nation-state was doomed terrified traditional politicians the world over. If the Russian Revolution spread, the nations of Europe would be threatened. Because Lenin seemed so eager to conclude a peace agreement with the enemy, the leaders of the Western states thought that in reality he was an agent of the German general staff. Something had to be done and done quickly by the Allies to neutralize the appeal of the revolutionaries. Wilson saw that the threat to the durability of European governments posed by Bolshevism represented an opportunity for the United States to exert leadership.

Wilson outlined an ambitious peace program, his famous Fourteen Points, in a speech to Congress on January 8. He demanded that "the world be made fit and safe to live in; and particularly that it be made safe for every peace-loving nation." Seven of the points called for specific territorial changes after the war. Wilson promised independence to the Czechs and the southern Slavs who were included in the Austrian empire. He pledged an end to Turkish control over its possessions in the Balkans. The Germans would also have some subject nations taken from them. An independent Poland with access to the sea would be made up of lands taken from Germany, Austria, and Russia. The remaining Fourteen Points formed the core of Wilson's progressive peace plan. He called for a "New Diplomacy" consisting of "open covenants openly arrived at." The secret treaties that had bedeviled European diplomacy in the years before the world war were to be cast aside by the United States and any other powers that advocated the liberal peace program. He advocated general disarmament after the war, free trade, freedom of the seas, and the impartial resolution of colonial disputes. The capstone of his peace plan was the creation of an international organzation, the League of Nations. This world body, open to membership to all independent states, was expected to regulate whatever peace treaty was adopted. It would supervise the disarmament of all the world's states and be in charge of the movement toward independence of colonies taken from the defeated powers. Moreover, the proposed League of Nations would have had power over all disputes among states, including those that did not arise from the peace treaty.

If the Fourteen Points speech was Wilson's way of stopping the spread of Bolshevism, the Allies had more immediate means of strangling that revolution. In June 1918 British, French, Japanese, and American troops intervened in the civil war in Russia in an attempt to topple Lenin. The war had broken out almost immediately after the Soviets had yielded about a quarter of their territory under the terms of their peace treaty made with the Germans at Brest-Litovsk in March 1918.

The old regime's supporters in Russia embarked on a civil war with the Bolsheviks in the spring of 1918. The counterrevolutionaries, or Whites, as they were called, were united by their hatred for the Reds, or Bolsheviks, and all the Whites wanted Allied support. The White forces promised they would continue Russia's war against the Germans, which would relieve the pressure on the Western powers. In June, therefore, the French, British, Japanese, and Americans sent troops to Siberia to help the anti-Bolsheviks in their war.

When Allied forces reached Siberia, they found that their mission had changed into offering protection to a group of Czech prisoners of war. Approximately 70,000 Czech members of the Austrian army had been captured by the czarist government of Russia, but the Czechs had never wanted to fight the Russians in the first place. Their own aims had been to see the establishment of a separate Czech state from the ruins of the Hapsburg Empire, and they wanted to fight against Austria. Once the chaos of the civil war in Russia broke out, the Czechs created a fantastic scheme to fight their way across eastern Russia and Siberia, embark at the Pacific port of Vladivostok for San Francisco, sail the Atlantic Ocean, and then join the Western allies fighting the Germans in France. As a measure of the nonchalance of the Americans stationed in Russia at this time, they saw nothing wrong with this plan. If only the Allies could secure the trans-Siberian railroad, the legionnaires would fight their way to the coast. The Bolsheviks in Moscow, of course, thought everything was wrong with the Czechs' ideas, and they watched angrily as the Allied forces joined with the White armies and the legionnaires. The Czechs, however, never did make it to the western front. They spent so much time fighting the Reds in Siberia that by the time they left the country the war against Germany was over.

THE WAR AT HOME

In the United States the war saw an end to Progressive reforms, a crusade against dissenters, and a propaganda campaign against Germans. At the president's request a former Progressive newspaper editor from Cleveland, George Creel, established a Committee on Public Information (CPI) to win the public over to the Allied cause. The CPI published pamphlets and placed newspaper stories about the threats to democratic institutions posed

Socialist leader Eugene V. Debs denounces a war of the plutocrats.
(National Archives)

by German aggressors. German soldiers were depicted as subhuman beasts who had embarked on a campaign of pillage, burning, rape, and murder in their occupations of Belgium and France.

A darker fate awaited radicals who dissented from the war. Congress passed a Sedition Act in June 1917 making it a crime to "encourage" opposition to conscription. Socialist leader Eugene V. Debs went to jail for shouting, "The master class has always declared the wars; the subject class has always fought the battles." Less famous leftists suffered more. Frank Little, a one-eyed organizer for the Industrial Workers of the World (Wobblies, or IWW), used crutches to mount a platform in Butte, Montana, to speak against the draft on July 30, 1917. Two nights later, a mob pulled him from bed and hanged him from a nearby tree. One of Montana's senators placed the blame on Washington, because "had [Little] been arrested and put in jail for his seditious and incendiary talk he would not have been lynched." In early September, Justice Department agents fanned out in raids on Wobbly headquarters across the country. They seized everything from correspondence to desks to furnishings. A treason trial opened in Chicago the following April, and a jury found them all guilty.

Congress passed a Selective Service Act on May 18, 1917, drafting men between the ages of 21 and 30 into the armed forces. In 1917 and 1918 3 million men were drafted. They arrived in training camps in the summer of 1917 to find no barracks and little military equipment. Instead of rifles, they trained with wooden sticks. The army had few horses available, so men pretended to ride wooden barrels. The army segregated African Americans into separate units. Many white army officers and southern officeholders feared that blacks would take up arms against segregation after the war, so they did not provide weapons training to them. Segregated African American regiments went to Europe in support roles.

THE END OF THE WAR IN THE WEST

The war in the west ended because the German strategy of overwhelming the Allies before the Americans could make a difference failed. Trench warfare, which had killed hundreds of thousands of men in a single day throughout the early years of the war, continued in 1917, and French troops, some of whom had mutinied during the horrible fighting of 1917, remained demoralized. But they held off the ill-fed Germans throughout the summer of 1917. Only in the spring of 1918 could the Germans release some of their troops from duty in Russia to try to overwhelm the Allies in the west. But the very harshness of the peace Germany exacted from the Russians worked in favor of the west. The kaiser had to leave more than 100,000 men behind to occupy the territory they had acquired from the Russian empire. The German spring 1918 offensive did not get underway until early summer, and by that time the American Expeditionary Force had reached France.

By August 1918 the Germans had pushed to within forty miles of Paris, the closest they had been to the French capital since the fall of 1914. Then the American troops began to make a difference, and for the first time in four years armies covered miles, not yards, every day. At Château-Thierry, American and French troops were able to throw back the German attack. Fresh and healthy Americans began a counteroffensive in late August that gathered momentum in September. By the end of the month, the German army fell back in disarray, and its leaders sought an end to the conflagration. Panic erupted among the general staff, who realized that the army was a spent force.

The German commanders and the government had paid attention to what Wilson had promised about war aims over the past nine months. Wilson had clearly distinguished the United States from the aims of the Allies, and the Germans also thought it very significant that the president had refused to join a formal alliance with the British and the French.

American doughboys in the French mud, 1918
(National Archives)

Germany's hope for lenient treatment ran afoul of a change of heart by the president. As combat had gone on, Wilson had adopted another cause and no longer considered the complicated system of alliances the sole root of the debacle. The enemy's own autocracy contributed to it, and Wilson now believed that, unless democratic governments were set up throughout Europe and the Americas, conflict would be continuous.

THE ARMISTICE AND THE ELECTION OF 1918

When Germany showed signs in October of wanting to end the fighting on terms Wilson had proposed the previous January, the president greeted the overtures coolly. He looked forward to an end of the carnage on the battle-field but was just as eager not to outrun the tenuous support given him by the British and the French. Because Wilson knew that his troops had actually been the major force that had turned the tide in battle, he could influence the British and the French. Therefore, in October Wilson tried to steer a mid-dle course between generosity and harshness toward the enemy.

When the Germans formally asked the Americans on October 24, 1918, if they could lay down their arms on the basis of Wilson's Fourteen Points, the president imposed tough conditions. He pointed out that the United States was only one of the three major states opposing the Germans. Before any cease-fire could be concluded, it had to be acceptable to all parties. In order to bring the European Allies into line, Wilson pressed their requirement that the Germans could not resume hostilities after the truce took effect. According to the French, protection rested on complete disarmament of the enemy and an Allied occupation of Germany. Wilson would not go so far, but he agreed that for the armistice to hold, the Germans would have to promise not to resume the battle. The enemy would be physically restrained from war through retention of the Allied blockade and by forcing the German soldiers on the western front to give up their guns. They would turn over their artillery, tanks, and airplanes to the victors and would keep their small arms for use against the rise of left-wing revolution.

Having set military conditions for acceptance of an end to the fighting, Wilson also demanded changes in Germany's "monarchical autocracy." The president sent word to the enemy through Col. House that the United States would not open any kind of negotiations with the German kaiser. Only if he abdicated and turned the government over to a republic would the United States consider a cease-fire.

Initially William II abdicated in favor of a regent, Prince Max of Baden, who would preserve the monarchy, but this solution proved unacceptable to Americans, republicans within Germany, and militarists. For Washington the idea of regency suggested an intact German autocracy, and that had been a cause of the war. For German republicans the regency of Prince Max looked equally unappealing. It meant that in the future some relative of the discredited emperor might wear the crown. The democratic parties would continue to have to watch from the sidelines as court and army conducted affairs. The republicans believed that if Germany's defeat could not force their countrymen into acknowledging the need for parliamentary democracy, nothing ever could. The army, strangely enough, took the side of republican politicians in this factional battle. In early November the generals needed someone to blame, and republican parties in parliament made excellent scapegoats.

On November 11, 1918, the Germans and the western Allies signed a cease-fire at 11:00 in the morning. After the guns fell silent on the western front, statisticians counted 10 million dead and 5 million wounded among the belligerents. France had suffered the most, losing one-third of its young male population. The British and Germans had done nearly as badly. It took another halfcentury before European nations recovered from this vast devastation.

The war left a legacy of national resentment, suspicion, and lust for vengeance. Young men who had served in the mud and slime, seen their friends die horrible deaths from the machine gun and suffer the crippling effects of gas attacks, and have gangrenous limbs amputated lost their faith in their officers and came to hate politicians. At the end of the war some French and British troops and a great many more German soldiers thought that the Bolshevik attempt to sweep aside the corrupt structure of international relations was the only sensible method of restructuring world politics. Far more of these disillusioned troops turned from their leaders and placed their hopes instead on the reforms of the American president, Woodrow Wilson. Thus, Wilson emerged as the most popular figure in Europe on Armistice Day 1918. Despite their growing disillusionment and desire for vengeance, many Europeans thought that Wilson could redeem them.

THE ELECTION OF 1918

But back home in the United States, Wilson did not enjoy the same appeal. He could have recognized the slide in his popularity, but he chose to ignore it. A few days before the armistice was signed congressional elections took place; the Democratic Party suffered a huge defeat and lost control of the Senate. The Republicans had already captured the House in the election of 1916. Consequently, Wilson did not possess a congressional majority to support his overseas moves.

Popular enthusiasm for Wilson's call for the United States to redeem world politics waned by the fall of 1918. Soldiers longed to return home, where their relatives heard horrifying tales of swindles in war plants and profiteering among defense contractors. Despite Wilson's pleas for Democratic candidates, voters took out their frustrations, war weariness, and impatience with the president's high-sounding rhetoric by electing Republican majorities in both the House and Senate.

If anything, the Democrats' electoral rout of 1918 augmented Wilson's self-confidence. He no longer needed to share power with congressional Democrats, and he would never yield to Republicans. A complicated mixture of moralist and partisan, he believed that many in his own party were small-minded time servers but that all Republicans put their party interests above the common good. Now that the Republicans controlled both houses of Congress, he felt no compunction about ignoring what they had to say about foreign affairs.

The American election reflected a movement toward political extremism that was experienced by all the victorious powers. Similar elections took place in Great Britain, France, and Italy in late 1918. In each case incumbent parties lost ground to militants of the right and left. As peace began, then, it seemed as if Wilson, with his liberal faith in the rational ability of human beings to resolve their differences, would be swept aside. Unwilling or even unable to admit that these elections represented a mockery of his "New Diplomacy," Wilson promised to go to the Paris Peace Conference to finish the job of making "the world safe for democracy."

PREPARING FOR THE PEACE CONFERENCE

Woodrow Wilson arrived in Brest, France, aboard the *George Washington* on Friday, December 13, 1918. He chose the delegation that accompanied him to Paris carefully. It included the secretary of state, Robert Lansing; his personal confidant, Edward M. House; the general who had represented the United States in the Supreme War Council, Tasker Bliss; and one experienced diplomat, Henry White, former ambassador to Italy and the only registered Republican among the group. Wilson brusquely turned aside suggestions that he include Republicans of stature such as former secretary of state Elihu Root and chairman of the Foreign Relations Committee Henry Cabot Lodge.

Before the conference opened, Wilson went on a triumphal tour of France, Britain, and Italy. Hundreds of thousands of well-wishers cheered him as the savior of Europe. Posters proclaimed "We want a Wilson peace." An American living in Paris said the "enthusiasm and affection" of the crowds

U.S. delegation to the Paris Peace Conference, 1919. (left to right) Edward M. House,
Robert Lansing, Woodrow Wilson, Henry White, Tasker Bliss
(Library of Congress)

was "the most remarkable demonstration...on the part of Parisians that I ever heard of." Wilson urged his admiring crowds to pressure their own national leaders to adopt the liberal program of the Fourteen Points, implying that he had come to Europe to save the Old World from its worst nationalistic tendencies. The leaders of Britain and France watched the spectacle of Wilson's tour with a mixture of wary hope, amused disdain, and envy. French foreign minister Stephen Pichon greeted Wilson in Paris with the words, "We are so thankful that you have come over to give us the right kind of peace." Georges Clemenceau, the French prime minister, was far more skeptical of Wilson's plans to reform world politics in ways that would make war unthinkable. Clemenceau told Wilson "we too came into the world with the noble instincts and the lofty aspirations which you express so eloquently. We have become what we are because we have been shaped by the rough hand of the world in which we have to live and we have survived only because we are a very tough bunch."

Once the president returned to Paris for the opening of the conference, he ignored the advice of dozens of experts in international relations on the staff of the American delegation. Wilson also succumbed to demands from the British, French, and Italians that the meetings exclude the defeated Germans. Clemenceau even refused his former enemies the right to have observers at the conference. Wilson was willing to keep the Germans from the deliberations, although he had come to Europe intending to create a peace of equals. Without Germans present to remind their victims of all the pain caused by the war, Wilson thought that he could soothe the passions of the Allies, explain that they had to look to the future, and

Germany left out of conference entirely

prevent hurt feelings among the defeated. The best way to assure the peace of Europe would be to agree that a new international organization committed to "open diplomacy" would stand willing to adjust all disputes after the treaty was signed.

THE FEAR OF REVOLUTION

Time was short in 1919. Wilson had taken an unprecedented step by leaving the country, and he knew that his domestic position would be challenged by a long absence. He wanted to draft the treaty as quickly as possible. The European leaders did not have to worry about absenting themselves from their offices, yet a more ominous specter disturbed their sleep—Bolshevism. Ray Stannard Baker, one of Wilson's trusted advisers, said that "Russia played a more vital part at Paris than [Germany]."

The revolution in Russia had not fallen under its own weight in 1918, nor had the White armies overcome the Reds. Revolution might spread to the rest of Europe, starting with the defeated countries. German sailors waving red flags had mutinied aboard their ships at Kiel when the war ended in November 1918. A more ominous event occurred in January 1919, when the left wing of the German Social Democratic Party tried to seize control of the government in Berlin. The rise of the left was crushed in Germany, but that did not give much comfort to other Europeans, who feared communism, Germany, or anything unpredictable.

In Paris the news of the revolt in Germany sent the diplomats into a frenzied search for a speedy peace treaty. Wilson, Lloyd George, and Clemenceau all knew that other revolutions could break out at any minute among other defeated powers. Britain's Winston Churchill, the secretary of state for war, proclaimed that "the essence of Bolshevism as opposed to many other forms of visionary political thought is that it can only be propagated by violence." For Wilson, Germany had to recover economically as quickly as possible. "So long as hunger continues to gnaw," he told his colleagues in Paris, "the foundations of government would continue to crumble." He wanted the French to permit lifting the blockade of Germany's ports, but French treasury minister Louis-Lucien Klotz refused to consider it until the Germans turned over their gold to the west.

WRITING THE TREATY

Fearing revolution, the diplomats at Paris reasoned that the quickest path to a treaty was to have it drawn up by the major powers and then presented to the entire assembly. As in Wilson's acquiescence to the exclusion of Germany from the entire conference, this decision made sense. Obviously, no one expected the plenary sessions, at which more than thirty nations were represented, actually to set down details. The solution was to let the great powers do the job.

A "Council of Ten" consisting of the leaders of the United States, Great Britain, France, Italy, and Japan and their foreign ministers was set up. Even this group proved too large to draft the language, so it was reduced to a "Council of Four" including the heads of government of the obvious big powers: David Lloyd George of Great Britain, Georges Clemenceau of France, Vittorio Orlando of Italy, and Woodrow Wilson of the United States. These men did the real work.

Once the idea of the Council of Four was firmly established in February, it dealt a serious blow to the hopes of the liberals who believed in the president's program. In a single stroke the leaders of the major powers denied the equality of all states. Now it was clear that the world was not only divided into victors and vanquished, which in itself was a departure from

The Big Four at Paris. (left to right) Vittorio Orlando, David Lloyd George, Georges Clemenceau, Woodrow Wilson

(Library of Congress)

the program of a "peace without victors," but also that four states were the important ones.

The Europeans came with concrete proposals to advance individual causes, while Wilson had to create general solutions to everyone's problems. Wilson had to compromise with the Europeans to gain their support for the centerpiece of his new system, the League of Nations. Unless all the nations of the world were willing to join the new international organization, Wilson feared that the entire structure would crash to the ground.

The president explained that the League of Nations would substitute a universal alliance, committed to something called "collective security," for the competitive, partial alliances he believed had been mostly responsible for the coming of the war. Under collective security each member of the general international organization agreed that a threat to another member represented a threat to its own interests, and each pledged aid, just as parties to a military pact promised to assist one another.

Wilson's call for national self-determination was difficult to put into practice in Paris. Secretary of State Lansing asked "when the President talks of self-determination, what unit has he in mind? Does he mean a race, a territorial area, or a community?" The secretary thought that promising independence to colonial peoples "will raise hopes which can never be realized." No government official among the European or Japanese victors spoke openly of yielding colonies, but they did agree to Wilson's proposal for a "mandate" system in which victors seized German and Turkish territories not for themselves but in the name of the world community, or League of Nations. The conference created three types of mandates, A, B, and C. "A" mandate status applied to Ottoman territory in the Middle East, for example, Palestine, Syria, and Iraq, places that "had reached a stage of development where their existence as independent nations can be provisionally recognized." Britain assumed an "A" mandate over Palestine and Iraq, while France took charge in Syria-Lebanon. Both promised eventual independence. "B" mandates applied to "peoples, especially those of central Africa …at such a stage that the mandatory must be responsible for the administration of the territory." No one expected such "B" mandates as Tanganyika in East Africa, given to Britain, or Cameroons in West Africa, placed under French administration, to rule themselves anytime soon. Eternal bondage awaited "C" mandates. These were forlorn places "such as southwest Africa and certain of the Pacific islands, which, owing to the spareness of their population or their small size or their remoteness from the centers of civilization," would forever remain under foreign control. The government of South Africa took over Germany's ownership of phosphate-rich Southwest Africa, Japan ruled Germany's Pacific islands north of the equator, and Australia and New Zealand divided the "C" mandate south of that line.

Wilson left Paris to return to Washington for three weeks in February and March 1919 to fortify his position with the Republican majority in Congress. Efforts at accommodation proved fruitless, and he suffered a rebuke when Massachusetts senator Henry Cabot Lodge led thirty-nine Republican senators in a round robin attack on America's participation in the League of Nations. Newspapers criticized the secrecy of the conference as a repudiation of his liberal New Diplomacy. His chronic headaches got worse, as they always did when he encountered opposition; he may even have suffered one of a series of ministrokes that had begun in his days as president of Princeton.

In April and May Wilson offered compromises on territory to the the leaders of France, Italy, and Japan. These agreements seriously undermined the president's promises of a nonvindictive peace. Japan's desire to maintain control over China's Shandong Peninsula proved especially troublesome.

Japan offered an article to the peace treaty recognizing the formal equality of all races in the world. The move reflected Japan's hope to expose the limits of Wilson's commitment to self-determination. Complaints came immediately from the Australian delegation, supported by Britain, who considered the pledge of racial equality a thinly veiled attempt to invalidate Australia's own laws excluding Japanese immigrants. To resolve the problem Britain's Lloyd George suggested that the conference not endorse racial equality but offer Japan confirmation of their hold over Shandong. Wilson felt relieved to go along with this proposal. In early May diplomats agreed that Japan could stay in China, running the government and railroads of the province, until a referendum took place in 1922. News of this agreement reached China on May 4, igniting an angry demonstration by thousands of student radicals who surged through the streets of the northern capital, Beijing, denouncing the agreement as a cowardly surrender to the Japanese.

French and British demands for Germany to pay for the cost of the war also threatened Wilson's generous peace terms. Wall posters in Paris proclaimed "Let Germany Pay First." Originally Wilson balked at the notion of Germany being compelled to pay the entire cost of the war, claiming that it would be vindictive, would imply that Germany had caused the war in the first place, and would cause the Germans to thirst for revenge. Besides, he thought that a requirement of huge reparations would exceed Germany's capacity to pay. Either Germany would default, or the United States, the only nation with a functioning economy, would pick up the tab. While Wilson was in Washington his adviser Edward M. House sought to purchase future French goodwill by agreeing that Germany would be held responsible for the cost of the war; what that price was would be decided later. Diplomats justified requiring Germany to pay by labeling it the aggressor in 1914 in Article 231 of the peace treaty. When the news of this "war guilt" clause reached Germany, all parties from the right to the left denounced it. To most Germans the war

Central European territorial changes after World War I

guilt clause meant that the treaty was solely a victor's political propaganda document signed to libel them.

For the next two months Wilson and the leaders of Britain, France, and Italy worked out the final details. Finally, in early May a document was ready to submit to the defeated Germans, who complained bitterly that the peace agreement was a harsh "diktat" toward the Germans. The Germans were not alone in castigating the treaty as a betrayal of Wilson's Fourteen Points. Several of the young, hopeful members on the American staff accused the president of violating his ideals. Joseph Fuller complained that America had "bartered away her principles in a series of compromises with the interests of imperialism and revenge," John Storck declared that the accords would make Germany "eager for revenge," and George Bernard Noble predicted that the result "would be provocative of future wars."

Staff members' doubts did not penetrate to the president, who believed that the draft's flaws could be cured when the League of Nations took shape. On Saturday, June 28, five years after the Austrian archduke and his wife were shot in Sarajevo, the peace treaty was signed in a ceremony in the Hall of Mirrors at the Palace of Versailles.

THE TREATY COMES HOME

When Woodrow Wilson brought the agreement home in July, he expected the Senate would ratify it quickly and give him credit for having negotiated it. A huge crowd of 100,000 people greeted him at Washington's Union Station. When he addressed Congress he asked, "Dare we reject [the treaty] and break the heart of the world?" Most newspapers also predicted ratification, and the public wanted the Senate to approve it. A majority of senators polled in July agreed that they would vote yes even if they had to make changes. Nevertheless, the leader of the opposition, Henry Cabot Lodge, grumbled, "I read [Wilson's] speeches and they are all in the clouds and all full of sentiments that lead nowhere." Lodge did not foresee a flat rejection of the document, but he had served notice when the president had returned to Washington in February and March that the Senate would insist on its own version. The senators wanted to see guarantees of American superiority in the Western Hemisphere expressed in acknowledgment of the Monroe Doctrine. They also opposed Article X of the League of Nations covenant, which required member states to use troops if called upon by the League. The senators, jealous of the prerogatives of Congress, saw the article as a way around their control of the war power.

In the summer of 1919 Lodge expected a delay in ratification would help Wilson's opponents. He wanted to give the accord the most exhaustive appraisal that any agreement had ever had. He personally read all 200 pages into the *Congressional Record* in a two-week marathon.

Lodge held hearings, something the Senate Foreign Relations Committee had never done before for a peace agreement. For six weeks in August and September the committee listened to experts highlight the flaws. Witnesses predicted a new war as a result of German resentment. Some said that the League of Nations would force the United States to engage in continuous warfare. One witness who testified was the Idaho Progressive Republican William Borah, who led a group of "Irreconcilables," so named because they would not accept the treaty under any terms. Borah worried that the United States would become the guarantor of the old empires of Britain and France. Germany and Russia, excluded from the new order, would conspire to wreck the settlement.

Faced with delays and mutterings about his lapses from idealism, Wilson decided to counterattack with a public speaking tour. In September 1919 he covered 8,000 miles in twenty-two days, delivering thirty-six speeches and standing in cars for a dozen parades. At every stop he appealed to the public for support and mocked opponents who predicted that the League would have American troops in combat in faraway places. American soldiers would go to war only in places where the United States had interests. As he told his audience in Salt Lake City, "If you want to put out a fire in Utah you do not send to Oklahoma for the fire engine. If you want to put out a fire in the Balkans…you do not send to the United States for troops." He brought his audience to tears when he told them that if the League of Nations were rejected, a war would erupt in which "there would not be merely seven and a half million men slain. The very existence of civilization would be in the balance." Finally, in Pueblo, Colorado, on September 26 he gave his last speech, recalling the mothers who had grabbed his hand, shed tears, and cried, "God bless you, Mr. President." "Why," he asked, "should they weep upon my hand and call down the blessings of God upon me? Because they believe that their boys died for something that vastly transcends any of the immediate and palpable objectives of the war. They believe and rightly believe that their sons saved the liberty of the world." At the end of his speech the president collapsed with a serious stroke, and four days later his life was in danger.

For the next six weeks Wilson could do no work, and he never recovered fully from this latest in a series of blood clots in his brain. Throughout October and early November, his wife, Edith Bolling Wilson, became, in effect, acting president. She shielded her husband from the importunities of his colleagues and grew jealous of his advisers. When Robert Lansing thought that as secretary of state he should hold a cabinet meeting in the president's absence, Mrs. Wilson was outraged. She reported Lansing's disloyalty to her husband, who summarily fired him and put Bainbridge Colby in charge of the State Department. Wilson also broke finally with Col. House during this period.

With Wilson on the sidelines, the Republican opposition grew. Lodge announced that he would vote yes only if provisions guaranteeing the Monroe Doctrine and the right of Congress to declare war and repudiating the Shandong agreement giving the peninsula to the Japanese went into law. The first roll call in November was on the agreement with the Lodge reservations. The Democrats joined with the Irreconcilables to vote it down fifty-five to thirty-nine. Then the senators took up the original treaty without the reservations. Lodge joined with the Irreconcilables, and the vote was thirty-eight for, fifty-three against. Wilson had recovered enough to know of the vote and, surprisingly, was not discouraged by the defeat, thinking that public pressure would force a reversal at the next session of Congress. The treaty came up again on March 19, 1920. This time Senate Democratic leaders begged the president to allow the loyal Democrats to vote for a version containing the Lodge reservations, but Wilson was adamant. To accept something amended by his brilliant enemy would mean that the final product would be Lodge's, not his. Besides, the president clung to the forlorn hope that he would win another nomination by his party for the presidency. Once nominated, he would turn the campaign into a "solemn referendum" on the Paris peace and the League. Under orders from the president to vote against the Lodge reservations, Democrats joined with the Irreconcilables to defeat it. In the March roll call, forty-nine voted for the treaty and thirty-five against it. Its supporters were seven votes short of a two-thirds majority.

THE ELECTION OF 1920

Wilson hoped the Democratic Party would nominate him for a third term in 1920, but they nominated the governor of Ohio, James M. Cox, a popular vote getter in an important state. As a governor Cox did not have wide experience in foreign affairs, which was just as well from the point of view of the party's leaders. As a vice presidential nominee the Democrats selected the former assistant secretary of the navy, Franklin D. Roosevelt. The Democratic Roosevelt had some international experience, and it was he who would carry the banner for the League of Nations in the "solemn referendum" of the 1920 election.

The Republicans selected another Ohioan, Sen. Warren G. Harding, whose principal qualifications were that he had no enemies and that he looked like a president. His campaign manager followed the advice of Sen.

Bose Penrose of Pennsylvania, who urged, "Keep Warren at home. Don't let him make any speeches. If he goes out on a tour, somebody's sure to ask him questions, and Warren's just the sort of damn fool to try to answer them." No one could tell where he stood on the League of Nations or the peace treaty. His only contribution during the campaign was a phrase that passed into the American political lexicon when he said that "America's present need is not heroics but healing, not nostrums but normalcy." In the last week of the campaign thirty-one prominent Republicans stated that they were sure Harding favored the League. The president of Columbia University, Nicholas Murray Butler, Henry L. Stimson, Elihu Root, and former nominee Charles Evan Hughes all expressed certainty that the United States would participate in some form of the League.

Harding himself was not sure. He swamped Cox with a majority of more than 60 percent of the vote. Upon learning of his landslide, Harding came to his front porch and told his supporters that the League of Nations was now "deceased." In office Harding did nothing to revive it, and the United States did not ratify the rest of the Versailles Treaty. Instead, on July 2, 1921, Congress ended the war with Germany. A month later the United States and Germany signed the Treaty of Berlin, which gave Washington all the rights it would have had under the Versailles agreement. American diplomats made similar agreements with Austria and Hungary the same month.

HISTORIANS' ASSESSMENTS OF WILSON

Wilson left office a broken man, with only a few loyal supporters to keep alive his vision of a new world order reformed through American efforts. By the time of the Second World War, the League of Nations seemed to have missed a chance to fill the peacemaking role Wilson had expected of it, and Americans looked back with a guilty conscience to their repudiation of the work of the Paris Peace Conference. Paul Birdsall, a journalist, took another look at the treaty making in *Versailles: Twenty Years After* (1940), which appeared on the eve of the Second World War. The peace no longer appeared as harsh as it had before the rise of Hitler, and Birdsall thought that the Allies under Wilson's direction had actually held back from excessive demands. Birdsall implies that Europe would have been safer in the 1930s had the United States participated in the League of Nations. Thomas Bailey makes the point more strongly in two books on the peace process written in the midst of the Second World War. Both *Woodrow Wilson and the Lost Peace* (1944) and *Woodrow Wilson and the Great Betrayal* (1945) try to apply the lessons of 1919 and 1920 to the plans for the end of the Second World War. While Bailey damns Wilson's stubborn refusal to reach an accommodation with his Republican opponents, which led to "the supreme infanticide" of the president—destruction of his own brainchild—the historian lauds the aims of Wilson's internationalism. After the Second World War, when American foreign policy became unashamedly "internationalist," Wilson's plans for the postwar order carried the day. Arthur Link, his fullest biographer, notes in *Wilson the Diplomatist* (1956) and *War, Revolution and Peace* (1979) that the world would have been a better place had the treaty been approved as drafted. Dissent concentrated on Wilson's methods, not his intentions. William A. Williams's *Tragedy of American Diplomacy* (1962) argues that Henry Cabot Lodge and William Borah offered alternative visions that might have cost less in the long run. William C. Widenor's *Henry Cabot Lodge and the Search for American Foreign Policy* (1980) maintains that Lodge had a vision of an active American diplomacy that acknowledged limits Wilson often ignored. By the beginning of the twenty-first century historians had once more come to believe, as John Milton Cooper put it in *Breaking the Heart of the World* (2001), that "For all their decency and intelligence, Wilson's opponents were wrong. For all his flaws and missteps, Wilson was right. He should have won the League fight. His defeat did break the heart of the world."

CHAPTER FIVE

An Era of Conservative Internationalism, 1921–1929

SEIZING POSTWAR ECONOMIC OPPORTUNITIES

Warren Harding cared little about foreign affairs, but he selected an accomplished team of cabinet secretaries to promote American power after the Great War. Charles Evans Hughes, the Republican standard bearer in 1916 and a leading internationalist, became secretary of state. Herbert Hoover, a former mining engineer with a reputation for humanitarianism acquired by feeding Belgium and Russia during the Great War, was the secretary of commerce. The president named Andrew W. Mellon, a wealthy Pittsburgh businessman, as secretary of the treasury.

Together Hughes, Hoover, and Mellon developed a foreign policy that would enable the United States to continue participating in the world's economic and political life while at the same time retaining a free hand in international relations. The new Republican leaders did not believe that their country could escape an active role in the world, but, instead of using the League of Nations as the balance wheel of international relations, Americans would stand apart from the general organization, remaining free to make whatever bargains with other countries they found advantageous at the moment.

Three Republican administrations of the 1920s all followed a foreign policy of "conservative internationalism" inspired by Henry Cabot Lodge, who doubted that the Great War signified a departure in world history. "Wars always happen," he snorted, and the one just finished was no worse than any of the others that had occurred over the centuries. For Lodge the alliance system of the past generation was the natural way that nations assured their own safety. The League was only a new sort of alliance, one which the United States could safely avoid. Lodge would, however, have the United States participate in world politics—especially economic affairs.

As the war ended, Lodge, Hoover, and Mellon joined with prominent bankers of the house of Morgan or the Rockefeller-backed Chase National Bank and important exporters in the National Foreign Trade Council to replace British merchants as the world's premier traders. Americans in the twenties challenged Europeans for international economic preeminence. Hoover took the lead as secretary of commerce in making the United States compete with Europeans. He sent out a corps of commercial attachés whose job was to return information about opportunities for American businesses, look for foreign firms that might like to trade with the United States, and spot changing markets where the Americans could introduce new products. Almost as soon as the first commercial attachés took up their posts in 1921, Hoover received complaints from foreign competitors and from the Department of State. Europeans resented being hustled out of overseas opportunities, and the professional diplomats of the Department of State watched in horror as their chance to direct foreign policy seemed to slip away.

The commercial expansionists also tried to break European barriers to trade. At the end of the war all industrial nations, including the United States, erected intimidating tariff laws against competition. The American contribution, the Fordney-McCumber Tariff of 1922, reversed Wilson's movement toward lower trade barriers as a response to Commerce Secretary Hoover's warning that "the time has arrived when we require either disarmament or defense" in the "trade war" with Europe. He took the lead in demanding that American firms receive an opportunity equal to those of the imperial nations to extract the raw materials necessary for the automobile age. The war had shown the importance of motorized vehicles, and now the race was on for rubber and petroleum. Hoover successfully beat back a British plan, drafted by James Stevenson, a Colonial Office functionary, to maintain high prices for rubber coming from Malaya and keep the companies who made up the Rubber Association of America from sharing in this lucrative business. Throughout his tenure at the Commerce Department, Hoover threatened to block the import of Malayan rubber into the United States until the American firms participated, and in 1928 the British abandoned the Stevenson plan.

OIL DIPLOMACY IN THE MIDDLE EAST

After the war petroleum began to assume the important role it would have later in the century. American oil firms sought the help of the State and

Commerce departments in their competition with the British. Hughes and Hoover led an assault on British privileges in Mesopotamia (modern Iraq). In May 1920 Britain and France secretly agreed at a conference in San Remo, Italy, to close the door to all outside companies in Iraq. The Republican administration objected, and tedious negotiations among representatives of American firms, the State Department, the Commerce Department, the governments of Britain and Iraq, and European oil companies took seven years. Finally, in July 1928 the Americans, incorporated as the Near Eastern Development Corporation, won the right to a 23.75 percent share of the Turkish Petroleum Company's concession in Iraq. It seemed on the surface that Hoover had vindicated the Open Door policy and ushered Americans through it to a share of the riches of Baghdad. The British worked behind the scenes with the government of Iraq to void the sublease arrangements of the Turkish Petroleum Company, which changed its name to the Iraq Petroleum Company (IPC). By 1931, when the first oil in any appreciable amount was pumped out of the Iraqi sands, the government there had given the IPC, dominated by the British, exclusive rights to future discoveries. No new American firms not associated with the IPC could produce oil in Iraq.

Visions of oil fortunes also helped create the first but not last American encounter with the hostile face of nationalism in Persia, now Iran. As a next–door neighbor of Iraq and sharing its geological formations, Iran seemed an ideal place for petroleum exploration, and Americans were welcome for a time. Perhaps the main advantage the Americans had was that they were not British, since the new ruler of Iran, Shah Reza Pahlevi, like most of his countrymen, deeply resented the encroachments on Iran made by Britain and Russia at the end of the nineteenth and beginning of the twentieth century. The shah appointed an American, Arthur C. Millspaugh, who had once been the economic adviser of the Department of State, to supervise the chaotic finances of the Iranian government. He was supposed to reorganize tax collections, supervise customs, and, most important, drum up American loans for projects in Iran.

Millspaugh arrived in 1922 and had a brief honeymoon before things went sour two years later. His American way of doing business clashed with the customs of the bazaar merchants, and his staff made no effort to accommodate the Shi'ite Muslim religious sensibilities of the Iranians. The American vice consul in Tehran, Robert W. Imbrie, infuriated a crowd when he tried to photograph a religious celebration on July 18, 1924, and the participants clubbed him to death. A representative of the Sinclair Oil Company used Imbrie's murder as an excuse to end his company's agreement to pump oil out of Iran's desert and transport it across the Soviet Union. In fact, the company withdrew because its owner, Harry Sinclair, no longer could make good on his promise to the Soviet Union to influence Secretary of the Interior Albert

Fall and Attorney General Harry Daugherty to grant American recognition of the Soviet government. All three men stood accused in the Teapot Dome scandal, an attempt to swindle the American government out of vast, profitable oil lands in Wyoming. Newspapers in Iran also claimed that Sinclair had bribed influential Persians to achieve his oil concession. Millspaugh, for his part, remained in Iran for another three years. Relations between him and Reza Pahlevi were never the same, however, with the latter saying, "There can be only one shah in Persia." Still, Millspaugh was not finished with the country, and he returned during the Second World War, from 1943 to 1945, to lay the foundations for even greater American involvement in the Iranian economy.

OVERSEAS LOANS AND GERMAN REPARATIONS

While Hoover and Hughes tried to get equality of commercial opportunity for the United States, their counterpart in the Treasury Department, Andrew Mellon, attempted to direct the lending of money overseas by American banks. In 1922 the Treasury Department drafted a set of rules governing overseas loans. The State Department immediately became alarmed at what the assistant secretary of state, Leland Harrison, saw as poaching on its territory. Harrison expressed concern that any regulations of overseas capital meant that the government would be offering protection to its bankers. Finally, the two departments compromised on a set of rules for the major American banks, requiring them to notify the State Department of any projected overseas loans. The department would check with officials at the Treasury to see if the loans violated any of the following provisions: no loans to countries in arrears to the United States, no loans for armaments, no loans to governments not recognized by the United States, and no loans to foreign monopolies maintaining high prices against Americans. Loans had to pay for themselves. If the project did not fall into one of these categories, then the State Department would simply write back that it had "no objection" to the loan. At the State Department Charles Evans Hughes hoped that no banker would read a guarantee into these chilly words.

Another international economic matter that complicated American foreign policy during the 1920s was the related question of reparation and debt. At the Paris Peace Conference the victors had not set a final figure for Germany to pay, agreeing instead that Germany bore the full responsibility for the war but that the exact amount it would pay would be determined by a reparations commission. In 1920 the commission assessed Germany 5 billion gold marks a year, with payments to be made every six months in gold. This system lasted for only two years. The German government refused to raise taxes to pay for the reparations bill, preferring to print money instead. In 1922 and 1923 an unprecedented inflation swept the country. Bread cost 2 million marks, and the savings of an entire middle class were wiped out. In January 1923 the German government suspended its payments of reparations to the victors, and the French retaliated by sending troops to occupy the Ruhr industrial area. The British, ostensibly allied to France, thought the invasion a blunder because they believed that Paris wanted to provoke a new war that none of the powers could afford.

But Americans could not ignore a threat to their entry into Europe's economy. As long as Germany did not pay its reparations to the British and the French, these governments would not be able to keep up the payments on their debts to the United States. European treasury officials and private American businessmen joined the State Department in selecting Charles G. Dawes, a midwestern Republican banker, to head a commission to revise the amount owed by Germany for reparations. In March the Dawes Plan became official. Germany's payments were scaled down to 2.5 billion marks over the next fifty years, and French troops left the Ruhr. Almost immediately the German economy stabilized and took off like a rocket. In the next five years Germany's exports tripled, people went back to work, and the country again became the foundry of Europe. German diplomacy also revived in the wake of the Dawes Plan as Foreign Minister and later Chancellor Gustav Stresemann negotiated the Locarno Treaty with Britain and France, formally acknowledging the western borders set by the Versailles Treaty. The same year, 1925, Germany joined the League of Nations.

Part of the German recovery was fueled by a massive injection of American loans. Ironically, bankers who had been shy of shipping money to the victors because they had debts to the United States felt no such compunction about funding the German revival. Over the next five years American banks sent $2 billion to Germany. The Germans used some of the money to build new plants, but more went to meet the reparations payments to the European governments, which in turn sent money back to the United States in fulfillment of the war debts.

IMMIGRATION, NATIVISM, AND FOREIGN RELATIONS

"A nation of immigrants" is the proud celebration of contemporary American multiethnic society, but life has never been easy for newcomers to the United States. Mostly poor, they worked for little, and the availability of a large supply of submissive laborers helped spark the awesome economic expansion of industrial America in the late nineteenth century. Since the earliest days of the republic, however, antiimmigrant "nativists" have railed against the religions, politics, racial physiognomy, languages, hygiene, intelligence, work habits, and cultures of new arrivals. Before the Civil War a political party, the American or Know Nothing Party, attacked Irish Catholic arrivals. After 1865 bigots lynched Italians in New Orleans and killed scores of Chinese in Rock Springs, Wyoming.

Most significant, perhaps, a movement emerged for legislation to restrict or eliminate immigration. Chinese were the first to be excluded, in 1885. In the aftermath of the First World War a nativist Congress passed immigration laws in 1921 and 1924 setting quotas on the number of immigrants each country could send to the United States. Quotas were based on the per-centage of each country's descendants in the total U.S. population in 1910 (for the 1921 law) and 1890 (for the 1924 revision). Britain and Germany, the homelands of many of the white Anglo-Saxon Protestants (WASPs) who urged restriction, had huge, unfilled quotas in excess of 60,000 per year, while the mostly Catholic and Jewish immigrants from southern and eastern Europe scrambled for space in quotas less than 5,000. The rest of the world fared worse, with some countries receiving token allotments of 100. The Japanese, who had voluntarily stopped emigration under the terms of the gentlemen's agreement of 1907, saw that accord abruptly terminated and discovered themselves excluded, like the Chinese they despised.

Not surprisingly, the discriminatory quota system caused difficulties in American relations with foreign governments that felt they had been unjustly singled out. Japanese politicians saw the abrogation of the gentlemen's agree-ment as further proof that the Caucasian nations would never treat them as equals. In Italy as well, the new fascist government of Benito Mussolini con-sidered immigration restriction an affront.

THE WASHINGTON CONFERENCE, CHINESE NATIONALISM, AND PEACE PLANS

One legacy of Wilson's diplomacy was the movement to reduce armaments. The president had believed that the arms race between Britain and Germany had helped bring about the world war. Republicans close to Theodore Roo-sevelt were not so worried about arms races leading to war as Wilson had been, but they also wished to reduce arms. They noticed how expensive it was to provide a modern armed force. The naval building program of the United States had cost $1.5 billion since 1915. The Harding administration's economic policies rested on a commitment to reduce taxes; Secretary of the Treasury Mellon worried about a naval construction program that would cause the government to continue the tax rates of the world war. There were also strategic reasons for the United States to advocate arms control and disarmament measures. The world war had seen the U.S. Navy grow from the fourth largest in the world to a fleet that rivaled the British, the greatest ever to sail. Along with the British, the United States was the only one of the great naval powers that maintained a fleet in both the Atlantic and Pacific oceans. The same fears of excessive naval spending also worried the finance ministers in each of the major naval powers—Great Britain, Japan, France, and Italy. All of them except Japan had suffered economically during the world war, and they could not afford to continue a naval arms race. For Europeans the fear of Germany's navy had been eliminated. The British, French, and Italians had been allied during the Great War and saw no need to continue a naval rivalry with one another.

A naval race could easily arise in the Pacific, however, where Japan wanted to preserve gains made in the war. Japan, an ally of Britain from 1902, fretted that the alliance would not be renewed in 1921. With Germany disarmed, London no longer needed a naval partner, and Australia and New Zealand anticipated Japanese expansion to the south. In 1920 Britain informed Tokyo that the alliance would not be renewed for another twenty years. Another issue was the future of China. While the Chinese had objected mightily to the Shandong settlement at the Paris Peace Conference, nothing had been done to protect them from Japan.

These interrelated questions of naval balance and the future of China became the subject of an international conference on the Far East and naval disarmament that opened in Washington in November 1921. The United States agreed to host the gathering of ten powers because Hughes convinced Harding that it was a good time to demonstrate that despite rejection of membership in the League of Nations, Americans still had an interest in world affairs. Furthermore, the United States wanted to preserve some stability in the Far East. If Japan's ambitions in China and the South Pacific were not checked, the American stake in the Philippines, Guam, and Samoa could be threatened.

Most of the delegates who reached Washington that fall believed that the conference would engage in tired rhetoric and solve nothing. Hughes astonished the diplomats and naval experts who met in November with an opening speech calling for the scrapping of 200,000 tons of capital ships built during the war. He proposed that after these vessels had been destroyed, rough equality should exist between the navies of Great Britain and the United States, with other nations trailing behind. Under the plan Japan would have a navy 60 percent as strong as that of the United States or Great Britain. However, because Japan used its fleet only in the western Pacific while the Anglo-Saxon powers sent their ships everywhere, the Japanese actually would be the premier naval power in their home waters. The conference continued until February 1922, with naval experts from

Secretary of State Charles Evan Hughes (at the head of the table) meets with the heads
of other nations' delegations to the Washington Naval Conference in 1922.
(Library of Congress)

each country pressing their political leaders to make certain that national
interests were advanced over those of the other participants. Still, once
Hughes suggested the reduction of the size of navies, most of the politicians present heaved sighs of relief. No longer would they have to borrow
from already strained financial institutions to create navies.

In February 1922 three treaties ended the Washington conference. The
first, the Five Power Agreement, set the relative naval strengths of the United
States, Great Britain, Japan, France, and Italy. The ratio among the powers
was fixed at 5:5:3:1.67:1.67. The United States, Japan, Britain, and France
signed another pact in which they agreed to respect one another's holdings
in the Pacific. Finally came a Nine Power Treaty in which all the states with
interests in the Far East sanctioned the territorial integrity of China.

Dramatic social changes were taking place inside China. The republic
created in 1911 persisted after the death of Sun Yat-sen in 1925. New leaders contended for preeminence but agreed on a central theme of the revolution: that the imperial powers had demoralized and humiliated China and
that all of them should go. One nationalist, Jiang Jieshi (Chiang Kai-shek),

educated by American missionaries, assumed leadership. Jiang, like other nationalists, hoped to rid China of foreign leaseholds, end the degrading practices of extraterritoriality, and regain autonomy in foreign policy. American diplomacy ignored Jiang and the list of nationalist grievances against the outside powers, because the United States tacitly assumed that Japan dominated China. Stung by the American rebuff, Jiang formed a temporary alliance in 1926 with the Soviet Union, another unhappy power left outside the Washington treaty system. The Chinese Nationalist Party, or Kuomintang, belonged to the Communist International for three years while leaders of the International in Moscow ordered the small Chinese Communist Party (CCP) to submit to Jiang's leadership. Surprised Chinese Communist officials meekly obeyed until April 1927, when Jiang suddenly ordered the massacre of thousands of CCP members and sympathizers. Over the next twenty years Nationalists and Communists waged an intermittent civil war, with the United States becoming increasingly involved on the Nationalist side after Japan invaded China in 1937. Throughout the nearly fifty years of relations between the United States and Jiang Jieshi, which lasted until his death in 1977, each side distrusted the good faith, honesty, and competence of the other.

The naval limitations treaty proved the first step in the movement for international disarmament, but Wilsonians also placed importance on the reduction of land armies. In fact, because most European wars had begun on the continent, a way had to be found to reduce the size of standing armies. Among the advocates of paring armies was a professor of international relations at Columbia University, James T. Shotwell, who had been with the American delegation at the Paris Peace Conference. In the 1920s, he strove to continue Wilson's ideals of disarmament. One of his many essays on the subject of international reform won a prize offered by Edward Bok, the editor of the *Saturday Evening Post*, for the best plan to end war. Shotwell called for a declaration making war illegal. The way to end war was to declare it unlawful.

Shotwell's plan became the official policy of the U.S. government in 1927. Unlike the Columbia professor, officials in the American government who advocated peace reform acted from cynical assumptions. What happened was this: in 1927 the French foreign minister, Aristide Briand, approached the American ambassador Myron T. Herrick with a request for a mutual defense agreement. The French had pestered successive American governments since 1917 with demands for a formal alliance. Each time the U.S. diplomats had put the French off with pleas that some international or collective agreement could substitute for a formal alliance. Once the United States had refused to join the League of Nations, the French complained that the security offered by their transatlantic ally had diminished. When the French tried again in 1927, Undersecretary of State William Castle thought of a way to end these constant demands. Why not change the proposal for a Franco-American alliance into a general program open to all the nations of the world declaring war illegal along the lines of Shotwell's plan? The pact then would not commit the United States any more than any other nation to the security of France, and both powers would appear to have taken a forthright stand in favor of peace. Castle sold this scheme to Secretary of State Frank B. Kellogg, a former senator from Minnesota who had taken over from Hughes in 1925. Consequently, in August 1928 Kellogg went to Paris to sign an agreement with French foreign minister Briand. The two powers invited every other nation of the world to join in the self-denial of the use of force, and all but five of them did. Later historians took a gloomy view of the proceedings. It was "an illusion and a deception," according to Robert Ferrell, who wrote a detailed history, *Peace in Their Time* (1952) from the soured perspective of someone who had experienced how little the pact had done to prevent World War II.

The Coolidge administration also pressed ahead with plans for disarmament. Although the Washington conference of 1921–1922 had set limits on the size of the battleships and aircraft carrier fleets of the major powers, it said nothing about smaller ships. The naval powers had taken advantage of this loophole to compete in the smaller categories. The Americans had stayed out of the race between Japan and Great Britain for budgetary reasons. In early 1927 the Coolidge administration called a new conference to expand the naval agreement. Meetings took place in Geneva, the home of the League of Nations, from June 20 to August 4. Nothing was accomplished. The United States, Britain, and Japan were the only nations represented. France refused to attend because it resented having been classed with Italy at the Washington conference, and the Italians would not come if the French stayed home. Britain and Japan, which were there, refused to halt their cruiser rivalry. By the time the conference broke up in August, European newspapers were filled with accounts of the American president's "insufficient preparation," a polite way of saying that Coolidge did not know what he was doing. While Europeans clucked over the Americans' ignorance, Congress joined the arms race on the seas. A few weeks before the Coolidge administration left office in March 1929, the lawmakers passed a bill giving the United States fifteen heavy cruisers and an aircraft carrier.

Herbert Hoover, nominally a member of the Society of Friends, or Quakers, who opposed war, succeeded Coolidge as president in March 1929. While he did not think that war was necessarily evil, he did believe it was always expensive. In October 1929, two weeks before the stock market crashed, sending the world economy into the greatest depression in modern history, Hoover met with the new British prime minister, Ramsay MacDonald, at a Maryland mountain retreat. MacDonald, the first leader of the Labor Party ever to serve as prime minister of Britain, also had a vaguely pacifist past. He had opposed Britain's entry into World War I, and as prime minister he wanted to end the arms race to divert funds to creating a welfare state. The old pacifist who wanted to fund unemployment insurance and the apostle of rugged individualism found they had much in common as they sat on a log under the crisp fall skies. They decided to convene another disarmament conference in London in January 1930.

Delegates met on January 21, 1930, as the world began its slide into depression. All governments present recognized that the best place to cut costs was in naval expenditures. The conference extended the Washington limits to the lighter categories of ships. America, Britain, and Japan agreed to limit all their navies at the 5:5:3 ratio. Italy and France also signed the agreement at the end of discussions in April. At that time the two states could not agree on exactly what the ratio between them should be, but they said they would resolve their disputes in the next two years. They did not.

Disarmament attracted sporadic attention in the 1930s, but the Depression eventually eliminated it as a major topic. In February 1932 the League of Nations sponsored another general disarmament meeting in Geneva. Despite the League's endorsement, the United States attended. President Hoover even offered another American plan for the scrapping of a third of all arms. No one responded favorably, however, and the talks dragged on inconsequentially through 1932. When Adolf Hitler came to power in Germany in January 1933, the first thing he did was begin to rebuild the German armed forces. In 1934 the Geneva meetings adjourned temporarily, and they were never held again. The next year, 1935, the London naval conference reconvened to try to stop a new arms race in the Pacific. The rise of a new German navy made the outlook for success exceptionally bleak, and these talks, too, accomplished nothing.

THE UNITED STATES AND LATIN AMERICA

While the American attitude toward Europe, the Middle East, and Asia was that the United States should be the equal of the European powers, the policy in the Western Hemisphere was to keep the United States on top. The United States preserved its influence under cover through direct investment, its control of the Panama Canal, the sanctification of the Monroe Doctrine, and, when necessary, the direct intervention of troops. By 1929 U.S. citizens had doubled their pre–world war investment in Latin America, from $1.26 to $3.52 billion. Americans owned railroads, electric utilities, oil, bananas, and sugar. The United Fruit and Standard Fruit Companies accounted for most of the revenue of Honduras, and U.S. firms benefited from more than half of Venezuela's oil production. From the world war to the Great Depression, American exports to Latin America tripled in value and accounted for 20 percent of all goods shipped abroad. While the U.S. economic role in the hemisphere grew, that of the Europeans, especially the British, slipped.

During his 1920 presidential campaign Warren Harding suggested that he would be less domineering in the Caribbean and Central America than his predecessors had been. He responded sharply to Democratic vice presidential candidate Franklin D. Roosevelt's statement that as assistant secretary of the navy he "wrote Haiti's constitution myself, and, and if I do say it I think it's a very fine constitution." In a Harding administration, the Republican candidate said, "I will not empower an Assistant Secretary of the Navy to draft a constitution for helpless neighbors in the West Indies and jam it down their throats at the point of bayonets borne by United States Marines." In fact, however, during the 1920s the U.S. government maintained troops in Haiti, the Dominican Republic, and Nicaragua. Americans controlled Cuban politics and on several occasions again came close to coming to blows with Mexico. The United States had occupied the Dominican Republic in 1915 as part of the Wilson administration's campaign to teach the Latin American republics to elect good men. By the time of the election of 1920, many people wanted to end the occupation. The Republican platform of

Yankees on guard in Haiti
(National Archives)

that year called for withdrawal because it cost too much to maintain a force on the island; once the Harding administration took office, liberals called on it to make good on its promise. The marines who occupied the Dominican Republic and ran the customs house had imposed a rough order there. A national guard trained by the Americans kept matters quiet. In 1924, therefore, the Coolidge administration carried out the 1920 pledge to withdraw.

In part, the removal of forces from the Dominican Republic was designed to steal the thunder of the Progressives. Faced with the prospect of another four years of the Coolidge administration, some of the old liberals organized a new political party in 1924. Calling themselves Progressives, they nominated Sen. Robert LaFollette of Wisconsin to run for president. Their platform demanded an end to Yankee intervention in the affairs of Latin America, as LaFollette maintained the opposition to an aggressive American foreign policy he had begun when he opposed the entry of the United States into the world war. LaFollette received only eight electoral votes in the 1924 election. However, he outpolled the hapless conservative Democratic nominee, John W. Davis, in California, and 1.5 million Progressive voters indicated that some citizens doubted the wisdom of dominating the Western Hemisphere.

Among LaFollette's supporters was William E. Borah of Idaho, who became the chairman of the Senate Committee on Foreign Relations at the death of Lodge in 1925. Borah, the old "Irreconcilable," waged a steady campaign against the interventionist policies of the United States in Central America. Nowhere was he more persistent than in his condemnation of American policy in Nicaragua. Partly in response to Borah's objections, the United States withdrew the marines from Nicaragua in 1925 but sent them back in 1926 during the war between the conservative church supporters led by Juan Sacassa and the liberal anticlerical party led by Emiliano Chamorro. When the marines returned, other senators complained. Burton K. Wheeler of Montana said "I wouldn't sacrifice ... one American boy for all the damn Nicaraguans." Senator George Norris of Nebraska said that President Coolidge had sent the marines "to burn villages, to bomb innocent women and children from the air." Opponents also charged, in the words of Alabama senator Thomas Helflin, that "our army is now being used to collect the debts of Wall Street financiers."

The opposition became so intense that Coolidge explained to Gen. Frank McCoy, the commander of U.S. occupation forces in Nicaragua, "there is a great deal of criticism in this country of the way in which these operations are being dragged out without any concrete results.... People cannot understand why the job cannot be done, and frankly I cannot understand myself." Coolidge sent Henry L. Stimson, secretary of war under President

William Howard Taft, as a special representative to end the war. With the aid of the 5,000 troops patrolling Managua, Nicaragua's capital, Stimson managed to arrange a tenuous peace between the liberals and the conservatives. This pact, the Peace of Tititapa, held with the American troops in place until 1934. The American marines trained a civil guard to take their place. One young sergeant in that guard, Anastasio Somoza, took control of the country when the Americans left in 1934. He and his family retained power until 1979. Somoza's first official act was to invite the leader of the guerrillas, Augusto Sandino, to the capital at Managua for peace talks. When he arrived, the civil guard killed him.

The United States also ruled Haiti directly from 1915 to 1934. When Franklin D. Roosevelt became president in 1933, he repeated his earlier boast that he had single-handedly written the Haitian constitution in 1918. Roosevelt then proceeded to withdraw the marines in 1934, reasoning that they had created a friendly government. In the nineteen years the marines ran Haiti, they built roads, bridges, hospitals, and power plants, created local army (the Garde d'Haiti), and carried with them their own racial prejudices. None of the improvements did much good for the Haitians, who remained the poorest people in the Western Hemisphere. American marines treated the Haitians little better than slaves. The ambitious road-building program was completed with a forced draft of labor. In 1919 many Haitians rebelled against being dragooned into chain gangs, and the marines responded by killing nearly 2,000 of them. The Americans also introduced racial segregation to Haiti and favored the mulatto elite over the black part of the population.

Throughout the 1920s, the United States ruled Haiti with compliant local presidents. When the depression began in 1929, the prices for Haitian coffee exports slumped, and the people of Haiti grew fed up with colonial rule. Strikes and protest marches swept across the country, and the United States responded with an inquiry chaired by the former governor general of the Philippines, W. Cameron Forbes. The next year, 1930, Forbes's commission reported that the Americans had failed "to understand the social problems of Haiti." It recommended training more Haitians for local authority and the eventual withdrawal of the American forces from the island. Roosevelt finished the removal in 1934. The Haitians celebrated a festival of "Second Independence" when the Americans left, but economic conditions did not improve with their own leaders.

ACCOMMODATING THE MEXICAN REVOLUTION

Mexico, richer, larger, and closer to the United States than Nicaragua or Haiti, presented special problems in the period of Republican ascendancy.

The Wilson administration's unhappy experience of direct military intervention left an ashen taste in the mouths of many Americans. The United States granted de facto recognition to the country in 1917, but a bitter legacy remained. That same year Mexico adopted a new constitution, part of which sent shock waves through the community of foreign investors. Article 27 affirmed that all "land and waters" and all subsoil minerals belonged to the Mexican nation. American mining and petroleum companies immediately began to experience heavy taxes.

In 1921 Harding's new Republican administration asserted that the Mexican constitution violated the principles of compensation in international law and claimed that American firms were entitled to "prompt, adequate and effective compensation." Secretary of the Interior Albert B. Fall (who went to prison for his role in the Teapot Dome oil scandal) announced that "no Mexican government will be recognized, with my consent, which does not first enter into a written agreement promising to promote American citizens and their property." In 1923 a more conservative president, Alvaro Obregón, negotiated the Bucerelli agreements with the United States. In exchange for formal recognition, Mexico acknowledged the right of ownership of American oil companies that had acquired lands before 1917. At that time Americans owned more than half the subsoil petroleum rights in Mexico. In 1925 Mexico lurched to the left with the election of Plutarco Calles, who believed that the Bucerelli agreements had sold out national interests to foreign investors who came to his country intending to "take everything and leave nothing." The Mexican congress repudiated the granting of foreign ownership to oil companies. Instead, the Americans had a lease of only fifty years. American oil companies complained loudly in Washington, begging for another intervention. Secretary of State Frank Kellogg said that the United States "will continue to support Mexico only so long as it protects American lives and American rights and complies with its international engagements and obligations." James R. Sheffield, the U.S. ambassador to Mexico, said privately that Calles and his supporters were "motivated by greed and a wholly Mexican view of nationalism, and an Indian, not Latin, hatred of all people not on the reservations."

Despite such strident calls for military intervention in Mexico, the Coolidge administration felt pressure from liberals not to send troops. In 1927 the president sent an old college friend, Dwight Morrow, as ambassador to Mexico. No one could accuse Morrow of neglecting the interests of international financiers, as he was a partner in the J. P. Morgan banking concern. Morrow believed that the long-term interests of American bankers and investors required that Mexican pride be assuaged. Himself a masterful conciliator, he astonished the Mexicans by learning a few words of Spanish. A romance between his daughter and Charles Lindbergh, the "Lone

Eagle" whose solo flight across the Atlantic in April 1927 had made the front pages in Mexico City, helped win the hearts of the Mexican leadership. In 1928 Morrow worked out a compromise under which Americans retained lands acquired before 1917 but leased those properties obtained afterward. This agreement continued in force until 1938, when another strongly nationalist Mexican president, Lázaro Cárdenas, expropriated the property of all foreign oil companies. However, it was a pyrrhic victory, because the major producers there refused to handle the Mexicans' own oil. As a result Mexico did not again become a major producer until the 1970s, when world demand for petroleum forced international firms to buy its oil.

THE RETREAT FROM INTERVENTION

Understandably, U.S. dominance of Latin America created a reaction. Latin Americans themselves complained that the United States had become the "New Rome." By the time the Western Hemisphere republics assembled for their triennial conference in Havana in 1928, the Latin American delegates were in no mood to allow the United States to set the agenda, as it had in the past. The Havana meeting took place in the shadow of the American troops landing in Nicaragua.

To head off denunciations of Washington's policy, the United States sent a most prestigious delegation to the conference. President Calvin Coolidge went to Havana to address the opening meeting, and Charles Evans Hughes headed the American contingent. Even the former secretary of state could not stanch the flow of criticism. The delegate from El Salvador introduced a resolution opposing the right of any state "to intervene in the internal affairs of another." Diplomats from Mexico and Argentina, two large republics that resented North American actions, backed nonintervention. Hughes first attempted to have the resolution suppressed, studied, or tabled for the next meeting. Finally, however, he had to defend American high-handedness, claiming that "we simply wish peace, order and stability and the recognition of honest rights properly acquired." Silence greeted his comments, but Hughes did manage to prevent the adoption of an anti–U.S. resolution.

The message of the Havana conference was clear: the United States had to do something to mollify its neighbors. During the Hoover administration the United States repudiated the Roosevelt corollary to the Monroe Doctrine while retaining the same informal control over the affairs of Latin America. The chief legal officer of the State Department, J. Reuben Clark, spent much of 1929 investigating the basis in international law for unilateral intervention. In 1930 he presented his memorandum on the Monroe Doctrine, which held that the right of intervention in the affairs of the Western Hemisphere advocated by the Roosevelt corollary was not a logical or legal derivative of the Monroe Doctrine. While the Clark memorandum stated that Theodore Roosevelt had erred in resting intervention on the Monroe Doctrine, Clark did not suggest that the United States would never again interfere in the internal affairs of nations of the Western Hemisphere. Instead, the Hoover administration would begin a policy, followed by Franklin Roosevelt's administration and every subsequent presidency, of securing the agreement of the other Western Hemisphere states whenever the United States found it convenient to meddle. Franklin Roosevelt called his overtures to Latin America the "Good Neighbor policy." Harry Truman extended the doctrine of containment of communism to the Western Hemisphere. John F. Kennedy had the Alliance for Progress but also the Bay of Pigs intervention in Cuba. Lyndon B. Johnson sent the marines to the Dominican Republic. Ronald Reagan pressed the Caribbean Basin Initiative and fought revolution in El Salvador, Nicaragua, and Grenada. George H. W. Bush sent U.S. forces to Panama. Throughout it all the Latin Americans themselves continued to resent the overbearing manner of the "Colossus of the North."

ASSESSING REPUBLICAN FOREIGN POLICY

When Americans came to reflect on the Republican ascendancy of the 1920s in the era of the New Deal and the Second World War, they found little to like. The twenties seemed a blotted decade in which frightened nativists slammed shut the door to refugees from eastern Europe with the immigration laws of 1921 and 1924; leaders ignored social ills; hypocrisy flowed with the gin brewed in defiance of Prohibition; and President Coolidge complacently took four-hour naps each afternoon. From the perspective of American commitment to a new international organization after 1945, the diplomacy of the 1920s represented, in the words of historian Manfred Jonas, an expression of a mean-spirited "isolationist impulse."

An almost inevitable swing of the historiographical pendulum took place as writers began to doubt the wisdom of the foreign policy undertaken by the Democrat Franklin D. Roosevelt (FDR) from 1933 to 1945. Although FDR's conduct had not been above reproach, perhaps his Republican predecessors had not made such a mess of things. William A. Williams set the boundaries of the debate in *The Tragedy of American Diplomacy* when he argued that the supposed "isolationism" of the twenties was a "legend" put forward by internationalist historians bemused by FDR's successes. Williams took the Republicans of the twenties seriously and insisted that they valued American participation in foreign affairs. Their concentration on the expansion of American commerce and demand that the door be opened to the United

States in Latin America represented a clever strategy to assume the role of an exhausted Great Britain. A few years later, in 1967, Joan Hoff Wilson presented a subtle rehabilitation of the twenties diplomacy of the 1920s in *American Business and Foreign Policy, 1920–1933*. Arguing that business did not speak with a single voice and that large and small manufacturers, exporters, and banks were often at one another's throats, Wilson discovered that business interests never turned their backs on foreign affairs. Their ideas were not frivolous, and they were united at least in a belief that the United States had to participate in foreign affairs.

By the 1980s historians no longer spoke of the 1920s as an isolationist period. Criticism of the Republican administrations did not take Harding, Coolidge, Hughes, Hoover, and Mellon to task for ignoring legitimate interests overseas. Instead, the debate followed the lines of the 1924 presidential election, with left-wing critics such as Jules Benjamin taking the Progressive position in *The United States and Cuba* (1974). Others thought that conservative internationalism made sense. William C. Widenor's *Henry Cabot Lodge and the Search for American Foreign Policy* (1980) presents a spirited defense of the Senate Foreign Relations Committee chairman's assessment of America's true interests in world politics.

At the turn of the twenty-first century writers employed the insights of students of gender, culture, and race to address enduring issues of American economic and military expansion. Mary Renda's *Taking Haiti: Military Occupation and the Culture of U.S. Occupation, 1915-1940* (2001) notes that U.S. attitudes toward racial hierarchies and subordination conditioned Americans to think of nonwhite people of the Caribbean as childlike and dependent but simultaneously highly sexualized, and in need of control. Emily Rosenberg's *Financial Missionares to the World* (1999) argues that American bankers and government officials saw borrowers in poor countries as feminine and childlike dependents who required instruction and control by white men from the prosperous United States. The twenties seemed to fit more neatly into the general course of the rise of American power in the twentieth century. The United States continued in the "prosperity decade" to scramble for a position of equality with the world powers of Europe. As those powers nursed their wounds from the Great War, an assertive America increasingly moved them aside.

CHAPTER SIX

The Diplomacy of Depression, 1930–1939

The Great Depression represented the most searing episode in modern economic history, and only the notorious bloodthirstiness of the twentieth century prevents identifying it also as the most important event in modern international relations. Nonetheless, it runs a strong second to the wars that devastated the world. It affected every aspect of American life, leaving what Caroline Bird calls a "hidden wound" on the minds of the generation that lived through it. Politically, it altered the balance of the two big parties, making the Democrats the majority for the next halfcentury. The New Deal began and the Second World War completed the process of enlarging the federal government and magnifying the power of the president to the point where he seemed to act at will in international affairs.

HOOVER CONFRONTS DEPRESSION

The Depression casts a giant shadow over the foreign policies of the Hoover and Roosevelt administrations. Herbert Hoover, who moved into the White House on March 4, 1929, with the hopes of applying the managerial skills of the "great engineer" to the problems of international relations, soon found himself grappling with an economic crisis no one understood and that he could do nothing to improve. As the depression worsened, international affairs took a back seat to finding a way out of the sickening slump that threatened an end to world trade, an end to profits, and an end to work.

Hoover's secretary of state, Henry L. Stimson, came to his job beautifully equipped, having served as secretary of war under Taft and going on to lead troops in the Great War, make a fortune during the 1920s, and mediate the civil war in Nicaragua. In his four years as the chief foreign policy adviser to the government, Stimson came to believe that Hoover was incapable of handling the profound international consequences of the Depression. Despite a forbidding exterior, Stimson was carefree compared to Hoover, who anguished over the economic crisis. Hoover wanted his cabinet members in his office every morning at 7:00. Once they got there, the president required them all to get into sweatsuits and shove a medicine ball into one another's ample stomachs. Afterward, they took breakfast together while Hoover's hounds climbed over them. Stimson, at sixty-three, had had enough exercise and complained that the cabinet meetings with Hoover were "like sitting in a bath of ink." Stimson lamented that no matter how much attention Hoover gave to the Depression, things got worse.

Although the Depression had been sparked by the crash of the New York Stock Exchange on October 29, 1929, Hoover looked to international solutions to worldwide distress. The value of international trade spiraled downward from $2.858 billion in 1929, to $2.327 billion in 1930, to $1.668 billion in 1931, to $1.122 billion in 1932. American policy contributed to the commercial slump when Congress passed the Smoot-Hawley Tariff in 1930, raising rates to their highest level in history and effectively closing the U.S. market to Japan. Protectionist sentiment swept other countries, too, as all European nations and Japan erected their own trade walls to shield endangered domestic industries.

An even darker economic cloud loomed over the future of international debts. American bankers had aggressively loaned money abroad in the five years after 1924, and no project, no matter how unlikely to be repaid, escaped the interest of eager bankers. Countries obliged to repay these loans could make gold shipments to the United States (which could not last long), export goods to America (a course blocked by the high tariff), or borrow more money at even higher rates of interest to repay the first loans. Once American banks ran out of money in 1930, foreign countries no longer could pyramid loans, and the house of cards of international finance collapsed in a roar of defaults.

European governments also threatened to stop payment on their public war debts to the United States. As had been the case in the Ruhr crisis of 1923, the United States received nothing until Germany sent reparations to the Allies. The German economy, in turn, had been badly shaken by the suspension of American loans and the high U.S. tariff. Germany attempted to revive its domestic economy in the spring of 1931 by establishing a common market, or customs union, with the independent state of Austria, but the French government immediately howled that this plan violated the Versailles Treaty's prohibition of a union, or *Anschluss*, between Germany and Austria.

The French believed that the common market was the first step toward unification of the two states. With fears of German nationalism a staple of French
politics, the government scuttled the *Anschluss.*

The reaction in Austria was the June 1931 collapse of the largest bank
in Vienna, the Creditanstalt, and a financial panic ensued. Germany suspended payments on reparations to the Allies and also threatened to stop
installments of its war debts to the United States. Hoover feared that an outright default by the Allies would enrage nationalist members of Congress,
who might retaliate with even higher trade restrictions against Britain and
France. He hoped to buy time, let the Depression reach bottom, and then
encourage Europeans to make good on the war debts. He therefore advocated a moratorium to last for a year and a half on the debts owed by the
Allies to the United States. The Allies were not going to pay, anyway, so he
put the best possible face on a bad situation. On June 21 Hoover declared
the moratorium.

The public's relief passed quickly, as the moratorium did little to stop
the economic slide. By September British unemployment reached a sickening 25 percent of the work force, and the Labor Party government of Ramsay MacDonald fell in an angry dispute with the Bank of England. Montagu
Norman, the bank's president, threatened the prime minister that the bank
would no longer maintain the value of the pound in relation to gold if the
government continued to pay unemployed workers. Faced with an ultimatum, MacDonald abandoned his Labor Party principles and joined with the
Conservative Party to form a national government committed to slashing the
budget. Even so, this move did not stop the Bank of England from taking
Britain off the gold standard.

THE MANCHURIAN CRISIS

News of the fall of the British Labor government reached Washington on
September 16, 1931. The president hosted a dinner that evening for Stimson, Secretary of Commerce Robert P. Lamont, and Treasury Secretary Mellon. The four men sweltered in 95-degree heat, and they sadly agreed that
the U.S. Treasury and Federal Reserve Board had no money to help bail out
Great Britain.

While the American government confessed its financial impotence, an
event took place 12,000 miles away that contributed to the paralysis of American foreign policy. In Manchuria, the northernmost province of China,
a small war broke out between Japan and China. For the remainder of the
Hoover administration, the president and his secretary of state had to cope with
a conflict that threatened to engage the United States and upset the stability

established by the Washington treaty system. Both China and Japan had suffered from the high American and European tariffs erected to stop the Depression. Leaders of the Japanese army, which had been stationed in northern China since the beginning of the century, saw the Depression as an opportunity to find a market for Japanese goods there without having to fear retaliation from the Europeans and Americans. Consequently, on the night of September 18, 1931, Japanese troops staged an incident on the South Manchuria Railway's main line a few miles north of the town of Mukden. They blew up a short section of railroad track, accused the Chinese of having set the explosion, and used the affair as an excuse for a military expedition against China in Manchuria.

Over the next month Japan waged war on China while the world watched. No Western government could afford to stop the Japanese by force, since war in the midst of Depression simply would cost too much. The League of Nations assembled in October 1931 and decided to send a commission of inquiry to China. Britain's Lord Lytton headed this commission, which literally took a slow boat to China, arriving early in 1932. While the Lytton commission dithered, Japan attacked the coastal Chinese city of Shanghai.

Japanese troops patrolling occupied Manchuria, 1932
(National Archives)

Secretary Stimson, flushed with indignation, concluded that the United States would act on its own if the League stood by. He drew upon the moralism of Woodrow Wilson and William Jennings Bryan to declare that the United States would not recognize any territorial changes brought about through the use of force. The so-called Stimson Doctrine of Nonrecognition was made public in a letter the secretary of state sent to Senator Borah, chairman of the Committee on Foreign Relations, on February 23, 1932. In it Stimson referred to the Open Door policy and the Nine Power Treaty of 1922. He told Borah that he was waiting for other powers to join in nonrecognition, "which, as has been shown by history in the past, will eventually lead to restoration to China of rights and titles of which she may have been deprived."

Stimson wanted to go beyond nonrecognition to threaten actual military force against Japan. He knew that he would be bluffing but thought that Japan might back off if all the Washington treaty powers bluffed together, yet Hoover rejected what he considered an empty warning as unworthy of the United States and unlikely to persuade Japan to withdraw from Manchuria. Abandoned by his chief, Stimson sulked. Over the next twenty years Hoover and Stimson engaged in a public row over whether the nonrecognition doctrine properly should be named after the secretary of state or the president. It hardly mattered, though, if it was called the Hoover Doctrine, the Stimson Doctrine, or the Hoover-Stimson Doctrine, because Japan remained in Manchuria, renamed Manchukuo, until 1945.

EARLY NEW DEAL DIPLOMACY

Foreign policy issues had little to do with the election of 1932, in which people were preoccupied with the economic crisis, but a sharp observer could detect differences on international relations between Hoover and his Democratic rival, Franklin D. Roosevelt. At every stop in the campaign, Roosevelt blamed Hoover for the Depression and accused him of doing nothing to end it. The Democrat suggested that the president's concentration on the international origins of the economic calamity was a way of lifting blame from his shoulders. Roosevelt also signaled other shifts away from his earlier commitment to Wilsonian internationalism. As a condition for his support in the general election, the influential newspaper editor William Randolph Hearst demanded and received assurances that FDR would drop his longstanding support for American membership in the League of Nations. When Roosevelt won a landslide victory of 22,800,000 votes to Hoover's 15,750,000, no one knew the exact shape his government's policies would take. Since the campaign had been fought and won on the domestic issue of the Depression, it was clear that the new president would devote the bulk of his attention to recovery from the slump.

The 1932 election was the last one in which the interregnum between the casting of the votes and the assumption of office lasted a full four months, from November to March. Never did the period seem longer or the results more catastrophic. The economy reached rock bottom in those four months. Thousands of banks closed, while hundreds of thousands of people lost their jobs. Hoover bitterly resented the charge of cruelty, insensitivity, and blundering Roosevelt had thrown at him in the fall. The relations between the two men worsened in the winter as Hoover begged Roosevelt to support ongoing foreign economic policies by endorsing the moratorium on debt and agreeing to attend an international economic conference. But Roosevelt wanted to keep a free hand to avoid blame for any failures in his predecessor's policies, and he had no power until March 4. He said nothing about the moratorium, which was allowed to lapse in December 1932. As for the international economic conference, Hoover did coax from Roosevelt a commitment to attend, but the president-elect refused to say what the United States would do once it got to the conference scheduled to open in London in June. Roosevelt wanted time to experiment with the domestic economy in isolation from the world's political turmoil. When Roosevelt stood on the steps of the Capitol on March 4, 1933, and proclaimed that "the only thing we have to fear is fear itself," he started the New Deal, but he did not start a new diplomacy. Roosevelt's choice for secretary of state was a sixty-one-year-old courtly senator from Tennessee, Cordell Hull, who had spent the previous twenty years in Congress advancing the cause of world peace through tariff reform. He believed, along with the liberal reformers of the nineteenth century, that the cause of war was trade dislocations. He thought that if all nations could trade freely with one another, their economies would become so interdependent that they could not risk going to war. As secretary of state, he pressed a Reciprocal Trade Agreements Act that would cut American tariffs in response to similar cuts by the other nations of the world, but on other matters Hull had little expertise, interest, or comment.

Despite the president's hints that the Depression had to be beaten at home before the United States could turn to international relations, he had committed the United States to participate in the international economic conference in London that would be held from June 12 to July 24. Sixty-four nations were supposed to fix a value for one another's currencies. After the British and several other European nations abandoned the gold standard, the rate of exchange fluctuated wildly. Any business intending to ship goods to another country had trouble knowing what to charge because no one knew what payment in a foreign currency, such as British pounds, would mean in terms of one's own money, such as dollars. Many merchants simply refused to trade, and the Depression got worse. The London conference was also supposed to reduce trade barriers and maybe even eliminate the war debts owed by the Europeans to the United States. Roosevelt sent a high-level delegation headed by Hull and the chairman of the Senate Committee on Foreign Relations, a tough-talking, hard-drinking Democrat from Nevada, Key Pittman. As befitted a senator from a silver-mining state, Pittman had no interest in resurrecting the gold standard, preferring instead silver-based money, which would raise the price of that metal. Moreover, in June 1933 Prohibition was still the law of the land. Pittman arrived in London like a man released from prison and headed to the nearest legal liquor store. At one point an astonished member of the American delegation fled in horror as the senator, stark naked and holding a bottle of whiskey in one hand and a knife in the other, chased him down the corridor of their hotel shouting that he should support the monetization of silver.

While Pittman enjoyed himself, Hull laid on the table a plan for across-the-board tariff reductions. The British replied by saying that trade revival had to be accompanied by currency stabilization. Hull warred with Pittman, so the matter was referred to the president, who dispatched Raymond Moley, an economist who headed the president's informal "Brain Trust," to end the bickering. Newspapers headlined this expedition with "MOLEY, MOLEY, MOLEY, HOLY MOLEY." The expectations were misplaced, because shortly after Moley arrived Roosevelt "torpedoed" the conference with a famous "bomb-shell" telegram of July 3. He announced, "The sound internal economic system of a nation is a greater factor in its well being than the price of its currency." Any plan for a fixing of the value of the dollar in relation to the currencies of other nations would have to wait until a majority of nations had recovered economically, could "produce balanced budgets," and could live within their means. With these bows to nationalism and economic orthodoxy, the London economic conference ended in disarray. Two years later, in 1935, the central banks of Great Britain, France, and the United States worked out an informal arrangement to fix the values of their currencies. Yet nothing was done to create a general international agreement on currency stabilization until the Bretton Woods Conference of 1944 set up the International Monetary Fund. The failure of the London conference signaled a retreat from international economic cooperation on the part of the United States.

Over the next few years Secretary of State Hull received presidential support for his plan of tariff reduction. In 1934 Congress passed a Reciprocal Trade Agreements Act that enabled the president to cut tariffs by as much as 50 percent. Hull wanted the president to use this immediately and across the board. Economic nationalists in the administration, however, thought that the United States should get something in return for its willingness to reduce its imports. George Peek, an agricultural economist and member of Roosevelt's Brain Trust, called Hull's plan "unilateral economic disarmament." While Hull favored multilateralism, a plan whereby all nations would reduce their tariffs at once, the nationalists preferred bilateral agreements, and their view prevailed. In the 1930s the State Department negotiated thirty agreements with other nations, mostly those in the Western Hemisphere, effectively tying their trade ever closer to the United States. The State and Treasury departments even went so far as to threaten the nations of Ecuador, Peru, Chile, and Argentina with limitations on their imports to the United States should they reduce their tariffs to other nations.

THE GOOD NEIGHBOR POLICY

In his inaugural address Roosevelt announced that "in our relations with the western hemisphere, we shall be guided by the principle of the good neighbor." In actuality, New Dealers followed the outlines of the policy set down by Herbert Hoover: the United States maintained control where it could over the Western Hemisphere but avoided the use of force. It would use persuasion and economic pressure to get the Latin American governments themselves to follow American leadership.

The United States would not, however, renounce the use of force for all time. At the seventh Pan-American Conference, held in Montevideo, Uruguay, in 1933, the resolution barring intervention again was presented. For the first time, the United States voted for such a resolution. Secretary of State Hull attached an important proviso, however. He said that the United States reserved its right to intervene "by the law of nations as generally recognized and accepted." Three years later, at the Buenos Aires conference, the United States went further and voted for an unequivocal renunciation of the use of force. Nonetheless, the Americans did not abandon the right to apply political or economic pressure throughout the hemisphere.

The first test of the Good Neighbor policy came early in the Roosevelt administration in its relations with Cuba. The United States had retained the right of intervention there through the Platt Amendment of 1902 (Sen. Orville H. Platt, R., Conn.). Throughout the twenties Americans had run the economy of the island with investments topping $1.5 billion in 1929. Americans controlled the treasury and tax collection and increased the size of the Cuban army. Gerardo Machado, an avowed admirer of Italy's fascist *Duce* Benito Mussolini, served as Cuban president from 1924 to 1933. In 1929 the economy of Cuba began to unravel with a crash in the price of sugar. Strikes and protest erupted that Machado quelled by jailing or murdering leftists, labor union leaders, and student activists. Edward Guggenheim, the American ambassador in Cuba, unsuccessfully attempted to calm Machado.

When Roosevelt came to power he sent a close friend from his Groton schooldays, Sumner Welles, to Cuba as ambassador. When Welles reached Cuba he concluded that Machado had to go but that the United States could not use its own troops to evict him. While American warships steamed off the coast, Welles conspired with the old politicians, looking for one of them to take power. Faced with the Americans' hostility, a general strike, and a student uprising, Machado fled the country in August. Welles's handpicked president, Carlos Manuel de Céspedes, had no control over events. Less than a month after he assumed office a group of army sergeants led by Sgt. Fulgencio Batista helped a liberal professor, Ramón Grau San Martín, take over the presidency.

Grau had long opposed the Machado government, which had forced him into exile, and the Platt Amendment. Soon after his elevation to the presidency, Grau abrogated the amendment, which gave the United States the right to intervene in the nation's internal affairs. He also suspended payment of loans to New York's Chase National Bank and began the expropriation of American-held plantations. Welles could not stand the independence and nationalism of Grau, nor could the military leaders who had helped him seize power. The fledgling Cuban Communist Party, on the other hand, thought Grau too moderate. At one point that fall, Welles had asked Secretary Hull to approve sending troops to evict their hand-chosen president. The secretary thought that would not be very neighborly and opted instead for a convoy of warships. Welles spoke to Batista, who with the support of the army seemed to be the major power in Cuba. The ambassador returned to the United States in December, and in January 1934 Batista led a coup against Grau, who left the country for Mexico.

Early in the "era of Batista," the United States abrogated the Platt Amendment, lowered the sugar tariff under the Reciprocal Trade Agreement Act, and granted Cuba loans through the Export-Import Bank. The United States also backed Batista's rule, either personally as president or through strong men, until his ouster by Fidel Castro's revolutionaries in 1959. In return for these favors, the United States was given the rights to a naval base at Guantanamo Bay on the south coast of Cuba.

While the United States ruled Cuba directly or indirectly into the 1930s, it reached an accommodation with the nationalists in Mexico. As had been the case in the Coolidge administration, a conciliatory ambassador was able to smooth the rough relations caused by Mexico's insistence on its rights to control its own mineral and petroleum wealth. Mexico's size, population, and militant nationalism prohibited the United States from seeking a military solution, although many would have wished it. In 1938 another strongly nationalist president came to power in Mexico. Lázaro Cárdenas abrogated the deal worked out by Dwight Morrow and declared that all of Mexico's mineral wealth belonged to its citizens. U.S. oil company executives fulminated, refused to sell Mexico the equipment to drill for oil, and boycotted Mexican products in the American market.

FDR's ambassador to Mexico, Josephus Daniels, had as secretary of the navy in 1914 sent the marines to Vera Cruz. As ambassador he seemed bent on repairing that wrong, and he became every bit as effective as Dwight Morrow had been. A soft-spoken North Carolinian who neither smoked, drank, nor swore, he had been preaching the gospel of the Good Neighbor since he arrived in Mexico in 1933. When faced with the expropriation of American oil properties, Daniels took a softer line than his boss in Washington, Cordell Hull.

The secretary of state prepared a stinging telegram on expropriation that Daniels refused to deliver. Hull contemplated sending the marines until his ambassador told him this would violate the Good Neighbor policy. At one point Hull ordered Daniels home, and the envoy ignored the request. Daniels had the support of the president, who believed that the United States needed Mexico's friendship in the coming global confrontation with Nazi Germany. Accordingly, Roosevelt allowed Daniels to accept the principle that Mexico owned the subsoil mineral rights. The Mexican government agreed to compensate the American firms that had been expropriated, and the United States provided Mexico with a credit of $30 million under the Export-Import Bank.

RECOGNITION OF THE SOVIET UNION

Since the Bolshevik Revolution of 1917 the United States had refused to extend diplomatic recognition to the Soviet Union. The Republican administrations of the 1920s thought that the Soviet Union was an outlaw state committed to the export of revolution throughout the world. Only the independent-minded chairman of the Senate Foreign Relations Committee, William Borah, kept up a steady campaign to send diplomatic representatives to Moscow. Secretary of State Frank Kellogg blamed the Soviet Union for sending arms to Nicaragua via Mexico. Washington also claimed that the repudiation of the czar's war debts to the United States prevented recognition.

When Roosevelt took office, however, conditions had changed. Depression caused business to look to every country of the world, no matter how unlikely, as a possible outlet for American goods. Henry Ford, who had built car factories in the Soviet Union in the early twenties, wanted to go back. So did Gerard Swope, the president of the General Electric Company, and several other business leaders urged diplomatic recognition as a way of opening trade. There were strategic reasons as well. One of the principal China experts in the State Department, Stanley Kuhl Hornbeck, had been frightened for years about the rise of Japanese power at the expense of China. For a short time in the mid-twenties, the Soviet Union had been allied with the Chinese, but relations had broken down in 1927. Hornbeck wanted to use the Soviet Union as a counter to Japan, but to do so there had to be some sort of official relations between the United States and the Soviets.

The government in Moscow also wanted to end its long period of diplomatic isolation. The rise of the Nazi Party to power in Germany had shocked the Soviets. Before Adolf Hitler became chancellor on January 30, 1933, the international communist movement denied a Nazi threat. The German Communist party had waged bitter street battles with the Nazis, but the German communists had not sought to ally with any of the "democratic" parties to stop the Nazi seizure of the state. On the eve of the Nazis' ascendancy, German communists were foolish enough to predict "after Hitler, us." Instead, communists were thrown into concentration camps, their party was outlawed, and Nazi foreign policy spokesmen called the Soviet Union the enemy. Consequently, Soviet leader Josef Stalin switched course, tried to find allies among the democratic nations of the West, and told Western communists to create "popular fronts" with noncommunist "progressive parties." In 1934 the Soviet Union joined the League of Nations, where its representative, Maxim Litvinov, became the foremost spokesman for collective security against Germany's military revival.

Before the Soviet Union joined the League, it opened diplomatic relations with the United States. Roosevelt appointed William C. Bullitt his special representative to the Soviet Union. Bullitt approached Boris Skvirsky, the principal Soviet representative in the United States, in early October 1933, offering an invitation from Roosevelt to a Soviet official to come to the United States. Skvirsky asked, "Does this mean recognition?" and Bullitt parried, "What more can you expect than to have your representative sit down with the president of the United States?"

The Soviets were pleased to send their foreign minister, Maxim Litvinov, to the United States for talks from November 8 to 16, 1933. Roosevelt used his legendary charm on the Soviet envoy. As became his custom later in his presidency, he told his cabinet how he had cajoled Litvinov into allowing religious freedom for Americans living in the Soviet Union. "You know Max, your good old father and mother, pious Jewish people, always said their prayers. I know that they must have taught you to say your prayers." Roosevelt went on: "Max blustered and puffed and said all kinds of things, laughed and was very embarrassed, but I had him." Roosevelt won from Litvinov the agreement that Americans in the Soviet Union could have religious freedom; this disarmed the criticism of the Catholic press in the United States. He extracted a pledge that the Soviet Union would pay from $70 to $150 million in war debts; this warmed the hearts of bankers. Businessmen were encouraged to believe that a vast market awaited them, and friends of China thought that finally a bulwark had been established against the Japanese.

These hopes proved illusory over the next five years. The Soviets did not allow freedom of religion. They did not repay the debts. Business and trade with the Russians went nowhere. And the Japanese continued their assault in the Far East. The enthusiasm for the Soviet regime of Bullitt, the first American ambassador to the Soviet Union, turned to equally unbalanced anticommunism within two years. He left in 1935 to become ambassador to France, leaving behind a staff of experts, led by George F. Kennan, most of whom grew disgusted with and frightened by the purges of old Bolsheviks that consolidated Stalin's rule. The Foreign Service experts on the Soviet Union thereupon began a campaign inside the State Department to alert politicians to the threat of communism.

NEUTRALITY

Robert Dallek, who has written a major study of FDR's diplomacy, *Franklin D. Roosevelt and American Foreign Policy* (1979), describes "his prevailing inclination to move slowly in foreign affairs." Only when the president could be certain of "an unequivocal popular consensus" behind him would he take a strong position, Dallek asserts. In the first Roosevelt administration, there seemed to be general agreement that the United States should steer clear of Europe's problems. The memory of the recent past and a fear of repeating unhappy experiences dominated policy. In the twenties Americans were already suspicious of the motives for entry into the world war. With the onset of the Depression and the election of Roosevelt, the conservative internationalism of the Republican twenties became an object of scorn. Liberals came to believe that recent foreign affairs had served the interests of international bankers and investors, two especially reviled groups in 1933. When Richard Whitney, the vice president of the New York Stock Exchange, went to jail in 1934 for swindling thousands of small investors, his disgrace highlighted the hypocrisy of the business community. These suspicions combined with the economic nationalism of the early New Deal to make a forward foreign policy seem the work of selfish, old-fashioned diplomats.

Americans reflected worldwide trends in their rejection of the Versailles Treaty and the policy of collective security. In Britain liberals who had had such high hopes for the success of Wilsonianism had come to believe that the world war had been a mistake. W. H. Dawson's *Germany Under the Treaty* (1932) and Lord Birkenhead's *Turning Points in History* (1929) joined John Maynard Keynes's *Economic Consequences of the Peace* (1920) in creating a widespread agreement that Germany had been mistreated by the Treaty of Versailles. The British Labor Party, having broken with Ramsay MacDonald in 1931, turned its back on international questions to concentrate its attention on complaints about the government's fumbling attempts to handle the Depression. Once the Conservatives came back to power in 1935, under the premiership of Stanley Baldwin, they too hoped to appease the German ambitions. Some prominent conservatives, such as Lady Astor, Lord Halifax, Neville Henderson, and Frank Ashton-Gwatkin, found virtues in the Nazi government. Some conservatives, terrified of revolution, liked the Nazis' anticommunism; others hated Jews and saw nothing wrong with Hitler's anti-Semitic ravings; and still others thought that Germany was a fertile market. Similar feelings arose in France in the midst of the Depression. Except for a brief interlude in 1936 and 1937 when a popular front government of liberals, socialists, and communists, headed by a Jewish politician, Léon Blum, was in power, France in the thirties had little stomach for a confrontation with Germany. Bled white by the world war, which had cost France alone 1.5 million lives, no government in the Depression wanted to spend money for weapons against Germany.

In the United States the revulsion at the memory of the world war took the form of neutrality laws designed to prevent Americans again being sucked into a war. Four such laws passed Congress: in 1935, 1936, 1937, and 1939. The first came as a result of hearings held by a Senate Select Committee in 1934. Sen. Gerald Nye, a Progressive Republican from North Dakota, chaired a committee especially empowered to look into charges raised in the book *Merchants of Death* (1934) that the United States had been fooled into fighting the war by an unholy alliance of bankers and munitions manufacturers. Dorothy Detzer, the head of the Women's International League for Peace and Freedom, had approached Sen. George Norris, a Progressive Republican from Nebraska, who favored an investigation. Norris asked Nye to assemble a committee, which met in late 1934 and early 1935. Nye's committee heard from businessmen, historians, and diplomats and concluded that the United States had not truly been neutral in the years before 1917. America could only have avoided conflict, the committee decided, by avoiding financial dealings with embattled countries.

The researches of the Nye committee became more than an academic enterprise in 1935. Fascist Italy under Benito Mussolini looked for a way to restore the glory of the Roman Empire. He found it in East Africa, where, from the end of 1934 until the fall of 1935, Italy made demand after demand on Ethiopia. Finally, Italy attacked Ethiopia on October 3, 1935. Alarms ran through European capitals, where politicians feared that the attack on Ethiopia signaled a crisis as grave as the one that had touched off the world war.

The answer of the Nye committee to these new tensions was to draft new laws with three provisions—a ban on travel by Americans to a war zone (to avoid another *Lusitania* incident), a ban on loans by Americans to belligerents, and, most important of all, an impartial embargo on arms to belligerents. Roosevelt spoke up for the authority to impose a discriminatory embargo, that is, one that would let him declare one nation an aggressor and embargo weapons only to that one. But Nye and his supporters would have none of a discriminatory embargo, and they filibustered against it on the Senate floor. At one point frantic members of the Committee on Foreign Relations found their leader, Chairman Key Pittman, barely sober enough to stand. Doses of coffee revived him enough to come to the Senate floor and announce that the president would agree to a bill that had an impartial arms embargo. Both houses of Congress passed the bill, and on August 31, 1935, President Roosevelt signed the Neutrality Law. When signing, Roosevelt did warn, however, that the impartial arms embargo "might have exactly the opposite effect from that which was intended. In other words, the inflexible provisions might drag us into war instead of keeping us out."

The next year, 1936, Congress passed a second neutrality law that simply extended the first for another year. In 1937 lawmakers had to contend with another European crisis—the civil war in Spain—when they sought to make the neutrality law permanent. The Spanish Republic, proclaimed in 1931, was led by liberals and moderate socialists. In July 1936 Gen. Francisco Franco, the commander of Spanish forces in North Africa, led an uprising against the republic. Fascist Italy and Nazi Germany quickly came to Franco's aid with troops and weapons. A few months later the Soviet Union enlisted on the side of the republic with smaller amounts of military aid. The British led an international movement to stay neutral in the fighting. Foreign Secretary Anthony Eden convinced the French, who had an agreement to aid the Spanish Republic, to stay out. Britain also wanted the United States to remain neutral, and President Roosevelt was happy to oblige. American opinion was deeply divided over the Spanish civil war, with liberals and leftists supporting the republic and conservatives and the bulk of the Catholic hierarchy backing Franco. Roosevelt had no wish to alarm Catholics or British diplomats, so he invoked the neutrality act to keep Americans from backing either side.

Crises in European politics seemed to come with increasing frequency; either they would lead to war, or they would become endemic. Whatever happened, advocates of neutrality wanted to find a way for Americans to continue to reap the benefits of trade with contentious and warring Europe while at the same time avoiding the risk of involvement in war. The next addition to the neutrality law was the brainchild of Bernard Baruch, a South Carolina self-styled adviser to presidents who had made millions in stock market "bucket shops," establishments in which customers bet on the price of common stock they happened not to own. Baruch, who had been the head of the War Industries Board during the Great War, believed that the threat to neutrality came from American ships being sunk. Ban shipping in a war zone, and there would be no chance of war. How then could Americans continue their trade? The answer: "Get the belligerents to pay for the goods beforehand and ship them home themselves." He expressed this cash-and-carry principle this way: "We will ship to any belligerent anything except lethal weapons, but the terms are '*cash on the barrel head and come and get it.*'" Roosevelt favored this plan because he knew that it subtly shifted the balance in favor of Great Britain, a state whose foreign policy he approved, and away from Germany. The British had the merchant marine that the Germans lacked. Advocates of strict neutrality such as Nye preferred a total embargo, but they thought that the cash-and-carry provision was the best they could get through Congress. Thus, on May 1, 1937, Roosevelt signed a permanent Neutrality Act. Under its provisions, whenever the president declared that a state of war existed anywhere in the world, he had to place three major restrictions on Americans—an arms embargo, a prohibition of loans, and a prohibition of travel on belligerent ships. It was also up to him to place all trade with belligerents on a cash-and-carry basis. The main provisions of the act were permanent, but the cash-and-carry feature was due to expire in May 1939. Robert Divine describes the Neutrality Act of 1937 in *The Reluctant Belligerent* (1965, 1979) as "a compromise that reflected the contradictory desire of the American people to remain economically in the world and politically out of it."

THE SECOND SINO-JAPANESE WAR, 1937–1939

On July 7, 1937, war broke out again between Japan and China, and Japanese troops attacked north of Beijing in an effort to extend Japan's domination of China's economy. The war continued until the final defeat of Japan in 1945; it involved the United States and, most important, hastened the revolution that swept the communists to power in 1949. American voices began calling immediately for an international condemnation of the Japanese. Henry L. Stimson, who had hoped for a stronger policy against Japan when he was secretary of state, led a movement for a boycott of Japanese goods, and the State Department's chief China hand, Assistant Secretary of State Stanley Hornbeck, also wanted a strong American stance in support of China. On the other side, however, American diplomats stationed in Tokyo, led by Ambassador Joseph C. Grew, who held the post from 1931 to 1941, thought that any American criticism of Japan would further inflame the Japanese against China.

Like Hoover before him, Roosevelt did not wish to risk war with Japan over China. He dismissed a trade embargo on Japan as unworkable in the midst of the Great Depression. At one point, on October 5, 1937, he delivered a speech in Chicago that seemed to condemn Japan as he called for a "quarantine" of aggressors, including Italy for its attack on Ethiopia, Germany for its violations of the Versailles Treaty, and Japan for its war on China. Reaction to the quarantine speech in the American press was surprisingly favorable. Even the *Chicago Tribune*, a staunch foe of any American involvement in European quarrels, said the prospect of economic and financial steps against Japan "would not lead to war." Having launched his trial balloon and not seen it explode, Roosevelt went no further in the direction of sanctions. He refused to believe that the public would actually support American military action in China and consequently did no more. His suspicions that few Americans wanted to be involved in an Asian war seemed confirmed the next month. On December 12, 1937, Japanese planes bombed an American naval gunboat, the *Panay*, patrolling the Chang Jiang (Yangtze) River in China on behalf of the Socony-Vacuum Oil (later Mobil) Company. Instead of calling for a punitive reaction against Japan, Arizona senator Henry Ashurst voiced the views of most Americans when he answered that "none of my" colleagues would vote for war with Japan. Indiana congressman Louis Ludlow took the opportunity to gain floor action on a constitutional amendment requiring a national referendum before declaring war. Peace groups wondered what an American gunboat had been doing in China helping Socony-Vacuum. They expressed a widespread sentiment that the government had no business bailing out businessmen who worked in dangerous regions and called for the withdrawal of the American navy from China. When Japan apologized and offered to pay for damages on Christmas day, the furor subsided. For the next two years American policy in the Far Eastern crisis was to give public lip service to the idea of the Open Door, to give private military and economic aid to Jiang Jieshi, and to maintain a precarious peace with Japan, but in 1940 and 1941 American policy toward Japan became more hostile (see chapter seven).

AMERICA: HITLER'S SILENT ACCOMPLICE?

After the Second World War broke out in September 1939, *appeasement* became a dirty word, and the Munich Conference of September 1938 came to symbolize everything that was wrong with the foreign policy of the Allies before the Second World War. Appeasement suggested naiveté, weakness, and wishful thinking. Neville Chamberlain, the British prime minister who orchestrated the Munich Conference on Czechoslovakia, became a pathetic figure of fun. Opponents of the abandonment of the Czechs for a time even refused to carry umbrellas because of the association with the prime minister, who carried one off the plane from Germany when he proclaimed, "This is the second time in our lifetime that a British prime minister has returned from Germany with peace and honor. I believe it is peace for our time." In 1938, however, the appeasement of Germany's "legitimate" desires to rectify the Versailles Treaty was seen as "a self-confident creed ... both utopian and practical," writes historian Martin Gilbert in *The Roots of Appeasement* (1966). The policy "sought to satisfy legitimate national aspirations without fomenting aggressive, destructive nationalism."

Since taking power in 1933, Hitler had systematically gone about reversing the judgment of the Versailles Treaty. In 1935 he began rearming the German military; in 1936 he established military bases in the Rhineland in violation of the treaty. In the fall of 1936 he provided an air force and tanks to fight on the side of Franco in Spain; in March 1938 he annexed Austria to Germany. All the while he denounced the Western democracies, Bolsheviks in the Soviet Union, and Jews everywhere, claiming that they were responsible for all the world's woes. Promising to restore Germany to its rightful place in the sun, he claimed that only communists, Jews outside of

Adolf Hitler receives the adulation of jubilant Nazis at a party rally.
(National Archives)

Germany, and a few professional German-haters and militarists wanted to wage war on the Nazis. In Great Britain, for example, Winston Churchill led an isolated fringe group of conservatives who called for British rearmament, but Churchill's views were ignored when they were not considered radical and at war with reality.

In the summer of 1938 a new crisis arose in central Europe. Hitler tried to join the Germans living in Czechoslovakia to the Reich, just as he had done with Austria. This time, however, Czech prime minister Eduard Beneš was more fiercely opposed than the Austrians had been, and war threatened to erupt late that summer. The Czechs had a security treaty with France and another with the Soviet Union and believed that they could resist the Germans. At this point Britain, also allied with France, stepped in to look for a peaceful solution. Prime Minister Chamberlain traveled twice to visit Hitler in his mountain retreat near Munich. At the second of these meetings the French also participated. Significantly, the Czechs, whose fate was being decided, and the Soviets, who were willing to fight the Germans, were not invited. The Munich agreement awarded one-third of Czechoslovakia to Germany in return for a promise not to take the rest. Chamberlain returned home with his umbrella. The Roosevelt administration reacted with pleasure to the Munich agreement. The president sent Chamberlain a two-word cable, "GOOD MAN," when he learned that the conference had averted war. Still in the Depression— the economy had taken another nose-dive in 1937–1938—the Roosevelt administration had no desire to confront the Germans directly. Less than six months later, in March 1939, Germany finished the job, annexed the rest of Czechoslovakia, and killed British hopes that Germany's leader was a traditional politician whose aims could be appeased.

The administration did little to aid the most direct victims of Nazism— Jews forced to flee their homes. American immigration policy remained hostile to Jewish refugees in the 1930s. The quotas passed in 1921 and 1924 had excluded eastern European Jews as of "low racial quality." One American diplomat in the 1920s suggested that the Jews who applied for visas to enter the United States gave his office "a smell no zoo could equal." The Roosevelt administration did nothing to lift barriers to immigration. Foreign Service officers retained their animosity to Jews after Hitler rose to power. In 1935 Germany passed the notorious Nuremberg racial laws, making it virtually impossible for Jews to make a living in the Reich. Thousands left Germany in the wake of these laws. More followed after November 1938, when a wave of violence against Jews swept over Germany. Throughout this period the United States resisted the idea of allowing more into the United States than would be permitted under the quota for Germany. In early 1939 a ship laden with refugees was forced out of Havana harbor in Cuba, where the authorities would not let it land. No other safe haven beckoned, and it had to go back to Germany.

No international action occurred to ease the plight of the refugees. A conference at Evian-sur-les-Bains, a comfortable resort town in central France, took place in 1938. The nations of Europe and Latin America, along with the United States, met to decide if any could accept more Jewish refugees. All agreed that because of the Depression their economies simply were too strained to make room for any more of the victims of Nazism. The conference ended with a pious declaration that the German government should stop the persecutions.

This apparent underestimation of the dangers posed by the rise of German power set off a mild flurry of controversy among historians, although it never became as heated as the arguments over American entry into the First World War. In the palmy days of consensus that American participation in the Second World War made sense, the complaint arose that the United States had become, in Robert Divine's words, a "silent accomplice" of Hitler's grand design for world conquest. Roosevelt, who became "the soldier of freedom" in political scientist James MacGregor Burns's estimate during the Second World War was viewed as having been too cautious in the thirties. According to some historians, by not raising the alarm Roosevelt actually encouraged Hitler to go further than he might otherwise have done. Written in the midst of the Cold War competition with Russia, the complaints about Roosevelt's apparent reluctance to get too far in front of the public justified confrontations with Russia. As doubts emerged about the Cold War, some New Left historians resurrected old criticisms of American diplomacy in the thirties. One of them, Patrick Hearden, presents a different picture of Roosevelt than as someone who feared leaving public opinion behind. In *Roosevelt Confronts Hitler* (1987) he argues that the president opposed Nazism in order to establish a Pax Americana of U.S. commercial dominion. While admitting that Roosevelt was "genuinely concerned about the plight of the Jews," Hearden states that ethical concerns did not move the administration.

WAR IN EUROPE: SEPTEMBER 1939

The desperate illusion that the Munich conference would promote peace in Europe was shattered early in 1939 when Germany annexed the rest of Czechoslovakia. That summer a crisis erupted over control of the German-speaking city of Danzig, the port that gave Poland access to the sea. Danzig was a "free city" under League of Nations supervision, and the residents were Germans who sympathized with the Nazi government in Berlin. They demanded the right to attach themselves to Germany, and Hitler backed them, threatening Poland with war unless it relented.

The Western powers, Britain and France, had realized with the conquest of Czechoslovakia that Hitler's word could not be trusted. Besides, the Poles had a history of fighting quixotic wars they had no chance of winning and, unlike the Czechs, were likely to oppose the Germans without allies. Therefore, British and French diplomats gloomily concluded that war was likely in the summer of 1939.

London and Paris clung vainly to the hope that the Soviet Union or the United States might force the Germans to back down. Britain and France conducted desultory talks with the Soviets in July. But reactionary Western officers did not have their hearts in these conversations, and the envoys took weeks getting to Moscow. A suspicious Josef Stalin, mindful of his exclusion from the Munich negotiations, feared being sucked into a losing battle with Hitler. He dropped his Jewish foreign minister, Maxim Litvinov, who advocated collective security, and responded to Nazi overtures. Hitler's foreign minister, Joachim von Ribbentrop, flew to Moscow on August 22. The next day he and his Soviet counterpart, Vyacheslav Molotov, Litvinov's replacement, stunned the world with the announcement that their governments had signed a nonaggression pact.

Official Washington reaction to the crisis over Danzig and the Nazi-Soviet pact was measured even though war seemed likely. Roosevelt did press Congress to lift the arms embargo required by the neutrality acts. The president preferred to allow belligerents to buy arms if they could pay cash and carry them away. Roosevelt retreated, however, in the face of a certain filibuster by senators who feared an arms trade would make the United States a quasibelligerent. The president was stirred to action by the Nazi-Soviet pact. Upon learning of the agreement on August 23, he telegraphed the king of Italy, asking him to intercede between Germany and Poland. The next day he sent similar messages pleading for restraint to Hitler and Polish president Ignacy Moscicki. None of Roosevelt's messages worked, of course. On August 25 Great Britain signed a formal alliance with Poland. Exactly one week later, on September 1, Hitler attacked Poland. Two days afterward the British and the French invoked their alliance with the Poles and declared war on Germany. The Second World War had begun. Unlike the First World War, no crowds plunged into the streets in any of the capitals of the belligerents. None had recovered from the first war, and most believed that the second would be even more brutal.

CHAPTER SEVEN

The Politics of Coalition Warfare, 1939–1945

Contemporary U.S. foreign policy came alive during the Second World War. In 1940 Henry Luce, the founder of *Time* magazine, proclaimed that "America is already the intellectual, scientific and artistic capital of the world." He assured the public that the world had entered "the American century" in which "we have that indefinable, unmistakable sign of leadership—prestige." Directors of American foreign policy from the president to the lowliest Foreign Service officer, army lieutenant, or congressman shared the view that their country would be the premier power in the world once the war ended.

NEUTRALITY

People who called themselves internationalists in the 1930s filled the two years between the outbreak of war in Europe in 1939 and the American entry in December 1941 with calls for military aid to France and Britain and preparedness for war. Later, advocates of aid to the Allies saw the two prewar years as a test of the moral fiber of Americans: would they assume their "rightful role" in world politics? For others, who called themselves noninterventionists in the thirties, the two years after 1939 bore a striking and sad similarity to the period between the outbreak of war in 1914 and the American declaration of war in 1917. Leading noninterventionists such as historian Charles Beard, air hero Charles Lindbergh, and Sen. Robert Taft insisted that the United States recapitulated the mistakes of earlier neutrality and grimly predicted the coming of a garrison state bereft of democracy and civil rights.

Both internationalists and noninterventionists organized politically to mold government policy and change public opinion. Advocates of American participation in the European war began a public campaign to support Britain and France. Encouraged by President Franklin D. Roosevelt and Secretary of the Interior Harold Ickes, William Alanson White, a well-known liberal Republican newspaper editor from Emporia, Kansas, organized the Committee to Defend America by Aiding the Allies in June 1940.

The White committee came to life as the Roosevelt administration sought to undermine the appeal of the America First Committee, a group born in the late spring of 1940 to keep the United States out of war. America First, the brainchild of Robert B. Woods, an heir to the Sears Roebuck fortune, included as prominent members Charles Lindbergh, Yale professor of international law Edward Borchard, and Sen. Burton K. Wheeler of Montana. It had a strong following in the Midwest and among college students opposed to war. It held public rallies, distributed literature, and lobbied public officials against American military support for the Allies.

While the White committee debated the America Firsters, accusing them of a cowardly refusal to admit that Germany threatened America, the Roosevelt administration was busy blackening the reputations of those who opposed aid to the Allies. The president had Ickes and the director of the Federal Bureau of Investigation, J. Edgar Hoover, launch a whispering campaign against the leaders of America First, suggesting that they took their orders from Berlin. The FBI followed members of America First, opened their mail, and concocted phony letters to prove they had the best interests of the Nazis at heart. By the fall of 1941 the campaign against America First had been successful, and public opinion polls showed that more than 40 percent of the American people were willing to fight. Roosevelt honestly perceived a threat to the United States in 1940 and 1941, but later presidents used the vilification of opponents in lesser causes.

While Roosevelt wanted the United States to fight the war on the side of Britain and France, he feared leaving public opinion too far behind. Remembering how the initial enthusiasm for Woodrow Wilson's program in war and peace had evaporated in the hard reality of the war, he wanted assurances that if the United States were to fight in the Second World War, the public would stay the course. He preferred to lead the public slowly to appreciate that the United States had to fight the war for self-interest, not for any grand program of international reform.

He began in the fall of 1939 when he tried once more to revise the neutrality laws. This time he succeeded in eliminating the arms embargo in favor of the ability to sell arms on a cash-and-carry basis. He suggested that the arming of the Allies would work to keep the United States out of the war, but he did not pretend that the end to the embargo gave equal access to all the belligerents. Cash and carry aided the British and French, who had the merchant marine, navy, and money to buy, while the Germans were effectively frozen out of the American arms trade. Making no secret of his sympathies for the Allies, Roosevelt offered no admonition to Americans to be neutral in thought or deed. Throughout the winter of 1939–1940 Americans shipped more than $50 million in arms to Britain and France.

WAR IN EUROPE

The president's warm feeling for Britain and France came partly from memory of his experiences as assistant secretary of the navy during the First World War. He had visited the front in 1917, spoken to government officials, and come home convinced that Germans fought with cruel, heartless tenacity. Americans who had been to Germany after Hitler's rise to power in 1933 saw with their own eyes storm troopers beating Jews, Nazi bonfires of books, and hate-filled faces of participants at the annual rallies of Hitler's followers in the Bavarian town of Nuremberg. Austrians and Czechs had gotten an unforgettable taste of life under Nazi rule in 1938 and 1939, and in September 1939 the world learned how Hitler's armies fought.

The Wehrmacht (war machine) moved hundreds of thousands of infantrymen behind thousands of tanks and under the cover of fighter bombers that seemed to emerge out of nowhere to terrify the enemy. This *Blitzkrieg* (lightning war) surprised military experts who expected any new combat would resemble the trench warfare of 1914 to 1918. Poland was crushed within six weeks, and the Nazis continued a brutal campaign of terror against Jews, local communists and socialists, and anyone connected with the old Polish government. Treating the Poles as *Untermenschen* (subhumans), commando squads of the SS (special security army) stripped, beat, and bludgeoned to death thousands of Poles in the autumn. This was only a foretaste of the systematic murder of 5 million Poles (including 3 million Jews) begun in 1941. Germany installed the sadist Hans Frank as military governor to extract as much labor as he could from the Poles. While Germany perfected new sorts of tyranny in the western two-thirds of Poland, the Soviet Union occupied the eastern part of the country under the terms of the Nazi-Soviet pact of late August.

Although Britain and France had declared war in support of Poland, they sent no troops and did not attack Germany in the fall and winter of 1939–1940. Hitler, contentedly digesting Poland, believed the Allies incapable of fighting, and Germans suggested that *Blitzkrieg* had turned to *Sitzkrieg* (sitdown war). Domestic opponents of the British government who urged action against Hitler charged that diplomats and generals throughout western Europe fought a "phony war."

The United States provided more than $50 million in arms to Britain and France from October 1939 to April 1940, but the primary target of American diplomacy was not Germany, but the Soviet Union, which sent its army against neighboring Finland in December. Roosevelt promised arms to the Finns, the one country to have fully repaid its First World War debts. The British government, baffled at ways to fight Hitler but eager to do battle somewhere, drew up unworkable plans to ship a division across frozen Norway to Finland. The League of Nations, unable to halt the spread of Nazism, responded to the Russo-Finnish winter war by expelling the Soviet Union. This was the only time in its history that the League evicted a nation for violating the covenant's prohibition of aggression. Japan, Italy, and Germany, each of which had sent its armies against other countries in the thirties, had all left before the international organization could throw them out.

In 1940 Germany and Italy created an alliance of their own as a ghastly mockery of the League. Mussolini called it the Rome-Berlin Axis because the world would now revolve around the Nazi and Fascist states. A new German *Blitzkrieg* exploded the phony war in April. Panzer tanks and Stuka dive bombers led 1 million of the best-armed foot soldiers the world had ever seen across Denmark, Norway, Holland, and Belgium. All these countries capitulated within six weeks. In London Neville Chamberlain reluctantly resigned in the face of a revolt by fellow Conservatives, one of whom stood up in the House of Commons, wagged his finger at the prime minister, and bellowed words spoken 300 years before by Oliver Cromwell, "You have sat too long in this place. In the name of God, go." Winston Churchill, for years regarded as an irritating romantic, in love with the empire, the king, and the products of the Uppmann Cigar Company, took over a coalition of the Conservative, Labor, and Liberal parties in May.

Churchill's warnings about the danger of German rearmament seemed vindicated by his elevation to prime minister, but he could do nothing to prevent the German army from rolling over France in early June. As the Wehrmacht surrounded the French troops, Churchill flew several times across the channel to encourage continued resistance. He went before the microphones of the British Broadcasting Corporation to offer France "indissoluble union" with Great Britain if only Paris would not surrender to Hitler. French president Eduard Daladier, shocked by the German success at out-flanking the supposedly unbreachable Maginot Line of defense, wanted no part of Great Britain. Most French people were bewildered by the collapse of their army, resented the dramatic escape of the 200,000-member British Expeditionary Force across the channel from the beach at Dunkirk, and thought the Germans invincible. The government fled Paris in front of tens of thousands of terrified refugees who clogged the roads to the south and west away from the approaching Nazis. Marshal Henri Pétain, a hero from the First World War, took over. The government surrendered on June 22. A jubilant Adolf Hitler accepted France's capitulation in the same railroad car the Allies had used to host the German officers who signed the armistice on November 11, 1918. The Nazi leader emerged smiling from the car and made his only visit to Paris, where he sped through the deserted streets to look down on Napoleon's tomb to remind the world that Europe had a new conqueror.

Now Britain stood alone expecting an imminent invasion. Exhilarated Britons compared themselves favorably to the French as they listened on the radio to the distinctive gravelly voice of their new prime minister promising "blood, toil, tears, and sweat"; they thrilled at the sight of his short, stubby form, arm upraised in the V-for-victory sign, and went about filling sandbags, sewing burn dressings, and encouraging their neighbors to keep the blackout. Camaraderie, defiance, and determination were not enough, however, as the British were desperate for American weapons by the summer of 1940.

AID FOR BRITAIN

In August Roosevelt readied a plan for temporary relief to Britain with a gift of fifty obsolete destroyers in return for bases for the American navy on British-owned Caribbean islands. Winston Churchill hoped for more direct aid, but he was mollified by Roosevelt's assurance that the destroyers-for-bases swap meant the death of official American neutrality. Encouraged to believe that the "English-speaking peoples" were now "somewhat mixed up together," Churchill could say that their friendship was "like the Mississippi, it just keeps rolling along."

Roosevelt also shook up his cabinet in the summer of 1940, turning his back on New Deal domestic reforms as he recruited important Republicans to fill key military assignments. On June 19 he named Henry Stimson and Frank Knox, two of the best-known pro-Allied Republicans, as secretary of war and secretary of the navy, respectively. Stimson, secretary of war for President Taft (1909–1913) and secretary of state for President Hoover (1929–1933), seventy-two years old at the time of his appointment, favored repeal of all neutrality laws and enactment of compulsory military training. Knox, the Republican vice presidential candidate in 1936, was even more ardent in his support of Britain, urging an army of 1 million Americans, the largest air force in the world, and the immediate shipment of hundreds of planes to Britain.

Later that summer Roosevelt moved to make a reality of the larger army. On August 2 he swung his support behind the moribund bill creating a Selective Service system to draft young men into the military. Roosevelt's announcement that he was "distinctly in favor" of the draft encouraged Congress to pass the law in September. The draft lasted for one year and included a provision that conscripts would serve only in the Western Hemisphere. Despite these qualifications designed to quiet the anxieties of peace societies and "Gold Star Mothers" (women whose sons had died in the last war), who had flooded Congress with mail opposing the draft, FDR's advocacy of Selective Service left little doubt that the president believed war was likely in the next year.

Roosevelt did nothing further publicly to aid the Allies before the election of 1940. He looked forward to an unprecedented third term. The Republicans, frustrated at having twice unsuccessfully run well-known officeholders against FDR, chose a newcomer to politics, Wendell Willkie of Indiana, who came from the internationalist wing of the Republican Party that supported the British in the war. During the campaign neither Roosevelt nor Willkie spoke of their true feelings about the need for the United States to come to the aid of Britain, and both promised peace. Willkie supported the destroyers-for-bases deal and the conscription law, yet in the heat of the campaign he blurted out, "If you elect me president, I will never send American boys to fight in any European war." FDR replied in kind on October 30 when he promised American mothers, "I have said this before and I shall say it again and again and again: Your boys are not going to be sent into any foreign wars." That was enough for the public; Roosevelt was reelected on November 5 with 55 percent of the popular vote. His margin of victory had declined since 1936, and a majority of people questioned by Gallup said they would have voted for Willkie had it not been for the war. Congress, too, was less heavily Democratic than the one elected in 1938, but FDR's fellow Democrats still enjoyed a margin.

Now that his authority had been renewed, Roosevelt returned to the problem of Britain. By December the British had exhausted their foreign currency reserves and could no longer pay cash for American arms. The neutrality laws and the Johnson Act of 1934 prevented floating private loans, but in a fireside chat on December 29, Roosevelt told the public that the United States should become "the great arsenal of democracy." When Congress convened the first week of January 1941, he let the senators and representatives know that the United States stood for Four Freedoms—freedom of speech, freedom of worship, freedom from want, and freedom from fear. He then explained that the United States would protect these freedoms by aiding the British and asked Congress to enact a "lend-lease" law. The bill proposing Lend-Lease, called H.R. (House Resolution) 1776, authorized the president to "lease, lend, or otherwise dispose of," to any country whose defense was vital to the United States, arms and supplies up to the astonishing amount for the time of $7 billion.

Noninterventionists immediately saw that their carefully constructed system of neutrality was about to come crashing down, and they railed against Lend-Lease. Democratic senator Burton K. Wheeler of Montana compared the proposal to an early New Deal program, the Agricultural Adjustment Administration, which had ordered farmers to plow under their crops to raise prices. "The lend-lease-give program is the New Deal Triple A foreign policy; it will plow under every fourth American boy," Wheeler charged. A stung Roosevelt used his outrage to vilify the noninterventionists, and he told a press conference that Wheeler's remark was "the most dastardly, unpatriotic thing that has ever been said. Quote me on that. That really is the rottenest thing that has been said in public life in my generation."

But the opposition kept at it. Testifying before a Senate committee, historian Charles A. Beard pleaded against enacting a law that was certain to lead the United States to war. He begged the senators to "preserve one stronghold of order and sanity even against the gates of hell." But this was the view of a minority. Internationalists made equally fervid appeals to pass Lend-Lease as a means of keeping the United States out of war. Finally, in mid-February Wendell Willkie, the titular head of the Republican Party, endorsed the law, making it a bipartisan issue. Both houses of Congress passed the bill, and on March 11 the president signed Lend-Lease. Within a month Congress appropriated the $7 billion Roosevelt requested for aid to Britain and its allies.

CONFRONTATION WITH GERMANY

Even as Congress debated Lend-Lease, the United States moved toward a military confrontation with Germany. From January 29 to March 27 high-ranking representatives of the British and American Chiefs of Staff met secretly in Washington to coordinate military strategy in the event of American entry into the war. The talks set a pattern that continued throughout the war. The two sides never saw eye to eye as the British clung to an empire the larger, richer, and more powerful Americans tried to pry loose. Whatever their political squabbles, the Chiefs of Staff did settle a military question, adopting the suggestion of the American chief of naval operations, Harold R. Stark, that in event of war with both Japan and Germany, the United States and its allies would fight against Germany first. When the talks ended on March 27, the two sides had adopted a plan, "ABC-1," under which they ratified Stark's ideas.

While these secret conversations went forward, Roosevelt tested the public's appetite for the American navy to escort the ships carrying weapons to Britain. On March 15 he made a cryptic remark in a radio address in which he said he would maintain "a bridge of ships" to Britain. Two days later the Committee to Defend America by Aiding the Allies, the William A. White committee, came out in favor of convoys. In his press conference of March 18, FDR was noncommittal about convoys, and at the end of the month two non-interventionist members of Congress, Sen. Charles Tobey of New Hampshire and Rep. Harry Sauthoff of Wisconsin, introduced a joint Senate-House res-olution against convoys. The resolutions never came up for formal votes, but enough opposition to convoys was expressed to give Roosevelt pause. Over the next month he distinguished between "patrols" and "convoys." He ad-mitted the navy conducted patrols but denied that convoys were part of the American operation. There was the same difference between a convoy and a patrol, he told his press conference on April 25, as between a cow and a horse. "If one looks at a cow and calls it a horse that is all right with the pres-ident, but that does not make a cow a horse."

Instead of publicly acknowledging that the navy was convoying American ships, Roosevelt moved stealthily to bring the American navy into the war zone. On April 9 an agreement was reached with the Danish foreign minis-ter placing Greenland inside the American "sphere of cooperative hemi-sphere defense." Three months later, on July 7, the United States made a similar pledge to Iceland, placing that island, 500 miles northwest of Britain, officially in the Western Hemisphere. The United States received the right to station its destroyers in naval bases in Iceland from which they escorted American ships bearing Lend-Lease aid to Britain.

The German reaction was predictable and maybe slower in coming than FDR had hoped for and expected. When the Nazis began attacking Ameri-can destroyers, Roosevelt used the incidents as reasons formally to convoy vessels bound for Britain. The first German episode occurred on September 4, when a U-boat fired torpedoes at the American destroyer *Greer*. Roosevelt indignantly announced in a radio broadcast of September 11 that the ship had been innocently engaged in carrying passengers and mail to Iceland when "she was then and there attacked by a submarine.... I tell you the blunt fact that the German submarine fired first upon this American destroyer without warning and with deliberate design to sink her." He then said that he had responded by ordering the navy to "sink on sight" hostile submarines and that the navy was now indeed convoying merchant ships.

The facts of the *Greer* case made the navy less the innocent victim of German aggression than Roosevelt had implied. The destroyer had actually received radio word from a British warplane of the presence of a German submarine. The *Greer* had then given chase for the next three and a half hours, radioing the position of the U-boat to the British plane. The warplane had joined the hunt, during which it dropped four depth charges that missed the submarine. The German boat fired a torpedo that crossed the American vessel about 100 yards behind. The destroyer responded with eight more depth charges, each of which missed; the submarine replied with another erring torpedo. The chase continued for a few more minutes with the destroyer dropping more depth charges. Finally, the American ship gave up and went on to Iceland.

A more serious incident involving an American destroyer and a German U-boat took place a month later, on the night of October 16–17. A German submarine fired a torpedo that hit the American destroyer *Kearney*, severely damaging it and killing eleven sailors. "America has been attacked," Roosevelt said on the radio on the evening of October 17. He neglected to mention that the *Kearney*, like the *Greer*, had been stalking the submarine and dropping depth charges when it had been torpedoed. Three days later a U-boat sank the tanker *Salinas*, and the same night the Germans torpedoed and sank the American destroyer *Reuben James*, with the loss of ninety-six sailors.

By November 1941 the United States was involved in an undeclared war with Germany. Beginning with the destroyers-for-bases deal and continuing with Lend-Lease and the extension of the hemisphere zone of defense eastward to Iceland, Roosevelt had aligned America's security with the British while publicly maintaining that these measures were defensive. When the conscription law came up for renewal in July 1941, Roosevelt asked that draftees serve for the duration of the war and requested the authority to send them any place in the world. Extension of Selective Service aroused more passion than the first law, as many congressmen said they had been deceived by a president who no longer would promise to keep conscripts out of harm's way. The America First Committee denounced extending Selective Service as an inevitable step toward war. The issue remained in doubt until the House of Representatives passed the extension by a single vote in mid-September.

THE FIRST SUMMIT

In the midst of these military moves, Roosevelt started a political friendship with British prime minister Churchill. They kept in touch nearly every day by telephone and cable until Roosevelt's death in April 1945. Churchill flattered Roosevelt before the United States entered the war. In their secret telegrams Churchill addressed him as "Former Naval Person" (referring to the president's stint as assistant secretary of the navy during the First World War). Roosevelt replied in kind, addressing Churchill as "First Sea Lord." Churchill spoke of a "special relationship" that bound the "English-speaking peoples." Churchill, the weaker partner, used these terms of political endearment more than did the president. Roosevelt recognized early on that the age of British domination of world politics had passed, to be replaced by a new "American Century." While happy to have the British support American plans for a "new world order," Roosevelt carefully avoided any commitment to restore Britain to its former position of influence.

This pattern became apparent in August 1941 when the two leaders met for the first time on two warships, the *Augusta* and the *Prince of Wales*, in Placentia Bay off the coast of Newfoundland, Canada. Both knew that the United States would someday join the war, and both hoped to create a warm relationship of mutual trust. Each recalled how Woodrow Wilson's hectoring of the Europeans during World War I had wrecked his chances to reform world politics.

The "first summit" lasted from August 9 to August 12, during which the two leaders took up the progress of the war, American participation, and what the postwar world should look like. On June 22, 1941, Hitler had attacked the Soviet Union, and Stalin had responded by obtaining an alliance with the British and sending a mission to the United States that received a promise of $1 billion in Lend-Lease supplies. Roosevelt and Churchill agreed at the conference to continue the pipeline of supplies to Stalin, thinking that Hitler had made a major mistake in tackling Russia.

Roosevelt surprised Churchill with a proposal for a new economic order ending the trading preferences Britain and other colonial powers enjoyed with their colonies. The president followed Secretary of State Hull's advice that the way to create American domination of the world's trade after the war was to break the stranglehold of the colonial powers, and he insisted on an end to imperial preference. Churchill was willing to include a statement about ending unfair trade relations so long as it was understood that the United States and Britain applied these provisions primarily to Germany and Japan and left the British system intact. In the final public version of the Atlantic Charter, postwar free trade became a vaguely worded hope. The future of the British Empire remained a constant irritant, as the Americans pressed for more commercial access against a determined but ultimately unsuccessful British effort to keep them out.

Roosevelt objected when the talk turned to the general international organization. He recollected how the controversy around the League of Nations had sparked a major reaction against Woodrow Wilson's internationalism. He avoided a specific pledge to join a new organization "because of the suspicions and opposition that such a statement…would create in the United States." He even encouraged the prime minister to think that he favored a joint Anglo-American peace force rather than a new universal organization to keep the peace. They then generated a statement pledging the freedom of the seas and the disarmament of aggressor nations "pending the establishment of a wider and permanent system of general security."

Franklin Roosevelt and Winston Churchill at the Atlantic Conference,
August 1941
(National Archives)

On August 14, two days after the meeting ended, the Atlantic Charter was made public. Noninterventionists howled that Roosevelt had had no right to meet with Churchill, and they were certain the two men had struck a private deal to bring the United States into the war. Had they known what Churchill said to the war cabinet upon his return to England, they would have had their worst fears confirmed. The prime minister assured his colleagues that "the president had said he would wage war, but not declare it." Roosevelt, he predicted, "would become more and more provocative... he would look for an 'incident' which would justify him in opening hostilities." That, of course, was precisely what Roosevelt looked for in the Atlantic in the fall, but he found his "incident" in the Pacific.

AMERICA'S ASIAN WAR

"For a long time I have believed that our best entrance into the war would be by way of Japan," Secretary of the Interior Harold Ickes confided to his diary in October 1941. Roosevelt, however, moved slowly. For example, he had refrained from cutting off Japan's oil supply, as Ickes urged, because "I simply have not got enough navy to go round, and every little episode in the Pacific means fewer ships in the Atlantic." At the Placentia Bay conference Churchill tried to get Roosevelt to issue a warning to Japan, but the president refused, saying again that he doubted that public opinion would support a public declaration of opposition to Japan. Roosevelt did, however, believe that the United States had to do something to stop further Japanese advances in China, South Asia, and the Pacific islands.

Japan had waged continuous warfare against China since 1937. The United States had done little publicly to stop the onslaught after Roosevelt had withdrawn from his quarantine speech of October 1937. Secretly, however, the administration had actively encouraged Chinese resistance to Japan. In 1939 Secretary of the Treasury Henry Morgenthau elaborated a scheme to send the Chinese government of Jiang Jieshi an air force bearing Chinese markings but flown by American pilots. At one point in 1940, Morgenthau, Gen. Claire Chennault, and Chinese foreign minister T. V. Soong suggested that these planes take off from Chinese bases and bomb the Japanese, who presumably would know that the United States had supplied the planes and pilots and back away from more war against China. The need to supply Britain with arms stopped this plan, but its serious consideration showed how far the United States would go to stop Japan.

In mid-1940, while the administration's attention was fixed on Europe after the collapse of France, the appointment of the militantly anti-Japanese Henry Stimson as secretary of war signaled opposition to Japan. Stimson, who had led the anti-Japanese boycott movement, continued to call for a firm resistance to Japan.

Japan formally aligned itself with Italy and Germany in the Tripartite Pact of September 1940. The next summer Tokyo continued its southward march. For the past decade Japanese expansion had rested on the assumption that the island nation was overcrowded and needed an outlet for its surplus products that the rest of the world could not provide. Europe, in the midst of war, held no prospect of becoming a reliable trading partner for Japan. While the United States might have filled the role, the jeers of friends of China disqualified America as a safe market. Furthermore, the Japanese were smitten with the hope of creating a new economic order, a "Greater Asia Co-Prosperity Sphere" accessible to their goods and emigrants to replace the dying European empires in Asia. By carefully playing upon anti-European nationalism in South Asia, Japanese planners thought they might generate local support for their economic domination of the region. Japan promised a modest development of South Asia, just enough so Indochina, south China, Malaya, and Indonesia might exchange their raw materials for Japan's finished products. While the remainder of Asia would become a subordinate "little brother," Japanese publicists argued that the rest of the Eastern Hemisphere had more to gain from voluntarily cooperating with a nonwhite Asian empire than from maintaining ties to Europeans who had purposely kept them poor. Japan airily dismissed as utopian dreams nationalist calls for Asian freedom from both European colonialism and Japanese commercial hegemony.

Such independence created "chaos" and would upset the "natural hierarchy" of international relations. The model for Japan's grandiose plans for Asia was U.S. dominance of the economic and political life of Central America and the Caribbean, and Japanese diplomats likened their Co-Prosperity Sphere to the Monroe Doctrine. Washington's complaints about Japanese expansion only seemed to confirm the worst racial suspicions of the Japanese that the white nations of Europe and North America resented the economic, political, and military accomplishments of a successful Asian competitor.

In the summer of 1941, Tokyo faced an impasse in its four-year-old war with China. Although Japan controlled all of the coast, one-third of the territory, and 40 percent of the population of China, the Chinese would not formally surrender. The Nationalists led by Jiang Jieshi and the Communists under Mao Zedong had even patched together an uneasy truce in their civil war in the interests of ridding their homeland of invaders. Unable to win decisively in China, Japanese generals proposed widening the war to China's neighbors in the hopes of further isolating Jiang and forcing him to give in. Natural resources from the rest of Asia (rubber and oil in the south and coal in the vast Siberian wilderness of the north) would help run Japan's industries and armed forces, so Japan's government, led by Prime Minister Hideki Tojo, had to choose between a strike north against the Soviet Union or south against the British, French, and Dutch colonies.

Eventually, the government settled on the southern route in the fall of 1941. Complicated relations with the Soviet Union, Europe, and the United States molded its choice. In 1940 Japan and the Soviet Union had signed a nonaggression pact, a mutual pledge not to attack each other, and the Japanese did not wish to break it even after the Germans invaded Russia in June 1941. Japan already had adequate if not abundant supplies of coal, so the booty of Siberia seemed less alluring than the riches available in Indochina, Malaya, New Guinea, and Indonesia. With France and Holland humiliated and occupied by Germany, neither could keep its grip on its Asian colonies, French Indochina (Vietnam, Laos, and Cambodia), or the Dutch East Indies (Indonesia and half of New Guinea). Britain, holding its breath for an expected invasion across the channel, could hardly defend Malaya or its half of New Guinea. In July 1941 Japan took the first step in its southern march by taking over control of French Indochina.

An alternately assertive and conciliatory American policy encouraged Japanese expansionists to strike before the United States could muster an effective military force. In July Roosevelt finally sided with the pro-Chinese boycotters and created an embargo of trade on Japan, freezing its assets in American banks and barring its access to American petroleum and scrap iron vital to a mechanized army and navy. Roosevelt balanced this threat with the promise of friendlier relations if the two countries could come to terms over the future of China. Rather than break all ties, the president preferred "to slip the noose around Japan's neck and give it a jerk now and then," Ickes reported. Secretary of State Hull spent the fall pressing Japan to accept a cease-fire in the Chinese war. In late November Japanese ambassador Kichisaburo Nomura learned to his horror that Hull wanted nothing less than the complete evacuation of all the Chinese territory, including the puppet state of Manchukuo (Manchuria) it had seized in 1931. Nomura, a former admiral who still had friends in the navy, told Tokyo that Hull's insistence on withdrawal represented an ultimatum and proof that the American government plotted war against Japan. Stimson watched the failure of the Hull-Nomura talks and noted in his diary the president's whispered warning "that we are likely to be attacked, perhaps by next Monday." The secretary of war decided that "the question was how we should maneuver them into firing the first shot without allowing too much danger to ourselves."

Japan had been readying just such an attack against American possessions in the Philippines, Guam, and Hawaii ever since the freeze order. On September 6 the war cabinet agreed to complete preparations for war against the United States, Great Britain, and the Netherlands. One planner predicted that "it would be well-nigh impossible to expect the surrender of the United States," but he hoped that initial successes might condition Americans to accept a secure Japanese sphere of influence in the Pacific. The naval chief of staff rallied his colleagues with the homely advice that "one cannot obtain a tiger's cub unless he braves a tiger's den." Prime Minister Tojo tried to cheer up a doubting emperor with the reminder that "sometimes a man has to jump with his eyes closed." The chief of naval operations likened Japan's condition to that of a seriously ill patient who could "find a way to life out of a seemingly fatal situation" with a drastic operation.

As negotiations stalled in Washington, plans went forward in Japan for a dramatic surprise attack throughout Southeast Asia and Hawaii. A carrier force destined for Pearl Harbor in Hawaii secretly set sail from Japan on December 2, and on Sunday morning, December 7, the admiralty radioed EAST WIND RAIN, the signal to bomb the American fleet. At 7:55 Hawaiian time, a wave of 170 Japanese planes struck the American fleet. Another wave of 190 planes took part in the two-hour-long raid that sank seven battleships, killed 2,403 Americans and wounded another 1,178, and destroyed or put out of commission most of the army and navy planes parked on the runways of the island of Oahu. Simultaneously with the attack on Pearl Harbor, the Japanese army launched invasions of the American-held Philippines and British-owned Malaya and Singapore.

Roosevelt went before Congress the next morning to denounce the "dastardly" attack, predicted that December 7 would become "a date which will live in infamy," and asked for a declaration of war. Stunned noninterventionists were left speechless, and the war resolution passed both houses with only one dissenting vote, that of Montana congresswoman Jeanette Rankin, who had also voted against the American declaration of war in 1917. Three days later Hitler, invoking his alliance with Japan, declared war on the United States to the great relief of Roosevelt, who wanted to be sure that the United States fought Germany as well as Japan.

[margin note: at war w/ Germany and Japan.]

A furious controversy about Roosevelt's complicity in the Japanese attack erupted immediately and continued unchanged for a generation. Revisionist historians of the entry into the Second World War—Harry Elmer Barnes, Charles Beard, and Charles Tansill—charged that the president knew of Japan's plan, baited the Japanese into implementing it, and refrained from warning the defenders of Pearl Harbor, all in the interests of maneuvering the United States into war with Germany by the "back door." Critics pointed to the American practice of deciphering Japanese secret cables for the previous decade and asserted that knowledge of the attack was available to FDR had he chosen to use it. Roosevelt had told Churchill that when America entered the fray, there would be none of the idealistic talk about a "war to end war" that had led to such disillusionment after 1918. The United States would fight in the forties to defend itself, and the attack on Pearl Harbor was the most dramatic demonstration that the republic was in peril. The America First Committee disbanded in a flurry of apologies, and red-faced noninterventionist congressmen publicly recanted their views in humiliating speeches that called to mind the confessions wrung from the old Bolsheviks during the Moscow purge trials of 1935–1938. From these tantalizing hints revisionists concluded that Roosevelt had secretly maneuvered the Japanese into administering the kind of shock to the American public he had been unable to find over the previous two years.

Such damning charges naturally alarmed the president's admirers, who hastened to his defense. Historians from Basil Rauch, who wrote *Roosevelt: From Munich to Pearl Harbor* (1950), to Herbert Feis, who weighed in with *The Road to Pearl Harbor* (1950), to Gordon Prange, who contributed the most thorough account of Japanese and American actions in *At Dawn We Slept* (1981), to Robert Dallek, who produced the standard synthesis of work on New Deal diplomacy in *Franklin D. Roosevelt and American Foreign Policy* (1979), all deny the particulars of the revisionists' indictment. A specialized study by political scientist Roberta Wohlstetter, *Pearl Harbor: Warning and Decision* (1962), absolves Roosevelt of the most serious charge, that of withholding warning from the naval commander at Hawaii, while detecting flaws in the way the government evaluated intelligence reports. Wohlstetter concludes that the decoded Japanese messages never made much of an impression on officials, who had trouble separating worthwhile information from the ocean of "noise" emanating from the broken codes. Not expecting an attack on Hawaii (they believed Japan might strike farther west in the Philippines and Malaya), the administration simply ignored the warnings about the attack on Pearl Harbor.

COALITION WARFARE

However bizarre the idea that Roosevelt conspired with the Japanese, the president was nonetheless relieved to end the anxiety over when the United States would join the fight. He enjoyed a suspension of partisan dissent, at least in the beginning, as the Republican national chairman pledged his support. The president went on the radio two days after the attack on Pearl Harbor to rally the public with the announcement that "every man and woman and child is a partner in the most tremendous undertaking of our American history." No one was happier that the United States no longer stood on the sidelines than Prime Minister Churchill. His immediate thought was "so we had won after all!" He telephoned Roosevelt on the afternoon of December 7. FDR remarked, "We are both in the same boat now," to which Churchill replied, "That certainly simplifies things." The two leaders arranged for Churchill to come to Washington over Christmas to produce a strategy for waging war and producing a peace settlement.

The White House conference of December 1941–January 1942, code named ARCADIA, was supposed to eliminate the friction that had made life miserable during the First World War. Instead of the United States issuing orders for the rest of the world to follow, jointly developed principles would be in order. Instead of the president remaining aloof, he would make friends with other wartime leaders. But instead of the American military following strategies laid down by the Europeans, U.S. admirals and generals would tell the Allies how to fight the war.

In practice Churchill and Roosevelt discovered that they could reach easier agreements on military questions than on political arrangements. Despite the shock of Pearl Harbor, Roosevelt, a committed Atlanticist, never wavered from Adm. Harold Stark's plan of winning the war in Europe before going after Japan. Roosevelt's inclinations were strengthened by the nearly unanimous view of the American generals that the German army was a more formidable foe than Japan. If the Germans lost, Japan would fall, but if the Allies knocked Japan out of the war, Germany would still remain a fighting force. Concentration on Europe first also promised political and personal advantages for the president as Asia had traditionally attracted more attention from Republicans than Democrats. Midwestern isolationist papers such as the *Chicago Tribune*, never friendly to Roosevelt, urged that war be conducted against Japan and Germany be ignored. The president thought there

War in the Pacific

was nothing to gain by following the *Tribune's* advice. Moreover, if Roosevelt wanted the public to maintain an interest in the active American foreign policy after the war, the United States had to look to Europe. Finally, an Asia-first strategy would mean that Gen. Douglas MacArthur, the imperious commander of the American forces in the Philippines, would take over the direction of the war. Roosevelt could not stand MacArthur, a vain authoritarian who wanted someday to be president. FDR did not relish the idea of having such a potential rival in charge of the major American offensive.

At ARCADIA Roosevelt and Churchill quickly agreed that the European war would take precedence, but they differed on what kind of attack to mount on Germany. The chief of the American staff, George C. Marshall, favored a second front on the continent as quickly as possible, but Churchill, with memories of the carnage of the First World War fresh in his mind, demurred. He offered an invasion of North Africa in which the British and the United States could test their forces but not suffer large casualties, hoping all the while that the Soviet Union would bear the brunt of fighting the Germans. Over the next year the most nettlesome question among the Soviets, British, and Americans was when and where the Western powers would open a second front against Germany.

Roosevelt and Churchill also parted company over the political goals to be pursued after the war. Seeking an accommodation with his major ally, Roosevelt urged Churchill to commit himself to an open trading system once the war ended, but the prime minister would not drop his fears for the future of the British Empire. Just as he had during his meetings the previous August off the coast of Newfoundland, he turned down the Americans' invitation to make specific pledges about a free trading system after the war. The two leaders merely issued a vaguely worded Declaration of the United Nations on January 1, and they invited all of the countries fighting the Axis to join the alliance (the United Nations) and pledge themselves to continue until the Axis powers were defeated.

The war in the Pacific went badly for the United States and Britain in early 1942. By March the Japanese completed their conquest of the Philippines, Malaya, and Singapore while increasing their hold on China. In June, however, one of the largest naval engagements in history took place near the island of Midway. In three days of aerial warfare, U.S. navy planes destroyed a Japanese fleet and stopped further Japanese expansion across the Pacific. After the battle the United States could contain Tokyo and wait for the day in which Germany was defeated.

Combat in Europe also turned in late 1942, as the Germans suffered setbacks in Russia and North Africa. The Nazis had gained against the Russians in their summer offensive, aiming at the oilfields of the Caucasus Mountains, but in November the Red Army counterattacked, surrounding the more than 1 million German troops at the Volga River city of Stalingrad on November 26. At that point the German army lost its invincible reputation, although two and a half years of hard fighting remained.

At the same time, a joint Anglo-American force invaded North Africa, sweeping the Germans out of Morocco, Tunisia, Libya, and Algeria within two months. The first American encounter with Germany demonstrated some of the political difficulties of coalition warfare. The U.S. commander, Dwight David Eisenhower, fearful that the untried American troops would do badly against German veterans, allowed local French authorities to continue in power in return for helping the Allies. Unfortunately, the head of the French military, Gen. Jean Darlan, represented the collaborationist government of Vichy France and had close ties to the Nazis. The "Darlan deal" angered American liberals and the Free French forces led by a former tank commander, Col. Charles de Gaulle, who denounced Eisenhower for helping a "traitor." But President Roosevelt supported the arrangement since he shared Eisenhower's apprehensions about the quality of the American troops. Moreover, Roosevelt deeply distrusted de Gaulle, whom he considered a sort of French MacArthur and a self-important potential dictator. The British, who had sheltered de Gaulle in 1940, had more tolerance for the commander of the Free French than did the Americans, and British officials begged Eisenhower to let de Gaulle take over in North Africa. Yet the American commander would not break his word to Darlan. A serious rift in the alliance was avoided only by accident in late December when a Free French supporter shot and killed Darlan. The new French leader, Gen. Henri Giraud, had fewer connections to the Germans and shared power with de Gaulle, who grudgingly accepted him.

PLANNING FOR THE POSTWAR ERA

The complicated relationship between the British, Americans, and Free French was followed by other more important imbroglios among the United Nations. While formally allied against Germany, the United States, Britain, and the Soviet Union each looked forward to ending the war in a way that would boost its own position in the postwar world. Roosevelt kept a tight rein over foreign policy during the war, relying upon personal advisers Sumner Welles (1933–1943) and Harry Hopkins (1943–1945) to get across his ideas for American domination of postwar diplomacy. The State Department, unable to do much about daily diplomacy, slipped into producing grand plans for the future that never got read. In poor health and fed up with being ignored by Roosevelt, Hull resigned in 1944. His successor, Edward Stettinius, formerly the president of United States Steel, tall, solid, and handsome, made up in white-haired dignity what he lacked in knowledge of foreign affairs.

While the secretaries of state were shunted to the sidelines, a variety of other government bureaus competed to set the postwar policies of the United States. The armed forces, under the leadership of Secretary of War Henry Stimson, developed a clear set of plans for the postwar world. So did the Treasury Department under Henry Morgenthau, who pressed proposals for international monetary reform shelved since the London economic conference of 1933. All of the plans tried to ensure American leadership of a stable, predictable postwar world.

In January 1943 Roosevelt met Churchill at Casablanca in recently liberated North Africa. They decided that the United Nations would insist upon an unconditional surrender from the Germans, Italians, and Japanese and that none of the Allies would sign a separate peace with the Axis powers. Churchill was unhappy with unconditional surrender, fretting that the plan took away a potential bargaining tool with the Germans, but accepted it as a way of buying Soviet friendship without opening a second front in Europe. In the 1950s, as well, Hanson W. Baldwin, the chief military correspondent for the *New York Times*, described unconditional surrender as "one of the great mistakes of the war." Both Churchill and Baldwin thought that unconditional surrender meant that U.S. government officials neglected the postwar period for the immediate goal of beating the Axis. Critics took pains to blame Roosevelt and his principal advisers for nonchalantly closing their eyes to the opening chasm between the Anglo-Saxon powers and the Soviet Union.

In fact, however, planning for the postwar period paid considerable attention to the shape of Soviet-American relations. According to the optimistic assessments of the State, War, and Treasury departments after the war, the Soviet Union, like every other power, would cheerfully acknowledge American leadership after beating the Axis. Roosevelt believed that the needs of the Soviet Union for reconstruction aid would be so great that Stalin would beg Washington for loans and credits. The president also thought that his own easy charm could make Soviet leaders support the American viewpoint. The president consciously wooed Stalin by telegram and at the two meetings they had at Tehran in November 1943 and at Yalta in early February 1945. At both these conferences Roosevelt befriended the Soviet leader, made jokes at Churchill's expense, and positioned the United States between Great Britain and Russia.

From 1943 on the United States worked out a plan for the future of Germany. Having twice experienced a German threat to the security of the western powers, some of Roosevelt's advisers wanted to render Germany incapable of again waging an aggressive war. Treasury Secretary Henry Morgenthau

The end of war in Europe

believed that Germany should be split into at least five different nations, each one of which would be stripped of its industrial capabilities. The Morgenthau plan won acceptance from the White House before a meeting with Churchill at Ottawa, Canada, in August 1944. The prime minister, however, thought that the dismemberment of Germany would leave a vacuum in central Europe—one that the Soviet Union might rush to fill. The American military leadership supported the British position, with Stimson and Marshall, chairman of the Joint Chiefs of Staff, distressed at the cost of occupying a Germany that no longer was the engine of central Europe. A permanent American presence might be called for. Marshall opted for a quick transition of Germany back into regular membership in the European community. To break up Germany smacked of the kind of vengeance imposed after the First World War, and it might inhibit a potential market for American goods.

THE HOME FRONT

The memory of the First World War affected domestic policy as well after December 1941. The government resumed control over production, prices, and wages. Business executives joined labor leaders on the War Resources Board, the War Labor Board, the War Production Board, the Office of Production Management, and the Office of Price Administration—all of which were designed to coordinate production and assure labor peace. In return for government guarantees of full employment and price stability, the American Federation of Labor and the Congress of Industrial Organizations (CIO) agreed to forgo strikes throughout the war. Acquiescence was not universal as John L. Lewis, head of the United Mine Workers and one of the founders of the CIO, a longtime foe of FDR, called his men out of the coal mines in early 1944. Threat of government takeover of the pits brought an end to the walkout but left a bitter legacy.

While inviting labor into the government, FDR acknowledged that the war signaled the end of efforts at liberal reform as he shifted from "Dr. New Deal" to "Dr. Win the War." Scores more business executives flocked to Washington, often serving as "dollar a year men" to award war contracts to plants only beginning to emerge from the Depression. Congress decreed that 25 percent of the value of all contracts go to businesses worth less than $2 million, but investigations by oversight committees revealed that many major firms such as General Motors, Ford, and General Electric had surreptitiously acquired orders slated for small businesses. During the war the federal government provided $1.5 billion annually for scientific research and development. Research teams in labs across the country developed radar, the first electronic computers, jet engines, synthetic fibers, and antibacterial drugs such as sulfa and penicillin. In addition, the government spent $2 billion on research to develop an atomic bomb.

While Republicans might privately take heart at the New Deal's demise, they did not make up as much electoral ground as their predecessors did in the 1918 mid-term election. They voiced few complaints over FDR's internationalist foreign policy. The president retained an uncanny knack for mollifying defeated foes, and he enlisted the 1940 Republican nominee, Wendell Willkie, in the campaign for public support. Willkie returned from a round-the-world trip in 1943 to publish *One World,* a book whose title expressed his and the president's hopes that the people of the world would unite around a program for a new world order after the defeat of Germany and Japan. The 1942 congressional elections drew the lowest voter turnout, 43 percent, in modern history. The Republicans narrowed the gap in the House of Representatives to 221 Democrats against 211 Republicans, while Senate Democrats held a 57-to-38 majority. In 1944 Roosevelt, concealing his failing health, ran for a fourth term. Roosevelt's immense popularity among soldiers offset his ebbing appeal in traditional Republican strongholds of the Midwest and enabled him to defeat New York governor Thomas Dewey with 53 percent of the popular vote, his lowest margin.

For vice president he dropped Henry A. Wallace, whose outspoken liberalism annoyed conservative southern Democrats. FDR coyly played with several potential vice presidential candidates, including Wallace, liberal Supreme Court justice William O. Douglas, and conservative South Carolina senator James F. Byrnes, before settling on a safe choice, Missouri senator Harry Truman. An apparently colorless product of the Kansas City Democratic machine, Truman had been a quietly loyal New Dealer whose only claim to fame had been chairmanship of the Senate committee investigating the conduct of the war. The president seldom consulted with him during the fall campaign and virtually ignored him after the fourth inauguration on January 20, 1945.

The government engaged in an ugly reprise of the persecution of minorities that had besmirched domestic life during the First World War. This time Americans of Japanese descent suffered the most. Anti-Japanese hysteria swept across the West Coast after Pearl Harbor as congressmen, state legislators, and mayors accused local Japanese citizens of espionage, sabotage, and sending radio messages to the imperial fleet supposedly standing offshore in preparation for an invasion. General John L. DeWitt, the army commander of U.S. forces in the western United States, investigated these claims. He found that "the very fact that no espionage or sabotage has taken place is disturbing and confirming indication that such action will take place." In February 1942 Roosevelt issued Executive Order 9066 to arrest all Japanese-Americans and send them to "relocation camps" scattered across the country from California to Arizona to Colorado to Louisiana. U.S. marshals pounded on the doors of some 110,000 men, women, and children, giving them seventy-two hours to close their shops and houses, collect one suitcase, and board buses and trains for the trip to the grim, isolated camps that would be their homes for the next two years. The only escape was offered to young men of military age who could join the armed forces for the war in Europe against Germany and Italy.

No similar actions were taken against Americans of German and Italian ancestry, and, naturally, the Japanese-Americans affirmed their loyalty to the United States and resented their mistreatment. Earl Warren, California's attorney general who had pressed for the deportations, became chief justice of the United States in 1954. As leader of a liberal Court devoted to protecting civil liberties, he privately acknowledged "a great injustice against the Japanese." Other officials were unrepentant. A House subcommittee held hearings on the subject in the summer of 1982. Former assistant secretary of war John J. McCloy, then eighty-eight, proudly defended the relocation camps as "necessary in time of war," but Congress did issue an apology and provided compensation for the camps' survivors.

Political dissenters fared better than the Japanese and better than their counterparts in the First World War. The nation had not grown more tolerant, but the fighting attracted broader support than the 1917–1918 involvement. The Communist Party of the United States earnestly backed the campaign to defeat Nazism and Fascism once Germany attacked the Soviet Union. Party secretary Earl Browder proclaimed, "Communism is twentieth-century Americanism." Many other former noninterventionists dropped their public dissent from official foreign policy in the aftermath of Pearl Harbor. While some shared the worries of gadfly historian Charles Beard that the war would "militarize" American society, most kept their doubts to themselves. Pacifists of military age who opposed all wars and refused service as noncombatants fared as poorly as the Japanese. Thousands went to jail.

REACTION TO THE HOLOCAUST

Opposition to Henry Morgenthau's plan for the dismemberment of Germany drew strength from a darker motive—anti-Semitism. Stimson and Marshall muttered that the treasury secretary was incapable of adopting an objective stance toward the problems of Germans because he was Jewish. Although Jews suffered the most from the Second World War and were the targets of the Nazi "final solution of the Jewish problem," the murder of all Jews in Europe, the United States did very little directly to relieve them. News of the death camps, which were killing thousands of Jews a day, reached Washington in 1942. Roosevelt received a continuous stream of impassioned pleas from

Jewish leaders in the United States to do something about the death camps. One described the gas chamber at Auschwitz: "It holds 2,000.... When everybody is inside the heavy doors are closed.... After three minutes everybody in the chamber is dead." Rabbi Stephen C. Wise asked the president at least to state publicly that he knew of the Nazi extermination policy and warn the Nazi leaders that they would be held accountable for their campaign of murder. Other Jewish leaders begged the secretary of war to send airplanes to bomb the extermination camps. Washington replied with evasions. The State Department did not change usual visa practices. The War Department refused to bomb the rail lines leading to the extermination camps. Assistant Secretary of War McCloy said attacking the camps would be "impracticable, because it could be executed only by diversion of considerable air support." He told the World Jewish Congress that Allied attention to the Nazi atrocities "might provoke even more vindictive actions by the Germans."

Even as American diplomats forwarded stories of unspeakable murders, they expressed disbelief. When the U.S. ambassador to Sweden cabled news of the killing of Jews in Warsaw, he ended his report with the words "so fantastic is the story... that I hesitate to make it the subject of an official report." Roosevelt knew how Americans had become disillusioned when they learned after World War I that reports of German atrocities in Belgium had been exaggerated. As Samantha Power writes in "A Problem From Hell": America in the Age of Genocide (2002), "the vast majority of people did not believe what they read.... A plot for outright annihilation had never been seen and therefore could not be imagined. The tales of German cremation factories and gas chambers sounded far-fetched." Roosevelt himself, while professing personal sympathy to Jewish leaders, may have also believed that he risked losing general American support for the war effort if he made a special appeal for the Jews. According to public opinion polls, anti-Semitism reached a new high in the United States in 1945, with 55 percent of the population expressing anti-Jewish prejudices. Roosevelt, a consummate judge of public sentiment, thought that if he were to make a special plea for Jews, other Americans would no longer think the war was their fight. In 1944 Roosevelt authorized the creation of a War Refugees Board to create camps to harbor victims of the Holocaust in neutral countries and U.S.-controlled territory overseas. Several hundred thousand refugees found safety in these camps, but only 1,000 were admitted directly into the United States during the war.

ECONOMIC PLANS

Treasury Secretary Morgenthau drafted plans for a postwar international monetary order at the conference of the major economic powers that convened at Bretton Woods, New Hampshire, in August 1944. Significantly, the Soviet Union, skittish about being swallowed by a capitalist economy, sent no representatives to this meeting designed to breathe life into the proposals for a multilateral trading order at the end of the war. The British sent a large delegation in which John Maynard Keynes, a prominent economist, took the lead in pressing a plan for a new international currency. Morgenthau would not go as far as Keynes in creating an international source of money, preferring instead that nations acknowledge American economic power and fix their money's value in terms of the dollar. This view prevailed in the new International Monetary Fund (IMF) created at Bretton Woods to assure that every nation's currency was freely convertible into that of every other potential trading partner. Backed with capital of $10 billion, half of which came from the United States, the IMF was supposed to lend money to nations that temporarily found themselves short of foreign reserves. In return for its loans, the IMF could demand changes in a borrower's economic and trade policies—insisting that it balance its budget, allow its citizens to hold foreign currency, permit convertibility of its currency into other money, and drop restrictive tariffs. At a time when the United States alone seemed in a good position to export goods, the IMF would help produce a congenial trading environment for American enterprise. Bretton Woods created a companion organization for the IMF in the International Bank for Reconstruction and Development, or World Bank, a multinational organization with power to finance longer-term programs than those covered by the IMF. The memory of abuses in private lending during the 1920s combined with the fear that the needs for reconstruction after the Second World War would be more than could be met by private banks to lay the ground for the government-sponsored World Bank.

IMF Created

THE FUTURE OF ASIA

American plans for the postwar Far East called for the replacement of the Japanese Empire with a stable and predictable region under the influence of the United States and a China backed by America. The president detected a "warlike" streak in the Japanese national character. He sustained a three-year correspondence with an anthropologist at the Smithsonian Institution about the advisability of "cross-breeding the Japanese" with "gentler" Pacific islanders. More practically, FDR encouraged the ambitions of China's leader, Jiang Jieshi.

Roosevelt had a soft spot in his heart for Generalissimo Jiang, despite discouraging reports coming from his adviser in China, Joseph W. Stilwell. In 1943 and 1945 Gen. Stilwell concluded soon after his arrival in Chungking that the Nationalist government was ridden with embezzlement and bribery and commanded no popularity. He mocked Jiang to all who would listen as "the peanut" and other epithets, some unprintable. By 1944 the complaints of the Nationalists were so loud that Roosevelt had to replace Stilwell as adviser to Jiang. He chose as ambassador one of the most unsuitable envoys in the twentieth century, Patrick C. Hurley. A former Republican governor from Oklahoma, Hurley knew nothing about China but compensated with loud rebel yells, slaps on the back, and viselike handshakes. The new ambassador decided that Jiang was indeed the savior of his country and that his reputation had been blackened by disloyal Foreign Service officers tricked by the Communists they had visited in their mountain headquarters in Yenan.

Roosevelt tolerated Hurley and may have shared his enthusiasm for the generalissimo, but the president also acknowledged Jiang's corruption and unpopularity. In a way, these deficiencies made the Chinese leader a more pliable friend of the United States. Roosevelt thought that someday China could become a great power like Britain or the Soviet Union; in the meantime, the Chinese depended on Washington for aid and political guidance. With Japan out of the picture, America could run the affairs of the Far East with the aid of the Chinese.

Roosevelt also looked forward to the end of the Dutch, French, and British empires in Asia, which had discriminated against American products. His scorn for colonialism strained European nerves. When British colonial secretary Oliver Stanley called at the White House late in the war, FDR taunted him: "I do not want to be unkind or rude to the British, but in 1841, when you acquired Hong Kong, you did not acquire it by purchase." An angry Stanley shot back, "Let me see, Mr. President, that was about the time of the Mexican war, wasn't it?" FDR knew that the United States would have to bear the cost of restoring the economies of the imperial powers in Europe, and he shrank from the prospect of American aid being squandered on their Asian territories. Finally, American experts on colonial matters considered the independence of the Asian possessions a foregone conclusion, so why waste the time, energy, and money restoring the Europeans' colonies, which soon would send them home?

The easiest colony to make independent was the Dutch outpost in the East Indies. The Netherlands, a minor power occupied by the Germans and dependent on the goodwill of the United States for its postwar recovery, could not hold Indonesia. The British and the French also could be persuaded to sacrifice the Dutch if they could maintain their hold on their own colonies. So in 1944 American policy was to evict the Dutch from Indonesia after the war, and this goal was accomplished in 1949.

The French in Indochina presented a more difficult case. Roosevelt, who could not abide Gen. de Gaulle and thought the French decadent for their

A haggard FDR flanked by Winston Churchill and Josef Stalin at Yalta, February 1945

(National Archives)

1940 surrender to Germany, approved a plan in 1943 for placing French Indochina under the trusteeship of China at the war's end. The Free French
objected and gained support from Britain, which hoped to restore its own
power in the Far East. Stimson's War Department and American headquarters in the China-Burma-India theater also thought the eviction of the French
from Indochina would make it harder to win the war against Japan. By the
middle of 1944, Roosevelt retreated from his plan for a Chinese caretaker
for Indochina, and at the Ottawa conference in August, he gutted his trusteeship plan and accepted the French return under the condition that they
promise eventual freedom for Indochina.

In the case of the British Empire in the Far East, the United States pressured Churchill for an early independence for India. Since previous British
governments had been willing to grant Indian independence, Churchill reluctantly went along. But the prime minister wanted to keep the remainder
of the British Empire intact. British experts on joint Anglo-American committees studying postwar problems fought a ferocious and ultimately successful rear guard action to keep their Asian possessions.

Americans continued their efforts to displace the British from the oil-
rich regions of the Middle East. American petroleum engineers discovered
vast reserves in the deserts of Arabia in the mid-thirties. By 1939 a consortium of American firms lifted 19,000 barrels of petroleum per day. Officers
of the Arabian-American Oil Company (Aramco) worried that the British
might reexert their traditional influence in Arabia once combat ended.
A 1944 Office of Strategic Services report concurred that the "century-old
policy of regarding Arabia as a British sphere of influence" hindered American interests. Noting a "delicate balance" of oil supply and demand, Interior Secretary Harold Ickes fought for the creation of an American-financed
Trans-Arabian Pipeline (TAP). Churchill objected to Roosevelt that "the
United States has a desire to deprive us of our oil assets in the Middle East."
FDR did nothing to ease British anxieties.

YALTA AND THE END OF THE WAR

On D-Day, June 6, 1944, 500,000 American, British, French, Canadian, and
other Allied troops successfully invaded northern France, and the end of the
war was in sight. Churchill, Roosevelt, and Stalin agreed to meet at Yalta on
the Crimean Sea in early February 1945 to decide what the future would
look like. In ten days of hard bargaining, the "Big Three" agreed that Germany would pay some reparations but not the entire cost of the war. They
decided that the new international organization, the United Nations, would
be a universal organization, but that the major powers—the United States,

Great Britain, the Soviet Union, France, and China—would be permanent members of the Security Council. Each of the great powers could veto any resolution of the body. They also seemed to agree on the future of eastern Europe, where the Soviet Union was guaranteed "friendly" governments on its borders. No end of problems were created by this provision, since the Soviet Union also agreed to permit "free elections" in Poland. In fact, the Yalta Conference left more issues unresolved than it settled. Roosevelt, however, had few reservations; he was sure that the personal bond between himself and the other leaders could smooth over the rough spots in the alliance. They would soon meet after Germany was defeated to tie up the loose ends of the war. Remembering the First World War experience, he favored a series of conferences at the end instead of one big peace meeting that all the major wartime leaders would attend.

The one thing finally settled at Yalta concerned the war in the Far East. In return for a Soviet pledge to enter the war against Japan three months after the war in Europe ended, the Western powers made territorial concessions to the Soviets in Asia, granting them the southern half of Sakhalin Island from Japan and a return of the old Russian railroad in Manchuria. Stalin sweetened the deal when he concluded a treaty of friendship with the Nationalist Chinese and restrained the Communists from resuming the civil war.

TRUMAN BECOMES PRESIDENT

Roosevelt was a sick man at Yalta. His face grew gray, and his strength was gone. Nevertheless, he hardly expected to die within two months of his return. When news of his fatal stroke flashed across the world on April 12, Hitler rejoiced, thinking it a sign of divine intervention for the Nazi cause. Vice President Harry S. Truman, a former haberdasher and Missouri senator chosen by Roosevelt as a safe, inoffensive running mate in 1944, told reporters that he felt "as if the sun, moon, and the stars" had just fallen on him and asked for their prayers. Untutored in foreign affairs and kept in the dark about the most important military secret of the war—the atomic bomb—Truman did not have Roosevelt's confidence that his personal conduct of diplomacy would preserve an effective anti-Axis coalition.

The new president determined to mask his uncertainties in international relations with displays of toughness and temper toward Allied diplomats who might take advantage of him. Barely a week in office, Truman met Soviet foreign minister Molotov in the White House and dressed him down for his government's hostility toward non-Communist politicians in liberated Poland. "I've never been talked to that way before in my life," Molotov complained when the new president finished his harangue. "Keep your agreements and you won't be talked to that way," Truman replied. The San Francisco meeting of the United Nations organization, which opened on April 24, saw more bad blood between the Soviets and the United States. The American assistant secretary of state for Latin America, Nelson Rockefeller, pressed for the admission of Argentina despite that government's fascist inclinations. Surprised Soviet diplomats saw the invitation to the Latin American republic as a signal that the Americans would have their way in the postwar world.

THE ATOMIC BOMB AND JAPAN'S SURRENDER

Two weeks later, on May 7, Germany surrendered, and the Big Three resolved to meet again in July at the former headquarters of the German general staff at Potsdam, outside Berlin. At that encounter they intended to discuss the future of Europe and the war against Japan. Although Germany had collapsed, some military planners thought that the war in Asia might take another five years and require an invasion of the home islands of Japan.

The plans did not account for the dreadful power of a new superweapon, the atomic bomb. Produced by the Manhattan Project, the most expensive weapons-development program undertaken to that time, the atomic bomb represented three years of work by approximately 120,000 people at a cost of $2 billion. American officials shared scientific information about atomic energy with their British counterparts, but they did not breathe a word to the Soviet Union. The first atomic test took place on July 16. As a light brighter than a thousand suns flashed across the desert sky, scientific director J. Robert Oppenheimer later recalled that he thought of a line from the *Bhagavad-Gita*, an Indian holy book: "I am become Death, Destroyer of Worlds." Gen. Leslie Groves, Manhattan Project supervisor, described the event in a cable to Truman, who was meeting the leaders of the Soviet Union and Great Britain at Potsdam.: "The test was successful beyond the most optimistic expectations of anyone.... I estimate the energy generated to be in excess of the equivalent of 15,000 to 20,000 tons of TNT." Stimson watched Truman read Groves's message and reported that "the president was tremendously pepped up by it."

Encouraged by a sense of American invincibility, Truman hardened his language toward Stalin. "I shall state frankly what I think," he told the Soviet leader. Churchill found him "emphatic and decisive...telling [the Soviets] as to certain demands that they absolutely could not have." At an informal break in the conversations, Truman mentioned to Stalin that the United States now possessed a weapon of "awesome destructiveness." The Soviet nonchalantly wished the Americans well against Japan. He probably knew of the

Manhattan Project through surreptitious agents, resented Anglo-American attempts to keep atomic secrets, and feigned indifference to bluff the Americans. Had Truman hoped to use "atomic diplomacy" to force the Soviets to accept American suggestions, the remainder of the Potsdam Conference disabused him. Like Yalta, Potsdam left unresolved many major issues, including the future of occupied Germany, the amount of reparations to be paid to the Allies, and an agenda for a peace conference. Unlike Yalta, the leaders could not agree to meet again. They never did.

Afraid of settling every problem in a grand assembly on the pattern of the 1919 Paris conference, Truman set his hopes on a series of more modest ministerial discussions. He authorized his newly appointed secretary of state, former South Carolina senator James F. Byrnes, who had been a rival for the 1944 vice presidential nomination, to reach accommodations with suspicious coalition partners. Like Truman, Byrnes erroneously assumed that "the bomb assured ultimate success in negotiations."

On August 6, two weeks after the Potsdam Conference broke up in disarray, the U.S. Army Air Force B-29 *Enola Gay* dropped an atomic bomb, nicknamed "Little Boy," on the mid-sized Japanese industrial city of Hiroshima, instantly killing at least 80,000 people. Later studies of the bombing indicated "that the whole city was ruined instantaneously." Survivors of the blast discovered "a heap of debris and corpses and a stunned mass of injured humanity." A grocer recalled a procession of thousands of injured people slowly leaving the site of the conflagration. "They held their arms bent and their skin...hung down... [they looked] like walking ghosts. They didn't look like people of this world." Another eyewitness observed people "so broken and confused that they moved and behaved like automatons."

The next day the Soviet Union made good its Yalta pledge and declared war on Japan as its armies crossed the border between Siberia and Manchuria. On August 9 another B-29 made the 2,500 mile flight from Saipan to detonate a plutonium-based bomb, nicknamed "Fat Man," on Nagasaki, and more than 60,000 Japanese died. Emperor Hirohito now told his government that the war was lost and that they had to move more quickly on surrender negotiations. Japan's military leaders had for months resisted the idea of surrender as a betrayal of Japan's cherished traditions despite the approaching Americans. Other officials argued that superior Western science, rather than military valor, had defeated Japan, so a surrender under these circumstances would not compromise Japan's ancient military code of honor. The government now dropped its request for reassurances that the emperor could keep his throne threw itself to the mercy of the Allies, and announced that it had accepted the principle of unconditional surrender. The United States agreed that Hirohito could remain emperor, but he had to acknowedge Allied control of his country. On September 2 a sad-faced Adm. Sadatoshi

Tomioka climbed aboard the American battleship *Missouri* to sign a surrender document and place himself and Japan at the mercy of Gen. Douglas MacArthur, who headed the Allied delegation and the following occupation authority.

In the decades after the end of the war, a controversy erupted over whether it had been necessary for the United States to drop atomic weapons. President Truman and Secretary of War Stimson asserted in the years after the war that the use of the bomb had ended the war before the United States would have launched an invasion of the home islands that might have cost as many as 500,000 American and more than 1 million Japanese lives. Later investigations indicated that these projections were far higher than the figures available to American planners in the summer of 1945. A variety of other explanations then arose for Truman's decision to drop the bomb. Some historians in the United States and Japan observed that Japan was defeated but not yet ready to surrender until the bomb was dropped. The bomb therefore shortend the war. Some pointed to the intense hatred of Japan and the desire for retribution after Pearl Harbor. Another explanation was that Truman wanted to send a message of enormous American power to the Soviet Union. Others noted the huge cost of the atomic research project and said

The devastation at Hiroshima
(National Archives)

that Truman decided to use the bomb to justify its cost. The most generally accepted explanation, summarized by the historian Barton J. Bernstein, was that the United States used the atomic bomb because it had it. "The older morality" of avoiding attacks on noncombatants "crumbled in the crucible of what became virtually total war. Almost any weapon (gas and biological warfare were usually exceptions) was generally used."

EFFECTS OF THE WAR

So ended the most destructive war in history. Some 40 million soldiers and civilians were dead, and an additional 10 million refugees wandered forlornly across Europe and Asia. Production had stopped in much of western Europe, Germany, the Soviet Union, and Japan. Hitler's "Thousand Year Reich" lasted only twelve, but it managed to commit such crimes as to numb the imagination and be summarized in a single capitalized word: Holocaust. Japan failed in its bid to organize East Asia, and the atomic firestorms that highlighted the end of the Japanese Empire also highlighted the dangers of the postwar world. Now humanity seemed nearly able to kill everyone on the planet.

The end of the war saw the United States finally become the world's foremost power, confirming what nationalist and internationalist thinkers had predicted, longed for, and fretted over. Unlike the end of the First World War, when Americans faced the prospect of sharing their newfound authority with European coalition partners who could not bring themselves to acknowledge their time had passed, American planners expected that other nations would beg for leadership from the New World. While the other belligerents had seen their cities bombed and plants leveled, the war enabled the United States to snap out of the depression. At the beginning of 1940, more than 10 million American adults had no jobs; in 1945 there was a shortage of workers. The armed forces had 14 million men and women in uniform, and an additional 5 million people had taken positions on the assembly lines producing the weapons for "the arsenal of democracy." While fearing a return to the breadlines, economic planners hoped that an open trading system would keep up high production. The war also continued the expansion of the federal government begun by the New Deal. The government spent more than $200 billion in each of the four war years, 1942–1945, nearly eight times more than it had spent before. More significant perhaps were the thousands of experts who flocked to the capital to wage war and prepare for peace. The State, War, Navy, and Treasury departments contended with each other and specially created agencies such as the Office of Strategic Service (the overseas espionage office), the Office of War Information (the propaganda service), the Office of Price Administration, and the War Production Board, whose functionaries hoped to continue their work in the peacetime era.

Franklin D. Roosevelt, who had presided over this explosive growth, no longer was alive to soothe hurt feelings in the United States or across the Atlantic with his good nature and ability to cement personal friendships with international leaders. President Truman was less secure in his grasp of the subtleties of international affairs and less comfortable with people who did not share his ideas. He demanded clear and precise solutions to problems, and few were available in the postwar years. In the decades after the end of the Second World War, some Americans believed that the change from Roosevelt to Truman caused many of the disappointments the United States encountered in the subsequent Cold War era. They expressed the hope that Roosevelt would have better managed the emerging competition with the Soviet Union. There is an element of truth to the idea that Roosevelt would have been more able than Truman to maintain a semblance of harmony in the wartime coalition after the war. But that coalition had been born of very special circumstances that no longer existed in September 1945. At the end of the war, Americans' hopes to create a harmonious world order under the leadership of the United States exceeded the ability of any nation to realize them. The real sense of obligation former coalition partners had to America could not mask equally strong feelings of envy and anxiety about the future.

CHAPTER EIGHT

The Early Cold War, 1945–1952

As Europeans and Asians poked through the rubble left by the Second World War, Americans hoped that their former partners would continue to accept aid and guidance from Washington. But the Soviet Union, suspicious of American intentions and with ambitions of its own, did not cooperate. The "Grand Alliance" that had defeated Hitler fell apart in a chorus of charges of bad faith, and the new United Nations organization did not become the instrument for peace its founders hoped. By January 1947 political leaders, diplomats, and publicists on both sides of the Atlantic knew that the United States and the Soviet Union had entered a Cold War, a global ideological struggle between Soviet-style communism and revolution and Western capitalism and democracy led by the United States. Two years later, in 1949, the United States broke its traditional ban against permanent alliances and concluded its first peacetime military pact with ten European countries and Canada—the North Atlantic Treaty. Shortly afterward the Soviet Union exploded an atomic bomb, and serious-minded Americans and Europeans trembled that a new world war, fought with atomic weapons, was about to break out between America and Russia. In June 1950 a different sort of war directly involving the United States but not the Soviet Union did erupt in Korea.

What caused the Cold War? Why did the world of 1950 look so different from the hopes of President Franklin D. Roosevelt and his foreign policy advisers that the post–World War II era would see a continuation of the cooperation among the Allies that had defeated Germany and Japan? Was it a failure of leaders to find satisfactory solutions to difficult, but not necessarily impossible, problems? Did the Cold War result from the belligerence and desire for control of Eastern Europe on the part of the Soviet Union and especially its dictator, Josef Stalin? Was American diplomatic rigidity and anti-Communist hostility toward the Soviet Union's legitimate security a major cause of the Cold War? Was it a combination of these reasons?

[handwritten margin note: causes of Cold war?]

These questions divided politicians and citizens at the time and for decades afterward. The battlefields ran between supporters of American foreign policy who argued that the Cold War came about because of Soviet imperialism and critics who laid much of the blame for postwar tension on American misconduct. Within the government there was little disagreement that the Soviet Union bore major responsibility for the outbreak of the Cold War, and the United States needed to respond to its aggressive behavior. Throughout the forty years of the Cold War, until the collapse of communist governments in Eastern Europe in 1989 and 1990 and the end of the Soviet Union in 1991, most U.S. officials believed that the principal aim of American foreign policy was the containment of Soviet power. Presidents and their advisers tried to avoid an outbreak of war between the United States and the Soviet Union, but they fought Soviet allies. They also employed a variety of secret and clandestine operations to disrupt communist and revolutionary activities in many areas of the world. They fostered a broad consensus that the Soviet Unoin represented a threat to the United States and to millions of people around the globe.

Popular support for U.S. government policies in the Cold War waxed and waned. The consensus that the Soviet Union posed a threat held until the mid-1960s, but it eroded as the Vietnam War lost popularity. During the Vietnam War era some historians reexamined the early days of the Cold War and criticized President Harry Truman and his foreign policy team for unnecessarily provoking the Soviet Union. These revisionist views attracted a significant following in the late 1960s and 1970s. But another trend also developed as part of the conservative political revival of the 1970s. When Ronald Reagan sought the presidency in 1976 and 1980, he argued that the United States needed to win the Cold War against the Soviet Union. He pursued an assertive anti-Soviet policy once he became president in 1981.

In the years after the end of the Cold War and the end of the Soviet Union, much of the passion dissipated from the debate over the origins of the Cold War. A new consensus emerged that Soviet-style communism was a brutal and unsustainable system. Americans agreed that their foreign policy makers did not always behave wisely during the Cold War, but they also believed that it was appropriate for the United States to have opposed the Soviet Union. Nearly all Americans welcomed the end of the Cold War, and most believed that the peoples of Eastern Europe and the states of the former Soviet Union were better off without communism.

THE FIRST YEAR OF PEACE

President Harry Truman came to office with little experience in foreign affairs and chose to rely on the advice of his cabinet and ambassador to the Soviet Union, Averell Harriman. Truman's newly appointed secretary of state, James F. Byrnes, resented Truman's accession to the presidency, believing that the Democrats should have selected himself as their candidate. The secretary, unlike the president, expected good relations with Moscow.

The Soviets could not easily be mollified in the second half of 1945; they remembered Anglo-American mistreatment during the war. The United States and Britain had delayed opening a second front in Europe until 1944. An American OSS (Office of Strategic Services) official, Allen Dulles, had held secret surrender talks with the German commander in northern Italy in April 1945, generating fears among the suspicious Soviets that the western powers might conclude a separate peace with the Germans. The Soviets resented the Americans for having informed the British of the Manhattan Project developing the atomic bomb but not having provided information to Moscow. Stalin and Vyacheslav Molotov worried that Britain and America would pay less attention to Soviet security needs now that Germany no longer posed a threat. American reliance on the monopoly of the atomic bomb to force the Soviets to see things Washington's way heightened Moscow's anxieties.

Byrnes failed dramatically to revive the coalition spirit in the fall and winter of 1945–1946. In September he met with the British, Soviet, French, and Chinese foreign ministers in London to write peace treaties for Hungary, Bulgaria, Romania, and Finland, all former allies of Germany. The Soviet Red Army had occupied the first three countries and part of Finland during the war, and Byrnes tried unsuccessfully to dislodge the Soviets at the London conference. Molotov refused to budge despite, or perhaps because of, Byrnes's ostentatious references to American atomic weapons, which the Soviets did not yet possess. The five foreign ministers could not even agree on the wording of a communiqué to be released to the press.

Byrnes dropped "atomic diplomacy" when he went to Moscow for conversations with Molotov and Stalin in December. Despite the chilly Russian winter, the secretary of state thought he achieved more than had been accomplished in London. The Soviet leaders reiterated their determination to have friendly governments along their borders, but Stalin allowed that "perhaps the Bulgarian parliament could be advised to include some members of the loyal opposition in the new government" and suggested "it might be possible to…satisfy Mr. Byrnes" about Romania. Byrnes perked up at these Soviet concessions, but the Russians remained firmly in charge in Eastern Europe. George Kennan, the second in command at the American embassy in Moscow, called the Bulgarian and Romanian accommodations "fig leaves of democratic procedure to hide the nakedness of Stalinist dictatorship."

The president also was less hopeful than his secretary, and Truman resented Byrnes's habit of not keeping him more abreast of ongoing negotiations than could be learned from reading the newspapers. "It was more like one partner in business telling the other that his business trip was progressing well and not to worry," Truman grumbled. The president got angrier when Byrnes made a radio report of his trip upon landing in Washington without first coming by the White House. When the secretary finally did present himself on the presidential yacht, he got a dressing down from Truman, who rebuked him for letting the public know things "I had never heard of." The chief executive went on to say that he "would not tolerate such conduct." Relations between the president and secretary of state barely improved for the rest of 1946.

Truman confronted serious domestic problems in 1946. The economy was in a mess, but not because depression had returned, as many economists had predicted. Instead, consumers rushed to buy the houses, cars, refrigerators, shoes, and clothes they had wanted during the 1930s but could not purchase because they lacked jobs and could not have during the war because of rationing. Prices shot up 18 percent in 1946 after Truman bowed to business pressures to disband the Office of Price Administration in the fall of 1945. Labor unions, freed of their no-strike pledge, stopped work in the steel, rail, and auto industries. Unlike FDR, Truman had no rapport with labor leaders. He toyed with the idea of drafting strikers into the armed forces to make them work and even wrote out the text of a radio broadcast to veterans urging them to help him lynch union leaders. His aides persuaded him that such demagoguery might not calm public passions, and he never delivered it.

Relations with the Soviet Union deteriorated further in 1946. On February 9 Stalin delivered a rare public speech in which he explained the fundamental incompatibility of communism and capitalism. The latter system, he stressed, needed war for raw materials and markets. The Second World War had only been the most recent in a chain of conflicts that could be broken only when the world's economy made the transformation to communism. Henry Luce's *Time* magazine concluded that the remarks were "the most warlike pronouncement uttered by any top-rank statesman since V-J Day."

Two weeks after Stalin's speech, George F. Kennan, the second in command at the American embassy in Moscow, sent an 8,000-word "long telegram" to the State Department explaining why the Soviets behaved the way they did. The Soviets saw the world divided into hostile capitalist and communist camps between which there could be no peace. They held as an article of faith that capitalism would collapse under the weight of its internal contradictions and that socialism would replace it. The Soviet leaders clung to their revolutionary outlook because "Marxism is the fig leaf [this image covered a lot for Kennan] of their moral and intellectual respectability. Without it they would stand before history, at best, as only the last in that succession of cruel and wasteful Russian rulers." Truman read this cable with intense interest and believed it explained why the Soviet leaders had been so belligerent and uncompromising since the end of the war.

Poland became the most emotional point of contention between the Soviet Union and the United States. Whereas Roosevelt had favored any cosmetic agreement over the future of Poland, which allayed the anxieties of the Polish-American community, Truman chose to interpret Soviet backing for a communist-led government in Warsaw as proof that Stalin sought dominion over all of Eastern Europe. When the new Polish government persisted throughout 1946 in denouncing opposition groups as "neofascist" and "Nazi collaborators," confiscated church lands, nationalized industries, and refused to join the new International Monetary Fund and World Bank, U.S. diplomats, churchmen, and politicians ignored earlier promises that Moscow would have a friendly Poland on its border. The United States, seeing only that it was frozen out of Eastern Europe, spent the next five years making certain the Soviet Union would have nothing to say about events west of the Elbe River, which separated the Soviet zone of occupied Germany from German territory held by American, British, and French forces.

Truman's animosity toward the Soviet Union neatly coincided with the opinions of the generals and diplomats in charge of the occupation of Germany. Nothing had come of the wartime plan for Great Britain, France, the Soviet Union, and the United States to administer Germany jointly. An Allied Control Commission met throughout 1945 and 1946, but the powers reached no agreement on German reparations, elimination of Nazi influences, or local governments. Often the French joined the Soviets in charging the Americans and British with softness toward former Nazi Party members. But Gen. Lucius D. Clay, commander of U.S. forces in Germany, rejected all complaints. He preferred to believe that the Soviets sought communist rule for all of Germany as a first step in their eventual subjugation of Western Europe. Convinced that Moscow looked toward displacing "bourgeois" governments, Clay toyed with the idea of a revived Germany blocking Russia's way.

Truman signaled his new toughness in September 1946 when he fired former vice president Henry Wallace as secretary of commerce. A thorn in the side of conservatives for years, Wallace in 1946 took a gloomy view of the name-calling between Moscow and Washington. After brooding for six months, he delivered a speech on foreign affairs on September 12 before 20,000 people assembled by the U.S.–Soviet Friendship Association in New York's Madison Square Garden. "The tougher we get, the tougher they will get," he predicted. He also denounced "namby-pamby pacifism" in the United States and criticized the Soviet Union for its repression and contempt for civil liberties.

His audience, mostly old popular fronters sympathetic to the Soviets, hissed and booed him for these remarks, but Byrnes had a different reaction. Attending a meeting of Soviet, European, and American foreign ministers, he thought that Wallace's criticism cut the ground from under him. Byrnes phoned Truman to insist on Wallace's muzzling or his head. These demands put the president in a ticklish spot, for he had actually read and approved Wallace's speech before he delivered it. Feeling sorry for himself, Truman unburdened his grievances with the commerce secretary to his diary. "Wallace is a pacifist 100 per cent," he wrote. "He wants...to give Russia our atomic secrets and trust a bunch of adventurers in the Kremlin politburo.... The Reds, phonies and the 'parlor pinks' seem to be banded together and are becoming a national danger. I believe they are a sabotage front for Uncle Joe Stalin." On September 20 Truman sent Wallace a letter as ill-tempered as his diary entry, firing him from Commerce. Wallace returned the smoldering document to Truman rather than embarrass him before posterity, cleared out his desk, and departed. Byrnes's victory lasted barely three months. In early January 1947 it was the turn of the secretary of state to get in trouble with Truman. When he went to Moscow and made conciliatory sounds, Truman fired him somewhat more gracefully than he replaced Wallace.

The choice to follow Byrnes as secretary of state was Gen. George C. Marshall, chief of staff during the Second World War. In December 1945 Truman had seen Marshall in China attempting to work out an accommodation between Communists and Nationalists. When he came home in January 1947, he said that no compromise was possible between the two sides in their ongoing civil war and that the Communists were bound to win. Marshall had a formidable reputation for integrity, and Truman chose him as someone immune from criticism.

THE TRUMAN DOCTRINE, CONTAINMENT, AND
THE MARSHALL PLAN

The Truman administration was on the defensive in 1947. The new Republican Congress had been elected in 1946 using two insulting slogans: "To err is Truman" and "Had enough?" An incident in the eastern Mediterranean in early 1947 sparked a new approach to the Soviet Union. On February 21 the British government told the United States that it no longer would pay the upkeep on Greek and Turkish efforts at fighting domestic leftist uprisings.

American officials had expected the financially strapped British to renege on their commitments to Greece and Turkey for some time, and they did not mind their leaving the Middle East to the United States. The British need for hard cash offered an opportunity for the United States to insist on an end to their exclusive control over the "sterling bloc" as a quid pro quo for American aid. In return for an American loan of $2 billion, the British had to agree that the currencies of their dominions would be fully convertible into dollars.

Events in Greece and Turkey also presented the United States with an opportunity to outflank the Soviets to the south. Although President Roosevelt had agreed to the British and Soviets sharing power in Greece, the Truman administration wanted to rid the country of the taint of communism. Americans had encouraged Britain to arm Greece's government in its civil war against the leftist National Liberation Front, known by its Greek initials EAM. Despite the fact that EAM had attracted 1.4 million, mostly noncommunist members in a country of 7.5 million people, the State Department considered the movement "not a 'friend' or ally of the USSR; it is an instrument of Soviet policy." The War Department's intelligence division decided that the Soviet goal was "to gain complete control of Greece." Loy Henderson, a State Department Soviet expert, reported that "the Soviet Union seems determined to break down [Britain's] great dam [blocking] the flow of Russian power to the south." Now that the British seemed reluctant to maintain that dam, the United States eagerly offered direct aid to Greece.

The question was whether the United States should announce its commitment to Greece and Turkey. George F. Kennan, the chief of the newly established Policy Planning Staff of the Department of State, advised simple support of these two governments without enlarging the commitment into a global confrontation with the Soviet Union, but Marshall and Truman believed the Greek and Turkish crisis presented the opportunity to explain the growing confrontation with the Soviet Union and communism across the globe.

On March 12 Truman went before Congress to ask for an aid package of $300 million for Greece and $100 million for Turkey to equip their armed forces to eliminate communist guerrillas. Assistant Secretary of State Will Clayton urged a militant speech, as "the United States will not take world leadership effectively unless the people of the United States are shocked into doing so." Informed by Republican senator Arthur Vandenberg that he had to "scare the hell out of the country," the president went beyond pleas to assist these two governments by promulgating a "Truman Doctrine," committing America to aid all governments facing domestic leftist insurrections. He rallied Democrats and drew grudging praise from most Republicans. The privately expressed doubts of George Kennan were joined by the public fears of the prominent newspaper columnist Walter Lippmann, who criticized the

Truman Doctrine as a "vague global policy, which sounds like the tocsin of an ideological crusade," one which "has no limits." Neither complaint altered the Truman's administration's increasingly confrontational stance toward the Soviet Union. Public concern that the the United States had embarked on an open-ended and potentially costly competition with the Soviet Union grew.

Later in 1947 two phrases—*containment of the Soviet Union* and *the Cold War*—became popular ways of describing relations between the United States and the Soviet Union. As an active foreign service officer, Kennan felt compelled to cloak his identity. Under the pseudonym "X" he published an article, "The Sources of Soviet Conduct," in *Foreign Affairs* in July. He zipped through 300 years of Russian and thirty years of Soviet history to demonstrate that Moscow's foreign policy rested on three pillars—traditional Russian imperialism, revolutionary Communist ideology, and the paranoid suspicions of Josef Stalin, whom "X" considered deranged. Only the first of these sources, traditional Russian expansion, was likely to endure, as Kennan doubted that a nation could maintain Marxism for long or forever submit to the whims of a dictator. "We are going to continue for a long time to find the Russians difficult to deal with...but the United States has it in its power to increase enormously the strains under which Soviet power must operate," he asserted. While waiting for the Soviet Union to abandon communism and behave like any other state, the United States had to exercise "the patient containment" of Soviet power to areas of Eastern Europe already under its control. Walter Lippmann responded in a series of *New York Herald Tribune* columns critical of containment as a "strange monstrosity" doomed from the start. He predicted that the United States would have to engage in "recruiting, subsidizing, and supporting a heterogeneous array of satellites, clients, dependents, and puppets"; the result would be perpetual "Cold War" with the Soviet Union.

The Truman Doctrine formed only one part of a concentrated strategy, the second half of which was announced by Secretary of State Marshall to the graduating class of Harvard University on June 6. He invited European nations to step forward with requests for reconstruction assistance from the United States. A radical reversal stood behind this innocuous-sounding proposal: no longer did American planners believe, as they had in 1945, that the United Nations should coordinate aid. The economic situation in Europe appeared desperate, and British inability to fund Greece and Turkey represented only one example. American travelers to Europe in the winter of 1946–1947 reported dark cities, cold houses, closed factories, empty treasuries, and starving people badly in need of dollars, coal, and food. Russell C. Leffingwell, a banker with the house of Morgan, came back in April 1947 to predict an inevitable seizure of power by French, Italian, and German

Occupation of Germany and Austria

communists unless the United States stepped in to revive the economies of Western Europe. Recovery there would encourage consumption from restarted American factories.

The fears of the post–World War I era returned, but this time the United States took the lead in crusading against revolution. The beauty of Marshall's plan was that it did not appear on the surface to be directed against the Soviet Union. The secretary of state never mentioned the dangers of communism or the Soviet Union, and he opened the program to all European nations. He knew, however, that the Soviet Union would reject the invitation as a transparent attempt to penetrate Eastern Europe with American commerce. The State Department expected the Soviets to prohibit their communist-dominated governments of Eastern Europe from joining others in asking for aid. The onus for dividing Europe into two hostile camps would fall on Moscow, not Washington.

The division occurred in the summer of 1947. Western European nations assembled in August to draft a European Recovery Program, the formal title for the Marshall Plan. The Czech government, not thoroughly controlled by the Communist Party, sent a representative, and the Poles tried to join. The Soviets quickly sent word that they believed participation by the Eastern European nations would marry their economies to the United States, and the Czechs and Poles retreated. The European Recovery Program took shape without any participation from the governments east of the Elbe River, and Marshall succeeded in launching reconstruction that linked the fortunes of Western Europe firmly to the United States.

Congress approved the Marshall Plan in the summer of 1947. Republicans who might have objected to a program calling for $23 billion in economic aid had no qualms at all about endorsing a package designed to thwart the Soviet Union. Republicans from Arthur Vandenberg to the staunchly conservative William Jenner of Indiana, an enthusiastic member of the China Lobby (which opposed Truman's Asian policies), joined a chorus of Democrats in supporting the appropriations. Truman had cut the ground from under the resurgent Republican majority in Congress, but he paid the price by publicly announcing that the two super-powers were on a collision course. No longer did he or any other important figure in the administration harbor any hope that the United States and the Soviet Union could reach an agreement on the future of Europe.

DOMESTIC POLITICS AND THE COLD WAR

While the phrase *Cold War* became a cliché in mid-1947, the conflict between the United States and the Soviet Union had existed during the Second

World War. It became obvious to the public in 1946 that the two former allies disagreed about every important issue in Europe and Asia. For the remainder of the Truman administration, the attitude of the public became central to the administration's conduct of foreign affairs. The Republican Party, which had been a loyal opposition during the Second World War, played a more complicated game after 1945. Sometimes it supported Truman in a proud display of bipartisanship, while other times it raised fears about the "subversives," "spies," and "security risks" it said penetrated the American government at the bidding of a communist conspiracy directed by the Kremlin.

At the beginning of the postwar era, the most prominent Republican spokesman on foreign affairs was Sen. Arthur Vandenberg of Michigan, who had expressed common Midwest isolationist sentiments and distrust of Franklin Roosevelt before Pearl Harbor. The Truman administration changed his mind on one important aspect of internationalism, however, when it secured his support for the United Nations organization in May 1945. Over the next four years Vandenberg, as the ranking minority member and then chairman of the Foreign Relations Committee, led his fellow Republicans in support of Truman's strong anti-Soviet stand in Europe, but the opposition had nothing good to say about the administration's response to events in Asia. The Chinese civil war between Nationalists and Communists resumed in early 1946, and American friends of Jiang Jieshi—conservative Republican members of Congress cheered on by Henry Luce's *Time* magazine and the *Chicago Tribune*—blamed Truman for weakening the Nationalists.

The administration tried to protect itself from criticism from anticommunists by introducing its own program for exposing and eliminating "subversives" working for the government. In the process Truman climbed on the back of a tiger and found it hard to dismount without Republican politicians accusing him of ignoring subversion. In July 1945 the Federal Bureau of Investigation (FBI) announced it had arrested the editors of *Amerasia*, a small-circulation journal devoted to academic articles on U.S.-Asian relations, and charged them with possession of classified government documents. The FBI also detained John Stewart Service, an American foreign service officer home on leave from his post in China. Service, later cleared of the charges in the *Amerasia* case, became the first of several American experts on China charged with disloyalty when their only crime was accurately predicting the demise of the Nationalists. The furor over *Amerasia* passed in a few months, but the Truman administration used the case to commence a program of loyalty investigations of government employees early in 1947.

A Loyalty-Security Board began inquiring into the political beliefs of all federal workers, hearing secret testimony it was not required to share with the accused. The board never defined what loyalty was, but all government functionaries knew that past association with communist or communist-led organizations could cost them their jobs. The loyalty-security program struck fear in the hearts of old New Dealers, but it did little to quiet the Republican clamor for stricter measures. In the summer of 1947, the House Committee on Un-American Activities, now chaired by Republican J. Parnell Thomas of New Jersey, conducted investigations of the motion picture industry in Hollywood. In four days of testimony broadcast across the country by radio, the committee discovered little more proof of communist influence than the ominous fact that smiles lit up the faces of Soviet children in the movie *Song of Russia*.

The Truman administration was happy to use the issue of the threat of domestic subversion as a way of generating public support for its foreign policy so long as it did not lose control of it to the opposition. By portraying a worldwide communist conspiracy operating inside the United States, the administration hoped to frighten the public into support for a forward foreign policy.

REORGANIZING THE FOREIGN AFFAIRS APPARATUS

Congress also remodeled the foreign affairs apparatus in 1946 and 1947. Ever since the Second World War, experts had worried about the confused lines of authority in the foreign affairs bureaucracy. President Roosevelt, with his personal style and his reliance on friends to conduct delicate negotiations abroad, had left the professionals in the State Department angry and humiliated. The armed services had engaged in bitter wrangling for turf, and the Office of Strategic Services—the espionage organization headed by a wealthy Republican, William J. "Wild Bill" Donovan—had been a virtually independent arm of the executive branch. Reformers thought that some order had to be brought to these fiercely competitive agencies. Members of each body wanted to preserve and expand their own authority at the expense of the others. Truman and his advisers wanted to make certain that the president could dominate foreign affairs even if he did not have the political appeal of his popular predecessor.

Two laws tried to bring order to the conduct of foreign affairs. The first, the Foreign Service Reform Act of 1946, represented an attempt by professional diplomats to recapture the center stage in the making of foreign policy. Ignored by Roosevelt, career officials looked forward to a fairer deal from Truman. During the war many officials from other agencies temporarily joined the State Department, and Foreign Service officers had served tours in Washington. The reforms of 1946 attempted to make these arrangements permanent by creating Foreign Service reserve officer classifications for officials who entered the service for short terms. It also merged the State Department and the Foreign Service into one single organization. Now diplomats and consuls would rotate back to headquarters in Washington between tours of duty. Time in the capital no longer would be considered a vacation or a punishment, as professionals learned about and helped formulate policies. The next year, 1947, the State Department set up a Policy Planning Staff made up of Foreign Service officers instructed to provide insights into the future.

While the Department of State attempted to seize the initiative, leaders of other foreign affairs departments resisted with plans of their own. The most successful were the armed forces. After all, the army and navy had more than 1 million men in uniform after demobilization, but the State Department numbered 2,000. The Pentagon spent more than $9 billion, and the appropriation for the State Department was less than $40 million. Insofar as the United States affected world events, the army and navy departments were central.

During the war military reformers had come to believe that the division of effort into a War Department and a Navy Department made little sense. The use of airplanes to bomb cities and battlefields had made military affairs more complicated. Pentagon advocates of air power encouraged congressional supporters who believed that a new age of warfare had begun with the explosion of the atomic bomb. Some members of Congress backed a new unified force amalgamating all three branches—army, navy, and air force—into a single service. Of course, generals and admirals of the traditional branches gulped in amazement at suggestions for them to give up their long-held commands. Their brethren who had served in the air forces of the army and navy also shunned a merger into a single service, predicting that a new air force would give them the opportunity to rise more quickly.

The National Security Act passed by Congress in late July 1947 compromised among these competing plans. On the military side no unified single service was set up, and a separate air force was carved from the old army air corps. Yet the planners did create a new Defense Department, presided over by a civilian secretary, to coordinate the work of the army, navy, and air force. To preserve civilian control over the military, no one could become secretary of defense who had been on active duty with the military during the previous five years.

The National Security Act also dealt with the problems of extralegal, or covert, operations of the government. The Office of Strategic Services (OSS) had been disbanded at the end of the war. A wide gulf had separated the upper echelons of the OSS, led by Donovan and peopled by mostly conservative Ivy Leaguers and lower-level analysts, who tended to be political liberals. When the OSS was closed, liberals lost influence, but now that the Cold War had erupted, the administration reasoned that a new spy organization was needed. The National Security Act created a Central Intelligence Agency (CIA) to place all spy activities under a single roof. Unstated in the act but clear in the minds of its authors was the notion that the CIA would be the arm of the government that would do those jobs too unsavory for the remaining branches.

The final provision of the National Security Act established a coordinating body, the National Security Council (NSC), headed by the president and including the chairman of the Joint Chiefs of Staff, the secretaries of state and defense, the vice president, and anyone else the president wanted to invite. Intended to eliminate the chronic squabbling among various foreign affairs and military bureaus, the early NSC had no permanent director nor any professional staff members. Truman used it to assess the shape of the world in the future. In 1950 it produced one of the most important memorandums since the Second World War, NSC-68, a prediction of the military requirements of the United States in the next five years. The paper called for a build-up of American conventional forces and the annual expenditure of $50 billion on defense, a rise of 300 percent, yet the NSC did not come into its own as an independent agency until the Kennedy administration.

IMMIGRATION POLICY AFTER WORLD WAR II

After 1945 only minute policy changes took place in restrictive immigration policies. From 750,000 to 1.5 million displaced persons (DPs), victims of the Holocaust, languished in camps supervised by the United Nations. Relief agencies lobbied Congress for the special displaced persons laws finally passed in 1948 and 1950. Ironically, the first law assisted the oppressors— Nazi officers and collaborators—more than the victims. One lobbying group decried "the unashamed cynicism displayed in legislating ostensibly for the relief of those who suffered most from the last war, while actually locking the doors against them." In Congress one bigot damned DPs as "the scum of the earth," and another characterized them as "bums, criminals, subversives, revolutionists, crackpots and human wreckage." Public outcry led to the removal of the most flagrant restrictions on DPs in 1950.

For the next thirty years the displaced persons acts served as models for other efforts at admitting refugees from governments the United States opposed. The most generosity was shown to people fleeing communist regimes. Congress made special provisions for anticommunist Hungarians after the unsuccessful uprising of 1956, Cubans after the revolution of 1959, and Indochinese after the communist victories in 1975. The national quota system as a whole, which had caused such resentment abroad, was scrapped in 1965 and replaced by an overall ceiling of 400,000 immigrants admitted annually, but the new law did not permanently settle immigration policy. Millions of noncitizens simply crossed the frontiers without official permission. By 1982 the Immigration and Naturalization Service (INS) estimated that as many as 12 million such "undocumented" aliens lived in the United States, where they took the worst jobs, found the poorest housing, and lived in terror of being turned over to the authorities. At the same time the government applied inconsistent standards to refugees who entered the country. While welcoming those from communist countries, it jailed and deported thousands from poor, dictatorial Haiti and strife-torn El Salvador. In the the 1980s, with immigration barriers offering few restraints and some Americans bitterly resentful of the new arrivals, additional legislation was introduced. It provided amnesty to some undocumented aliens already in the country while imposing stiffer penalties on any future migrants who attempted to seek their fortunes in America without proper visas or work permits. Fears of immigrants subsided in the 1990s, but they revived in the twenty-first century after the attacks on the World Trade Center and the Pentagon by al-Qaeda extremists in September 2001.

THE MIDDLE EAST

While relations with the Soviet Union dominated Truman's foreign policy, the administration also expanded its interests in the Middle East. The establishment of the Jewish state of Israel in the British mandate of Palestine in 1947 and 1948 set the stage for a dispute that has not been resolved to this day. Jewish settlers in Palestine had decided during the Second World War that they would fight simultaneously with the British against the Nazis and against the British for the establishment of a separate Jewish state. At a meeting of the World Zionist Congress at the Biltmore Hotel in New York City in 1942, political representatives of the settlers agreed to seek immediate independence after the war, but British authorities continued their prewar practice of restricting the entry of Jews into the mandate. This prohibition of immigration was made all the worse by the memory of the murder of 6 million Jews and the miserable sight of hundreds of thousands of death camp survivors and refugees languishing in displaced persons camps throughout Europe.

American policy during the war had been to encourage the Jews of the United States to believe that FDR supported the idea of their creating a Jewish state in Palestine. Truman continued to raise hopes in May 1946 when he backed the Jewish demand for the immediate admission of 100,000 Jews to the Holy Land. Then, spurred by a desire to remove an issue from the Republican opposition, Truman for the first time announced his support of the Jewish state in Palestine in early October on Yom Kippur, the holiest day of the Jewish year. He had received word shortly before that the Jews of New York would desert the Democratic Party for the Republicans in the upcoming congressional election unless he made some dramatic gesture and that the Republican governor of the state, Thomas E. Dewey, the party's presidential candidate in 1944 and the front-runner for 1948, planned to make a statement favoring the admission of several hundred thousand European Jews to Palestine. Nativism also played a part in nudging Truman toward sympathizing with the plight of the Jewish victims of Hitler, as British foreign secretary Ernest Bevan, a visceral anti-Semite, projected some of his prejudices onto the president when he said Truman badgered Britain to admit more Jews into Palestine "because he did not want 100,000 Jews in New York."

In mid-1947 in response to American pressure as well as the Jewish revolt in Palestine that killed more than 100 British troops, the British government announced that it was abandoning its mandate by December 31 and turning the issue over to the United Nations, which established a Special Commission on Palestine. The commission traveled to the area to hear testimony from Arabs and Jews and recommended the partition of Palestine into two states—one Jewish and one Arab—to the General Assembly. The Jewish Agency accepted partition; the Arabs did not. On November 27, 1947, the General Assembly voted by a two-thirds majority to partition Palestine, with American ambassador Warren F. Austin joining the European and Latin American nations and the Soviet bloc in voting for the creation of Jewish and Arab states in mid-May 1948.

In the intervening six months American policy underwent dramatic reversals. State Department experts on the Middle East had never been happy with the idea of Jewish aspirations. One diplomat called American support of Zionism "a major blunder in statesmanship; it might even threaten world security." Another offered a cold assessment of why the United States should support the Arab claims: "As for the emotions of the Arabs, I do not give a dried camel's hump. It is, however, important to the interests of this country that these fanatical and overwrought people do not injure our strategic interests through reprisals against our oil investments." Officials also predicted a bloodbath should the Jewish Agency go ahead with its plans to declare independence in the face of Arab hostility. In February 1948 the State Department presented a radical reversal of course to Ambassador Austin at the United Nations headquarters at Lake Success, New York. Instead of a Jewish state, the United States would agree to act as trustee for all of Palestine. Austin dutifully presented this scheme to the Security Council, thinking it had the backing of Truman. Jewish leaders were astonished and depressed. Chaim Weizmann, longtime head of the world Zionist movement, in New York for the UN session, rushed to Washington to convince the president to reaffirm

President Harry S. Truman (right) and Secretary of State George C. Marshall take
a look at the Middle East.
(Harry S. Truman Presidential Library)

the American commitment to an independent Jewish state. Truman, fearing
reprisal from Jewish voters in 1948 and convinced that the Jews needed a state
of their own, explained that Austin did not speak for the administration. A
chastened UN ambassador gamely accepted this presidential dressing down
and reported that the United States accepted a new Jewish state.

On May 14, 1948, David Ben-Gurion, the head of the Jewish Agency, proclaimed the independence of the Jewish state of Israel. Five Arab nations immediately attacked and looked forward to pitching the Jews into the sea
within weeks. On the day of the declaration of independence, the Truman
administration, hoping to beat the Soviets to the punch, announced it had
extended de facto recognition. By summer the Israelis had beaten back the
invasion forces from Egypt, Jordan, and Syria, and negotiations opened for
an end to the war. The next year, 1949, saw an armistice between Israel and
its Arab neighbors. No peace treaties followed that agreement until the
Egyptian-Israeli treaty, negotiated with the help of the United States, was
signed in March 1979. Israel and Jordan also signed a peace treaty in 1994.
The political status of millions of Paestinians displaced by the creation of

the state of Israel remained unresolved. In 1993 the United States helped Israel and the Palestine Liberation Organization, representing the Palestinian people, arrange a framework to end the conflict. The hopes created by this peace process went unrealized, relations between Israel and the Palestinians deteriorated, and they did not reach a peaceful settlement.

American policy throughout this crisis demonstrated caution, hesitation, and vacillation. Torn between a sense of relief that the British had left the Middle East, a genuine concern for the Jewish victims of Nazism, fear of the power of Jewish voters, and an equally strong urge to please the Arab states, the Truman administration sought to satisfy each of the quarreling parties. In the end the British resented American moralizing, and the Arabs distrusted American support of Israeli independence. The new government of Israel was delighted, of course, that the United States had been the first foreign power to extend recognition, but the Israelis tempered their gratitude with boasts that they had won the war with their own arms and military prowess. American diplomats struggled with the problem of reconciling fiercely competitive interests in the Middle East into the twenty-first century.

THE ELECTION OF 1948, THE BERLIN CRISIS,
AND THE CREATION OF NATO

Bipartisan agreement over foreign policy unraveled in the aftermath of the presidential election of 1948. Republicans, believing that the inept Harry Truman would be an easy target, expected to win handily, and practically everyone else agreed. In early 1948, fearing a debacle at the polls, some liberal Democrats led by Eleanor Roosevelt sought out war hero Gen. Dwight David Eisenhower to see if he would consent to run for president as a Democrat. The general refused, and the Democrats faced the gloomy prospect of losing the presidency as well as the Congress. The Republicans, supremely confident, chose New York governor Thomas E. Dewey, who had lost to Franklin D. Roosevelt in 1944. Dewey spent much of his campaign assembling his cabinet, so sure was he of victory. On foreign policy he supported the Truman administration's policy of confrontation with the Soviet Union in Europe, and coming from the eastern internationalist wing of the party, Dewey did not indulge in any baiting of the Democrats for the decline of Jiang Jieshi in China.

The campaign took place in the midst of growing European tensions and the revival of Republican charges of spies among the New Dealers. In September 1947 the Soviet Union, responding to the American and British introduction of a new form of currency in their zone of occupied Germany, cut off land access by the Western powers to their zones of Berlin, officially under the joint control of the Allies. The confrontation over Berlin represented the final episode in the ill will between East and West over the future of Germany, which had been building since the Potsdam Conference. Unable to reach agreement on reparations, the Allied Control Commission, which was supposed to formulate policy for all the occupied zones of Germany, produced only an endless series of acrimonious meetings among representatives of the Soviet Union, Britain, France, and the United States. Many of the confrontations pitted the three Western powers against the Soviet Union, but there were also occasional outbursts of bad feeling between the French and the two Anglo-Saxon powers. Britain and the United States consequently decided to combine their two areas of occupied Germany into a single "Bizonia" capable of putting to good use the billions of dollars in reconstruction loans expected under the Marshall Plan.

The creation of Bizonia in mid-1947 persuaded the Soviet Union that the United States and Britain contemplated a revived German state, possibly armed and assuredly hostile to its eastern neighbors. The Soviets bided their time until the Western powers reformed the currency of their parts of Berlin without first securing the approval of the Allied Control Commission. Then Russian troops turned back all traffic, including soldiers, goods, and foods bound from the western zones of occupation to Berlin. The American commander in Germany, Gen. Lucius D. Clay, told Truman that the Soviet move was the opening shot in the Third World War and asked for authority to enter Berlin by force. Cooler heads held the day in Washington, however, and Truman ordered Clay to organize cargo flights from the western zones of Germany to Berlin. The airlift continued for the next seven months, allowing the citizens of West Berlin to survive. The Soviets were forced to acknowledge the right of the Western powers to remain in Berlin, and they ended their blockade of the city in late April 1949. After the United States succeeded in breaking the Soviet stranglehold on Berlin, Washington ended the formal occupation and encouraged the creation of the Federal Republic of Germany. This new West German state, made up of British-American Bizonia, the French section, and the three western sectors of Berlin, signaled the official end of the occupation and the fiction of Allied cooperation.

The Berlin airlift gave Truman a boost during his reelection campaign, but new charges about "spies" and "subversives" arose in the late summer and fall to shake the president's equanimity and alarm the remnants of the New Dealers. In August the House Committee on Un-American Activities heard Whittaker Chambers, a former communist, senior editor of *Time*, and the translator of *Bambi* from German to English, testify that he had recruited into the Communist Party Alger Hiss, in 1945 director of the State Department's Office of Special Political Affairs and then head of the Carnegie Endowment for International Peace. Hiss hotly denied party membership, said he had never met Chambers, and sued for libel. Committee members, loving the publicity, arranged a dramatic confrontation between Hiss and Chambers in a room at Manhattan's Roosevelt Hotel. Hiss repeated his denials under oath, making clear that he expected the committee to challenge the veracity of his tormentor, Chambers, whose story seemed preposterous. Throughout the fall the committee dithered, not wishing to lose its star witness but lacking evidence to proceed against Hiss. After the election killed Republican hopes, Chambers's greatest supporter on the committee, Richard M. Nixon, a second-term Republican representative from California, helped the *Time* editor publicize a far more damaging charge against Hiss. Not only had the former high State Department official been a member of the Communist Party, Chambers now claimed, but he was also a spy who had passed secret State Department memorandums to Chambers to transfer to Soviet officials. To prove his charge, Chambers led Nixon and a posse of reporters to a pumpkin patch on his Maryland farm, where he extracted from the hollowed-out orange vegetables several rolls of microfilms containing pictures of the documents Chambers claimed to have received from Hiss. The statute of limitations having expired for the crime of espionage (all the documents bore the dates 1937 or 1938), a New York grand jury indicted Hiss for perjury for denying under oath that he had been a communist or knew Chambers.

At a hearing before the House Committee on Un-American Activities, Alger Hiss (right) denies that he spied for the Soviet Union. Elizabeth Bentley, who admitted membership in a Soviet spy organization, is at the left.
(Library of Congress)

The Hiss case threw the Truman administration into an uproar, with the president agreeing to a reporter's description of the charges as a Republican "red herring" dragged across the trail of the election. The U.S. attorney general looked into the possibility of indicting Chambers, not Hiss, for perjury, before the *Time* editor pulled the films from the pumpkins. Chambers's revelations unnerved Truman, who approved the indictment against Hiss. He was tried twice—the first trial ending in a hung jury—convicted in 1950, and sentenced to a five-year prison term. More than a former State Department official stood in the dock, though. As Alastair Cooke, a long-time American correspondent for the British Broadcasting Corporation, described it, the case put "a generation on trial." All former New Dealers who, like Hiss, had hoped for a continuation of goodwill between the United States and the Soviet Union seemed accused. While he was on trial for acts committed in the late thirties, Hiss's enemies in the newspapers made much of his presence as a diplomat at the Yalta Conference in February 1945. Hiss steadfastly maintained his innocence and denied that he was ever a Soviet spy for more than thirty years. Some New Dealers stood by him as an honorable man smeared by disreputable opponents. Documents made public after the fall of the Soviet Union, however, demonstrated that Hiss had been a Soviet agent.

Truman's reelection surprised the political experts and infuriated Republicans, who lost the presidency, Congress, and something else—the sense that they would be rewarded for their bipartisan support for the president's foreign affairs initiatives in Europe. Republican stalwarts again saw themselves shut out of power as Democrats ran things. In April Truman submitted the North Atlantic Treaty (NATO) to the Senate for ratification. Made up of twelve countries—the United States, Canada, Denmark, France, Iceland, Italy, Portugal, Norway, Great Britain, and the three Benelux nations—NATO was to be both a military and political alliance. Gen. Omar Bradley, the chairman of the Joint Chiefs of Staff, told the Senate Foreign Relations Committee that the Western European countries had insisted on NATO as a more effective defense against the Soviet Union than the United Nations. Dean Acheson, appointed secretary of state in January 1949, argued that NATO would do more than maintain a "balance of power" and would give the West a "preponderance of power" over the Soviet Union. Even with the alliance, however, the Soviets enjoyed superiority in conventional forces, which the United States outweighed with its monopoly on the atomic bomb. Acheson explained NATO's political importance to the senators. He considered it a demonstration to the Eastern Europeans of American concern for their welfare, thereby preventing a revival of "neutralism" or "appeasement" in Europe. Utah Republican senator Arthur Watkins opposed the pact as providing little additional military security for Western Europe. Watkins noted that the "constitutional processes" clause of the treaty required that each nation declare

Secretary of State Dean Acheson (second from right) greets British
prime minister Winston Churchill.
(National Archives)

war in the legally defined manner, and he predicted that the Soviet Union
could overrun Europe before Congress declared war. Sen. Robert Taft, the
Ohio Republican who had consistently opposed American participation in Europe's conflicts since the late thirties, added his voice to the opposition to
NATO as a departure from traditional American avoidance of entangling alliances. But only eleven senators cast votes with Watkins and Taft, and the Senate ratified the treaty by a vote of eighty-two to thirteen in July. Upon signing
the treaty Truman sent Congress a Mutual Defense Assistance Act with a price
tag of $1.5 billion for one year's worth of military equipment for Europe.

THE FAR EAST: CHINA, JAPAN, AND INDOCHINA

Having failed to dent Democratic successes in molding policy in Europe, Republican scored heavily as they criticized Truman's confused responses to
changing circumstances in Asia. By the middle of 1949, it was clear that the
communists led by Mao Zedong would win the Chinese civil war. Friends of
Jiang Jieshi in the Republican party—William Knowland of California, Walter

Judd of Minnesota, and William Jenner of Indiana—complained that Democrats had let the communists win. Joined by Henry Luce, this China Lobby wondered aloud why the Truman administration had stopped supplying weapons to Jiang after the Marshall mission of 1946. So annoyed were the president and the new secretary of state, Dean Acheson, by this barrage of criticism that they responded by making public the record of American aid to China. Acheson, immaculate and tall with an upturned mustache and well-appointed suits, was the son of the Episcopal bishop of Connecticut. Supercilious in his bearing, tone of voice, and even his face, he enraged former isolationist Republicans. One Republican congressman surveyed the secretary's clothes and bearing and wanted to shout, "Get out, get out. You're all that's been wrong with the United States for twenty years." For his part, the secretary had no respect for Congress, calling the conservatives "primitives" who knew nothing of foreign affairs but kept him away from his job by testifying before them.

In August 1949 the State Department sought to silence opponents by publishing a white paper on China, a two-volume edition of the diplomatic correspondence between the United States and China over the previous generation. The documents indicated that the United States had done everything possible to aid the Nationalist government. If Jiang had lost the civil war, it was because of his own failings: his corruption, unpopularity, and reluctance to fight. In the end the white paper concluded that the Chinese civil war had been lost by the Chinese Nationalists themselves. The volumes came equipped with a covering "letter of transmittal" produced by Assistant Secretary of State for Far Eastern Affairs Dean Rusk, in which he accused the Chinese communists of being puppets of Moscow. Rusk looked forward to the day when the Chinese would free themselves of "foreign domination."

While his assistant secretary fretted about Moscow's long reach, Acheson looked for ways to open diplomatic relations with the new Chinese government in Beijing. The secretary of state thought that the United States and China should maintain their embassies, as he had received reports from Foreign Service officers serving in China that the communists looked forward to demonstrating independence from the Soviets. Moreover, Acheson expected the Nationalists, who had escaped to Taiwan in the fall of 1949, to become a drain on American resources with persistent demands for arms and money to apply to pointless assaults on the mainland. Acheson told the Senate Foreign Relations Committee that the government of Jiang would quickly succumb to the communists. After "the dust settled" the United States and Beijing could resume diplomatic relations. In fact, the Korean War, which started in June 1950, changed the picture.

On September 23, 1949, the president announced that a "nuclear explosion"—he carefully avoided uttering the dreaded words *atomic bomb*—had occurred earlier that month in the Soviet Union. This news sent shock waves through Washington and set off a search for a scapegoat. No one had predicted that the Soviet Union would be able to have a bomb so quickly, so it seemed that spies must have slipped atomic secrets to the soviets. The arrest in 1950 of Julius and Ethel Rosenberg, one of whom, Julius, had worked on the Manhattan Project, added to the espionage furor.

The Soviet bomb also forced a revision in American strategic planning, which had rested since 1945 on a monopoly of what Bernard Baruch called "the winning weapon." In late 1949 and early 1950 officials of the departments of State and Defense and the National Security Council defined a new mode of competition. They completed their work before the new year, and it became official policy in April 1950 with the adoption of National Security Council Memorandum 68 (NSC-68). As previously mentioned, this document, largely the work of Paul Nitze of the State Department's Policy Planning Staff, predicted what the world would look like over the next five years. Asserting that the Soviets could not mount a military challenge before 1955, NSC-68 called for an extraordinary increase in the defense budget, from $13 billion to $50 billion a year, to maintain American superiority. To prepare the United States to wage a land war against the Soviet Union, the army had to be increased through a revived and expanded Selective Service system.

While NSC-68 did not foresee a major war for the next five years, small outbreaks were possible. Where would these wars occur? NATO's creation coincided with a relaxation of fears in Europe, so new conflict over Germany seemed remote. The Far East, however, was less tranquil. With the fall of Jiang's Nationalists, the United States looked for another nation to act as surrogate. Japan filled the bill. As early as 1947 the policy of occupation pursued in Japan had taken a "reverse course." No longer did the independent, arrogant Gen. Douglas MacArthur have a free hand in remolding Japanese society. Now Washington took an increased interest in Japan. Liberal plans for breaking up the giant Japanese trusts, or *zaibatsu*, were shelved in favor of revitalizing Japanese industry to trade with the remainder of Southeast Asia. Such trade would reduce the subsidy from the United States to Japan and prevent the Japanese from coming to terms with the Soviet Union.

Indochina, where the French had fought a guerrilla war since 1946, also attracted American attention in early 1950. Immediately after the Second World War the United States had helped the French return to power in Indochina. For the first two years of the insurrection against the French, the United States had not taken an active interest. Then, after Jiang's collapse, American policy shifted as Washington saw the French standing in the way of a communist sweep of Southeast Asia. In February 1950 the Truman administration agreed to send $18 million in military aid to fight the war against the Vietminh nationalists in Indochina.

WAR IN KOREA

The last place in Asia where Americans became interested in 1950 was Korea. At the end of the Second World War, the Americans had occupied the southern half of the country, while Soviet troops took over north of the thirty-eighth parallel. According to the Yalta accords, this division would end with the eventual unification of Korea. But the same divisions between communist and noncommunist governments that had arisen in Eastern Europe also became the rule in Korea. North Korea set up a People's Republic led by Kim Il Sung, while South Korea became the Republic of Korea led by Syngman Rhee.

The United States substantially reduced its Korean military mission in 1949. Gen. MacArthur wanted troops in Japan, and military planners believed the South Korean armed forces could resist an attack. In early 1950 the Korean issue became embroiled in the partisan wranglings over the "loss" of China. Congressional Republicans held up a bill to aid Korea until the Truman administration agreed to supply weapons to the Nationalists in Taiwan. Dean Acheson also commented on the situation in Korea at an address to the National Press Club on January 13. He admitted that the United States had drawn a "strategic defense perimeter" in the Pacific that ran from Japan through Taiwan, through the Ryukyu Islands, to the Philippines. He did not include Korea because the Joint Chiefs of Staff denied its military value. The generals, led by MacArthur, believed that a major buildup of American troops on the mainland of Asia would divert resources from where they were needed—Japan. Acheson acknowledged, however, that an assault against Korea would be met with a United Nations response.

That attack came unexpectedly on June 25, 1950. At dawn about 110,000 North Korean soldiers crossed the thirty-eighth parallel and immediately overpowered the South Korean forces. Within forty-eight hours, Gen. MacArthur flew to the battlefield to assess the chances of the South Koreans. Truman returned to Washington from his home in Independence, Missouri, convened a meeting of his principal advisers, and decided that the United States would commit troops to fighting the North Koreans. On Tuesday, June 27, the United Nations Security Council, fortunate in having the Soviets absent as a protest against the refusal to seat or recognize legitimacy of the mainland Chinese government, adopted an American-sponsored resolution to send forces to Korea.

American newspapers widely applauded Truman's decision to fight in Korea. From the independent *New York Times,* to the Republican *New York Herald Tribune,* to the old isolationist *Chicago Tribune,* to the liberal *Christian Science Monitor* came editorial support. Republicans who had attacked the administration for neglecting Asia hopped on board. Sen. William Knowland of California thanked Truman for drawing a "line" in the Far East. He said that Truman "should have the overwhelming support of all Americans

The Korean War, 1950–1953

Gen. Douglas MacArthur strikes a pose on the Korean battlefield.
(*National Archives*)

regardless of their partisan affiliations." Republican senators Leverett Salton-stall of Massachusetts, H. Alexander Smith of New Jersey, Wayne Morse of Oregon, and Henry Cabot Lodge also praised Truman's decision to send troops. The war also made the defense expenditures proposed by NSC-68 politically feasible.

Widespread public fervor for the war lasted until December. In mid-September Gen. MacArthur led the American troops on an amphibious invasion of the Korean peninsula at Inchon near the capital of Seoul. Within days Americans and Koreans had recaptured Seoul and forced the North Koreans to retreat. MacArthur's forces did not stop, however, at the thirty-eighth parallel. They pressed north to eradicate communist rule throughout Korea.

In October Truman flew to Wake Island in the Pacific to consult with MacArthur about the future of the war. The general treated the president as his inferior while assuring him that there was no danger of Chinese intervention if the Americans went north. The president, buoyed by American military accomplishments, gave the general the go-ahead.

The U.S. and South Korean forces overcame North Korean resistance in October and November, and near Thanksgiving they had nearly reached the Chinese border. In Beijing the Communist Party panicked. What if the Americans crossed the Yalu River, the border between Korea and Manchuria? Zhou Enlai, the Chinese premier, sent word through the Indian government that China would not accept an American army on its borders. In Washington the administration ignored the warning.

Then, on November 27 a Chinese army of 400,000 men attacked the American forces in North Korea. A rout ensued, and by Christmas the Americans stood south of the thirty-eighth parallel again. The initial Chinese victory came so fast that Truman wondered whether the United States should use the atomic bomb on China. This offhand remark sent a frightened British prime minister, Clement Attlee, scurrying to Washington to warn against using the weapon. Truman hastily withdrew the threat.

In early 1951, with the American forces back in South Korea, one of the most dramatic confrontations between civil and military authority in American history occurred. Truman fired MacArthur. The general had been a thorn in the flesh for years. MacArthur spoke to reporters when told to keep quiet, tried for the Republican presidential nomination in 1948, and sent long-winded telegrams to veterans' groups outlining his own personal foreign policy for the Far East. The general provoked a "cold fury" in Truman, who concluded that "there were times when he was…I think out of his head and didn't know what he was doing." The president told MacArthur to clear all public statements with Washington, but the general continued to press for air force attacks on China. He wrote Joseph Martin, the House minority leader, supporting the use of Nationalist Chinese troops against the mainland and insisting, "We must win." Martin released the letter. Truman exploded, "If what MacArthur had proposed had happened…we would have wound up being at war not only with Red China but with Russia too and…it might have meant the destruction of a good part of the world." Knowing that there would be some public uproar but determined that MacArthur had to go, Truman called in Gen. Omar Bradley and told him, "The son of a bitch isn't going to resign on me. I want him fired." On April 3 the White House press secretary read a statement relieving MacArthur of his command.

At first Truman seemed to have miscalculated the warrior's grip on the public imagination. He returned to a hero's welcome in San Francisco, and millions crowded downtown Manhattan for the largest New York ticker-tape parade since Charles Lindbergh's triumphal processional in 1927. Republicans blamed Truman for betraying the troops. Sen. Joseph McCarthy, the junior Republican from Wisconsin, and Joseph Martin called for impeachment proceedings against the president and Dean Acheson. Other senators invited MacArthur to Washington to testify before the Foreign Relations and Armed Services committees about how the president had forbidden him to win. He addressed a joint session of Congress, leaving not a dry eye when he finished with "Old soldiers never die, they just fade away." The old army song, "Old Soldiers Never Die," played over the radio within two weeks. Truman did not attend the speech, "and there wasn't any law that I knew of that could make me listen to it" on radio or watch it on television. He summarized his reaction to it in a brisk two-word Anglo-Saxon expletive and later remembered that "I knew that once all the hullabaloo died down, people would see what he was."

Truman predicted a six-week uproar over MacArthur, and that was about how long the spotlight focused on the aging general. His testimony to congressional hearings dragged through May with newspapers devoting less and less space to it. He retired to an expensive suite at New York's Waldorf Astoria to await a call to the Republican presidential nomination in 1952. Much to his surprise, no one asked him to run.

THE ELECTION OF 1952

As MacArthur's star faded, other Republicans kept alive the issue of the Democrats' overseas failures. The opposition rallied around Sen. McCarthy's year-old charges, made before a Republican dinner in Wheeling, West Virginia, in February 1950, that he held in his hands a list of 57 or 205 (he kept changing the number) communists in the Department of State. His accusations had not made news until the Korean War began. Then he used his chairmanship of the permanent investigations unit of the Senate Committee on Government Operations to attack Foreign Service officers who had been in China, demanded to know "who lost China," and stressed that the Democrats had presided over "twenty years of treason." He threatened to make the 1952 election a referendum on his remarkable accusation that some Democrats and professional diplomats had served Moscow's interests.

Another Republican who had a chance at the 1952 nomination, Robert Taft, also denounced the administration's foreign policy. Taft criticized the way Truman conducted diplomacy as well as what he did. Writing in *A Foreign Policy for America* (1951), Taft charged that Truman's "moral position" in the Korean War was unassailable, "but he did not recognize the implications of what he had started." The senator resented that the president had not asked for a declaration of war in Korea. He thought that Truman had violated the Constitution and abrogated far too much power to the White House. These were the same criticisms that isolationists had leveled at President Roosevelt before the Second World War. Taft believed that the United States should defend itself and wage unrelenting war against the Soviet Union in the Far East. He opposed, however, the alliances Truman had developed. He expressed the traditional American view of foreign policy as something intermittent to be abandoned in peacetime. According to Taft, the policy of containment spelled a recipe for continuous American involvement in foreign wars.

Buffeted by these complaints, the Truman administration watched morosely as the public grew to detest the stalemated war in Korea. Talks opened with the North Koreans in mid-1951, but they seemed to go nowhere. Unresolved issues included the future of prisoners of war and whether Korea would be unified.

In early March 1952 Truman lost the New Hampshire primary election to Tennessee senator Estes Kefauver. He announced that he would not run again for president. The last year was a sad time for his administration. Acheson had to testify continuously before Congress, and he lost his cool reserve in the face of hostile questions from Republicans who smelled blood. At one point he took a "swing" at Nebraska's Kenneth Wherry. The secretary felt the sting of Sen. Nixon's assault on "Dean Acheson's cowardly college of Communist containment."

The Republicans, not wishing to be denied the White House again, turned their back on the conservative Taft and embraced the hero of World War II, Gen. Dwight David Eisenhower. Ike had finally become a Republican, and he wrested the nomination from the Ohio senator with the help of the eastern internationalist wing of the party. He defeated Taft, but he mended fences with his rival shortly thereafter by appointing a conservative New York lawyer, John Foster Dulles, as the principal Republican spokesman for foreign affairs. He also kept his lines open to the strident critics of Truman, selecting California's junior senator, Richard Nixon, as his vice presidential nominee. He also chose not to repudiate Sen. McCarthy for his denunciation of Gen. George C. Marshall as "an agent of the Communist conspiracy."

He clinched the election when he promised to "go to Korea" if elected. His Democratic opponent, Adlai Stevenson, governor of Illinois, could only lamely promise that if the voters chose him, he, too, would visit the fighting. A general made more sense on the battlefield. Public weariness with "K_1C_2" (Korea, communism, and corruption), a sense that the Democrats were tired and the Republicans deserved a chance, and happy memories of smiling Ike leading the invasion of Europe in 1944 gave the former general a landslide victory, with more than 55 percent of the vote. He called it a "mandate for change."

CHAPTER NINE

Eisenhower's New Look, 1953–1960

President Dwight Eisenhower's principal speechwriter, Emmet John Hughes, described the new president's advisers as "bound and united...in a few elemental convictions....All of them believed the national government to be languishing in a state of decay and disorder, calling for swift remedy. They thought the world menace of communism had been so idly abetted by American irresolution that some show of resolution—spiced with some specific, but not too costly, show of force—would change matters considerably." The president himself vowed to clean up "the mess in Washington" left by twenty years of rule by Democrats.

Eisenhower as president maintained the approach to foreign affairs of the Truman administration. The United States continued a policy of containment of communism and confrontation with the Soviet Union. The Cold War continued without the victory over communism many of Eisenhower's supporters hoped for in 1952, but neither did it worsen into a nuclear war between the United States and the Soviet Union. America stopped fighting in Korea but only postponed a full-scale war in Southeast Asia. Relations with China remained frozen. The ongoing tension in the Middle East proved impervious to American mediation. The rest of the world took on new importance. By the end of the decade, independence movements had swept the European powers out of Africa and Asia, catching the United States unaware. A revolution succeeded in Cuba, to Washington's consternation. Throughout it all Ike expanded the use of covert operations, toppling unfriendly governments in Iran in 1953 and in Guatemala in 1954 and propping up weak ones such as South Vietnam after 1956. After eight years in office Eisenhower

President Dwight D. Eisenhower (left) confers with Secretary of State John Foster Dulles. *(Dwight D. Eisenhower Presidential Library)*

left with a warning that a "military-industrial complex" had strained the American economy and distorted its diplomacy.

ASSEMBLING THE TEAM

Eisenhower selected as secretary of state John Foster Dulles, a New York lawyer with Sullivan and Cromwell and one-time Republican senator, a foremost Republican spokesman on foreign affairs, and a member of the right wing. Dulles, a dour and ambitious man, savored apocalyptic statements about the future. He claimed that Soviet Communists believed "that human beings are somewhat superior animals…and that the best kind of world is that world which is organized as a well-managed farm is organized, where certain animals are taken out to pasture, and they are fed and brought back and milked, and they are given a barn over their heads." Contemporary observers claimed that he dominated foreign policy. Sherman Adams, Ike's chief of staff, categorically asserted that "Eisenhower gave Dulles a free hand and wide responsibility in conducting foreign policy." Later observers disagreed. The president, serenely self-confident in his own grasp of foreign affairs, employed the secretary of state as a spokesman and lightning rod. Dulles protected Eisenhower from conservative Republicans who had vowed to "liberate" Eastern Europe from the grasp of the Soviet Union. The president remembered how Acheson had exhausted himself testifying before congressional committees. Ike gave Congress a secretary of state so militant in his rhetoric that it would be appeased.

Dulles went a long way toward satisfying Sen. Joseph McCarthy, the angriest of the congressional critics of the Truman administration's Cold War policies, who had called for a purge of "comsymps" (communist sympathizers) from the State Department. Throughout the first eighteen months of the new administration, McCarthy leaked word to favored newspaper reporters about sedition within the Foreign Service. Dulles, who did not credit lurid tales himself, offered no public protection to beleaguered Foreign Service officers. Instead, he helped the senator's cause with the appointment of Scott McCleod, an admirer of McCarthy, to the post of inspector general for personnel. McCleod conducted his own secret security investigations in which accused officials could not examine the evidence against them. The inspector general ordered the firing of three highly qualified professional diplomats who had served in China in the 1940s: John Paton Davies, John Stewart Service, and John Carter Vincent. Their crime was to have exposed the ineptitude and corruption of Jiang Jieshi's government and predicted its fall to the better-organized Communists. For years afterward fear gripped Foreign Service officers as they wondered what controversial statements in their dispatches later would be used against them. Rarely outspoken in the best of times, they became almost invisible in the 1950s.

For secretary of defense, Eisenhower selected Charles E. "Engine Charlie" Wilson, the president of the General Motors Corporation. During his confirmation hearing a senator asked Wilson if he foresaw any conflicts of interest between government service and his career as head of the world's largest industrial corporation. He replied, "What's good for the country is good for General Motors and vice versa." Wilson entered the government vowing to cut the budget and get "more bang for the buck." As Senator Taft argued during the 1952 campaign, the United States faced bankruptcy if it did not slash its taxes and budget and eliminate the deficit. Secretary of the Treasury George Humphrey agreed that the voters of 1952 had instructed the new government to reduce the budget, including defense expenditures. How could this be done while still following a tough stance against the Soviets?

THE NEW LOOK IN DEFENSE

The Eisenhower administration developed a "New Look" as a military posture to reconcile the competing claims of the military for more money and the Treasury Department for smaller deficits. The New Look required the Defense Department to reduce the size of conventional forces and rely upon nuclear weapons to terrify the Soviet Union into accommodation. The air force, with its heavy bombers, would win the race for more defense expenditures, while the army, especially the infantry branch, was cut from twenty to fourteen divisions, a slash of 500,000 men. Eisenhower, a former commander of the army, believed that he alone could make such severe cuts in the size of the defense establishment. No one could accuse an old war hero of being indifferent to the needs of the military.

John Foster Dulles gave his own interpretation of the New Look in a publicly aired speech before the Council on Foreign Relations in New York on January 12, 1954. He announced that in the future the United States would no longer be bound to use conventional arms to fight the Soviet Union. Instead, he proclaimed a policy of "massive retaliatory power" to halt aggression. Simply put, the United States now threatened to use the most awesome weapons in its arsenal against the cities of the Soviet Union in cases such as the war in Korea. Massive retaliation ignited a firestorm of protest. Editorialists in the *New York Times* and Walter Lippmann in the *New York Herald Tribune* accused Dulles of going to the "brink of war" to threaten the Soviets. But the president refused to join the debate. He told reporters that Dulles was "merely stating what, to my mind, is a fundamental truth." Later he informed a March 17, 1954, press conference that the beauty of the policy of massive retaliation was its purposeful vagueness. No one "would undertake to say exactly what we would do under all that variety of circumstances."

A NEW ASIA POLICY

The new administration had its first chance to demonstrate its differences from Truman in Asian affairs. Eisenhower moved quickly to end the deadlock in Korea with a combination of negotiations and threats to use the atomic bomb. Peace talks, begun in 1951, had been stalled over the issue of North Korean prisoners of war. The North Korean government wanted them repatriated, while the government of South Korea asserted that the prisoners wanted to remain in the south. In June South Korean president Syngman Rhee broke the deadlock himself by releasing the prisoners in the south. Some Americans also wanted to stay in North Korea, which caused great embarrassment to the United States. Still, with the end of the prisoners issue, an American negotiator, Adm. C. Turner Joy, worked out an armistice arrangement with his Chinese and North Korean counterparts. The final agreement, signed at the border at Panmunjon in early July 1953, called for a division of Korea at approximately the same lines that had existed in June 1950—the thirty-eighth parallel. The partition would not be permanent, however, as the two Koreas promised to open talks aimed at unification. U.S. forces under the auspices of the United Nations remained until an agreement could be worked out to send them home. A demilitarized zone five kilometers wide separated the two parts of Korea until reunification.

With the war settled, the first real test of the doctrine of massive retaliation came in Indochina in 1954. The civil war raging in Indochina since 1946 had attracted increasing American attention. In May 1950 the Truman administration had begun the process of paying for the French war effort. The same spring National Security Council (NSC) Memorandum 64 described Indochina as vital to the United States. Three years later, in August 1953, the NSC warned that "the loss of Indochina would be critical to the security of the United States." The council urged full support for the French war effort because "any negotiated settlement would mean the eventual loss to communism not only of Indochina but of the whole of Southeast Asia."

Encouraged by American backing, the French adopted the Navarre Plan, a creation of the new commander in Indochina, Gen. Henri Navarre. He proposed an army of 550,000 French and Vietnamese troops to launch an offensive against the Vietminh. The United States would pay $385 million for the operation. Secretary of State Dulles assured a press conference that the Navarre Plan would "break the back of organized Communist aggression" by the end of the 1955 fighting campaign. A month later, in January 1954, Navarre forced a showdown with the Vietminh by trying to hold Dienbienphu, a Vietnamese outpost near Vietnam's borders with China and Laos. Dienbienphu, a major crossroads in a deep valley, was not a natural fortress. Some 12,000 French troops were surrounded by the Vietminh and several divisions of Chinese Communist troops who had been relieved by the end of the Korean War. In March the French government sent the chief of staff, Gen. Paul Ely, to Washington to ask for more aid. His American counterpart, Adm. Arthur Radford, was more forthcoming than Ely could have dreamed. The admiral offered an American air raid against the Vietminh attackers. Radford proposed a plan, code-named VULTURE, in which sixty American bombers based in the Philippines aided by 150 carrier-based fighters would attack the Communists. This massive air raid, possibly including tactical nuclear weapons, would break the siege and rescue the French from certain defeat. Vice President Richard Nixon enthusiastically backed the suggestion of possible use of atomic weapons to lift the siege.

Operation VULTURE never left the ground. President Eisenhower scrapped it in April. He believed that the future of Indochina was highly important for the United States. He called Vietnam either a "domino," the fall of which would set in motion a chain reaction, or a "cork in the bottle" containing communism. But he also had little faith in the French. He decided that they had badly mishandled the affairs of Indochina by clinging to their imperial role. Moreover, Eisenhower would not act without support from the British and Congress. British prime minister Winston Churchill refused to give his country's assent to an international force to rescue the French, and congressional leaders in the United States proved unwilling to engage in another Asian land war. Senate minority leader Democrat Lyndon Johnson of Texas railed against "sending American GI's into the mud and muck of Indochina on a bloodletting spree." Massachusetts senator John F. Kennedy proclaimed that an American war in Indochina would be "dangerous, futile and self-destructive."

On May 8 the French garrison at Dienbienphu surrendered to the Vietminh forces under Gen. Nguyen Giap. A new French socialist government under Prime Minister Pierre Mendès-France came to power in June vowing to end the war in one month. France agreed to open negotiations with the Vietminh and the British, Soviets, and Chinese at Geneva to end the war. American policy was ambiguous in late May. Eisenhower briefly approved a Joint Chiefs of Staff plan for "employing atomic weapons, whenever advantageous...against those military targets in China" in case the Chinese entered the war. Eisenhower was careful, however, to link his acceptance of the plan to European support. He told Robert Cutler, his national security adviser, that "unilateral action by the United States in a case of this kind would destroy us.... If we intervened alone in this case we would be expected to intervene alone in other parts of the world."

Instead of dropping bombs, the United States reluctantly allowed the Geneva conference to proceed with Britain and the Soviet Union acting as cosponsors. The Soviets and the Chinese applied pressure to the Vietminh to accept a division of Vietnam at the seventeenth parallel, even though the Communist forces controlled two-thirds of the country. The Chinese and Soviets reasoned that it was only a matter of time before Ho Chi Minh's forces completed their unification of the country. Faced with a lack of support from his two principal allies, Ho agreed to withdraw. He expected elections to be held within two years, and these polls would give his forces complete control of the entire country. The United States never signed these accords. Dulles only announced that the United States would support "free elections supervised by the United Nations."

Shortly thereafter the United States began a program of direct aid to the government of South Vietnam. In late September and early October 1954, Dulles said that American aid would go directly to the government of South Vietnam and not through the French. America would not permit the French to maintain their "protected preferential market," and Japan could not now sell directly to South Vietnam. In November an American military mission headed by Gen. J. Lawton Collins came to Saigon to help train the South Vietnamese army. That fall the United States also brought Ngo Dinh Diem, exiled at the Maryknoll mission's headquarters in Ossining, New York, to Saigon to take over the government of South Vietnam over the strenuous objections of the French.

The next summer the French evacuated South Vietnam, and President Diem announced that he would not hold the elections called for in the Geneva accord. The United States supported this decision, arguing that Diem's government had not signed the Geneva agreement. More to the point, Dulles thought that Diem would have a difficult time defeating Ho in any election. Subsequently, the United States continued to arm and supply the government of South Vietnam.

Americans were everywhere in South Vietnam from 1956 to 1960. Military men helped create the Army of the Republic of South Vietnam (ARVN). Col. Edward Lansdale arrived in Saigon to apply lessons learned in the Philippines war against communists. He soon recruited an army of secret agents to harass, arrest, and kill revolutionaries. The U.S. embassy in Saigon housed university and government law enforcement experts who instructed local policemen in controlling crowds, checking passports, and interrogating suspicious characters. Economic assistance officers scurried into the countryside to tell bewildered villagers how to increase crop yields, pay their landlords, and open their ears for antigovernment remarks.

Immediately after the Geneva agreements temporarily split Indochina, Eisenhower faced a flare-up of fighting between the Communist and Nationalist Chinese. On the morning of September 3, 1954, Communist artillery on the mainland began shelling Nationalist positions on the offshore island of Quemoy. Two American soldiers died in the assault, and the Eisenhower administration found itself in the midst of a dilemma.

During the campaign of 1952, Republicans had complained that the Truman administration had hamstrung Jiang Jieshi in his campaign to recapture control of China. They resented the Democrats' sending the Seventh Fleet to the Formosa Strait for the purpose of preventing Jiang from invading China while the Korean War went on. Vowing to "unleash Jiang Jieshi," the Eisenhower administration had removed the fleet in 1953. In August 1954 Chinese Communist foreign minister Zhou Enlai renewed the pledge to liberate Taiwan from the Nationalists. Eisenhower responded by remarking that "any invasion of Taiwan would have to run over the Seventh Fleet," which now returned to protect the Nationalists. But the islands of Quemoy and Matsu, a few miles off the coast of the mainland and directly opposite its port city of Amoy, were a different matter. They had always been a part of mainland China, and American moves to resist the Communists there might seem to be a direct assault on the mainland.

Eisenhower resisted calls from the Joint Chiefs of Staff to bomb the mainland. He sent Dulles to Taiwan to restrain Jiang. The secretary of state worked out a defense treaty with the Nationalists under which the United States pledged to defend Taiwan. In return, the Nationalists agreed not to use force against the mainland without first consulting the United States. By signing a defense treaty with the Nationalists, Eisenhower wrecked what chances remained for a rapprochement with the Communists. At the same time, the defense pact was Ike's payment to the right wing of the Republican Party, which had demanded that the administration blockade the entire coast of China.

In mid-January 1955 the crisis in the Formosa Strait reached a new height when the Communists attacked the Tachen Islands, about 200 miles northwest of Taiwan. Ike's military advisers told him that the Tachens were not vital to the security of Taiwan. Consequently, he helped the Nationalists evacuate them while asking Congress for a joint resolution authorizing the use of force to protect the island of Taiwan and the nearby Pescadores chain. Congress passed a resolution at the end of January, leaving vague whether the United States had made a commitment to defend the offshore islands of Quemoy and Matsu as well as Taiwan itself.

A little more than a month later, Secretary of State Dulles returned from a trip to Asia to announce that the situation in the Formosa Strait was worse than he had realized. He told a Washington news conference on March 10 that he feared a Communist attack on Quemoy and Matsu as a prelude to an invasion of Taiwan. The secretary then touched off a major war scare by remarking, "If we defend Quemoy and Matsu we'll have to use atomic weapons." Two days later, on March 12, Dulles informed reporters of "clean" nuclear weapons "of precision which can utterly destroy military targets without endangering unrelated civilian centers." His aides checked with the Pentagon and found that such weapons did not exist and that the smallest nuclear attack on China would cost a minimum of 12 million civilian lives. Eisenhower heightened the war tension with a remark to the press on March 15. He said that he saw "no reason why [tactical nuclear weapons] should not be used exactly as you would use a bullet or anything else." Over the next week hawks rallied to the president. Gen. James Van Fleet, the former commander of the Eighth Army in Korea, advocated sending more American troops to Quemoy and Matsu. If the Communists continued their shelling, the Americans should "shoot back with atomic weapons." Doves were less certain. Majority leader Lyndon Johnson feared an "irresponsible adventure." Former Democratic presidential candidate Adlai Stevenson infuriated Eisenhower when he accused him of "risking a third world war for the defense of these little islands."

With war fever running high, Eisenhower had to backtrack. His press secretary, James Hagerty, advised him to duck questions about the nuclear warning to China at his March 23 press conference. "Don't worry, Jim,...I'll just confuse them." The president then told a reporter who asked about the use of atomic bombs to defend Quemoy that he could not make any predictions. "Every war is going to astonish you in the way it occurred, and in the way it is carried out." Eisenhower thereby managed to warn the Chinese without at the same time saying what he would do. Ike's critics accused him of bringing the country to the brink of war and allowing his secretary of state to get out of hand.

COVERT OPERATIONS: IRAN AND GUATEMALA

Eisenhower and Dulles's threat to use atomic weapons in Asia was part of a careful strategy of public diplomacy. At the same time, the United States moved secretly to pursue its goals in international affairs. The Central Intelligence Agency conducted these operations in Iran and in Guatemala.

The American involvement with Iran represented one aspect of American petroleum policy in the Middle East. Since the 1940s American petroleum companies had become active in the Persian Gulf, a region traditionally the preserve of British, French, and Dutch corporations. During the Truman administration the government developed a deliberate policy of noninterference in the international activities of the oil companies. In 1950 the State Department came up with a "golden gimmick" to lessen the tax burden on the four American companies—Standard of California, Texaco, Mobil, and Esso (later Exxon)—that made up Aramco (Arabian American Oil Company). Under Acheson's plan Aramco could deduct the amount of royalty it paid to the Saudi Arabian government from its U.S. income taxes. The State Department then informed Saudi Arabia that the $50 million it received from the oil companies really would have been foreign aid from the United States. In this way the government of the United States could offer aid to Saudi Arabia without annoying supporters of Israel who would not like to see the United States underwrite the Saudi monarchy.

The Eisenhower administration inherited this free rein for the oil companies. It saw the policy tested first in Iran in 1953. Two years earlier Dr. Mohammed Mossadeq had become Iran's prime minister. An enthusiastic opponent of foreign domination of Iran's wealth, Mossadeq had nationalized the holdings of the Anglo-Iranian oil company. The international oil companies had responded with a boycott of Iranian oil. American firms active in the Persian Gulf and Saudi Arabia happily cooperated with the boycott, for it made their own holdings in other countries more valuable. Faced with the united hostility of the international oil companies, the Iranian government considered turning to the Soviet Union. On May 28 the prime minister cabled

Eisenhower that the boycott of the international oil companies might force him to turn to the Soviet Union for aid. Eisenhower waited until July to reply. When he did he refused to provide any aid, and he warned Iran that it should undertake a "reasonable settlement" with the British.

As a nationalist, Mossadeq distrusted all outside powers' attempts to control Iran's source of wealth, oil, and its territory. Soviet troops had occupied his country from 1942 to 1946, when they had withdrawn under threats from the United States. Washington had looked on sourly as London and Moscow agreed in 1942 jointly to control Iran's foreign policy until the war ended. The arrangement seemed to revive the old Anglo-Russian condominium in the Persian Gulf, and American oilmen resented a British grab of Iran's vast petroleum reserves. As the Cold War spread in 1946, the United States used its majority in the United Nations to force Soviet troops to return home from Iran. While Tehran feared their eventual return, the grip of foreign oil companies seemed a more pressing problem.

Throughout these maneuvers Shah Mohammed Reza Pahlevi, the official head of state, remained quiet. Installed by the British in 1941, he replaced his father, Reza Pahlevi, who had dallied with the Nazis in hopes of evicting the British. During the war Britain and the Soviet Union curbed the monarch's powers. Once foreign troops left, he agreed to a constitutional monarchy. The hostility of Prime Minister Mossadeq to Britain and his adoption of Soviet rhetoric, however, offered the shah his chance to gain absolute power. His personal interests coincided temporarily with those of American oil executives and diplomats who wanted for reasons of their own to take over Britain's place in the confrontation with the Soviets in the Persian Gulf.

Secretly, Eisenhower moved to overthrow the government of Iran. He authorized the CIA to carry out a coup against the government and restore the power of the shah. Kermit Roosevelt, grandson of President Theodore Roosevelt and a veteran of the World War II spy agency the OSS, became the organizer of the coup on the scene. Arriving in Tehran in early August, he found Gen. Fazollah Zahedi eager to lead the operation with the approval of the shah. Roosevelt then recruited a mob made up of circus performers— weight lifters and trapeze artists—and army and police NCOs dressed in civilian clothes who took to the streets in antigovernment demonstrations. An enraged prime minister, seeing the hand of a figurehead shah behind the scenes, moved to arrest the monarch, who fled to Rome. Then Roosevelt conducted a "James Bond–type" operation in which the army staged an assault on the parliament, arrested the prime minister, and installed Zahedi in his place. In Washington Eisenhower publicly congratulated Zahedi and the shah on September 5 and announced that the United States would offer $45 million to the new government. He secretly awarded the National Security Medal to Kermit Roosevelt.

Among the great winners in the American-sponsored coup were U.S. oil companies. Eisenhower chose Herbert Hoover, Jr., as the negotiator between Tehran and the British oil companies. Hoover had earlier advised Iran on its dealings with the British oil companies, and he knew that the shah would lose support of his subjects if he simply restored the old contracts. Furthermore, as an old American oil man, Hoover saw an opportunity for American firms in the oil fields. At first the American firms demurred. Their own holdings in the Persian Gulf and Saudi Arabia had done well when the major companies had refused to handle Iranian crude oil. Nonetheless, Hoover asked them to "serve the national interest" and move into Iran. They agreed if the American government promised to exempt them from antitrust actions for acting together in Iran. The president himself told Attorney General Herbert Brownell that "the enforcement of the anti-trust laws of the United States against the Western oil companies operating in the Near East may be deemed secondary to the national security interest."

Hoover then assembled a new consortium of Western companies to distribute Iranian oil. The negotiations took a year; the Iranian Parliament ratified the final terms in October 1954. Under the agreement the Iranian National Oil Company retained control of the oilfields and refineries, while the consortium of eight Western companies purchased the oil and agreed to distribute it. Anglo-Iranian Oil, the old British company, received a 40 percent share of the new consortium; the five American companies also got 40 percent, and the remaining 20 percent was divided between a Dutch and a French company. Faced with a glut of oil from the Middle East, the Western firms secretly agreed to limit the amount of oil they would buy from Iran. The Eisenhower administration's oil policy in the Iranian crisis enhanced the power of American firms. As of 1954 the United States stood poised to supplant the British as the major Western power active in the Middle East.

The Eisenhower administration used a similar covert technique to overthrow the government of the Central American country of Guatemala in 1954. That nation experienced a nationalist-liberal revolution in 1944. The new administration, made up of middle-class army officers and urban intellectuals, wanted an end to the large plantations that dominated the country's agriculture. They also called for a more democratic government with regular elections. These were duly held, and Juan José Arevalo took office as the first freely elected presidenct since 1821. Arevalo began a program of political, labor, and land reforms. Calling his policy "spiritual socialism," he pushed a new constitution guaranteeing political rights and laws allowing agricultural laborers to form unions and strike. Limited by the constitution to a term of six years, Arevalo supported Jacobo Arbenz Guzmán, his defense minister, in the 1950 election. One of Arbenz's conservative opponents, Francisco Javier Araña, met an assassin's bullet in July 1949, leaving only Miguel Ydígoras

Fuentes, a fierce reactionary, as a conservative candidate. Arbenz won an overwhelming victory in 1950, and his government enacted an agrarian reform law that expropriated idle land and gave it to the poorest of the peasants.

The Eisenhower administration decided to rid Guatemala of Arbenz shortly after his government took over 400,000 acres of unused land owned by the Boston-based United Fruit Company (UFCO). La Fruitera, as it was called in Latin America, profited handsomely from concessions granted earlier by conservative governments. It paid few taxes, had protection from competition, charged what it wanted for its port facilities, sent all of its profits back home, and was permitted to expand its operations at will. UFCO paid an intermittent wage of $1.36 a day for seasonal work. Laborers purchased company-supplied medical care, bought necessities at a company store, and rented cramped but clean living quarters from their employer. As they walked to the outhouses, they could peer over the high wire fence separating them from the opulent single-family homes, swimming pools, and golf courses of their North American bosses.

State Department officials joined publicity agents for United Fruit in asserting that Arbenz was a communist and an agent of the Kremlin. The American ambassador to Guatemala, John Peurifoy, told a House committee, "I spent six hours with him one evening, and he talked like a Communist, and if he is not one, Mr. Chairman, he will do until one comes along." The United Fruit Company launched a campaign to channel this fear of communism into sympathy for its cause. It sponsored junkets to Guatemala for reporters, editors, and publishers. Well aware that the American government probably would not intervene by force solely to stop expropriation, United Fruit's public relations counsel, Edward Bernays, emphasized the supposed international communist conspiracy. On May 3, 1954, the *New York Times* editorialized that the "constant harassment here [in Guatemala] to which the company [United Fruit] now is being subjected is largely a Communist tactic."

In the summer of 1953, Eisenhower authorized the CIA to develop a plan to overthrow the Arbenz government. Code-named PBSUCCESS, the operation established a field headquarters at Opa Locka, Florida, near Miami. The project cost between $5 million and $7 million, which was used to pay about 100 Americans and an equal number of mercenaries recruited from Guatemala and neighboring Central American nations. These men received military training, while other CIA operatives cast about for a suitable Guatemalan figurehead for the invasion. The CIA's experts rejected defeated presidential candidate Ydígoras Fuentes as too reactionary and finally settled on forty-year-old Carlos Enrique Castillo Armas, a military man who had trained at the U.S. Army School at Fort Leavenworth, Kansas. The CIA provided Castillo Armas with money, a radio station in neighboring Nicaragua, and an "army" made up of the mercenaries trained in Florida.

Certain that the United States was conspiring with the dictator of Nicaragua, Anastasio Somoza, to overthrow him, Arbenz sought military aid from communist countries. The Kremlin, sensing an opportunity to embarrass the Americans in their own hemisphere, authorized the Skoda works in Czechoslovakia to send weapons to Guatemala. The Swedish freighter *Alfhem,* carrying 1,900 tons of small arms and light artillery, reached Puerto Barritos, Guatemala, on May 15. The CIA knew the shipment was on the way, and its arrival determined the date of Castillo Armas's uprising. The arms shipment drew denunciations from officials in Washington. Senate Foreign Relations Committee chairman Alexander Wiley (R., Wis.) insisted that it represented "part of the master plan of world communism," and President Eisenhower snapped that 1,900 tons went beyond "any legitimate, normal requirements of the Guatemalan armed forces." CIA director Allen Dulles assured the National Security Council that the arms shipment demonstrated Soviet contempt for the Monroe Doctrine and an intention to establish a military base in the Western Hemisphere.

On June 18, 1954, Castillo Armas's "army" of 1,950 men crossed the Honduran border into Guatemala. They settled down in a religious shrine six miles from the border and confidently awaited the collapse of Arbenz. The Guatemalan president believed the propaganda broadcasts of the Voice of Liberation radio stations. His nerves cracked as he envisioned Castillo Armas leading an effective fighting force backed by U.S. troops. The CIA had never intended to commit American forces, predicting that Arbenz would not fight. The clandestine radio stations broadcast an appeal by a liquor-laden defector from the Guatemalan air force for his fellow pilots to follow his lead and join Castillo Armas's forces. Faced with the imminent defection of his army, Arbenz considered arming the peasantry. The prospect of an armed popular militia gave the final push to the army officers, who saw their traditional privileges eliminated. The chiefs of the armed forces deserted Arbenz and demanded his resignation. On June 27 the president complied, fled the country, and left power to Castillo Armas. Guatemala slipped again into dictatorship. The lands of the United Fruit Company were restored. In Washington the astonishing ease of the CIA's victory in Guatemala boosted the reputation of the agency and laid the groundwork for a later clandestine operation against Cuba in April 1961.

RELATIONS WITH THE SOVIET UNION

While the Cold War became a global conflict during the Eisenhower administration, relations with the Soviet Union remained the central issue. On March 5, 1953, barely six weeks after Ike took office, Josef Stalin died. His replacement as premier, Georgi Malenkov, departed from Stalin's foreign policy by seeking a relaxation of tension with the United States. Locked in a power struggle with the secretary of the Communist Party, Nikita Khrushchev, Malenkov wished to concentrate on internal political problems. He hoped that a bid to end the Cold War would encourage the Western European allies to reduce their reliance upon the United States. In April he called for the opening of talks between East and West on reducing forces in Europe.

The initial response to Malenkov's peace initiative was cool. No one in the State Department wanted to incur the wrath of Sen. McCarthy. Secretary of State Dulles, clinging to a belief in an "irreconcilable conflict" between "Godless communism" and the West, was loath to respond favorably to Malenkov's offer. Eisenhower offered the formal answer to the Soviet premier's new tactics on April 16 when he admitted that détente could come if the Soviets ended communist revolts in Malaya and Indochina, allowed "a free and united Germany with a government based on free and secret elections," "free choice" of governments in Eastern Europe, and a treaty restoring Austrian independence. Dulles testified before the Senate Foreign Relations Committee the next day. The *New York Times* headlined his remarks: "DULLES BIDS SOVIETS COOPERATE OR FACE VAST WEST ARMING."

This belligerent approach drew fire from a surprising source, the old anticommunist and opponent of appeasement Winston Churchill, who on May 11 called for a "summit conference" for world leaders to solve problems. A call from Churchill, the most respected leader in the Western alliance, unsettled officials in Washington. Senate majority leader William Knowland assumed that Churchill favored a "Far Eastern Munich." Eisenhower himself had explained why the official reaction was cool. In words that bewildered reporters, he muttered, "The world happened to be round and it had no end and he didn't see how you could discuss the problems, the great basic problems of today, which were so largely philosophical in character, without thinking in global terms." Whatever the president had in mind, the result was that no meeting with the Soviet leaders took place before 1955.

In the meantime, the arms race between the atomic powers became more heated. The United States pressed forward with the development of the "superweapon," the thermonuclear hydrogen bomb, despite the misgivings of J. Robert Oppenheimer, the scientist who had headed the research project that created the atomic bomb. Oppenheimer lost his security clearance for his refusal to be "enthusiastic" about the hydrogen bomb, a charge that provoked *Washington Post* cartoonist Herbert Block to produce a drawing of a workman entering a scientist's office and replacing the sign urging "Think" with one demanding "Enthuse." On March 1, 1954, the Atomic Energy Commission detonated an H-bomb at Bikini Atoll in the South Pacific. Twenty-three

H-bomb

Japanese fishermen aboard the *Lucky Dragon* had the bad luck to be trolling about eighty miles from the blast. They all suffered radiation poisoning, and one of them died shortly thereafter. Their plight awakened the world to the dangers of radioactive fallout. Atomic Energy Commission chairman Lewis Strauss compounded the problem by saying that fallout was not much of a problem since most of it fell in the direct vicinity of a blast. And how big might that blast be? reporters asked. "An H-bomb can be made as large enough to take out a city...to destroy a city."

By the fall of 1954, the Soviets had exploded their own H-bomb, eliminating the hopes of Americans to enjoy a few more years of nuclear superiority. The Eisenhower administration now responded to the growing international pressure for a summit conference with the Soviet leaders. The Russians announced in April that they were willing to sign a peace treaty for Austria, something they had resisted since 1945. The former wartime allies quickly signed an agreement creating a neutral Austria in May. Later that month the Soviet delegate to the UN Disarmament Conference presented a new plan to end the arms race. The Soviet proposal moved closer to Western plans for reduction of conventional forces as well as nuclear arms. The ground was now prepared for a summit conference of the heads of government of the Western alliance and the Soviet Union.

Eisenhower met with the new Soviet leaders, Prime Minister Nikolai Bulganin, who had replaced Malenkov, and Party Secretary Nikita Khrushchev, the third week of July 1955 in Geneva, Switzerland. The president came equipped with a plan for mutual aerial inspection of Western and Soviet nuclear facilities. This "Open Skies" proposal emerged from a committee of arms experts headed by presidential assistant Nelson Rockefeller. Secretary of State Dulles objected to the plan since it seemed to depart from his hard line. The president told Dulles he would not announce Open Skies before the conference, but he annoyed the secretary of state by raising the hopes of the public before his departure for Geneva. In a nationally televised speech before he left, Eisenhower predicted that the summit conference would "change the spirit which has characterized the intergovernmental relationship of the world during the past ten years."

Relations were cool between the Soviet Union and the United States at the opening of the conference. Bulganin and Khrushchev refused to budge on the issue of the reunification of Germany. On the fourth day of the conference, Eisenhower showed the Open Skies proposal to British prime minister Anthony Eden, who immediately gave his approval. He then presented it theatrically to the entire assembly. Taking off his glasses and speaking directly to the Soviet leaders, he proposed regular and frequent aerial inspections of American military facilities in return for the same privilege from the Soviets. A thunderstorm dramatically punctuated the president's

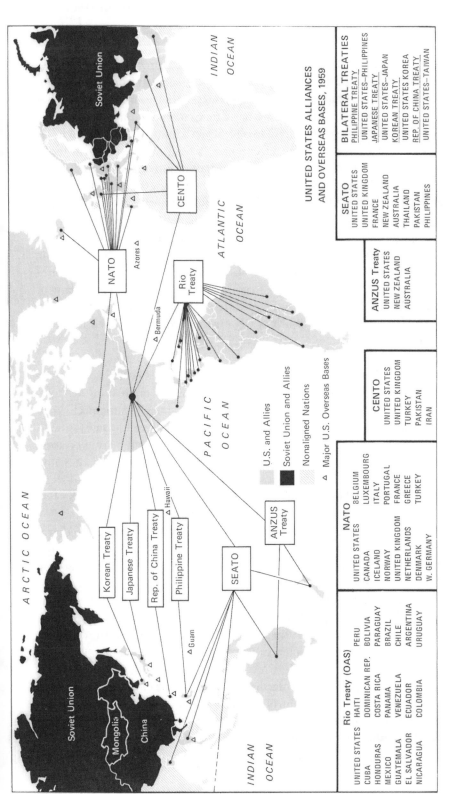

U.S. alliances and overseas bases, 1959

performance; as soon as he finished speaking, lightning flashed, and the lights went out in the room.

The British and the French predictably voiced approval of the American plan. The Soviets, finding themselves upstaged, seemed nonplussed. They made no public response to Open Skies, but that evening Khrushchev drew Eisenhower aside at a cocktail party that ended the day's session. The translator, American ambassador to the Soviet Union Charles Bohlen, recalled the Soviet leader asking Eisenhower "whom was he trying to fool?" Khrushchev called Open Skies a "very transparent espionage device." Eisenhower seemed to agree since the Russians already knew the locations of most American military facilities. He told Nelson Rockefeller that "mutual agreements for such overflights would undoubtedly benefit us more than the Russians, because we know very little about their installations." Ten years later Eisenhower told an interviewer who asked about Open Skies, "We knew the Soviets wouldn't accept it. We were sure of that." The Geneva conference ended with no agreements on the major issues of the future of Germany or disarmament. East and West did conclude a cultural exchange agreement, and newspapers wrote of a "spirit of Geneva" that reduced the tensions over the arms race.

The new spirit survived barely a year after the conference. In February 1956 Khrushchev, having banished Bulganin, consolidated his hold on the party apparatus with a speech before the Twentieth Congress of the Communist Party denouncing the crimes of Josef Stalin. Despite attempts to keep the address secret, news leaked to Eastern Europe, where reformers hoped that the Soviets would permit a relaxation of repression. In June riots erupted in Poland, where opponents of the regime demanded the ouster of Stalinists. A reformer, Wladislaw Gomulka, took power pledging an end to some of the excesses of the secret police. In the fall Khrushchev thought he had gone too far, and he told Gomulka to rein in the reforms. Instead, the Polish leader threatened to call out the Polish public. Khrushchev backed down, a retreat that encouraged anti-Communists in Hungary. Students took to the streets in Budapest on October 23, demanding the replacement of long-time Stalinist Erno Gëro with Imre Nagy. When the secret police sought to crush the demonstrations, workers struck. The Soviets sought to stem the tide by agreeing to the exchange of Nagy for Gëro, but the crowd no longer could be mollified. They demanded the removal of Soviet troops, which was done on October 28. Three days later, in the midst of an Anglo-French-Israeli attack on Egypt, the Soviet leaders reversed themselves. The new Hungarian government had withdrawn from the Warsaw Pact on October 29; that was too grave a threat to Soviet control over its Eastern European empire. As the Anglo-French army moved toward the Suez Canal on November 4–5, Russian tanks crushed the Hungarian uprising.

The United States did not help the Hungarians throw out Soviet rule, although American statements encouraged the revolutionaries to try. Republicans had called for the liberation of Eastern Europe during the election campaign of 1952. Eisenhower marked "captive nations week" each year with reminders of the brutality of communist rule in Eastern Europe. American Radio Free Europe headquartered in Munich and funded by the U.S. government supported the uprising. At the height of the crisis, on November 3, John Foster Dulles, who had gone to the "brink of war" with the Soviets, underwent emergency surgery on the stomach cancer that eventually killed him in 1959.

All of this activity, or handwringing, took place in the midst of the presidential election of 1956. Eisenhower had delayed announcing his candidacy until early 1956. He had suffered a heart attack in mid-1955, and Democrats were encouraged that the genial, grandfatherly Ike would step aside for the sharp-tongued and not especially popular Richard M. Nixon. The prospect of a Nixon bid for the White House alarmed Republican regulars who thought that Ike was the only choice to continue Republican rule. For their part, the Democrats again chose Adlai Stevenson. Foreign policy played a small but important part in the campaign of 1956. Ike ran on his record of ending the war in Korea and the nascent spirit of Geneva. Stevenson opposed him from both the left and the right. On the more liberal side the Democratic candidate called for disarmament, an end to the testing of atomic weapons, and study of the possible end to the draft. With the crisis in the Middle East and Hungary at full boil, Stevenson accurately pointed out that the Eisenhower administration had been slow to recognize "a vast new upheaval in the balance of world power." At the same time Stevenson attacked from more nationalist assumptions, reviving old Cold War rhetoric. He faulted Ike for letting half of Indochina "become a new Communist satellite," and he contrasted Harry Truman's toughness with the Soviets with Ike's neglect of "great opportunities to exploit weaknesses in the Communist ranks and advance the cause of peace." Whatever Stevenson said was to little avail. A popular president running against an opponent with little difference to offer except style, he defeated Stevenson with 57 percent of the vote.

SUEZ AND LEBANON

Another of America's gloomy encounters with revolutionary nationalism occurred in the Suez crisis of 1956. Four years earlier the corrupt and inept Egyptian monarchy of King Farouk had been toppled in an army coup led by Col. Gamal Nasser. The rebels had been angry and humiliated at the defeat inflicted on the Arabs by the Israelis in 1948. Israeli military superiority over Egypt continued after the coup as the Israelis launched an attack across the border into the Gaza Strip in 1955. Nasser wanted arms to rebuild his defenses. The Western nations proved unwilling to supply them, so in September 1955 Egypt concluded an agreement with Czechoslovakia to supply tanks and artillery.

At this point Dulles became interested in bidding for Nasser's friendship with American financial support for the planned Aswan Dam. This project would stop the waters of the lower Nile, providing electric power for all of Egypt, open new land for cultivation, and demonstrate to the world that Egypt had entered the world of electric modernity. In December the United States and Great Britain agreed in principle to help finance the Aswan project. In February 1956 Nasser reached an agreement with Eugene Black, the president of the World Bank, for funds from America, Britain, and the bank. Nasser then formally requested $100 million in aid from the United States. He heard nothing for the next five months.

In the meantime Dulles changed his attitude toward Nasser. The Czech arms deal was followed in April by a military alliance with Saudi Arabia, Syria, and Yemen, the obvious target of which was Israel. In May Nasser dropped his diplomatic relations with Jiang Jieshi and recognized the government in Beijing. An outraged China lobby allied with southern congressmen from cotton-producing states who feared the Aswan Dam would depress cotton prices to block the American support for the project. Dulles reasoned that he could teach Nasser a lesson if he withdrew American support for the Aswan Dam. Ignoring a warning from Eugene Black that "all hell might break loose" if he reneged on his promise, Dulles on July 19 bluntly declared that the United States would not send money to Egypt for the project.

One week later Nasser struck back by nationalizing the British-owned Universal Suez Canal Company. The Egyptian leader promised to keep the canal open to all former users of the waterway, but the British and French did not believe him. Nearly all of Europe's oil came through the canal, and the Europeans feared that an intense nationalist such as Nasser might interrupt this flow. Dulles tried to reduce tensions between the Europeans and Egyptians with a solution that pleased neither side. He proposed a users' association to manage the canal. Nasser did not want to share power with the foreigners, and the Europeans distrusted any Egyptian control. At the end of July the British foreign minister let Dulles know that the Europeans would move militarily against Egypt if the crisis were not resolved quickly.

By October Egypt still operated the canal on its own, and the British and the French secretly adopted a plan to go to war. They coordinated their strategy with the government of Israel, which believed that the European anger at Nasser was the perfect cover by which they could rid themselves of the irritating foe. In mid-October Israeli prime minister David Ben-Gurion flew secretly to an airfield outside of Paris where he reached an agreement with the British and French governments for a joint assault on Egypt. The Israeli army crossed the frontier into the Sinai Desert on October 29, and the next day the British and French announced that they would join the war "to protect the Suez Canal," already closed by sunken vessels. French and British paratroopers landed in the zone on November 1 and demanded that the Egyptian and Israeli forces withdraw to a zone five miles on either side of the waterway.

The Anglo-French statement of protection for free passage through Suez fooled no one. Opposition parties in France and Britain raised a howl, and the British Parliament erupted in shouts. The assault failed in its underlying purpose of evicting Nasser. It could not keep the ships moving, and the Western alliance underwent its greatest strain. In Washington Dulles, who heartily disliked British prime minister Eden, thought the British had purposely misled him. The United States joined with the Soviet Union in condemning the Western powers and Israel at the United Nations, where the General Assembly voted a resolution demanding a cease-fire. This alignment between the Americans and the Soviets came at an especially embarrassing juncture, for Soviet tanks were at that moment crushing the counterrevolution in the streets of Budapest.

With the sinking of ships in Suez, Europe lost access to Middle Eastern oil. Dulles thereupon pressed Latin American nations not to send petroleum to Britain and France as long as they remained in Egypt. In December the Europeans caved in to American pressure and announced their withdrawal from Egypt. American-European relations were badly shaken, and the French especially rethought their policy toward Arab nationalism. Instead of trying to overcome nationalists like Nasser, the French moved over the next few years to make an accommodation with them.

So did the Americans. In January 1957 Eisenhower asked Congress for a resolution endorsing the president's use of force in the Middle East "to block Communist aggression." This so-called Eisenhower Doctrine required Congress to yield its traditional war-making power to the president, and friends of Israel in the Senate complained that the president sacrificed support for the Jewish state by posing as the protector of anticommunist Arab nations. Still, Ike, like Truman before him, chose to use the fear of the Soviet Union to gain his foreign policy objectives; the Eisenhower Doctrine sailed through the Democratic-controlled House and Senate in March. That same month the administration also terrified Israel into withdrawing fully from the Sinai Desert and Gaza Strip captured from Egypt the previous November. In return for a pledge of a UN buffer force in the Sinai and UN control over Sharm el Sheik, the point controlling the access to Israel's Red Sea port of Eilat, Israel agreed to leave the Sinai. Lurking behind the UN proposals was an American threat to embargo the millions of dollars American Jews sent in aid to Israel.

The Eisenhower Doctrine received its major test in mid-1958. In the spring Nasser formed a United Arab Republic (UAR) of Egypt, Syria and Yemen. Two months later, on July 14, a nationalist coup occurred in Iraq, where Gen. Abdel Karim Kassim toppled the monarchy. Kassim's first move was to announce the opening of talks with Nasser about joining the UAR.

Iraq was important for its oil, but its location made it inaccessible to American pressure. Dulles wanted to demonstrate American power in the Middle East, and he found a convenient arena in Lebanon. On the day news of the Kassim coup reached Washington, the United States received a request from the president of Lebanon, Camille Chamoun, a Maronite Christian, for help in Lebanon's civil war. Eisenhower immediately ordered 14,000 American soldiers to Lebanon to quell what was portrayed as a threat and as a "Communist-inspired" coup d'état. Sunbathers on the beaches of Beirut, Lebanon's capital, watched in astonishment as a division of combat-clad marines waded ashore looking for communists. This large force had its effect on the new government in Iraq and on Nasser in Egypt. Over the next few months Iraq assured Western oil companies that their properties were safe, and Kassim dropped his bid for membership in the UAR. Nasser as well had to back down after flying to Moscow in the midst of the crisis and learning that the Soviet Union would not move beyond verbal support.

SOCIAL CONFORMITY IN THE COLD WAR

Consensus over foreign policy from 1945 to 1960 was bought at the cost of enforced silence and social conformity. A "silent generation" of college students looked forward to quiet suburban houses and unchallenging, secure, and well-paid jobs in large, anonymous organizations. Political issues of war and peace and capitalism, socialism, and communism seemed curiously old-fashioned. One sociologist, Daniel Bell, himself a former radical in the thirties, noted an "end of ideology." Nowadays, he claimed, all political questions could be easily resolved through good public administration.

Some social critics lamented the blandness of the times. David Reisman, a Harvard sociologist, noted in his 1950 study *The Lonely Crowd* that the American national character had been transformed from the rugged individualism of "inner-directed," self-confident sorts to a mindless, timid herd of "other-directed" conformists. William H. Whyte, the editor of Henry Luce's *Fortune* magazine, decried the sheeplike behavior of modern managers who had recruited a phalanx of fearful "organization men" to take over large corporations. John Kenneth Galbraith, a liberal economist at Harvard, attracted wide public comment with his 1958 study *The Affluent Society*, in which he worried about America's "private affluence and public squalor." Reisman, Whyte, and

Galbraith represented the limits of acceptable dissent in the fifties. But other, outside voices also spoke, even if respectable opinion paid little attention. As in the twenties, some of the most pungent criticism came from poets. Whereas the "lost generation" of expatriates excoriated American culture from Paris cafés, "beatnik" poets, wearing black turtleneck sweaters, goatees, and berets, settled into coffeehouses in New York, San Francisco, and Denver to listen to jazz, smoke marijuana, and read their works. One of the best known of the beats, then and later, was Allen Ginsberg. In one 1956 poem he howled, "I saw the best minds of my generation destroyed by madness." In another, more directly political effort called "America," he mocked "the impression I get from looking at the television set":

America you don't really want to go to war.
America it's them bad Russians.
Them Russians them Russians and them Chinamen. And them Russians.
The Russia's power mad. The Russia wants to eat us alive. She wants to
    take our cars from out our garages.
… That no good.

Few people interested in foreign affairs took Ginsberg seriously in the 1950s. Ten years later many more people concerned about the United States' role in the world voiced disillusionment with the course of the Cold War in terms that sounded very similar to the angry mockery of the beat poets.

THE REVIVAL OF FEAR, 1957–1960

The second Eisenhower administration saw a revival of the fear of the Soviet Union. Opposition Democrats, searching for an issue for the 1960 election, seized upon the supposed growth in Soviet military power. They decried decline in American "prestige" in Latin America, Asia, and Africa, and they accused the Eisenhower administration of a weak and vacillating response to the inevitable changes in world politics.

The renewed concern over Soviet might began on October 4, 1957, when the Soviets launched the world's first space satellite, called *Sputnik*. American education experts were stunned at what they saw as proof of Soviet technological superiority. They also saw an opportunity to boost American spending on technical education in the wake of *Sputnik*. An alliance of educators, defense contractors, and Democrats in Congress passed the National Defense Education Act in 1958. It called for the spending of $5 billion on higher education in the sciences, foreign languages, and humanities over the next few years to counter a perceived threat from the Russians.

American defense planning underwent one of its periodic reversals in the second Eisenhower administration. Army generals had resented Ike's cutback on their service in favor of air power and nuclear weapons. In 1959 retired general Maxwell Taylor published a scathing indictment of the Republican defense posture, *The Uncertain Trumpet.* Taylor charged that the reduction in size of the conventional armed forces made it impossible for the United States to fight any war but a nuclear one. He predicted that the next wars the United States would encounter would be small "brush-fire" encounters, not in Europe, but in Asia, the Middle East, Africa, and Latin America. He warned that the decline of the European empires meant the United States would soon find itself fighting wars of "national liberation" against nationalist forces, sometimes sympathetic to the communists, in Asia, Africa, and Latin America. The army had to be enlarged and a new strategy of "counterinsurgency" developed to fight such wars.

While Taylor advocated a revival of interest in nonnuclear weapons, nongovernmental strategists took another look at the policy of massive retaliation. The obvious flaws of this approach—its inflexibility and its consequent lack of believability—led civilian students of conflict to search for other means of nuclear warfare. One of them, Henry Kissinger, published *Nuclear Weapons and Foreign Policy* in 1957, arguing that massive retaliation by itself was not enough. These fears were increased with *Sputnik* because it now appeared that the Soviet Union had the capacity to hit the United States with atomic bombs mounted on top of missiles.

Democratic candidates for the presidential nomination of 1960, led by Missouri's Stuart Symington, a former secretary of the air force and an expert on air power, insisted that the Eisenhower administration increase its spending for missiles as well as for everything else. By the middle of 1959, Democrats accused Eisenhower of wholesale neglect of national defense. Reluctant to choose the cheapest among a variety of weapons systems or strategies, Democrats assured the public that the wealthy United States could afford any weapons its scientists could invent and that Ike's stinginess could imperil the nation.

In the middle of 1958, an episode in Latin America gave the opposition the chance to complain about the decline in American "prestige" abroad. Vice President Nixon, never one of the opposition's favorite politicians, had his motorcade stoned and spat upon when he traveled to Venezuela and Peru. To the Democrats this rough treatment at the hands of local student leftists proved that the administration lacked the ability to put the American case before the non-European world.

The events of 1959 seemed to prove the critics' complaints that the rest of the world rudely intruded on American foreign policy. On the first day of the year, a nationalist revolution in Cuba led by Fidel Castro sent Fulgencio Batista fleeing from Havana to Miami. Batista, the real power in Cuba since 1934, had close ties to the American government as well as to organized crime within the United States. Havana had become a haven for gamblers, drug dealers, and prostitutes. Immediately on seizing power Castro commenced executions of Batista's henchmen, closed down the gambling casinos, and threatened expropriation of American sugar holdings. Initially, liberals in the United States were pleased at Castro's victory over what they considered a disgraceful dictatorship. In a whirlwind trip to the United States in April, Castro addressed a huge audience at Harvard's Soldiers' Field, but he received a chilly reception from Eisenhower. By the end of the year, many liberal Democrats had stopped praising Castro's government and pointed instead to the prominence of Communists in it. They accused the Eisenhower administration of weaknesses and, just as the Republicans had done a decade earlier in the case of China, muttered about the "loss" of Cuba to the Communists. Isolated radicals continued to present Cuba's case. C. Wright Mills, a sociologist at Columbia, returned from the island in August 1960 to fire off *Listen, Yankee!*, an angry indictment of American misbehavior in the Caribbean. Yet his demand "Hands off Cuba!" and his plea "for a completely new United States approach to the problems of the hungry world" fell into a lake of indifference.

John Foster Dulles died in April 1959, leaving the conduct of foreign relations completely in Ike's hands. A new secretary of state, Christian Herter, a member of the Republican internationalist establishment, never sought the limelight the way Dulles had. Eisenhower sought to use his last eighteen months in office to undertake a series of personal visits around the globe to create a peaceful world. He thought that relations with the Soviet Union might be improved and the arms race ended. To this end he invited Nikita Khrushchev to the United States for a visit in September 1959. Khrushchev had consolidated his power in the Soviet Union in 1958. He had quickly announced that the deadlock over a split Germany, which had persisted since the close of the Second World War, must end. On November 10, 1958, he demanded that the United States and its Western allies withdraw 100,000 troops from West Berlin, make the former German capital a "free city," and negotiate access to it with the East German government. By the time Khrushchev reached the United States the following September, he had dropped that demand, and he spent his time touring an Iowa corn farm and unsuccessfully seeking admission to the newly opened Disneyland. Eisenhower and Khrushchev's meeting at Camp David did not resolve their differences, but they agreed to another summit in Europe the following spring. After the meeting of all the major powers, Eisenhower planned to travel to the Soviet Union.

Ike's return visit never occurred. On May 1, 1960, on the eve of the summit conference in Paris, the Soviet Union shot down an American espionage plane flying 70,000 feet above Soviet territory. The CIA pilot of this U-2 plane, Francis Gary Powers, safely parachuted but was captured. These flights had been going on from bases in Turkey for the previous two years. The president first denied that the United States was conducting aerial spying on the Soviets and then admitted it, saying that national security demanded such overflights. He refused to apologize, and the Soviet leader cancelled his visit. This was not the only trip the president had to erase from his schedule. A visit to Japan was blocked when rioting students made a visit by the president appear unsafe.

Khrushchev and Eisenhower never met again, but the Soviet prime minister did come to the United States in the fall of 1960 to attend the United Nations General Assembly. Fidel Castro came as well, got evicted from the Waldorf Astoria for keeping chickens in his room, and moved to Harlem's Hotel Theresa, where he addressed a crowd from a balcony. Khrushchev, wearing an impish grin for most of the session, drove American television

Nikita Khrushchev, chairman of the Soviet Communist Party, takes time from his visit to the United Nations to pay his respects to Eleanor Roosevelt at Hyde Park, New York. Mrs. Khrushchev stands at the left, and Soviet foreign minister Andrei Gromyko is in the background.
(Franklin D. Roosevelt Library)

viewers wild with rage when he took off a shoe and banged the table in carefully planned anger.

Khrushchev's visit took place in the midst of the presidential election in 1960. Democrats tried to create the public impression of a bumbling, sleepy, remote president who had never taken charge of the foreign affairs bureaucracy. Washington senator Henry Jackson invited academic foreign affairs experts, many of whom had served in previous Democratic administrations, to tell what was wrong with Ike's organization of foreign relations. For two weeks in the spring of 1960, Democratic senators nodded sagely in agreement to attacks on the Republicans' National Security Council as ignorant, slow, "only reactive," unable to plan, and insufficiently "tough-minded."

Democrats chose the youngest man ever to run for the presidency, Massachusetts senator John F. Kennedy. He campaigned on a platform of waging the Cold War with more "vigor" than the Republicans. The Republicans were led by a man almost as young as Kennedy, the forty-seven-year-old vice president, Nixon. Each candidate outbid the other in his anti-Soviet militance. Kennedy ran on more defense, more missiles, a larger army, and more action in Latin America and Africa. Cuba and Fidel Castro became his bête noire. Nixon, recalling his seven-hour shouting match with Nikita Khrushchev in a model American kitchen in 1959, reminded voters that he actually had the experience of "standing up to the Russians." In foreign policy the election of 1960 replayed 1952 with the parties reversed. Democratic outs charged that the Republican ins had squandered opportunities and predicted that if given the chance they would vanquish the Soviet Union. For their part Republicans asked the country to rely upon the experience of their leaders in actually waging Cold War.

Eisenhower himself played little part in the election. When asked to explain what Nixon had done to help in his administration, he begged, "Give me a week and I'll explain it." After Kennedy won by the narrow margin of 112,000 votes, Eisenhower delivered a famous speech warning against an excessive militarization of the Cold War. He explained that the United States was in the grip of a "military-industrial complex" that might distort the country's democratic institutions. That speech, like so much of Ike's foreign policy, was long on promise but short on performance. Coming to the office to end containment, he expanded it with "liberation." He missed opportunities to deal with a post-Stalinist Russia. Europe remained a divided and armed camp. The United States maintained an outmoded China policy and ignored nationalism in the Middle East, Africa, and Latin America. But the United States avoided foreign combat for eight years. The same could not be said for the following decade, which saw Americans engage in their longest, most divisive, and most futile war.

CHAPTER TEN

Cold War Dangers, 1961–1968

American hopes to shape world events soared to their highest levels in the 1960s before the war in Vietnam made the United States reconsider its Cold War policies. Exuberant, energetic, and vigorous representatives of the United States appeared in the remotest regions of the world carrying the message that the American styles of government, economic system, and social values should sweep away all alternatives. Convinced of the rightness of their cause, the evils of communism, and the poorer nations' longing for guidance, the Kennedy and Johnson administrations waged Cold War assertively.

Harry Truman's containment policy seemed too defensive, Secretary of State John Foster Dulles's "brinkmanship" too blustery, and Ike's appeals to end the arms race too defeatist for the Democrats who took over in January 1961. They put into practice global theories developed in government service, academic offices, and private research organizations. The results surprised them and nearly tore the country apart as the "consensus" on foreign policy, imposed on the public after the Second World War, collapsed. From Africa to the Caribbean to Vietnam, Americans learned hard lessons about the cost of global competition with communism. They confronted each other in angry street clashes by the end of the Johnson administration. For both those who continued to believe in an American anticommunist mission and those who preferred an end to foreign interventions, the optimism of 1961 seemed only a memory in 1969. The mood of government officials, the general public, and foreign observers soured as people around the world discovered the limits of American power.

KENNEDY IN POWER

John F. Kennedy took Washington by storm in January 1961. Arthur Schlesinger, Jr., a historian who served on his staff, seemed awestruck by his style and grace under pressure (a phrase borrowed from Ernest Hemingway) and thrilled to be part of history in the making. The thousand-day administration came to be called "Camelot," after King Arthur's mythical court where the weather was perfect, no one argued, and everyone had a good time. The president cultivated a sense of youthful activity that he thought stood in sharp contrast to the lethargy of his seventy-year-old predecessor.

This desire to take command and demonstrate a contrast to his predecessor also dominated Kennedy's foreign policy. The president set the tone in an inaugural address memorable principally for its nationalistic call for intervention around the world. The country was prepared "to pay any price, bear any burden, meet any hardship, support any friend, oppose any foe to assure the survival and success of liberty."

Kennedy filled his top posts with advisers whom the writer David Halberstam called "the best and the brightest." They were relatively young, many in their forties, had been edcated at some of the nation's finest colleges and universities, and had substantial records of achievement in business, academia, and government. Unlike Eisenhower, Kennedy chose to concentrate foreign policy in the White House instead of sharing it with his secretary of state. For that office he selected Dean Rusk, the assistant secretary under Truman, who had urged an uncompromising policy toward China before the Korean War. Not a friend or long-time supporter of Kennedy, Rusk had spent the 1950s as president of the Rockefeller Foundation. He had good connections with the foreign policy establishment, which respected him as a man who knew when to keep his peace. Rusk rarely asserted himself in the councils of the new administration, preferring to sit impassively while members of the White House staff discussed the issues.

With his secretary of state reduced in influence, Kennedy relied on the advice of a group of "action intellectuals" in the augmented National Security Council, the White House, the State Department, and the Defense Department. For the previous decade academic specialists in foreign affairs had argued that the Cold War was too important to be left to politicians, diplomats, and generals. In Cambridge, New York, and Berkeley a tightly knit group of political scientists, military strategists, and "development" economists created theories they hoped to apply to the endless competition with the Soviet Union. They took pride in their "hard-headed realism," their "tough-mindedness," and their "lack of sentimentality."

For national security adviser the president chose McGeorge Bundy, former dean of the faculty at Harvard, a liberal Republican and the son of a major aide of Secretary of State Henry L. Stimson. Bundy's brother William, the son-in-law of former secretary of state Dean Acheson, served as assistant secretary for international security affairs in the State Department. Another academic, MIT professor of economic history Walt Whitman Rostow, became the head of the Policy Planning Staff of the State Department. Earlier Rostow had written an influential study, *Stages of Economic Growth*, the subtitle of which, *A Non-Communist Manifesto*, explained how professors could wage Cold War among the world's poor. The Kennedy administration proved some of Rostow's notions about how the "development" of the poorer countries could be brought about.

WAGING COLD WAR IN LATIN AMERICA

Latin America was the first place in which the Kennedy administration tried to set a new tone. On March 13 Kennedy announced the Alliance for Progress with the Latin American nations. Kennedy would add $20 billion in foreign aid for the hemisphere over the next ten years. However, bureaucratic infighting and corruption in Latin America limited the effectiveness of the alliance over the next five years. The Peace Corps, made up of idealistic young men and women—recently graduated from college and without gainful employment—who would go abroad to teach and perform technical service, would pay special attention to Latin America. At the same time the Pentagon and the CIA increased the training of Latin American police and paramilitary outfits in order to help them fight guerrilla wars. The Pentagon set up a Jungle Warfare School in the Panama Canal Zone and at Fort Bragg, North Carolina, to train Latin American units. The Agency for International Development brought some 500 Latin American policemen to the Canal Zone school to learn how to infiltrate leftist groups and control the crowds of the type that had taunted Vice President Nixon on his trip to South America in 1958.

The alliance and the training of police were designed to prevent the rise of another Castrolike nationalist revolution. But what to do about the revolutionary government in Cuba itself? The Eisenhower administration had broken diplomatic relations with Castro in January 1960. Throughout the election campaign Kennedy had accused the Republicans of doing nothing about Castro, and he threatened some sort of an invasion if he were elected. Nixon, an old anticommunist and Red baiter par excellence, found himself in the uncomfortable position of opposing military action as a violation of international law, even though he knew that the CIA had plans underway to attack Cuba. Nixon suspected that Kennedy knew of these proposals and had mentioned them for the rankest sort of political advantage, knowing Nixon could not reveal or discuss the operation.

Whether or not he learned of them before the election, Kennedy was briefed by CIA director Allen Dulles on the agency's complicated and secret plan to train Cuban exiles in Florida and Central America and then ferry them into Cuba. Some of the same CIA men who had plotted the Guatemalan adventure in 1954 thought that an invasion of Cuba would be accomplished as easily. In January 1961 the new president gave his approval for the CIA to continue with the planned April invasion. He even convinced the *New York Times* not to publish a report of the impending operation, arguing that to do so would compromise the "national interest." On April 17 a force of about 1,600 guerrillas landed at the Bay of Pigs in southern Cuba. The CIA's director of operations, Richard Bissell, had assured Kennedy that this force would encourage a general rising of the Cuban population against Castro. Even if there were not an immediate rush to the anti-Communist colors, the invaders could withdraw to the mountains, which Bissell said were nearby. In fact, the poorly supplied and inadequately prepared force landed in a swamp with no mountains for miles. No uprising greeted them, as Castro was popular throughout the whole island and nowhere more so than the Bay of Pigs, where he frequently went on holiday. Within forty-eight hours of their landing, the brigade was captured by the Cuban army. Kennedy admitted responsibility but then fired Allen Dulles as head of the CIA. Over the next year the United States ransomed the invaders with $10 million in medical supplies.

Undaunted, the CIA spent the next eighteen months trying to embarrass, confuse, or murder Castro. The agency planned to drop depilitating powder into his shoes to make his beard fall out. Strategists suggested slipping him a cigar laced with LSD, offering him a pen with a poison tip, or blowing his legs off with exploding clamshells while he snorkled in the blue Caribbean. Five times the agency approached underworld figures, eager to regain control of prostitution, gambling, and narcotics in Havana, about sending a gunman to shoot the Cuban leader. The Cuban people became

Fidel Castro
(Library of Congress)

targets of Operation MONGOOSE, developed by Edward Lansdale, the former head of covert activities in Saigon. He suggested sending a submarine
to the shore where it would illuminate the night sky with incendiary shells
to convince the peasantry of the imminent Second Coming of Christ. E.

Howard Hunt, who had helped plan the overthrow of the Arbenz government in Guatemala in 1954 and later recruited the Watergate burglars in 1972, undertook a series of nighttime commando raids on the beaches. They managed only to rally the Cuban public to the revolution and encourage Castro to ask Moscow for military aid.

KHRUSHCHEV AND THE GERMAN QUESTION

The public rallied to Kennedy's support after the Bay of Pigs disaster. This customary rise in the polls in the face of adversity did little to bolster the president's self-confidence, however. He wanted some way to recover control of foreign affairs, and he thought he found it in a confrontation with Soviet premier Khrushchev at a summit meeting in Vienna. The Soviet leader again wanted a solution to the question of the division of Germany and Berlin. When the two leaders met in Vienna in May 1961, Kennedy was unyielding on the question of German reunification and believed that the Soviet chairman considered him a weak, inexperienced youngster.

The Berlin crisis in 1961 culminated a series of East-West confrontations that arose from the two nations' inability to reach agreement on Germany's future after 1945. Even after presiding over the birth of the Federal Republic of Germany (FRG) in 1949, the United States insisted upon reunification of Germany into a single, presumably noncommunist, state. No Western nation extended diplomatic recognition to the Democratic Republic of Germany (DRG), created as a Soviet response. Instead, the NATO countries persisted in calling the DRG an illegitimate creature of the Soviet Union and argued that having its capital in the Soviet-occupied sector of East Berlin violated the Yalta and Potsdam agreements. The FRG tried to ostracize its East German counterpart by breaking diplomatic relations with any noncommunist nation bold enough to open an embassy in East Germany. After Stalin's death successive Soviet governments urged a general European security conference to settle the German question, but the West refused, fearing recognition of the DRG and the end of the illusion of reunification.

Kennedy returned from Vienna in a somber mood and soon asked Congress for an increase in the defense budget of $3.25 billion. In words not heard since the days when John Foster Dulles had spoken of going to the brink of war, Kennedy said, "We do not want to fight, but we have fought before. And others in earlier times have made the same dangerous mistake of assuming that the West was too selfish and too soft and too divided to resist invasions of freedom in other lands." Relations with the Soviets plunged throughout the summer. On July 25 Kennedy called up the reserves to protect Western access to Berlin. When asked if he thought that the call-up was fair, he replied, "Life is unfair." The Communist response to this saber-rattling caught Washington by surprise. On the night of August 13, the Soviet government erected a heavily guarded wall between East and West Berlin. The drain of refugees, which had reached 100,000 in the previous year, abruptly stopped. Khrushchev dropped plans to sign his own peace treaty with the East Germans since the wall effectively sealed the eastern zone from the western. Kennedy's show of force had done nothing to prevent the final division of Germany. The United States protested the wall, and the president later made a highly publicized visit to the divided city to proclaim *"Ich bin ein Berliner"* (I am a Berliner). But the wall remained standing until 1989, a testimony to the failure of both communism and also of imagination on the part of American diplomats.

THE CONGO

As if to provide a test of the theories of the academic foreign affairs specialists, events on the periphery consumed the attention of the Kennedy administration for the next year. In Central Africa the United States participated in some shabby intrigues in the newly independent state of the Congo. This former Belgian colony had gained its independence in mid-1959, when the former colonial rulers abruptly left. Unprepared for independence and with fewer than 200 college-educated people in the country, the Congo quickly became a battleground for several tribal and political factions. Patrice Lumumba, leader of the ardent nationalist faction, became the prime minister. The Belgians hated Lumumba, hoping a puppet leader would invite them back to run the mines and profit from the country's immense mineral wealth. As a civil war broke out in the Congo, the United Nations sent a peacekeeping force to separate the armies of the Lumumba government and the Belgian secessionists in the mineral-rich southern province of Katanga, led by Moise Tshombe. The United States gave lip service to supporting the UN force but actually favored secession. The CIA saw Lumumba as a Moscow puppet since he had received training in the Soviet capital. If Katanga seceded, the gold, diamonds, and uranium of the area would stay under Western control. Days before Kennedy took office in January 1961, Lumumba was assassinated with the help of the CIA. The civil war dragged on for another year, but eventually a pro-Western government under the lead of Joseph Kasavubu took power. Shortly thereafter Joseph Mobutu, leader of the armed forces, became president. For the rest of the 1960s, rumors were rife in Africa about American complicity in the murder of Lumumba. Mobutu assumed dictatorial power, which he used to enrich himself and a small group of supporters while impoverishing his resource-rich country. He renamed the Congo Zaire, and he allied himself with the West during the Cold War. After the collapse of the Soviet Union, the United States withdrew its support for Mobutu's increasingly despotic misrule, and he was overthrown in 1997.

THE CUBAN MISSILE CRISIS AND ITS AFTERMATH

According to the foreign policy experts of the Kennedy administration, the best thing a government official could do was called crisis management. Their criticism of Ike's handling of foreign affairs concerned his desire to avoid conflict; they welcomed it, hoping to prove their toughness. They met their severest test in October 1962 in the controversy with the Soviet Union over missiles in Cuba. Kennedy's reputation as a steely leader, able to overcome foes with his careful assessment of a complicated situation and craft innovative solutions, rests on his handling of the Cuban missile crisis. Critics, however, accused him of endangering the safety of the world by a display of machismo.

Soviet intermediate range ballistic missiles (IRBMs) in Cuba assaulted American pride more than they threatened the physical security of the United States. Based ninety miles from the southernmost tip of Florida, the weapons could reach targets in the eastern and central United States in fewer than eight minutes, cutting the already minuscule reaction time of twenty-five minutes after the launch of intercontinental ballistic missiles (ICBMs) based in the Soviet Union or the United States. America had for years pointed its own IRBMs at Soviet targets from bases in neighboring Turkey. A Soviet base in Cuba seemed to reply in kind to the American strategy of ringing the Soviet Union with troops and weapons, but retaliation for Western encirclement may not have been uppermost in Khrushchev's mind. Moscow moved at the urging of frantic pleas from Cuban president Fidel Castro to do something about the CIA's continuing clandestine war against his person and his government.

The crisis took place in the midst of the congressional election of 1962, in which the Republicans expected to make the typical gains of the opposition party in nonpresidential elections. New York Republican senator Kenneth Keating said that the Soviets "had the power to hurl rockets into the American heartland." Congress passed a resolution advocating the president "by whatever means necessary, including the use of arms" to prevent the installation of missiles in Cuba. Kennedy also issued a warning to the Soviets in September. U-2 flights in August had revealed Soviet construction of a missile site, but CIA director John McCone was honeymooning on the French Riviera and could not be reached to confirm the data.

In early October, with McCone back in Washington, the CIA presented Kennedy with evidence that the Soviet Union had indeed constructed a missile base. With the election barely three weeks away and new Republican calls for action, Kennedy convened his leading foreign policy advisers. They secretly met in a side office of the State Department so as not to attract attention of the press. Former secretary of state Dean Acheson, chairman of the Joint Chiefs of Staff Maxwell Taylor, and Air Force Chief Curtis LeMay urged an immediate air strike against the missiles. The president's brother, Attorney General Robert Kennedy, supported the position of Undersecretary of State George Ball, who recommended a blockade of Cuba. Ball thought that if the blockade failed, an attack could always be ordered later, and Robert Kennedy opposed a Pearl Harbor–type preemptive strike. The president, he recalled, did "not want to be known as another Tojo." Secretary of State Dean Rusk kept silent, resenting having to share the limelight with other advisers. The president held his own views during the meetings, not wishing to inhibit discussion.

On Monday, October 22 Kennedy publicly announced the presence of the Soviet missiles in Cuba. He imposed a blockade of the island to prevent the Soviet Union from arming the missiles with atomic warheads. He gave the Soviets no deadline but made it clear that the missiles themselves had to be withdrawn. Two days later a blockade line went up, and Soviet naval ships en route to Cuba were turned away. On Friday the 26th, sailors from the U.S. destroyer *Joseph P. Kennedy* boarded a Soviet-chartered freighter bound for Cuba. Then, on October 28 Kennedy announced that the Soviet Union had agreed to crate up its weapons. Kennedy's supporters exulted, and the world drew back from the brink of nuclear war. Secretary Rusk summarized his feelings with a cowboy metaphor when he recalled that "we were eyeball to eyeball, and the other fellow blinked." As a result of the confrontation, the United States and the Soviet Union set up a direct teletype link, the "hot line," to use in the case of crises. The United States promised not to invade Cuba and intimated that it would withdraw its outmoded missiles from Turkey. This last pledge came easily, since at the beginning of the crisis Kennedy had not known that the United States had these weapons stationed near the Soviet border.

Not surprisingly, Castro was furious at the Soviet betrayal. He refused to see Moscow's special envoy who came to Havana to explain the benefits of the deal. The Soviets, unwilling to confront superior U.S. military power, saw merits in the American pledge not to attack Cuba, but Castro expected the secret war to continue, as it did until the assassination of President Kennedy in November 1963. Nor would the furious Cuban leader publicly agree to renounce support for revolutionary activity in the Western Hemisphere. Khrushchev had his own problems with his Politburo colleagues, who squirmed in embarrassment at their chairman's humiliation at the hands of the Americans. They resolved to remove him at the earliest opportunity, which occurred two years later, in 1964. They embarked upon a rearmament program to match the American naval and air superiority that had forced their surrender.

The European allies had publicly given their support to the United States during the crisis. Even France's president, Charles de Gaulle, long a critic of the United States for its arrogance and reluctance to consult with Europeans, had told roving ambassador Averell Harriman of his full support during the height of the tensions. Privately, however, Europeans expressed grave misgivings about the way the United States had behaved in October. De Gaulle, most notably, saw the episode as proof that the United States would act in its own interests. Even as he reassured Harriman, de Gaulle worried that Washington's unilateral actions meant that Europeans had to watch impotently from the sidelines. De Gaulle decided that the best way for France to assert itself in international affairs was to build its own *force de frappe* of atomic weapons. Later, in 1966, France withdrew its armed forces from the unified command of the NATO alliance. British reaction to the Cuban missile crisis was more muted, but the results were the same: Britain was shown to be the idle bystander to great events.

British prime minister Harold Macmillan prided himself on his friendship with the new president. In December 1962 Macmillan met Kennedy at Nassau in the Bahamas and learned a stinging lesson in power politics. The British wanted the United States to supply their armed forces with an air-launched ballistic missile, the Skybolt, to deliver their own nuclear arms. Secretary of Defense McNamara thought that Skybolt cost too much and could not deliver a weapon, and he believed that the British should not have an independent nuclear force anyway. Kennedy agreed that the British should join an American-sponsored multinational force, a group of ships made up of the navies of all the NATO allies with the U.S. command having final say over the use of these weapons. Hidden beneath the rhetoric of cooperation between the allies lurked the need to get the Germans involved in nuclear defense. No European power wanted West Germany to have nuclear weapons on its own, but the U.S. defense planners recognized that Germany was the most robust power in Europe. The British accepted the demise of Skybolt and agreed to join the multinational organization. The prime minister had trouble, however, convincing his countrymen that the "special relationship" with the United States did much good.

THE TEST BAN

While Kennedy moved on one front to bring the powerful West German army into the nuclear arms race, the administration also sought to reduce nuclear competition. During the fifties private groups in the United States such as the Committee for a Sane Nuclear Policy (SANE) and well-known scientists led by chemist Linus Pauling and physicist Edward V. Condon had complained about the effects of radioactive fallout on people's health. One radioactive isotope, Strontium 90, which was discovered in cow's milk, was found to cause a rise in cancer. While the Atomic Energy Commission sought to minimize fears during the fifties, its own scientists admitted to a congressional hearing in 1956 that "any quantity of radioactive fallout is undesirable."

Pressure mounted during the Kennedy administration for a ban on testing nuclear weapons in the atmosphere after the Soviet Union exploded a bomb of fifty megatons and threatened to explode one of 100 in late 1961. The United States responded with atmospheric explosions of its own hydrogen bombs in 1962, setting off thirty-three shots that year. By the beginning of 1963, public alarm over the health dangers of radiation worried officials. Furthermore, arms experts in the Defense Department assured the president that nothing could be learned from atmospheric testing that could not also be discovered from explosions set off in underground caverns. Kennedy had established an Arms Control and Disarmament Agency in the State Department in 1961 with the purpose of organizing efforts at reducing the arms race. The agency had opened talks but accomplished little in the first two years of his administration, so the possibility of a test ban seemed to present a way of making use of it.

In the spring of 1963, the United States and the Soviet Union negotiated seriously to stop testing atomic weapons in the atmosphere. Both sides realized the potential health hazards, and both recognized that their arms programs would not suffer if they switched to subterranean experiments. In mid-June they concluded a treaty banning future tests in the atmosphere. Either country could abrogate the treaty by giving one year's notice. Both agreed to continue the search for a complete ban on atomic explosions and to confer on reducing nuclear arms in general. Over the next decade hundreds of meetings took place at disarmament conferences in Vienna, but the hopes of 1963 for an expansion of the first agreement into a real sort of disarmament proved illusory. The United States tried to maintain its superiority over the Soviet Union, which in turn hoped to narrow the gap between the two powers.

SOUTHEAST ASIA

By the summer of 1963, the Kennedy administration was spending an increasing amount of time wrestling with the war in South Vietnam. In 1961 and 1962 American interest in Indochina had focused on Laos, where a civil war raged between a right wing general, Phoumi Nosavan; a neutralist prince, Souvanna Phouma; and a Communist prince, Souphanou-vong. At various times confused Americans provided aid to all three. In the spring of 1962, a new Geneva conference had opened cochaired by France and Britain. This time the United States, as full participant, and the parties had agreed to neutralize Laos. The Kennedy administration heaved a sigh of relief that the Communists had not won the war and was gladdened that the United States would not fight in as remote a place as Laos.

While Laos drew the headlines in 1961 and 1962, the civil war grew in South Vietnam. As a senator Kennedy had been a member of the American Committee for a Free Vietnam, which had boosted the reputation of President Ngo Dinh Diem. Upon taking office one of the first briefings the president had received concerned the new insurgency of the remnants of the Vietminh in South Vietnam. His newly appointed chairman of the Joints Chiefs of Staff, Gen. Maxwell Taylor, believed that Vietnam would be an excellent place to test new counterinsurgency fighters, the special forces called Green Berets. President Kennedy himself went to Fort Bragg, North Carolina, in 1961 to see a display of firepower and watch a demonstration of snake-eating and tree-swinging by a contingent of Green Berets.

In 1962 the Defense Department sent a team of advisers into the field with the South Vietnamese army, the ARVN, to live off the land with it as it rooted out the insurgents. Other advisers from the Agency for International Development and the State Department went into the countryside to build an "infrastructure" of social institutions, in the words of the academic specialists who planned their tours. Michigan State University continued its training of the police force of South Vietnam, and other universities sent specialists in "nation-building" into the countryside to assist the process.

By the middle of 1963, the United States had more than 10,000 troops stationed in Vietnam, and the fiction that they were engaged only in "advising" no longer carried weight. In June the public's attention was riveted by a Buddhist monk in Saigon who poured gasoline over his body and set himself on fire. This self-immolation climaxed a series of demonstrations by the

Buddhists, some 80 percent of South Vietnam's population, who deeply resented the control exercised by the Catholic 10 percent who backed Diem. While Americans watched the public burning in horrified fascination, Madame Nhu, the sister-in-law of the president and wife of the head of the South's secret police force, accused American television reporters of having staged the suicide. She charged that the Buddhists were Communists and cruelly joked that she would "supply the mustard for the monks' next barbecue."

For Kennedy and his advisers the Buddhist rebellion suggested that the Diem government no longer had the confidence of the country and was unlikely to quell the insurrection. That summer another 5,000 American soldiers disembarked in Vietnam, while the American government looked for alternatives to Diem. In August Kennedy appointed an old political rival, Henry Cabot Lodge, the grandson of the Republican opponent of Woodrow Wilson and the Republican vice presidential candidate in 1960, as ambassador to South Vietnam. Hoping to enlist Republicans into a bipartisan agreement on Vietnam, Kennedy saw Lodge as shoring up his position with the opposition. Immediately on arrival in Saigon, Lodge learned from the CIA chief in South Vietnam that the ARVN's top generals no longer had confidence in Diem's leadership. Along with his brother, the Vietnamese president seemed more interested in siphoning American aid than waging war. The army itself was a shambles that fled at the first sign of the enemy. To American diplomats the complaints about Diem seemed depressingly like those voiced in China against the corruption of Jiang Jieshi before 1949. CIA operatives in Saigon thought that the replacement of Diem with a group of less corrupt military men could improve the morale of the troops and lead to a suppression of the insurrection. Lodge forwarded these hopes and fears to Washington with a recommendation that the United States provide tacit support for a coup against Diem. Lodge's proposal found favor in the White House, where National Security Adviser McGeorge Bundy reasoned that nobody could be worse than Diem.

Word went back to Saigon in September that the American government would approve a change in leadership. On November 1 the plotters, led by Gen. Duong Van Minh, toppled Diem's government, seizing the president and his brother. Both were taken to the outskirts of Saigon and executed. Kennedy expressed surprise that the two men had been killed, and historians still argue over whether the CIA had ordered or knew about the plans to eliminate the Vietnamese president. Whether the actual directive received approval from the American embassy in Saigon is less important than the fact that the U.S. ambassador and the national security adviser had decided that the government of Vietnam had to be replaced.

On November 22, 1963, barely three weeks after Diem's murder, John F. Kennedy himself was gunned down in Dallas. He died profoundly uneasy about the future course of the war in Vietnam. He likened the U.S. military buildup in Vietnam to an alcoholic who takes a drink. The effect wears off, and you have to take another one. Protectors of the president's memory took heart from such remarks and a casual comment made by Kennedy to a political aide, Kenneth O'Donnell, about withdrawing U.S. forces from Vietnam after the presidential election of 1964. The idea that Kennedy anticipated the end to American involvement in the Vietnam War gripped the popular imagination with the release of Oliver Stone's film *JFK* in 1991. The movie strongly implied that a wicked conspiracy of militarists and defense contractors murdered Kennedy because they favored getting the United States more deeply committed to fight in Vietnam. This idea is clearly false. Kennedy did have doubts about the ability of South Vietnam to prevail. He resisted committing U.S. ground forces to the war. But he always believed that the stakes for the United States were very high in Vietnam. Southeast Asia remained a vital arena in the Cold War competition with the Soviet Union and its allies. In the late 1980s Kennedy's secretary of state, Dean Rusk, recalled that he "talked with

Ngo Dinh Diem, president of South Vietnam (center), meets President Dwight Eisenhower and Secretary of State John Foster Dulles (second from left). The United States provided massive military support for Diem's government from 1955 to 1963.
(National Archives)

John Kennedy on hundreds of occasions about Southeast Asia and not once did he suggest or hint at withdrawal." In the speech scheduled for delivery at the Dallas Trade Mart the day he was murdered, Kennedy was prepared to say that "we...are the watchmen on the walls of freedom.... Our assistance to...nations can be painful, risky and costly, as is true in Southeast Asia today. But we dare not weary of the task."

The horror of the president's death and the nostalgic longing for his cheerful good nature, his eloquence, and his probing intelligence created a small industry of laudatory accounts of his brief tenure in office. Theodore Sorensen, his principal speechwriter, lamented in his 1965 biography that Kennedy "had only begun, he was given so little time." The Cuban missile crisis became a source of studies showing how to make decisions under pressure. Even painful failures such as the Bay of Pigs invasion won Kennedy points for demonstrating how the president could learn from his mistakes. Kennedy's obvious anguish and skepticism over Vietnam came to be seen as part of the emerging American awareness of the limits of the country's military power. The Kennedy administration did not fulfill its soaring promise. Yet, as Robert Dallek, a recent biographer concludes, "the Kennedy thousand days spoke to the country's better angels, inspired visions of a less divisive nation and world, and demonstrated that America was still the last best hope of mankind."

LYNDON JOHNSON TAKES CHARGE, 1963–1964

Lyndon Johnson never wanted to be vice president; few people do. He had taken the job when Kennedy asked at the 1960 convention because he saw no way of continuing as an effective majority leader of the Senate if he turned it down. A great bear of a man, Johnson seemed to shrink physically as he went through the ceremonial duties of the vice presidency. He never gained admission to the inner circle of Kennedy's advisers, who shunned him as a rude Texan given to telling dirty jokes and emitting uncouth noises. Johnson delighted in the opportunity to escape from Washington as a goodwill ambassador. He went around the world as if campaigning for office. Europe, Latin America, the Indian subcontinent, and Indochina all got the Johnson "treatment." He astonished a Pakistani camel driver with a hug and an invitation to visit his ranch on the Pedernales River in Texas. In Vietnam he called President Diem the "George Washington of Southeast Asia."

Johnson had deep insecurities about his own grasp of international relations that he covered with bravura and by twitting "experts." Once he became president, he poked fun at the "Harvards" who had advised Kennedy while at the same time relying on their advice. Robert McNamara particularly won his heart with his "stacomb on his hair and his flow charts." Johnson had strong, sometimes unprintable, views on the foreign leaders he met. After a dinner with the king of Norway, he whispered to an aide, "That's the dumbest king I ever met. I didn't know they made kings that dumb."

For all of his defensiveness, Johnson appreciated the delicacy of his position as an unelected president. Kennedy supporters thought him nearly a usurper, and he wanted to calm their nerves by following the policies of the fallen hero to the letter. Despite Johnson's mockery of the "Harvards," he insisted that they remain in their jobs. All of them stayed for at least the first eighteen months of his presidency. In domestic affairs, where Johnson had a sure touch, he soon surpassed Kennedy's record. In 1964 and 1965 Congress enacted the most sweeping social reform measures since the New Deal and the most effective civil rights laws since Reconstruction. Johnson felt less confident in foreign policy. He resolved to determine exactly what Kennedy would have done and continue along the same lines.

VIETNAM AND THE ELECTION OF 1964

In Vietnam Johnson thought that meant continuing the role of the U.S. advisers in the hopes that the new government of Gen. Duong Van Minh could do a better job than Diem. Not that Johnson was very optimistic. Like Kennedy before him, the new president worried about committing ground troops. He had opposed the coup d'état against Diem. On November 30, 1963, Johnson expressed his misgivings about Ambassador Lodge, whom he thought "doesn't know one damn thing about" running the war. But Johnson also staked his personal reputation on success in Vietnam. He told Lodge's deputy chief of mission "Lyndon Johnson is not going down as the president who lost Vietnam." In December Secretary of Defense McNamara and National Security Adviser McGeorge Bundy worried that General Minh might negotiate with Hanoi to end the war, creating a neutral government in the Republic of Vietnam. At the end of January 1964, the United States helped Gen. Nguyen Khanh seize power in another coup, but Khanh's government proved no more able to pursue the war than had earlier ones. ARVN troops continued to hold back from the fighting, and American attempts at "nation building" stalled. In the summer of 1964, the U.S. Navy began accompanying South Vietnamese patrol boats as they sailed north of the seventeenth parallel to attack the coast of North Vietnam. For General Khanh these patrols were a prelude to a "march north" to carry the war into the Democratic Republic of Vietnam. The U.S. escorts came along to demonstrate Washington's backing of Khanh and also to discourage him from embarking on a dangerous and provocative invasion of the North. Sometimes the American naval vessels sailed within the territorial waters claimed by Hanoi.

On the night of August 2, three North Vietnamese torpedo boats fired at the *Maddox*, a U.S. Navy destroyer on patrol in the Tonkin Gulf, which was monitoring the electronic communication of the North Vietnamese. The damage was a bullet hole 1 inch in diameter, and the *Maddox* failed to hit any of the attackers with its return fire. Johnson yelled at his red-faced admirals "you've got a whole fleet and all those airplanes, and you can't even sink three little old PT boats." Two nights later, on August 4, another destroyer on patrol in the Tonkin Gulf, the *C Turner Joy*, reported that North Vietnamese PT boats had launched torpedoes against it. The night was stormy, the sonar operators inexperienced, and the whole crew jittery, and the navy expected an attack. Navy aviators flying over the *Maddox* reported seeing no North Vietnamese boats in the vicinity. No physical evidence of an assault on the *Maddox* appeared, and the "return" fire from the destroyer hit nothing. A few years later Johnson acknowledged his own doubts that a second attack ever took place. "For all I know," he said, "our navy might have been shooting at whales out there."

It hardly mattered what actually had happened in the Tonkin Gulf, for the Johnson administration wanted a reason for some dramatic gesture against both North Vietnam and the conservative Republican presidential candidate, Arizona senator Barry Goldwater, who accused Johnson of meekness in the war. As soon as news of the incident with the *C. Turner Joy* reached Washington, Defense Secretary McNamara ordered an air strike against North Vietnam's coast. As the planes were in the air, McNamara announced the American attack, and Johnson sent to Congress the text of a resolution offering support from the House and Senate for the "defense of American forces in Southeast Asia." The National Security Council had prepared the text of a "general or permissive" resolution two months before, in June, and the approach of the Democratic National Convention the third week in August made the timing right. The chairman of the Senate Committee on Foreign Relations, J. William Fulbright of Arkansas, who later became one of the harshest critics of the war in Vietnam, led the debate for the Gulf of Tonkin Resolution. He later apologized to the two senators who voted against it, Wayne Morse of Oregon and Ernest Gruening of Alaska, saying it was "the dumbest thing I've ever done." At the time Morse and Gruening were pilloried in the press for their criticism, *Newsweek* magazine calling them "gadflies" and "lightweights." The resolution passed the House without a single no vote, without hearings, and with only one hour of debate. For the next six years, until Congress repealed it in 1970, the Gulf of Tonkin Resolution became the legal basis Presidents Johnson and Richard M. Nixon used for the American war in Vietnam.

The air strike and resolution caused Johnson's popularity to shoot up in public opinion polls, which showed him defeating Senator Goldwater with more than 60 percent of the vote. The election campaign of 1964 saw Johnson accusing Goldwater of being a "trigger-happy" menace who would let American field commanders use atomic bombs without consulting the president. A Johnson television ad, used once, showed a little girl picking petals from a flower, counting down from ten to one as the scene shifted to an atomic bomb–caused mushroom cloud. On Vietnam the president's supporters accused Goldwater of favoring a buildup of hundreds of thousands of American troops and favoring a war against North Vietnam that would inevitably bring China and the Soviet Union into a fight with the United States. Goldwater offered an inviting target with his offhand remarks on how to conduct military operations in Vietnam, "I would turn to my Joint Chiefs of Staff and say, 'Fellows, we made the decision to win; now it's your problem.'"

Liberals swallowed their misgivings about Johnson's personality and his conduct of the war because of their fear of Goldwater, and they enlisted in

MY WARMEST GREETINGS, DETERMINED TO WIN / Ho Chi Minh / Hanoi, July 1969

North Vietnam's Ho Chi Minh
(Library of Congress)

LBJ's election campaign. Several public figures who later became active opponents of the war in Vietnam—Dr. Benjamin Spock, David McReynolds of the Socialist Party, and Prof. H. Stuart Hughes of Harvard—signed public appeals to "go part of the way with LBJ." On election day Johnson overwhelmed Goldwater with 60 percent of the vote, carrying forty-four of the fifty states. Johnson could claim that he represented general agreement, both foreign and domestic, and that he had been chosen "president of all the people." In practical terms, though, Johnson's victory left unanswered precisely what course the United States would follow in Vietnam. A majority of voters chose Johnson because he was not Barry Goldwater, and they hoped and expected him to avoid a ground war in Asia. As Fredrik Logevall observes in *Choosing* War (1999), "if Johnson's mandate provided for any kind of dramatic policy change on Vietnam it was in the opposite direction of escalation, toward disengagement."

ESCALATION AND THE COLLAPSE OF
THE COLD WAR CONSENSUS, 1965–1968

The election of 1964 represented the high-water mark of the consensus that had dominated discussion of international relations since 1945. Over the next three years Americans lost their unquestioning faith in the president's right to conduct foreign affairs as he saw fit, they began to doubt his word, and eventually they would not let him show his face on a college campus. The specter of communism and the "loss" of another country to radicals no longer could elicit fear. Whereas once academic experts had drawn up plans to wage wars of counterinsurgency, now professors denounced America's war as "genocidal" and drew unflattering comparisons between American behavior in Vietnam and Nazi conduct in Europe. The works of historians critical of the course of American foreign policy found a new respectful audience. William Appleman Williams's *Tragedy of American Diplomacy*, published to negative reviews in 1959, became a standard of a new school of revisionist writers. David Horowitz called the United States *The Free World Colossus* (1965), and Ronald Steel told the story of the *Pax Americana* (1967) that had ruled the world since 1945. Richard Barnet searched for *The Roots of War* (1972) and found them in the way Americans had sought to run the world to their liking. College campuses erupted into violent riots fueled by student disgust with the war and fear of the military draft. By 1967 hundreds of thousands of mostly young Americans took to the streets in demonstrations attacking American foreign policy in Vietnam and around the globe. Even Congress, which had offered its support for nearly every presidential departure in foreign affairs for twenty years, proved balky. It questioned

Johnson's assumptions about world politics and threatened to develop a foreign policy of its own.

All of these changes took place while the number of American troops in Vietnam grew from 50,000 in early 1965 to 535,000 in early 1968 and while American planes dropped 3 million tons of bombs on North and South Vietnam. The air war eventually ignited more explosions than Allied planes set off in Europe and Japan during the Second World War. The bombing of the North began in February 1965 after North Vietnamese commandos attacked the marine garrison stationed at Pleiku in South Vietnam. Again, Washington used a North Vietnamese attack as a justification for military action long in the planning. McGeorge Bundy muttered, "Pleikus are like streetcars; there's one every ten minutes." In early 1965 the Joint Chiefs of Staff had told President Johnson that the South Vietnamese army could not be expected to defend itself for at least another year. They recommended a commitment of U.S. combat troops and bombing of the North to lift morale in Saigon and stem the flow of supplies to the South. Johnson approved the ROLLING THUNDER bombing of the North in late January, but he stipulated that he personally would select the targets for the American planes. The president feared Chinese intervention if the planes came too close to the border, and he had small respect for the mental capacity of his air force commanders. "The generals only know two words—bomb and spend," he complained to a visitor.

Johnson continued his habit of giving the generals some but not all of what they wanted throughout the next three years as the United States "escalated" the war. The term *escalation* itself originated with academic strategists in the Office of Operations Research of the Pentagon, and it meant that a gradual increase in force would "exceed the enemy's threshold of pain." Presumably, the North Vietnamese would quit before the Americans. Secretary of Defense McNamara, an ardent believer in these theories at the beginning, returned from Vietnam in 1965 and 1966 with reports that he could "see the light at the end of the tunnel," and victory was "just around the corner." President Johnson used earthier language as he sent a group of GIs off to the war with the command that they come back and "nail the coonskin to the barn door."

In April 1965 the president outlined his war aims at a speech at Johns Hopkins University, one of the last times he could safely appear before an audience of college students. He offered to negotiate with the North Vietnamese about their withdrawal of troops from the South. He held out the prospect of more bombing and more American troops if they refused and promised a "TVA [Tennessee Valley Authority] for the Mekong Delta and North Vietnam" should they accept. Ho Chi Minh, observing the United States had simply taken over from the French as the major imperial power, flatly refused to negotiate while the United States bombed North Vietnam. The American proposal seemed especially impudent to him as it was the United States that fought 10,000 miles away from home while the North Vietnamese sent soldiers south to take part in a "civil war." Ho's position, constant throughout the war, was that the United States should stop bombing and withdraw its troops, and then negotiations could begin.

The Johns Hopkins speech boosted Johnson's standing in the polls, but it drew ominous warnings from domestic critics. Walter Lippmann, now seventy-five, saw it on television and was dismayed that the president ignored his advice to call an unconditional halt to the bombing. He predicted the United States courted disaster in Southeast Asia because Johnson had "not taken to heart the historic fact that the role of the white man as a ruler in Asia" had ended in 1945. Senator Fulbright started his journey into opposition by complaining that the Johns Hopkins speech offered nothing new.

INTERVENTION IN THE DOMINICAN REPUBLIC

These qualms grew with another American military operation in April 1965: the invasion of the Dominican Republic to stop a "Communist-inspired" coup there. The Dominican Republic emerged from thirty years of despotism when Rafael Trujillo, the dictator of the country since 1931, was assassinated in 1961. The Kennedy administration had sent a naval squadron to the republic to prevent the return to power of the dictator's son, Ramfis, and in December 1962 the reformers elected Juan Bosch president with more than 60 percent of the vote. Bosch lasted only ten months before he was ousted by an army coup that installed Donald Reid Cabral as the head of a conservative junta. The new Johnson administration disdained Bosch as a "poet and dilettante" and backed Reid Cabral, just as his junta lost support from both the army and businessmen. When Reid Cabral announced his decision to run in the presidential election of 1965, the opposition groaned, and the United States extended a loan of $5 million to the unpopular government.

Faced with an unfair election, the supporters of deposed President Bosch staged a coup of their own on April 24. Four days later, after word from Ambassador John Barlow Martin that fifty-eight or fifty-three (the number kept fluctuating) "identified Communist or Castroite leaders" were in the rebel force, the United States dispatched 33,000 marines and army troops to crush the rebellion. Johnson announced that "we don't intend to sit here in our rocking chair with our hands folded and let the Communists set up any governments in the Western Hemisphere." Newspaper reporters accompanying the troops believed the embassy's list of subversives was spurious, and they gave wide publicity to Bosch's complaint that "this was a democratic revolution

U.S. Marines land on the beach at Danang, South Vietnam, March 1965.
(National Archives)

smashed by the leading democracy of the world." The Johnson administration coaxed a reluctant vote of support for its operations from the Organization of American States. Privately, diplomats from other Western Hemisphere countries indicated that U.S. actions demonstrated the Yankees' contempt for their southern neighbors. Had these officials heard Johnson's comments on the regional organization—"The OAS can't pour piss out of a boot if the instructions were written on the heel"—they would have had their worst fears confirmed. Foreign Relations Committee chairman Fulbright exploded that "the whole affair...has been characterized by a lack of candor." An aide later explained that the chairman "realized that if LBJ was lying to him about the Dominican Republic, he might be doing the same about Vietnam."

RIDING THE TIGER IN VIETNAM

Over the next year the Arkansas Democrat broke with the administration over the endless war in Southeast Asia. In early 1966 he denounced the "arrogance of power" of American diplomacy since the Second World War. Mocking the nightmares of American strategists, he reported that "certain pledges must be repeated every day lest the whole world go to rack and ruin—e.g., we will never go back on a commitment no matter how unwise." He nudged the committee into probing the extent and purpose of participation in the war in Vietnam. In the midst of two weeks of televised hearings,

Secretary of State Rusk explained that the United States found itself in "the process of preventing the expansion and extension of Communist domination by the use of force against the weaker nations on the perimeter of Communist power." He lectured the committee that "the war in Vietnam is as much an act of outside aggression as though the Hanoi regime had sent an army across the seventeenth parallel rather than infiltrated armed forces by stealth." Fulbright seemed unmoved, and a plaintive Rusk asked, "Senator is it not just possible that there is something wrong with them [the North Vietnamese]." The chairman replied, "Yes, there is something wrong with them....They are primitive, poor people who have been fighting for twenty years and I don't understand myself why they continue to fight, but they do." Some members of the foreign policy establishment who testified before the committee—former diplomat George Kennan, the father of containment; former army general James Gavin; and "realist" professor of international relations Hans J. Morgenthau—agreed with Fulbright. They thought that the United States diverted precious resources from Europe, the proper focus of diplomatic attention, by waging a fruitless, costly, unwinnable war in Southeast Asia. These misgivings provoked President Johnson's denunciation of "Nervous Nellies...who become frustrated and bothered and break ranks under the strain and turn on their leaders, their own country and their fighting men."

The heaviest buildup in American forces in Vietnam occurred after July 1965, when Johnson accepted his generals' request for more ground troops. For the next three years the conflict became America's war, fought by draftees who quickly learned to despise all Vietnamese, both friend and foe. The city of Saigon became an American outpost, resembling any town adjacent to a base. Brothels, bars, and opium dens catering to Americans sprang up, and the metropolis grew to a population of more than 1.5 million. Some of the new immigrants came to work for the Americans, and others fled in terror from the war in the countryside. The Americans may not have welcomed them in town, but they were delighted to have them leave the land. The new American commander in Vietnam, Gen. William C. Westmoreland, favored a strategy of "search and destroy" in which the American troops scoured the countryside looking for the enemy and killing them. The fewer friendly Vietnamese the better, and the Americans cleared "free-fire zones" in which anything that moved was fair game. In a war without traditional front lines or regular enemy units, the "body count" became the means of measuring progress. Secretary of Defense McNamara required numbers from commanders to judge the success of the war. From the lowliest lieutenant to the colonels and generals, the number of dead on the other side was exaggerated until it appeared that the United States was slaughtering 300,000 Vietnamese a year.

Indochina during the Vietnam conflict

These reports convinced the secretary of defense until the middle of 1967, when he noticed that the North Vietnamese had no trouble replacing their losses in the South even though commanders had told him that more men were being killed than could be drafted. At the same time McNamara was wracked with doubts about the morality of the bombing campaign in the North and the South. He asked an assistant, Leslie Gelb, to compile a documentary history of the American involvement in the war. *The Pentagon Papers*, which emerged from this study, concluded that U.S. leaders since Roosevelt had deceived the public into supporting an unwinnable war. In the fall McNamara, ashamed of his participation in the war and convinced that it could not be won, asked Johnson for another job. LBJ, furious at his defection, let him become president of the World Bank. Few doubts assailed the president. His principal concerns in the war were not to lose, not to allow the Chinese or Soviets to intervene, and to keep the public behind him. He hoped to maintain popular support by making the fighting as painless as possible. Despite repeated pleas from the Pentagon, Johnson refused to call up reserves. While nearly 2 million draftees went into combat, they served a tour of twelve months rather than for the duration of the war. Even as the cost of the war soared to $50 billion per year, Johnson refused a plea by his chief economic advisers to raise taxes to pay for it or ask Congress to curb spending for the war on poverty. Instead, the administration paid for the war with public borrowing, causing inflation to rise in the United States from less than 3 to about 5 percent a year and flooding Europe with unwanted dollars.

INTERNATIONAL REPERCUSSIONS

Allied governments did little to help as they watched the economic and political results of the war in Vietnam with a combination of horror and some secret delight at America's discomfiture. The United States persuaded no Europeans to join the war effort as it had in the Korean War. Small contingents from South Korea, the Philippines, Australia, and New Zealand, all handsomely paid by the United States, joined the fight. The Koreans especially acquired a reputation for fierceness bordering on savagery in combat. But the European nations criticized the United States on several fronts. German chancellor Ludwig Erhard, a former finance minister, believed the United States was exporting inflation. French president Charles de Gaulle voiced the harshest criticism when he predicted in a 1966 speech in the Phnom Penh, Cambodia, soccer stadium that "there is no chance that the peoples of Asia will subject themselves to the law of the foreigner who comes from the other shore of the Pacific, whatever his intentions, however powerful his weapons." Back in Paris he blasted the "bombing of a very small people by a very large one" and condemned American actions as "unjust… detestable war, since it leads a great nation to ravage a small one." He offered to arrange a swift cease-fire and American withdrawal.

Dean Rusk shrugged off de Gaulle's proposals to mediate as the sour grapes of the leader of a country that had lost in Vietnam and wanted the Americans to suffer a similar humiliation. But Americans had a harder time responding to other concerns often voiced in Europe during the Vietnam years: namely, the war had diverted American attention from other more important world events. This objection seemed borne out when a war erupted between Israel and three of its Arab neighbors—Egypt, Jordan, and Syria— in June 1967. In May President Gamal Nasser of Egypt evicted the United Nations force from the Sinai Peninsula and closed the Strait of Tiran to ships bound to and from the southern Israeli port of Eilat. The United States, which had become a major supplier of arms to Israel in the Kennedy administration, tried to arrange an international force of warships to test the Egyptian guns at Sharm el-Sheik, which blocked the Strait of Tiran. To the chagrin of Johnson, Rusk, and McNamara, none of the fifty states approached was willing to join the United States in challenging the blockade. At the end of May, Johnson begged Israeli foreign minister Abba Eban for more time to reach a peaceful settlement. His government waited two weeks, but when it became apparent that the United States could not force Nasser to back down, Israeli warplanes struck at dawn on June 5, destroying Egypt's air force on the ground. The war lasted only six days, with Israel humiliating the combined armies of Egypt, Jordan, and Syria. Israel captured the Sinai Peninsula from Egypt, the West Bank of the Jordan River and eastern Jerusalem from Jordan, and the Golan Heights from Syria. Israeli bombers sank ships in the Suez Canal the first morning of the war, thereby closing that waterway for the next seven years. European powers were furious that their supply of oil would now have to make the 10,000-mile trip around Africa, but the United States found some comfort in the canal's blockage: now Soviet ships had a longer voyage on the way to carrying supplies to Vietnam.

In the aftermath of the Six Day War, Soviet prime minister Alexei Kosygin came to New York to attend a special session of the United Nations. While in America the Soviet leader met President Johnson for their only conference at the small college town of Glassboro, New Jersey. Johnson wanted Soviet help in pressuring the North Vietnamese to negotiate with the Americans. The Soviet leader was noncommittal, but Johnson at least came away with the relieved sense that Kosygin desperately wanted to avoid a direct military confrontation with the United States in Vietnam. The two men also agreed to do more to limit the race in strategic arms between the super-powers.

COVER ACTIONS AND U.S. FOREIGN POLICY

As the foreign policy consensus collapsed under the weight of the Vietnam War, Americans took a hard look at clandestine activities by their intelligence operations—the Central Intelligence Agency, the Federal Bureau of Investigation, the Defense Intelligence Agency, and the National Security Agency. Reports surfaced in 1967 that the CIA had funneled funds to foreign political parties, labor unions, newspapers, and publishers. In violation of its 1947 charter, the agency spied on American citizens in the United States, opening their mail, tapping their telephones, and tracing their friends. The CIA had secretly paid the bills of the liberal anticommunist National Student Association from 1951 to 1966 and provided subventions for publishing books on international affairs that subtly supported the American point of view. The CIA also plotted the assassination of foreign leaders, hatched a coup in Iran in 1953, invaded Guatemala in 1954, planned the Bay of Pigs invasion in 1960–1961, "destabilized" the socialist governments of Chile after 1970 and Nicaragua after 1980, and helped scores of anticommunist governments crush domestic rebellions and undermine opposition parties. More than $5 billion yearly went to the various intelligence operations, but the appropriations were hidden in innocuous-sounding programs in the Defense, State, Commerce, Treasury, and Agriculture Department budgets. Few members of Congress beyond a trusted inner circle knew how much money went for intelligence.

Fierce battles raged within the intelligence community itself. While the 1947 National Security Act supposedly centralized information gathering under the authority of the director of central intelligence, the CIA never managed to keep the field to itself. The FBI under the leadership of the prickly, maybe paranoid, J. Edgar Hoover, its only director before 1971, resented the CIA. Hoover despised its use of noncommunist liberals and socialists in foreign countries to achieve its ends. Suspecting that the well-connected Ivy Leaguers the CIA recruited as its operatives harbored liberal sentiments of their own, Hoover forbade the FBI agents from sharing information with their counterparts in the CIA. The FBI persisted in its own domestic espionage activities, code-named COINTELPRO (Counter-Intelligence Program), under which it infiltrated the American Communist Party, the Socialist Workers Party, the Students for a Democratic Society, the Black Panthers, and other dissident groups.

The CIA also encountered competition from intelligence operations in the armed forces, the State Department, and the National Security Agency. During the Vietnam War the CIA consistently presented accurately pessimistic estimates of the chances for success. Alarmed generals, admirals, and diplomats ordered their own departments to prepare more cheerful forecasts.

The National Security Agency, created in 1946 as a code-breaking operation, soon exceeded that technical function. After the United States began launching communications spy satellites, the NSA could intercept and decipher telephone conversations around the globe. "We know what Brezhnev says to his chauffeur," boasted one official. Instead of providing the raw data to the CIA for analysis, the NSA acquired its own staff of specialists to explain what the messages meant.

During the 1975 congressional investigations of covert intelligence activities, Idaho Democratic senator Frank Church, chair of the Select Intelligence Committee, charged that the CIA had become a "rogue elephant," plunging uncontrolled into a steamy jungle of deception, assassination, and counterrevolution. The charge that intelligence agents had become the masters rather than the servants of foreign policy was too simple. Political leaders often welcomed the "deniability" offered by entrusting "dirty tricks" to secret agents. Because they were outside the scrutiny of press, public, or Congress, covert operations permitted officials to avoid the second-guessing of democracy, which makes life harder for people at the top. Moreover, the confusion within the intelligence community mirrored the competition in more visible parts of the foreign policy bureaucracy. Intelligence agencies had the same types of parochial interests that the other offices pursued in the decades that the United States had global interests. The CIA, NSA, DIA, and FBI have been no more the servants or masters of foreign policy than other groups. All have been part of the vast, untidy apparatus that has projected American power.

JOHNSON'S FALL

Lyndon B. Johnson lost ground politically in 1967. He no longer spoke about being "president of all the people" and retreated to "I'm the only president you've got." While he met with Kosygin, a National Conference for New Politics opened in Chicago, hoping to form the first left-wing political party in America in twenty years. Martin Luther King, Jr., the most prominent of the nation's black civil rights advocates, opposed the war in Vietnam as needlessly causing the death of black draftees and called on Johnson to step down. In November as many as 100,000 demonstrators marched on the Pentagon to hear calls for immediate American withdrawal from Vietnam. Rejecting pleas for "moderation," "responsible debate," and "negotiated settlements," speakers told the crowd "the only thing to negotiate is the route American troops use out of Vietnam." While some demonstrators listened to the speeches, others followed the lead of poet Allen Ginsberg in attempting to levitate the Pentagon through mystical incantations. Others, such as Norman

Mailer, participated in mass arrests to emphasize opposition to the war. Calls went out throughout the antiwar movement to make the transition "from dissent to resistance."

Conventional politicians also looked for ways to "dump Johnson." Allard Lowenstein, a moderate antiwar activist, persuaded Sen. Eugene McCarthy of Minnesota to challenge Johnson for the Democratic nomination in the primary elections upcoming in the spring of 1968. Robert F. Kennedy, elected to the Senate from New York in 1964, had come out against the war in 1966, and he waited for the right opportunity to enter the fray against Johnson. Another dissident Democrat, Gov. George C. Wallace of Alabama, expecting to capitalize on the "white backlash" to the civil rights movement and the public weariness with the small progress in Indochina, announced his candidacy. Among Republicans Richard Nixon, Nelson Rockefeller, George Romney, and Ronald Reagan all hoped to run against "Lyndon Johnson's war." While the Republican contenders said little about what they would do differently, they all agreed that Johnson had mishandled affairs.

A U.S. Marine carries a wounded Vietnamese woman to a hospital in the midst of the fighting in Hue during the Tet Offensive, February 1968.
(National Archives)

The last hope the administration had of persuading the public that the war could be won vanished when the North Vietnamese launched the Tet (New Year's) Offensive on January 31, 1968. In two weeks of fighting, the North Vietnamese captured eight provincial capitals, blew up the wall surrounding the U.S. embassy in Saigon, and held the grounds for several hours. American television viewers saw the police chief of Saigon put a bullet through the head of a Vietcong suspect, and they heard an American officer proclaim the awful words "We had to destroy the village in order to save it." On March 16, a month after the Americans and the ARVN beat back the offensive, Lt. William Calley led an army company that gunned down about 500 infirm men, women, and small children in the hamlet of My Lai. No calming remarks from Gen. Westmoreland about having crushed the Tet Offensive could change the public's disgust with the endless bloodshed.

By March Johnson was severely shaken. Sen. McCarthy nearly defeated him in the New Hampshire primary, which caused a wavering Robert Kennedy formally to enter the race. The president knew that Kennedy would defeat him in the Wisconsin primary. Johnson's newly appointed secretary of defense, Clark Clifford, supported by a group of "wise men" led by the former secretary of state Dean Acheson, let him know that they believed the war could not be won. Having only hardliners such as Rusk and Walt Whitman Rostow behind him, Johnson reluctantly turned down Gen. Westmoreland's request for 206,000 additional troops. On March 31 the president shocked the public by announcing his withdrawal from the presidential race so he could devote himself full time to negotiating a settlement. He stopped the bombing north of the nineteenth parallel in an effort to open peace talks in Paris.

Things got worse before they got better. Several American cities erupted in flames after Martin Luther King, Jr., was murdered on April 4. Johnson called up thousands of regular army troops to suppress the insurrection in Washington. Two months later another assassin shot Robert Kennedy, shocking the world and stripping antiwar Democrats of the only dissenter who had a chance of gaining the party's presidential nomination. When the Democratic Convention met in Chicago in August, Vice President Hubert Humphrey, the president's choice, became the nominee in the midst of massive antiwar demonstrations. A total of 6,000 troops joined hundreds of Chicago police in clubbing antiwar activists who chanted, "The streets belong to the people" and "The whole world is watching" while trying to march on the convention hall. President Johnson, fearful of the chorus of boos that would greet his appearance (despite Chicago mayor Richard Daley's packing the gallery with loyal sanitation collectors), did not come to the convention.

The Democrats emerged from Chicago in such disarray that even the resurrection of Richard Nixon as the Republican nominee could not unite them. Liberals thought Nixon had committed political suicide when he lost the governorship of California in 1962 and told reporters, "You won't have Nixon to kick around any more." Now there was a "new Nixon," the foremost Republican statesman on foreign policy, who would take the high road while his running mate, Maryland governor Spiro Agnew, pictured Humphrey as soft on communism.

Nixon won in November by a mere 500,000 votes, a margin nearly as small as the one by which he had lost to John Kennedy in 1960. Many antiwar Democrats decided to support Humphrey at the last minute, after he announced that he would suspend all bombing of the North to get peace talks started. A few days before the election actual discussions between the United States and North Vietnam did open in Paris after the diplomats resolved a months-long dispute over the shape of the negotiating table. More voters probably wanted to escalate the war than wanted withdrawal. George Wallace received 8 million votes as an independent running on a prowar platform with former air force general Curtis LeMay, who expressed the wish to "bomb them [the North Vietnamese] into the stone age."

Nixon's own proposals for ending the Vietnam War were even more obscure. During the campaign he indicated that he had a secret plan that would assure "peace with honor," but to reveal it publicly would ruin Johnson's chances of ending the conflict. Privately, he doubted that the war could be won. A month after the election he chose Henry Kissinger, a Harvard political science professor who formerly had been foreign policy adviser to Nelson Rockefeller, to be the head of the National Security Council. Nixon and Kissinger together spent the next four years looking for ways to conclude America's war in Vietnam and silence the voices challenging the assumptions on which American foreign policy had rested since 1945.

 Lyndon Johnson departed Washington a broken man on January 20, 1969. His leadership in the most controversial war in American history coincided with the end of the era of American dominance of world politics.

CHAPTER ELEVEN

The Rise and Fall of Détente, 1969–1976

Richard Nixon had no secret plan for ending the war in Vietnam, but he knew that the war had taken a heavy toll on the country and its president. The war had wrecked Johnson's ability to act freely in foreign affairs, and the new president wanted to restore the authority of the White House. The bewilderment of the Europeans with the American preoccupation in Vietnam meant that the United States no longer could count on automatic agreement from its allies. For example, French president Charles de Gaulle assured fellow Europeans that the war in Vietnam hastened the day when "the Americans would no longer have any reason to stay on this side of the ocean." Nixon declared in his inaugural address on January 20, 1969, that "after a period of confrontation, we are entering an era of negotiations" with Cold War adversaries.

The excessive commitment of American power in Vietnam prevented the United States from responding to other changes in the world balance. For years Americans had denied the split between the Soviet Union and China, and Secretary of State Dean Rusk explained that the United States fought in Vietnam to meet the threat of "a billion Chinese armed with nuclear weapons." By 1969, however, with China convulsed in a "Great Proletarian Cultural Revolution," American diplomats no longer ignored the fact that the People's Republic went its own way. American and Soviet influence seemed to ebb in the rest of the world, too. This "diffusion of power," as Johnson's undersecretary of state Eugene Rostow called it, reflected the changes in the world's economy. No longer did the United States sit alone as the world's only wealthy country, as it had at the end of the Second World War. There was nothing Nixon could do to restore American economic dominance, but he reasoned that extrication from Vietnam would provide greater maneuverability in a competitive world.

ASSERTING CONTROL OF FOREIGN POLICY

Nixon's first objective regarding the Vietnam War was to silence domestic and foreign critics. Then, perhaps, government could govern without having to answer opponents it could never satisfy. Nixon's style of making foreign policy—his dramatic reversals, his reliance on trusted staff members, and his sanctimony—helped lower the rhetoric over Vietnam. His collaboration with National Security Adviser Henry Kissinger set the tone. They complemented each other, secretly directing relations with other nations while one of Nixon's oldest friends in political life, William P. Rogers, made the public appearances as secretary of state from 1969 to 1973. Rogers had been the man Nixon turned to when Eisenhower had wanted to drop him from the 1952 ticket as a result of the controversy over the "secret fund" provided by Nixon's business friends. Throughout the Eisenhower administration Rogers remained one of the few men who liked Nixon and retained his own sense of decency. His reward for befriending Nixon was appointment to the premier spot in the cabinet, where he suffered the indignity of being kept in the dark on important issues. Kissinger, who bested Rogers in the bureaucratic wars and could afford to appear generous, recalled that "Rogers was in fact far more able than he was pictured; he had a shrewd analytical mind and outstanding common sense."

With Rogers put forward to give an impression of well-intentioned honesty, Nixon and Kissinger went about their own work of creating an "illusion of peace," as former *New York Times* reporter Tad Szulc described it. Nixon's reliance on Kissinger rested on more than both men's enthusiasm for manipulation and secrecy. Both acknowledged the problems of bureaucratic rivalry that had plagued American foreign policy for half a century. They realized that the National Security Act of 1947 had built a framework for presidential control over foreign policy, but it had not eliminated interagency warfare. Things had gotten worse in the sixties when the Pentagon under Robert McNamara assumed an increasing share of the business of foreign policy. Kissinger proposed to Nixon to make the National Security Council "the principal forum for issues requiring interagency coordination, especially where presidential decisions of a middle or long range are involved." On the first day of the new administration, Kissinger seized control of the planning function for the National Security Council by demanding in the president's name that all policy papers receive clearance from him and his staff. He bombarded the State, Defense, and Treasury departments with requests for information. He set up special working groups to coordinate policies on Vietnam, southern Africa, and the Middle East.

LIQUIDATING VIETNAM

Nixon also took a visible part in setting a new course. In May 1969 he met South Vietnamese president Nguyen Thieu on the island of Midway to discuss the future of the war. Nixon told Thieu that American troops no longer could be as obtrusive in the war, that American forces had to be withdrawn with the South Vietnamese soldiers doing more of the fighting. So began the disengagement of American ground troops, a process as awkward as the new word Vietnamization Nixon invented to describe it. While the United States gradually reduced the troop level from 535,000 to 400,000 over the next year and American casualties fell from more than 300 men to less than 100 men killed a week, the air war increased. In 1969 and 1970 the United States dropped tons of bombs on battlefields in South and North Vietnam up to the nineteenth parallel and in Cambodia. From Midway Island the president flew to Guam where he promised a new "Nixon Doctrine" designed to limit American engagement in future wars. The United States would use small nations as surrogates, he asserted. America would provide the arms, advisers, and financing for other countries to wage guerrilla or conventional wars against domestic insurgents or foreign enemies.

Despite its promise of reducing American participation in overseas conflicts, the Nixon Doctrine changed little in the way the United States dealt with other lands. First, the president indicated that the United States would move to this new strategy only after the war in Vietnam ended. Moreover, the United States had modestly increased its sale of weapons throughout the sixties, but these activities mushroomed 150 percent in the early seventies. In 1970 the United States exported $1.8 billion worth of arms. That figure rose to $4.3 billion in 1973 and then skyrocketed to $11 billion in 1974 and $15.2 billion in 1976. While fewer Americans fought wars, the level of violence rose. Some regions, notably the Middle East, developed voracious appetites for sophisticated, deadly equipment. By 1977 the nations from the Mediterranean to the Persian Gulf absorbed 39 percent of all military sales, more than the purchases of the NATO and Warsaw Pact countries combined. These tools of destruction brought greater insecurity, not peace, to the region. A major war broke out between Israel and the Arab states in 1973, and the region was in flames again at the end of the decade.

The negotiations to end the war in Vietnam proceeded along two tracks. The public conversations begun a week before the 1968 election by the Johnson administration continued in Paris with Philip Habib, a career Foreign

Service officer, leading an American delegation in endless hours of fruitless conversation with the National Liberation Front contingent headed by Madame Nguyen Thi Binh. While these talks failed to hasten the coming of peace, they did explain to the world that the United States was talking with, and listening to, an exasperating foe. The North Vietnamese insisted that the diplomats resolve the military question of when the United States would withdraw its troops and stop the bombing. In reply Americans linked the military and political sides of the war. The United States was willing to withdraw troops, but only if the North Vietnamese did the same. Each time Nixon took to the air to announce withdrawal of more troops, American negotiators hoped to obtain North Vietnamese consent to a political deal. Instead, the adamant North Vietnamese stayed put, and with each reduction in the size of the U.S. army in South Vietnam, American leverage over the future of Indochina diminished.

While the public talks went nowhere, Kissinger began in August 1969 a series of secret negotiations with Xuan Thuy, the principal representative from the North Vietnamese delegation. The national security adviser would fly from Washington to unnamed airbases in France or West Germany and be whisked to private retreats on the outskirts of Paris. There, in villas owned by members of the Communist Party of France, where priceless Picassos hung on the walls, the national security adviser and Thuy spoke privately. At one point in the conversation, an enterprising reporter learned of Kissinger's presence, but the West German government put out a cover story that the plane carrying the American to Paris actually bore a mistress of French president George Pompidou. The national security adviser appeared more flexible in private than did the official team. He suggested that the United States was heartily sick of the war, but America could not leave immediately for fear of alienating President Thieu and being seen as weak. He indicated to Xuan Thuy, however, that the Americans would be willing to separate the military and political issues in the war if the North showed similar willingness to hold back in its eventual takeover of the South. Xuan Thuy did not encourage Kissinger in the early days of their conversations, but the American could be as menacing as he could be generous.

The United States signaled the North Vietnamese that it would enlarge the air war while it reduced the troop level. In April 1969 Nixon ordered the secret bombing of Cambodia, a traditional neutral that had managed to stay out of the war for the previous five years. Led by Prince Norodom Sihanouk, the Cambodians had allowed the North Vietnamese to use their territory as staging areas for the war in the South. American generals had wanted for years to cross the border into Sihanouk's country and eliminate what they thought was a secret command headquarters for the National Liberation Front. Lyndon Johnson had always resisted the expansion of the war beyond

Vietnam, but Nixon and Kissinger believed that a "sideshow" in Cambodia would keep the generals happy while the United States brought troops home. If the prince did not complain about the bombing, which was to be kept secret, then it would indicate that the Cambodians actually supported the Americans. The North and South Vietnamese would also know about the attacks, but news would be withheld from the press and public. Even the men who flew the giant B-52s were under the misconception that they dropped their bombs in South Vietnam. Whenever there was a special order for the MENU bombing, the code name for the operation, enlisted men secretly adjusted the coordinates on the airplanes' computers without the pilots' knowledge so they would fly over Cambodia. When the *New York Times* broke the story in April, a brief flurry of public opposition arose. Nixon and Kissinger offered bland assurances that the Cambodians did not object and continued with the bombing.

Prince Sihanouk, chief of state of Cambodia since 1945, never found favor with official Washington, which found him too fond of good wine, fast cars, and France, where he had spent much of his life. A proud nationalist who worried that the United States, Vietnam, and China each had designs on his land, the prince had tried, not always successfully, to stay aloof from the war in Vietnam. He closed his eyes to North Vietnamese troops in his land while at the same time uttering no protest when American B-52s bombed them. He drew the line, however, at American or South Vietnamese ground troops on Cambodian soil. But an ambitious anti-Communist army general, Lon Nol, had fewer qualms about inviting outsiders. When Sihanouk made his yearly visit to the French Riviera in March 1970, the general deposed the prince and made himself prime minister. In Washington Kissinger and Nixon cheered the news of a more compliant Cambodia that would actively join the war against North Vietnam.

The cavalier disregard of the public's objections continued in the fall when the antiwar movement tried once again to end the fighting. A broad coalition ranging from moderate Republicans to revolutionary supporters of the Vietcong scheduled a demonstration in Washington for the weekend of November 14. A week before the march, which drew close to half a million people, Nixon announced the withdrawal of an additional 75,000 troops. He also called upon the "great silent majority" of the American public to support him in the war. On the day of the demonstration itself, buses ringed the White House to prevent any of the demonstrators from getting too close to the president, who, his aides announced, spent the afternoon watching television as the Notre Dame football team defeated Michigan State. The November demonstration was the high-water mark for massive, peaceful marches on the nation's capital. Seemingly having no effect on the administration's policies and with the larger public happy that the troops were being withdrawn, the antiwar movement cast about for new techniques. Activists on college campuses suggested that student strikes occur each month, with the duration increasing.

The antiwar movement revived in May 1970, when the Nixon administration became convinced that the bombing of Cambodia had done little good and that an invasion was necessary. On the evening of April 30, Nixon took to the airwaves with the announcement that American and South Vietnamese troops had crossed the border to find the "headquarters of the North Vietnamese." Campuses erupted across the country. National guardsmen, summoned by Ohio governor James A. Rhodes to Kent State University, killed four and wounded twenty-two students attending a rally called to get the militia off the campus. In mourning, stunned undergraduates across the country refused to attend classes. Rhodes lost a close primary the next week, hundreds of television reporters descended on the town of Kent, and novelist James A. Michener produced a 600-page book on the incident. The public paid much less attention when Mississippi national guardsmen shot and killed two student antiwar protestors at Jackson State College, a black institution, the week after the massacre at Kent.

President Nixon offered no condolences to the families of the slain demonstrators, but he did ask his chauffeur to drive him to the Lincoln Memorial on the night of May 7 to talk about the war to some of the thousands of college students who had flocked to Washington to express their outrage. Senators John Sherman Cooper, a Kentucky Republican, and Frank Church, an Idaho Democrat, angry at the widening war, introduced legislation repealing the Gulf of Tonkin Resolution. Several members of Kissinger's staff submitted resignations, while the national security adviser himself confronted angry Harvard students and professors. "They were as wrong as they were passionate," he recalled. He told them he had restrained Nixon from even more forceful acts and begged his former colleagues for patience, but he concluded he "would get no help" from his old colleagues. Eager to demonstrate his loyal support for the Cambodian operation, Kissinger thereupon authorized the Federal Bureau of Investigation to install taps on the telephones of aides suspected of speaking to reporters. The taps revealed little. Nixon later explained to White House counsel John Dean at the height of the Watergate scandal, "Lake and Halperin [two staff members under surveillance], they're both bad. But the taps were too. They never helped us. Just gobs and gobs of material: gossip and bullshitting."

The invasion proved a fiasco. The Americans and South Vietnamese found no headquarters because none existed. Nixon shortly thereafter announced that the troops would leave Cambodia by June 30, thereby eliminating the small hope that the mission made military sense. In Cambodia the results of the invasion were worse. With Sihanouk deposed, a long-smoldering civil war erupted in full flame between the Cambodian Communists, or Khmer Rouge, and Lon Nol's government. Both sides used boys as young as twelve as soldiers. These untrained, frightened youths, imbued by officers with implacable hatred of the other side, engaged in murderous assaults. The better-led Khmer Rouge conducted some of the worst atrocities of the Indochina war. After their victory in April 1975, they forced hundreds of thousands of Cambodian city dwellers to leave their homes and live off the land. A total social breakdown ensued, and as many as 3 million innocent people, nearly 40 percent of the population, were starved to death by the new government. The unhappy country's troubles continued for years. In 1979 the new Communist government of Vietnam invaded Cambodia and installed a less brutal regime, but one that was a virtual puppet of Hanoi. Prince Sihanouk, now living in Beijing as a guest of the Chinese government and bitterly opposed to Vietnam, made another of his startling shifts of alliances and backed the remnants of the Khmer Rouge, despite their having murdered several of his children. The United States, too, decided that anything, including the odious Khmer Rouge, was preferable to Vietnamese domination of Cambodia. After 1979 American representatives at the United Nations continued to vote for the seating of the vestiges of the Khmer Rouge in the General Assembly. Prince Sihanouk, whom Washington had airily dismissed, returned for a triumphal American tour in 1981, in which private church and relief groups publicly promised aid and public officials privately expressed their understanding and support for his attempts to regain his throne with the aid of the butchers of his kingdom.

The American army began to disintegrate as troop withdrawals mounted. No soldier wanted to be the last man killed in action. Platoons refused to go on patrol, officers were murdered by their own men, and marijuana smoking increased. The absurdity of the wartime experience increased the disillusionment. As a disgraceful character in the antiwar novel *Dog Soldiers* put it, "When elephants are hunted by armed men in helicopters, the only solution is to get high." Interracial hatred mounted, as black soldiers believed they bore the brunt of the fighting and dying, and race riots broke out on navy vessels. In the midst of this, the massacre at My Lai came to light, and Lt. William J. Calley stood trial for murder. Although a court-martial convicted Calley in 1971 and sentenced him to a prison term of fifteen years, Nixon spoke out in favor of reducing the sentence. The president hoped to align himself with the prowar segment of the population who thought that Calley had been unfairly accused by the antiwar movement.

A year after the invasion of Cambodia hastened the destruction of that country, the United States helped the Vietnamese army move into another neutral neighbor, Laos, in May 1971. American television viewers saw the reality of Vietnamization as the Vietnamese troops scrambled for cover instead of fighting. The invasion turned into a rout, with ARVN soldiers rushing back home without clearing out another supposed headquarters of the insurgency. What had been planned in Washington as a means of demonstrating how well the South Vietnamese could fight became instead proof that they could not hold their own.

At the same time, the American economy seemed ill, with inflation running at an unacceptable rate of 5 percent per year, and Europeans were angry that the United States had exported the cost of the war to them. German and French central bankers made their distress known by demanding payment in gold for the dollars they held. On August 15, 1971, Nixon made a dramatic about face in economic policy, announcing the imposition of wage and price controls, something he had previously said he would never do. He also cut the remaining link between the dollar and gold; no longer would the U.S. Treasury repay foreign dollar holders with the precious metal. Nixon had little choice, for foreigners held four times as many dollars as the U.S. possessed gold. He devalued the dollar by 10 percent in terms of other currencies. Nixon hoped for a decline in the value of the American currency, which would accordingly decrease the flood of exports from Japan and Europe. The Japanese economy had, in fact, boomed during the Vietnam War as the United States used that nation's facilities to repair equipment.

AN OPENING TO CHINA

Nixon also moved in 1971 and 1972 to isolate Vietnam from China and the Soviet Union, reasoning that if the North Vietnamese lost their major backers, they would make peace on America's terms. Accordingly, Nixon and Kissinger recognized the Soviet-Chinese split while at the same time attempting to become friendlier with both Communist powers. The negotiations with the two nations went along at the same time, although the opening to China was the more dramatic. Secret talks began in Warsaw, Poland, between the American and Chinese ambassadors in 1970. During that year Kissinger took over the negotiations, letting Secretary of State Rogers know what he was doing only when he found it convenient. In March 1971 the Chinese sent friendly signals to the United States by inviting a traveling American Ping-Pong team to visit China. The same month he became the first American president to use the formal name "the People's Republic of China" in a speech in which he voiced his hope to "establish a dialogue" with the PRC. When the American Ping-Pong squad played in Beijing in April, Chinese premier Zhou Enlai said "your visit has opened a new chapter in the history of the relations between Chinese and American peoples."

In June Zhou sent a secret message to Nixon through Pakistan that Chinese Communist Party chairman Mao Zedong approved a secret visit by Kissinger to Beijing. Kissinger and Nixon were thrilled at this message, which they described as "the most important communication that has come to an American president since the end of World War II."

Kissinger went to Beijing on July 9 after first disappearing from sight on a visit to Pakistan. The press reported that the national security adviser had a stomachache, and the next day he showed up in the Chinese capital to announce that the president of the United States would be coming to China to open "normal" relations between the two countries. Kissinger formed a bond with Zhou Enlai, describing him as "one of the two or three most impressive men I have ever met." The national security adviser offered China "strategic reassurance" that the United States would not join with the Soviet Union in encircling China. He also said that Washington did not support a policy of two Chinas (the PRC and the Republic of China on Taiwan) or an independent Taiwan. He instantly became a celebrity in the press. *U.S. News and World Report* thought that "Kissinger's secret mission to Red China [had] few parallels in the annals of U.S. diplomacy." One of the security adviser's admirers proclaimed that his secret trip confirmed his standing as "the smartest guy around."

Officials in other countries experienced genuine pain at the handshake between him and Chinese premier Zhou Enlai. The Japanese, who had followed American suggestions and improved relations with the Nationalists on Taiwan, were caught unaware. They read of the American reversal in the newspapers. Secretary of State Rogers played no part in the planning for the trip to China, and he had to watch the most important departure in recent American diplomatic history from the sidelines. H. R. Haldeman heard the national security adviser complain that "Rogers is trying to stop Kissinger as the negotiator with the Chinese." The prospect of the old anticommunist warrior, Richard Nixon, breaking with the government of Jiang Jieshi (Chiang Kai-shek) also astonished the right wing of the Republican Party. Ohio representative John Ashbrook vowed to fight Nixon for the party's presidential nomination in the 1972 primaries. In Taiwan Jiang reacted with sputtering rage. That the American president who had hailed him earlier would now open relations with Mao Zedong flabbergasted Jiang. In Pakistan, where Gen. Ayub Khan had been the intermediary between Kissinger and the Chinese, the news won applause, for it seemed as if Pakistan were now an indispensable ally of the United States. Six months later, in December 1971, Gen. Khan called on Kissinger for something in return when the eastern province of Pakistan broke away and declared itself the independent nation of Bangladesh. Khan's army fought a war with India in which the United States "tilted" toward Pakistan. India triumphed, while the

President Richard Nixon with Mao Zedong, chairman of the Chinese Communist
Party, in Beijing, February 1972
(National Archives)

United States, unlike its Western European allies, supported the defeated
Pakistanis. Kissinger kept control of American policy toward the India-
Pakistan war. He told the president, "I can't turn it over to Rogers. We can't
be frivolous about this," because it is "the one area that will screw up the
trip" to China.

In February 1972 Nixon flew to Beijing. As he stepped off the plane, he
shook hands with Premier Zhou. The photograph of the two leaders reversed
an old snub; Secretary of State John Foster Dulles had refused Zhou's hand at
the Geneva conference of 1954. Nixon's trip to China proved a huge success.
He met with the aging Mao and accepted the Chinese leader's complaints
about the "hegemonism" of the Soviet Union. The two pledged to end their
thirty years of hostility and move toward "normal" relations. Before the decade
was out America and China had full diplomatic exchanges. On the touchy
question of Taiwan, the United States went a long way toward acknowledging the Chinese claims to the island. The Shanghai communiqué, announced
at the end of the meeting, indicated that the United States recognized that
both Chinese governments claimed that Taiwan was part of China, and that

the United States acknowledged the Beijing government as the sovereign power in China. Both sides pledged to work for a "peaceful resolution" of the dispute over Taiwan. No one knew precisely what that meant, and the phrasing was purposely ambiguous. Kissinger outshone Rogers in Beijing. The national security adviser helped fashion the final communiqué. His preeminence even threatened to overshadow the president. One of Nixon's other staff members worried that reporters had "built HAK to the point where people wonder whether he makes foreign policy or the president." Nixon minded less, however, as Kissinger helped the administration's reputation. The president used the national security adviser to generate support among the press for the Shanghai communiqué. "Deep six Rogers," the president commanded as he ordered Kissinger to explain the implications of the agreements with the People's Republic.

WHITE HOUSE ABUSES

While Kissinger decried leaks from NSC staff, other Nixon aides were appalled by certain stories in the press. In June 1971 Daniel Ellsberg, a former Pentagon analyst who had cast off his hawkish ideas on the war, turned over copies of the special Pentagon history of the Vietnam War to Neil Sheehan of the *New York Times*. Despite orders from Attorney General John N. Mitchell not to publish the documents, the *Times* did so on June 21. Immediately thereafter, the special assistant to the president for domestic affairs, John D. Ehrlichman, created a White House "plumbers" unit to plug leaks of embarrassing information. Their first stop was a break-in at the office of Ellsberg's psychiatrist to find discrediting information. Soon the plumbers cast a wider net. By the fall they were following Dita Beard, a lobbyist for the International Telephone and Telegraph Company, who had slipped documents to Jack Anderson suggesting that her company had paid $500,000 to the president's reelection campaign in return for help around the world, especially in Chile. While Beard recovered from a nervous breakdown at a Denver osteopathic hospital, E. Howard Hunt, one of the planners of the Guatemalan invasion in 1954, the Bay of Pigs operation of 1961, and the commando attacks on Cuba, dressed in a red fright wig and entered her hospital room to persuade her to recant her damaging allegation.

The Democratic National Committee's headquarters at the Watergate office complex in Washington appeared next on Hunt's ridiculous agenda. He recruited five anti-Castro Cubans to obtain Democratic Party secrets. While attempting to do so, they were apprehended at the building complex on the night of June 18, 1972.

DÉTENTE WITH THE SOVIET UNION

That "third-rate burglary," as Nixon's press secretary, Ronald Ziegler, dismissed it, created barely a stir in the summer of 1972 as Nixon successfully
relaxed tensions with the Soviet Union, proclaiming the beginning of an era
of détente. In late May he became the first American president to visit the
Soviet Union since FDR went to Yalta in 1945. Nixon's trip to Moscow was
all the more surprising as it came on the heels of another major escalation
of the war in Vietnam by the United States. A North Vietnamese offensive
in the spring of 1972 had once again exposed the weakness of the ARVN
troops. Nixon, politically unable to rush more American soldiers into battle,
responded instead by spending an evening watching the movie *Patton* and
then ordering American bombers to attack the ports of Haiphong and Hanoi
in Operation LINEBACKER. Nixon expected that Soviet ships would be hit
in these raids, which dumped 112,000 tons of bombs on the North. But if
the Kremlin leaders offered no formal protest and did not cancel his proposed visit to Moscow, he would conclude that they wanted an accommodation with the United States despite their friendship with North Vietnam.

Soviet president Leonid Brezhnev went ahead with the invitation to Nixon
for reasons of his own. With the scheduled opening of the Twenty-Fourth
Congress of the Soviet Communist Party at the end of June, the Soviet premier
desired some international success to show his docile delegates. The Soviet
economy was in far worse shape than the American, with the consumer goods
promised under Khrushchev still in short supply and chronic food shortages
threatening stability. The Soviet invasion of Czechoslovakia in August 1968
had temporarily stopped the Eastern Europeans from showing their independence, but the Soviets had constantly to worry about the loyalty of their
allies. The conditions on the Chinese border were even worse, with Mao
Zedong officially calling the Soviet Union a "revisionist" power that had
betrayed the revolutionary heritage of Leninism. (Mao had shown how much
of a revolutionary he was by embracing President Nixon!) Economically,
the Soviet Union could gain immensely by opening trade relations with the
United States. New technology would help the struggling consumer industry, and imports of American grain could raise meat production. If the United
States and the Soviet Union worked out a limit to the arms race, the Soviet
Union, already spending twice as much of its gross national product as the
Americans on arms, could divert resources to consumer goods. Finally, an
agreement with the United States in the face of the opening to China would
mean that the Soviet Union had effectively countered the pull of Beijing.

Accordingly, both sides had much to gain from an agreement in Moscow.
The two leaders culminated years of disarmament conversations in Vienna
when they signed a Strategic Arms Limitations Agreement (SALT I). In return

for a mutual pledge to drop production of an antiballistic missile (ABM) system, Nixon and Brezhnev set upper limits on the number of offensive missiles each side could husband. The Soviet Union would have 1,600, and the United States would be allowed 1,054. Despite these lopsided numbers, the United States actually gained in the exchange. The antiballistic missile system, a project with a price tag in excess of $50 billion, was given little chance by experts of accomplishing its difficult mission of shooting Soviet missiles out of the sky. The idea had been floated in the Johnson administration and dropped since weapons specialists did not believe it would work and a financially strapped government could not afford it. The ABM was resurrected by Nixon's secretary of defense, Melvin Laird, in 1969 as a way of showing that the new administration would be tougher with the Soviets than its predecessor had been. Henry Kissinger, whose academic work had included a discussion of the role of nuclear weapons, had backed the system for diplomatic, not strategic, reasons. The United States could threaten to complete the ABM as a bargaining chip that it would return to the Soviets for an agreement limiting the number of missiles.

In the case of intercontinental ballistic missiles (ICBMs), the United States actually came out ahead. While SALT I froze the number of missiles, it said nothing at all about the new technology of multiple warheads, in which the United States had a huge lead over the Soviet Union. With the introduction of MIRVs (multiple independently targeted reentry vehicles), the United States possessed a new weapon that had several warheads, each capable of hitting targets miles apart. The MIRVs gave the United States a two-to-one lead in deliverable warheads.

The arms race continued in the seventies, with each side trying to outdo the other in new technology. The United States developed a new strategy for avoiding a nuclear holocaust with the Soviet Union. Instead of protection, the United States and the Soviet Union would follow a MAD (mutual assured destruction) plan. The strategy was as frightening as the acronym that described it. Each side supposedly held the weapons of its adversary hostage, and each knew that an attack would be met with the assured destruction of its capacity to wage war. The Soviets never accepted the American definition of how the next war would be fought, but American planners dismissed Soviet complaints about "inhumanity" of the strategy as hypocrisy and proclaimed that the job of American defense intellectuals was to "raise the Soviets' learning curve" about modern strategic thinking.

In fact, the SALT agreements did not arrest the slide toward destabilizing weapons. Barred from some fields by the treaties, weapons planners on both sides turned their inventive energies to areas left uncovered by the agreements and sped up production of new generations of missiles not covered by SALT. The Soviets went to work on highly accurate land-based missiles—the SS16s. The United States worked on an invulnerable, accurate land-based missile of its own, the MX.

The two leaders also agreed to a twelve-point statement of Basic Principles of Relations between the United States and the Soviet Union, a document that broadly defined the ways in which they would treat each other in an era of détente. They promised to conduct "normal relations" on the basis of "peaceful coexistence" and the principles of "sovereignty, equality, non-interference in internal affairs, and mutual advantage." They promised to avoid seeking "unilateral advantage at the expense of the other" and to recognize each other's security interests "based on the principle of equality and the renunciation of the use or threat of force."

THE ELECTION OF 1972 AND THE VIETNAM NEGOTIATIONS

Nixon returned from Moscow to a coronation ceremony at the Republican National Convention, which had been hastily moved from San Diego to Miami after the whiff of scandal came from Dita Beard. Thugs from the Committee to Reelect the President (CREEP) had planned to kidnap radical leaders of demonstrations scheduled to disrupt the proceedings. The assembled Republicans cheered a man they expected easily to defeat the Democrats' Sen. George McGovern, a left-liberal who had been one of the first to oppose the war. CREEP had done what it could to disrupt the campaigns of the other Democratic candidates in the hopes that McGovern's liberal views went beyond those of most voters.

The election proved no contest. McGovern's campaign self-destructed early with the selection for vice president of Missouri senator Thomas Eagleton, who admitted having received shock treatments for depression. McGovern pledged "1,000 percent support" for Eagleton and then dumped him unceremoniously from the ticket. The public distrusted McGovern's economic proposals to guarantee $1,000 annually to every American, and they ignored his warnings that the Nixon administration had not moved to end the war in Vietnam. Instead, voters were heartened by Henry Kissinger's announcement in the last week of October that he had arranged a settlement with the new negotiator for North Vietnam, Le Duc Tho. "Peace is at hand," Kissinger assured a press conference, and a week later Nixon rode the euphoria of the war's end to a crushing defeat of McGovern. He carried every state but Massachusetts and captured nearly 61 percent of the vote.

Peace was not at hand in late October, and Kissinger received a severe dressing down from H. R. "Bob" Haldeman, the grim-faced, crew-cut chief of staff at the White House, for his indiscreet revelation on November 2 of why the public admired him. "Americans like the cowboy who leads the wagon train by riding ahead alone on his horse," the national security adviser informed an Italian journalist. Haldeman, wondering what role Kissinger saw for the president if his principal diplomat "rides into town and does everything by himself," temporarily banished him from the White House and forbade him to meet the press until an agreement was signed.

The snag in the negotiations arose from objections by South Vietnamese president Thieu to a peace settlement that would have the United States remove the last of its troops while the North Vietnamese agreed only not to introduce any new forces in the South. The United States had separated the military from the political aspects of the war by permitting the North Vietnamese and the Provisional Revolutionary Government (the new name for the National Liberation Front) to work out the best deal they could with the Thieu government. The United States had resisted the calls to depose Thieu, but still the South Vietnamese president did not want to face the armies of his enemies alone. He had a sinking suspicion that the United States had fled Vietnam and let the North know that it awaited only a "decent interval" before the Communists could take over the country. Thieu therefore rejected the importunities of Kissinger's deputy, Gen. Alexander M. Haig, who scurried to Saigon to secure South Vietnamese assent to the peace treaty before election day. Thieu was rude to Haig and refused to sign.

The Paris talks were at a standstill in November and December, when the president decided that a dramatic demonstration could loosen the South Vietnamese and frighten the North. Two days before Christmas Nixon ordered the B-52s, which previously had seen service only in the South and over Cambodia, to attack North Vietnam. Every city in the North came under fire, hospitals were exploded in Hanoi, and hundreds of civilians were killed. Denunciations came in from the usual peace groups, but Nixon treated their complaints with disdain. He justified the bombing by saying that it would secure the release of the American prisoners of war held in the North despite the fact that thirteen of the B-52s were shot down over the North and forty-five of their crew members held captive. While Nixon sought support from the silent majority, diplomats were at work on both the North and South Vietnamese. Kissinger continued his talks with Le Duc Tho and indicated that his boss might be mentally unhinged. Nixon himself carefully cultivated the fears that he might go to irrational lengths to get his way. Chief of Staff Haldeman later dubbed this procedure the "madman strategy": if the North Vietnamese doubted that Nixon felt bound by conventional restraints, they would sign before risking destruction. While Kissinger played upon these fears, Haig returned to Thieu in Saigon with some brutally frank messages. The United States was determined to have a settlement, withdraw all of its troops, and get its prisoners back. If Thieu refused, the United States would make peace anyway, leaving the South in the lurch. If, however, Thieu swallowed his misgivings, the bombing of the North offered only a taste of what the United States might do later to back its friend in the South. In a secret memorandum, which he later denied writing, Kissinger pledged the reintroduction of U.S. troops should the South need them. The United States also assured North Vietnam of future reconstruction aid if it would sign.

Thieu agreed to peace the second week of January 1973, and a smiling Henry Kissinger and a grinning Le Duc Tho put their initials on a treaty on January 23, three days after Nixon was inaugurated for a second term. The news that Nixon had actually withdrawn American troops may have been the final blow to an ailing Lyndon Johnson, who died at his ranch on the Pedernales on January 22. Kissinger was luckier, winning the Nobel Peace Prize in December 1973 along with Le Duc Tho.

The North Vietnamese diplomat refused to share the prize with Kissinger, whom he blamed for prolonging the war. Benjamin A. Schwartz, an expert on China and a former Harvard colleague, observed, "I'm no fanatical enemy of Kissinger, but this is a bit much. I think he's done some good things, but the Peace Prize? There's no peace, and we stayed too long." The *Los Angeles Times* expressed "some surprise," since "Southeast Asia is still not associated in most people's minds with peace," but, the paper went on, the prize was earned by "a professional and brilliant feat of diplomacy by two remarkable men."

In September Kissinger received the prize he really wanted when Nixon dropped William Rogers as secretary of state and appointed his national security adviser in his place. Since becoming a public figure with his trip to Beijing, Kissinger had delighted reporters, who loved his leaks, his wit, and his ability to mock his own German accent. Upon his appointment the liberal *New Yorker* praised him as "prodigiously intelligent, articulate, talented." One foreign service officer predicted, "we'll consider ourselves God's chosen children for a couple of months." The *Christian Science Monitor* reported that Watergate "may have been a catalyst in President Nixon's decision to make the change. It has already enabled him to say that he is 'getting the work out' in the departments where it belongs."

CHILE'S AGONY

Immediately upon appointment Kissinger became involved in the overthrow of the socialist government of Chile. Salvador Allende Gossens, the candidate of an alliance of socialists, communists, and radicals, had been elected president of one of the most thriving democracies of Latin America in 1970 with about 36 percent of the vote in a three-candidate race. The CIA followed its usual practice and funneled money to the Christian Democratic candidate, who came in third. When it became clear that Chile's congress would fulfill its traditional role of confirming as president the candidate with the most votes (Allende), the CIA station chief in Santiago panicked. He sent frantic messages to the Forty Committee, the Washington interagency body that supervised the CIA, asking for authorization to "destabilize" the government. Despite a secret CIA assessment that "no vital U.S. economic interests" would be threatened by Allende's accession to the presidency, the Forty Committee believed that his victory "created considerable political and psychological costs." The agency's deputy director for plans recalled that Secretary of State Kissinger "placed the heaviest of pressures" on him to block Allende's elevation. Accordingly, the agency developed a proposal to bribe Chilean congressmen to vote against Allende and, should that fail, encourage the military to mount a coup. The congress in Santiago confirmed Allende, and the military plot resulted only in the murder of Chile's chief of staff.

No coup followed, and for the next three years Allende embarked on a course of equalizing the gross inequalities in wealth plaguing his country. He nationalized the American-owned copper mines and expropriated the telephone system owned by the International Telegraph and Telephone Company (ITT). In Washington the American government responded by cutting off economic aid and using its influence with the World Bank and Inter-American Bank to refuse further credits to Allende's government. The aim, Kissinger explained, was "to make the economy scream." Despite the hostility of international business, Allende's government actually increased its share of the popular vote in the 1972 congressional elections, in which leftist candidates gained 42 percent of the vote. By the beginning of 1973, however, the Chilean middle class had joined with the elite and the foreign businesses in wanting the socialists out. CIA operatives were generous with their money, supporting demonstrations by angry middle-class housewives and a strike by truckers and taxi drivers, the best-paid members of the Chilean working class.

The military, proud of its long history of political neutrality, began plotting Allende's overthrow in the summer of 1973. The Chilean left insisted that Allende provide arms for the population, but the president, fearing a civil war and trusting the assurances of his military advisers that they would stand by him, refused to open the armories. On September 17 the generals who had given their pledge led the attack against Allende, and the president is supposed to have committed suicide. The United States helped the insurgents and immediately recognized the new regime. When asked about the morality of the overthrow of a duly elected democratic government, Kissinger replied that he saw no "right for people to vote in Communists" since presumably once they were in power they never left.

THE MIDDLE EAST WAR

Maintaining American domination over the Western Hemisphere came easier than asserting influence in the Middle East. A new war broke out between Israel and its neighbors when Syria and Egypt attacked on October 6, 1973, on the holiest day of the Jewish year, Yom Kippur. The Nixon administration had done little to defuse tensions since 1969. It had become the major arms supplier to Israel while at the same time floating a scheme in the summer of 1970 to have the Israelis withdraw to their 1967 borders. So little interested in the problem were Nixon and Kissinger that the American proposal for an Israeli retreat bore William Rogers's name, a sure sign that the men at the top had better things to do. Kissinger himself may have been reluctant to inject himself into the Arab-Israeli dispute because he was Jewish, but the Yom Kippur War jolted him into action. The Middle East became a region where the United States could block the Soviet Union.

In the first three days of the war, Egyptian troops crossed the Suez Canal, forcing the surrender of hundreds of surprised Israeli soldiers. In the north Syria's army posed an even graver threat to the Jewish state. It nearly broke through Israeli defenses on the Golan Heights to cut the country in two. Israeli prime minister Golda Meir telephoned urgent requests for American military aid and considered using the Israeli atomic bomb against the Arabs. American military officers were split over the kind of aid that should be offered to the Israelis. Some agreed with the European assessment that the Israelis should be brought down a few notches since they had not reached an accommodation with the Arabs after the 1967 Six Day War. If the United States were seen to be too enthusiastic in its support for Israel, whatever leverage America had with the Arab states would disappear. Still, Israel retained considerable support among the American public, and American Jewish leaders worried that the war seemed to be going so badly for the Jewish state.

Accordingly, Nixon and Kissinger devised a strategy of helping Israel repel the attack while simultaneously pressuring the Meir government to acknowledge its dependence upon the United States. A war that resulted in a stalemate between Arabs and Israelis might make both sides ask America to act as an honest broker. Nixon authorized an airlift of replacement arms and ammunition to Israel on October 21. Sure that they could receive additional supplies from the Americans, the Israelis committed the remainder of their equipment and turned the tide. They threw the Syrians back beyond the original line of the Golan Heights, and they crossed the Suez Canal and surrounded the Egyptian Third Army. At this point the Soviet Union threatened to intervene on the Egyptian side, while Nixon countered with an alert for American troops around the world. In October both the United States and the Soviet Union stood down, and they joined in a United

Nations Security Council resolution demanding a cease-fire. The Israelis reluctantly agreed despite their hopes of delivering a telling blow to the Egyptians. As Israeli defense minister Moshe Dayan explained to his country's parliament, "I tell you gentlemen, the tanks and ammunition our forces are firing in Egypt three weeks ago were in the United States."

With a cease-fire in effect between the Arabs and Israelis, Secretary of State Kissinger moved to have the United States become the major go-between in the dispute and to evict the Soviet Union from the Middle East. Egyptian president Anwar Sadat had begun the process a year before when he had thrown out 10,000 Soviet advisers. In mid-December a United Nations peace conference opened in Geneva with the United States and the Soviet Union as cochairs. For the first time in the history of the Arab-Israeli dispute, both sides sat down at the same table, but this icily correct meeting had only one session. Neither Israelis nor Egyptians wanted the Soviet Union involved. Instead, Kissinger began a process of "shuttle diplomacy" in the spring of 1974, flying from Cairo to Jerusalem and back to obtain a disengagement between the two armies. Since the Israelis stood on the west bank of the canal, while the Egyptians held positions on the east, both had reason to withdraw. After months of subtly shading what each had to say, Kissinger prodded them to an agreement in May. Negotiations between Israel and Syria were harder to carry off, as the Syrians were closer to the Soviets and hated the Israelis more than the Egyptians did.

WATERGATE'S IMPACT AND THE FALL OF RICHARD NIXON

The Yom Kippur War occurred as the Watergate scandal reached new heights. In his announcement of the international alert, Nixon tried but failed to divert attention from the resignation of Attorney General Eliot Richardson, the firing of the deputy attorney general, the dismissal of the special prosecutor, Archibald Cox, and the closing of his office in the "Saturday night massacre" of October 20, 1973. Immediately, calls went up for the impeachment or resignation of the president. Kissinger had the sickening sense that Nixon no longer could control a docile Congress. These premonitions were confirmed on November 7, when the House and Senate passed the War Powers Act over the president's veto. The new law represented a pendulum swing of congressional resentment over the "imperial presidency" that had stripped Congress of its right to make war. Under the terms of the War Powers Act, the president had to inform Congress whenever he committed American troops overseas. After sixty days the use of military power had to win specific congressional approval. The law had been introduced by Sen. Jacob Javits (R., New York) as a means of preventing any

Secretary of State Henry Kissinger briefs the new president, Gerald Ford.
(Gerald R. Ford Presidential Library)

open-ended commitment, such as the Gulf of Tonkin Resolution, from besmirching the reputation of the Congress, but critics charged that the act actually enhanced the president's power. Now, as never before, the president had a legal authorization of sixty days in which to do what he wanted in foreign affairs.

While the shuttle between Damascus and Jerusalem slowed, the Watergate scandal threatened finally to topple the president. Nixon's popularity fell steadily in 1973 and the spring of 1974 as the House Committee on the Judiciary prepared an impeachment bill against him. By June 55 percent of the public thought that Nixon should resign or be impeached. His approval rating stood at a minuscule 23 percent. Believing that his success at arranging détente with the Soviet Union retained some support among a public that believed the new vice president, Gerald Ford, lacked the stature to continue diplomacy, Nixon traveled to the Middle East and Moscow in June. The cosmetic character of these trips seemed obvious, and the histrionic effect of Nixon's suffering from a potentially fatal blood clot in his leg did not arouse the public sympathy he wanted. Millions of Egyptians turned out for a campaign-style swing from Cairo to Alexandria, but the Israelis who watched his motorcade from Tel Aviv to Jerusalem were more subdued. Some bore signs reminding the president of the hot breath of the impeachment process: "MR. PRESIDENT, YOU CAN RUN, BUT YOU CAN'T HIDE." Others expressed more basic fears: "DON'T SELL US OUT." En route to another summit with Premier Brezhnev, who thought that the Watergate impeachment process had been created by "right-wing enemies of détente," Kissinger erupted into an angry denunciation of the press. Documents leaked from the House Judiciary Committee's investigations indicated that the national security adviser had directed his deputy, Col. Haig, to install taps on his subordinates' phones. Accusing the newsmen traveling with his party of wanting to undermine his ability to direct foreign policy, he refused to answer any questions about this electronic eavesdropping. He promised to resign if they kept insisting, a prospect all reporters present agreed would leave the country without its most respected diplomat.

The House Judiciary Committee opened public debate on Nixon's impeachment in late July, and the Supreme Court ruled that the president had to hand over possibly incriminating tape recordings. The next week the committee voted three counts of the impeachment indictment—abuse of power, obstruction of justice, and contempt of Congress. Significantly, the charges of violating Congress's power to make war by the secret bombing of Cambodia failed to carry. On August 4 the White House released the transcripts called for by the Supreme Court order. One of them contained a "smoking gun," Nixon's directive for H. R. Haldeman to make the CIA stop the FBI's inquiry into the Watergate break-in. Kissinger, Haig, and Republican Senate leaders convinced Nixon that his position looked hopeless. The House surely would go along with the Judiciary Committee, and the Senate would convict the president. The secretary of state reportedly fell to his knees and joined the president in prayer on the floor of the White House's master bedroom on August 7, the night before Nixon announced his resignation.

The new chief executive, Gerald Ford, did not pretend to challenge the preeminence of Secretary of State Kissinger, who retained his title as national security adviser. While Ford's own popularity sank after he issued a blanket pardon of Richard Nixon in early September 1974, Kissinger continued to work his magic with reporters. That fall he revived his shuttle between Syria and Jerusalem.

THE OIL EMBARGO AND IRAN

Part of the urgency of the shuttle resulted from a Middle Eastern embargo on petroleum to the United States as punishment for its support of Israel. All Arab oil producers joined in cutting shipments to the United States, causing the lights on the national Christmas tree to be darkened and drawing a pledge from President Nixon "to make the United States energy-independent by 1980." Iran continued to provide petroleum to the United States, but the shah realized that here was an excellent opportunity to raise the price. By the spring of 1974, Iran had led the Organization of Petroleum Exporting Countries (OPEC) into a 300-percent rise in the price of crude oil, from $2 to $8 a barrel. To offset the costs for Iranian petroleum, the Nixon administration augmented the already huge arms shipments to Iran. "In the future," Nixon ordered, "arms requests from Iran should not be second guessed." The United States had forwarded $1.2 billion worth of war materials to Iran from 1950 to 1971. In the next seven years sales hit $21 billion. The shah's government spent 25 percent of its budget on the longest weapons shopping list in the world. The most advanced airplanes in America's arsenal—225 F-4s, 41 F-5s, 80 F-14s, 160 F-16s, and more than 900 helicopters—went to Iran accompanied by 5,000 military instructors for their use. Another 40,000 civilians went to the oil-drenched country to build the telephone system, construct modern airports and seaports, and operate the petroleum fields and refineries. They lived in ranch-style houses in isolated American colonies, bought imported food at familiar-looking supermarkets, refused to learn Farsi, the local language, and sowed seeds of nationalist resentment. At the same time nearly 100,000 Iranian students, supported by their nation's oil profits, enrolled in technical courses at universities in the United States. While in America they discovered that they could not get jobs at home. They blamed the shah's government for corruption, arrogance, and surveillance of their personal activities and enlisted in the opposition to the monarch's rule.

THE END IN VIETNAM

Lost in the excitement of presidential and secretarial travel and the fall of Richard Nixon was the continuing war in Southeast Asia, which reached a climax in the spring of 1975. President Thieu had broken the cease-fire in March 1973, and the North Vietnamese responded by sending thousands more troops south. The ARVN had fought as badly in 1973 and 1974 as it had while the Americans were there to assist it. In early 1975 Ford asked Congress for an additional $1 billion in aid in South Vietnam, Laos, and Cambodia. The Pentagon flew a delegation of congressional doves to Vietnam to show them how badly the situation had deteriorated. But old opponents such as New York congresswoman Bella Abzug were not persuaded that they should throw good money after bad. In February Congress voted to cut off all further aid to South Vietnam, Cambodia, and Laos. An angry Henry Kissinger asked newsmen, "What kind of people are we?" when he heard the news of Congress's cutoff.

Even congressional doves seemed astonished at the swiftness of the South Vietnamese collapse. In March North Vietnamese troops captured Danang in the north, and ARVN troops clamored aboard U.S. chartered aircraft for

Thousands of desperate Vietnamese crowd near the gates of the U.S. embassy in
Saigon during the final days of the war, April 1975.
(*National Archives*)

the flight south to Saigon, throwing women, children, and sick men off the
planes. Even worse chaos awaited the fall of Saigon in late April. American
"relief" operations spirited hundreds of supposed "orphans" out of the country. One giant C-5A transport crashed, killing more than 200 children, and
Vietnamese critics claimed that well-meaning but misguided Americans were
stealing babies from Vietnam. When it became obvious that Saigon would
fall, thousands of employees of the Americans feared for their lives at the
hands of vindictive Communists. They crashed the gates at the American embassy in Saigon, demanding visas to enter the United States. Marine guards
threw them back, but some managed to secure places on helicopters bound
for the American aircraft carriers off the coast. To make way for refugees,
the navy pushed millions of dollars worth of planes into the ocean. Finally,
the last helicopter, bearing Ambassador Graham Martin, left from the roof
of a building near the American embassy in downtown Saigon. About the
same time Communist forces triumphed in Laos and Cambodia, writing

another tragic chapter in the history of the latter country. Immediately upon seizing control of Phnom Penh, the Khmer Rouge began a mass evacuation of the capital, forcing city dwellers onto the land. As noted earlier, perhaps 3 million Cambodians died in the next three years.

In Washington the fall of Southeast Asia was greeted with recriminations from Ford and Kissinger, who blamed Congress for not providing more aid. They also made use of the Cambodian seizure of the American cargo vessel *Mayaguez* on May 12 to demonstrate their continued toughness. As soon as word reached Washington that the Cambodians had captured the ship, Ford ordered an American assault to free the crew. Thirty-eight American marines lost their lives in a needless rescue launched after the Cambodians had already set the crew free. Ignoring the War Powers Resolution, Ford had authorized the rescue without notifying Congress. No one complained, however, as lawmakers joined the applause for the show of resolve. Kissinger himself announced, "We did not do this to show our macho," but careful observers noted an element of guilty conscience: no one had publicly raised the suggestion. A week after the *Mayaguez* rescue President Ford received a standing ovation from students at the University of Pennsylvania, formerly a center of antiwar demonstrations.

COMING TO TERMS WITH VIETNAM

As the first war the United States clearly lost, the Vietnam debacle produced an anguished emotional response among politicians, diplomats, and observers looking for ways to avoid future entanglements. Congress, shaken by the sordid revelations of Watergate, spent 1975 and 1976 investigating the CIA. Subcommittees led by Congressman Otis Pike (D., N.Y.) and Sen. Frank Church (D., Idaho) poked through the evidence of twenty-five years of covert CIA operations in Asia, the Middle East, Europe, Latin America, and the United States. President Ford appointed his own task force, chaired by newly named vice president Nelson Rockefeller, to look into intelligence activities and quiet Congress. While none of these investigations aroused the intense public attention the earlier Watergate or impeachment hearings had created, they did build a case that foreign policy since the Second World War had often gone down a second, secret track, outside the scrutiny of the public, Congress, or the State Department.

For a generation after 1975, Americans wrestled with the proper lessons to be drawn from their Vietnam experience. Nearly everyone agreed that the war ended badly for the United States, but that was the limit of consensus. In the late 1970s policy makers and ordinary citizens sought to avoid U.S. military intervention. By 1980, however, a revisionist view of the Vietnam

War emerged. When Ronald Reagan ran for president in 1980, he characterized the Vietnam War as a "noble cause." He argued that the only mistake the United States had made in Vietnam had been timidity in the use of military force. Reagan and his more conservative supporters decried what they characterized as a "Vietnam syndrome," the reluctance to use America's military power to achieve its foreign policy ends. The Reagan administration pursued a more assertive foreign policy, especially in Central America, where it hoped to eliminate vestiges of the Vietnam syndrome. Yet the Reagan administration also recognized the limits of public support for prolonged U.S. military engagements. In 1984 Secretary of Defense Caspar Weinberger laid down a set of principles under which the United State should deploy its military. Under this "Weinberger Doctrine," the United States would commit its military only when the goals were clear, the military force could quickly achieve the stated ends, and the public would remain committed to the cause.

The memory of the Vietnam War reverberated as the Cold War ended. Reagan's successor, George H. W. Bush, referred to America's Vietnam experience in his 1989 inaugural address. He said that "the final lesson of Vietnam is this: no great nation can long be sundered by a memory." Bush returned to the theme of the legacy of the Vietnam War in the midst of the crisis with Iraq in 1990–1991. "This isn't going to be another Vietnam," he said when he dispatched 500,000 U.S. troops to Saudi Arabia to oppose Iraq's invasion of Kuwait. Gen. Colin Powell, the chairman of the Joint Chiefs of Staff who had first seen combat in Vietnam, expressed grave reservations about committing American forces to war against Iraq without adequate public support. Bush assured Powell that the military would have a freer hand waging war in the Persian Gulf than it had had in Vietnam. After the United States and its coalition partners evicted Iraq's army from Kuwait in 1991, Bush jubilantly proclaimed "by God, we've kicked the Vietnam syndrome."

Memories of Vietnam arose during the presidential election campaign of 1992. Arkansas governor Bill Clinton, the Democratic candidate, had opposed the Vietnam War as a graduate student at Oxford University in 1969. Advocates of President Bush assailed Clinton for having avoided military service during the Vietnam era. Clinton's opposition to the Vietnam War paralleled that of many Americans, and voters did not hold his lack of military service against him. As president Clinton deployed U.S. military forces to achieve humanitarian goals. In his last months in office, Clinton reflected that his own experience as president led him to soften his earlier harsh judgment of President Lyndon Johnson's decisions. "I now see how hard it was" for Johnson, Clinton remarked. "He did what he thought was right."

ASSERTIVE OUTBURSTS AFTER VIETNAM

The search for a place to show American resolve continued in 1975, and the site selected was one of the most remote in the world, the southwest African country of Angola, formerly a colony of Portugal. The right-wing government of Portugal fell in a coup led by army officers fed up with the grueling, unwinnable guerrilla combat in Africa in 1974. Despite Kissinger's fears that the triumphant generals actually were disguised communists, Portugal emerged as a democratic government after liquidating its African colonies of Mozambique, Guinea-Bissau, and Angola. In the latter, a struggle erupted for control of the new government between three factions. The alignment of outside forces defied conventional expectations, with the United States, South Africa, and China on one side opposing the Soviet Union, which backed the strongest of the three rebel groups, the MPLA (Popular Movement for the Liberation of Angola). Kissinger ordered the Central Intelligence Agency to give covert support to pro-Western factions, but the memory of Vietnam remained strong. A cartoonist had a sergeant remark, "If you liked Vietnam, you'll love…Angola." A balky Congress feared any aid might become the beginning of another wholesale commitment, and in December it passed an amendment to an appropriations bill by Sen. Dick Clark of Iowa prohibiting the use of CIA funds for the war in southern Africa.

The Angola crisis indicated that the détente with the Soviet Union was limited to Europe. There at least the East-West tensions seemed to ease in August 1975, when the two nations met with thirty-three others at the European Security Conference in Helsinki. They produced a treaty that finally ended the border disputes festering since 1945. In effect, the Helsinki accords became the peace treaty that had eluded diplomats since the Second World War. East and West agreed to respect the divisions that now existed. The United States exchanged ambassadors with East Germany. The Western powers also extracted from Moscow guarantees about the protection of human rights within the Soviet sphere, including the rights of citizens to emigrate. The last guarantee proved especially gratifying to congressmen who wanted the United States to aid Jews wishing to leave the Soviet Union for Israel, Europe, and the United States.

THE DECLINE OF DÉTENTE AND THE ELECTION OF 1976

The Helsinki accords could not arrest the decline in Kissinger's prestige among conservative members of the Republican Party. They criticized the extension of the SALT agreement worked out at a summit between Ford and Brezhnev in Vladivostok in November 1974. Ronald Reagan, the former governor of California who was challenging Ford for the presidential nomination, kept up a stream of denunciations of Kissinger's détente with the Soviet Union and the treaty being negotiated to turn the Panama Canal over to Panamanian control. Partially to satisfy conservative criticism and to make Kissinger a less visible figure, Ford stripped him of his title of national security adviser, which he had retained since being named secretary of state. An air force general, Brent Scowcroft, replaced Kissinger in his national security job in December 1975. Newspapers were filled with rumors that Kissinger himself would step down as secretary of state if Ford won reelection. Early in the campaign of 1976, Ford acknowledged that *détente* had become a term of abuse, and he banned it from his vocabulary. For a conventionally conservative Republican, Ford found the attack from his right distressing and unfair. He manfully defended Kissinger's détente without using the word, and he repeated that the Panama Canal Treaty was the only way the United States could maintain its standing among nationalist states of the Western Hemisphere. Using all the powers of incumbency, he barely beat back the challenge of Ronald Reagan at the Kansas City convention.

In the election itself Ford faced a formerly unknown ex-governor of Georgia. Jimmy Carter's anonymity proved his principal advantage in campaigning against the "Washington establishment," which he accused of having been responsible for the Watergate scandal. After leaving the governorship of Georgia in 1974, Carter had received some brief exposure to international affairs when David Rockefeller, the chairman of the Chase Manhattan Bank, had invited him to join the Trilateral Commission, a private group of business leaders, academics, and politicians from North America, Europe, and Japan. The executive director of the group was a Columbia University political scientist, Zbigniew Brzezinski, who had complained about the "Lone Ranger" style of Kissinger's diplomacy. In the campaign of 1976, Carter used symbolic language carefully constructed to appeal to the sensitivities of whatever group he addressed. In a masterpiece of unintended irony, he promised to "give America a government as good as its people." He chided the style of Kissinger's diplomacy for its flamboyance and sudden shifts, suggesting that he would be more attuned to the needs of America's allies. He supported the arms treaties negotiated with the Soviets but intimated that the Republicans had taken insufficient interest in human rights violations in the Soviet bloc. He denounced the "almost completely unrestrained" arms transfer policy for being "as cynical as it is dangerous." During the televised debates with Ford, Carter flashed a self-satisfied grin as the president blundered into suggesting that Poland no longer felt the sting of control by the Soviet Union. Carter's apparent sincerity, his promise "I'll never lie to you," and his ostentatious Christianity won many supporters early in the campaign; late August polls showed him ahead of Ford by more than

30 percentage points. Then disillusionment with both candidates set in as voters had to decide whether, in Arthur Schlesinger's words, to choose a candidate afflicted with the "dumbness factor" (Ford) or the "weirdness factor" (Carter). They chose a change, with Carter's fellow southerners carrying the day. Shortly after the election Carter's aide Hamilton Jordan explained that the new administration's diplomacy would mark a clean break with the discredited policies and tired individuals who had led American diplomacy since the Second World War. "If after the inauguration you find a Cy Vance as secretary of state and Zbigniew Brzezinski as head of national security, then I would say we failed. And I'd quit....You're going to see new faces, new ideas." In December Carter selected Vance for secretary of state and Brzezinski as national security adviser. Jordan did not quit. A new administration came to town vowing to put Vietnam behind the United States, open a dialogue between the rich and the poor nations, recapture the American commitment to human rights, place the Soviet Union on the defensive, and reduce the American role as the major arms supplier to the world.

CHAPTER TWELVE

A Respite and a Renewal of the Cold War, 1977–1980

By the middle 1970s the world had changed. Twenty years of rapid economic growth in Western Europe and Japan allowed those industrial nations to produce twice as much as the United States. Robust expansion stopped, however, in the wake of a tripling of energy costs. Poorer nations, concentrated mostly in the Southern Hemisphere, demanded greater shares of the world's prosperity. They pressed for a "new international economic order" to replace sterile Cold War competition between East and West as the centerpiece of world politics. Some Americans, stung by the bad memory of Vietnam, also hoped to focus attention on social and economic issues rather than military confrontation. Cyrus Vance, the new secretary of state, had grown dismayed by the waste of resources in Vietnam when he served as a delegate to the peace talks in 1968. Harold Brown, Jimmy Carter's choice as secretary of defense, a physicist who once served as secretary of the air force, also doubted the relevance of the application of military force to social questions. Zbigniew Brzezinski, Carter's national security adviser, sought to combine a commitment to advancing the interests of postindustrial Western societies with competition with Soviet-style communism. The new ambassador to the United Nations, Andrew Young, a black former congressman from Carter's home state of Georgia, looked forward to improved relations with the southern, nonwhite regions of the world.

At the outset the Carter administration seemed to press a new agenda, "the management of interdependence." Campaigning for the presidency in 1976, Jimmy Carter demanded that "we replace balance of power politics with world order politics." He predicted that "in the near future issues of war and peace will be more a function of economic and social problems than of the military security problems which have dominated international relations since World War II." In May 1977 he told a commencement day crowd at Notre Dame University that "an inordinate fear of communism has led us to embrace any dictator who joined in our fear." He suggested that his administration would pay more attention to human rights wherever they were threatened.

The commitment to "world order politics" lasted about two years. From 1977 to 1979 the United States pressed human rights, sought a "North-South dialogue" on economic issues, and moved to limit the global arms race. None of these initiatives reached its goals. And two of Carter's successes—concluding agreements with Panama over the canal and mediation of formal peace between Israel and Egypt—followed traditional, not novel, diplomatic practice.

Within the administration National Security Adviser Brzezinski raised alarms over a Soviet threat. In 1979 the president returned to assertive themes of the early Cold War. The seizure of the American embassy by Iranian revolutionaries in November and a Soviet invasion of Afghanistan in December 1979 completed Carter's conversion into a Cold Warrior. Yet his new course did not save him at the polls in 1980. Voters selected Republican Ronald Reagan to be the most conservative president since Calvin Coolidge. He provided an assertive foreign policy that confronted the Soviet Union, communism, and revolution. In the first few years of the Reagan administration, American combativeness raised fears of war at home and abroad. After 1985, however, Reagan shrewdly adapted to changes in the Soviet Union fostered by Mikhail Gorbachev. By 1988 Reagan, the most ardently anticommunist president of the post–World War II era, formed a close personal friendship with the leader of the Soviet Union. The Cold War was about to expire.

HUMAN RIGHTS, IMMIGRATION, AND THE LAW OF THE SEA

The Carter administration's advocacy of human rights in other countries recorded some achievements but was riddled with inconsistencies. Congress created a Bureau of Human Rights within the State Department. Headed by Patricia Derian, a former professor and political activist, the bureau published a yearly account of the state of civil and political liberties abroad. It denounced nations previous Republican administrations had wanted to use as surrogates against the Soviet Union under the terms of the Nixon Doctrine. The Philippines, South Korea, Chile, Brazil, and Argentina all came under the lash. The administration cut economic aid, pressured the World Bank, the International Monetary Fund, and the Inter-American Development Bank to curtail assistance; and publicly called for the release of political prisoners.

The administration did not, however, follow a consistent human rights policy. Old ideas of national security, presumably outmoded in the new era, led Carter to support several unsavory rulers. The need for oil prompted an embrace of the shah of Iran. Carter praised the shah for having created an "island of stability" in the turbulent Middle East. The administration muted criticism of human rights violations despite reports from Amnesty International, a respected London-based human rights group, that SAVAK, Iran's secret police, held as many as 50,000 political prisoners. In 1977 the United States sold the shah $5.7 billion worth of weapons, two-thirds of his country's arms imports.

Joseph Mobutu, ruler of Zaire in Central Africa, also received help from the new administration despite an appalling record on human rights. Gen. Mobutu had consolidated his hold on the former Belgian Congo in 1967. He created a single-party state, jailed opponents, and encouraged friends and relatives to loot the wealth of the country. On the verge of bankruptcy, kept afloat only by the willingness of foreign bankers to "roll over" loans to avoid a default, Zaire also faced the secession of Shaba province in the spring of 1978. Rebels based in neighboring Angola mounted an invasion in June. Immediately, the Carter administration ordered the air force to ferry French foreign legion and Moroccan troops to the town of Kolwesi, headquarters of a huge copper mine, to rescue 200 white missionaries and mining engineers.

The Carter administration also ran into difficulties applying consistent human rights standards at home, where the issue was immigration, always a complicated mixture of diplomacy and domestic politics. Immigration policy became a way of punishing unfriendly, usually communist, governments, rather than of assisting individual refugees. The United States opened its doors to 200,000 "boat people" fleeing the Communist governments of Vietnam, Laos, and Cambodia. State Department officials pressured European and South Asian nations to accept their share of refugees. American officials took the floor at international refugee meetings to assail the Vietnamese practice of demanding gold bribes before frightened citizens could disembark on a fleet of leaky, rotting, unsanitary small boats.

Carter also used the plight of refugees to score points from an old American nemesis, Cuba's Fidel Castro. In April 1980 10,000 disgruntled Cubans flooded the Peruvian embassy in Havana asking for asylum. From the middle of April until the middle of June, a flotilla of boats ferried more than 100,000 Cubans from the island to Florida, and by the time it was over the administration wished it had never raised the issue. The government sent the Cubans to sports stadia and army bases, where they set up tent cities, became hot and bored, and demanded to leave. Some Americans wanted them to stay incarcerated.

While the Carter administration made a show of welcoming the Cubans, it tried to deport thousands of Haitians who fled a government that maintained the traditional standards of tyranny for that unhappy island. Yet the State Department was reluctant to offer refugee status, fearing that it would offend the friendly government of Jean-Claude "Baby Doc" Duvalier. Civil rights groups in the United States charged that the State Department did not want Haitians because they were blacker than Cubans.

A failed attempt to reach international agreement regulating the use of the world's oceans also dashed hopes that the Carter administration could focus attention on nonsecurity issues. In 1972 a UN-sponsored Law of the Sea Conference had opened to resolve differences among 130 nations over warship rights, fishing, and deep seabed mining. Talks stalled under Nixon and Ford, but Carter appointed Elliot Richardson as his special representative to breathe life into the law of the sea. Despite these high sentiments and his acceptance of the fact that the oceans represented the "common heritage of mankind," Richardson was unable to reach agreement before the election of 1980.

THE PANAMA CANAL TREATIES AND CENTRAL AMERICA

Carter found more success following a traditional path of negotiation to heal the seventy-year wound left by Theodore Roosevelt's high-handed actions during the Panamanian revolution of 1903. Each American president since 1965 had conducted desultory talks with Panama over the future of the canal. In that year street demonstrations broke out in Panama City and Colón protesting the haughtiness of the U.S. residents of the Canal Zone— the five-mile-wide strip of territory bisecting the isthmus in which the U.S. acted "as if it were sovereign." Panamanians could be jailed under U.S. laws by American courts using English, a language they did not understand. While Panamanians took low-paying, unskilled jobs in the zone, none was found operating the locks or piloting ships through the canal. The government of Panama argued that the behavior of the "Zonians" represented the worst sort of "Yankee colonialism."

After ten years a deal was nearly struck in 1975. The United States was willing in principle to yield its perpetual lease. Panama insisted that the United States leave in twenty or thirty years, while the Pentagon held out for longer, perhaps another fifty. An ominous note was sounded, however, when conservative South Carolina Republican senator Strom Thurmond got the signatures of thirty-eight senators (five more than needed to block ratification) on a letter opposing any release of sovereignty. During the 1976 Republican primary season, Ronald Reagan charged Gerald Ford and Henry Kissinger with "giving away our canal." Ford quietly shelved negotiations during the heat of the campaign, leaving the nearly completed treaty for his successor. During the lull in the talks, Panama's leader, Omar Torrijos, engaged in a "banana war" with the United Fruit Company, and new riots broke out in September 1976.

Carter appointed Sol Linowitz as head of the American negotiating team. Within seven months he produced two treaties. The first returned legal jurisdiction over the zone to Panama. The United States would continue to operate and defend the canal until December 31, 1999, after which Panama would take over. The first treaty also protected the jobs of the Americans operating the canal. The second agreement gave the United States the permanent right to defend the "neutrality of the waterway."

When Carter presented the treaty to the Senate in August, it provoked a storm. Public opinion polls revealed that 78 percent of those who took a stand opposed yielding the canal. The administration spent the next six months changing attitudes in the hopes of gaining Senate ratification. Carter enlisted major establishment figures such as Averell Harriman, John J. McCloy, and former Republican Senate leader Hugh Scott to form a Committee for the Ratification of the Panama Canal Treaties. The president took questions about the canal on a radio call-in hookup. Noting that the United States had never had sovereignty, he predicted the "assured capacity of our country in guaranteeing that the Panama Canal would be open." Over the winter public opinion seemed to change.

The battle shifted to the Senate in February and March while Democratic leader Robert Byrd (W. Va.) and Republican Howard Baker (Tenn.) carried the brunt of the argument. Carter had more trouble with Democrats Richard Stone (Fla.) and Dennis DeConcini (Ariz.). Stone, who described Torrijos as a "Left-leaning, rickety, tin-horn dictator," agreed to vote yes out of the close ties his home state held with Central America. Deconcini offered his support only after Carter accepted a "condition" allowing the use of American forces *in Panama* to keep the canal open after 1999. Torrijos held his tongue about this violation of his country's sovereignty. On March 16 sixty-eight senators, one more than required for ratification, voted for the treaty. Ratification did not ensure good relations with Central American republics, but it did offer the hope of reduced tensions.

After some hesitation the Carter administration also accommodated a revolution in another Central American state, Nicaragua. Andrew Young's mission to the UN, which tried to steer American diplomacy toward the interests of the poor southern states, pressured Secretary of State Vance and National Security Adviser Brzezinski gracefully to accept the end of the Somoza dictatorship. The Somoza family had virtually owned Nicaragua ever since the departure of U.S. Marines in 1934. Anastasio Somoza took power in 1965. By the mid-seventies he had alienated the church and the small middle class as well as the traditionally exploited peasantry with his thievery and the brutality of the National Guard. Rebels, calling themselves the Sandino Liberation Front after Augusto Sandino, the insurgent murdered by the first Somoza in 1934, took up arms in 1976. In August 1978 a band of Sandinista soldiers, led by a dashing Eden Pastora, "Commander Zero," took over the national assembly building and held Somoza's hand-picked legislators for a ransom of $25 million. Commander Zero became a hero as he waved to a crowd of well-wishing Nicaraguans before boarding a plane for asylum in Venezuela. Shortly afterward national guardsmen murdered the editor of *La Prensa*, a moderate opposition paper.

On June 23 the OAS called for the "immediate and definitive replacement of the Somoza regime" by "a democratic government [and] the holding of free elections as soon as possible." The United States reluctantly endorsed this resolution, and Lawrence Pezullo, American ambassador to Nicaragua, spent the next several days trying to arrange Somoza's exile. Somoza temporized for three more weeks, as Washington scrambled to sponsor a new government in Nicaragua that would keep the Sandinistas from power. The revolutionaries would hear nothing of that. On July 18 Somoza fled Nicaragua for exile, first in the Bahamas, then in Miami, and finally in Paraguay, where he was murdered in 1980. On July 20 the Sandinistas in Managua triumphantly proclaimed a new revolutionary government. The new regime was a coalition of opponents of Somoza, but within months it became clear that a nine-member Directorate of Sandinistas had real power.

Over the remainder of the Carter administration relations between the United States and Nicaragua deteriorated. According to Robert Pastor, the administration's specialist on Central America on the National Security Council, "at the beginning the United States government deliberately suspended its suspicions about the Sandinistas." By the end of 1980, however, "the Carter administration was on the verge of terminating its aid program." In September Carter greeted Daniel Ortega of the junta at the White House and told him, "If you don't hold me responsible for everything that occurred under my predecessors, I will not hold you responsible for everything that happened under your predecessors." Everyone smiled. The United States promised to maintain a program of $80 million of economic assistance. Four days later Carter's expression soured when Ortega told the United Nations that "the most aggressive circles of the United States and of Central America dream of restoring Somozaism to our country."

In Nicaragua itself the revolution began to split as more conservative members of the junta distrusted the Sandinistas. By the summer of 1980 several moderates resigned, threatening to take up arms if the revolution did not mellow. In Washington, though, Carter still sought an accommodation.

The CIA found no conclusive evidence before November that the Sandinistas were arming revolutionaries in El Salvador. He continued economic aid to Nicaragua in the midst of the 1980 election campaign, despite Republican charges that he was permitting the development of another Cuba in Central America. After Ronald Reagan won Washington shifted course in the winter of 1980–1981. The Sandistas began shipping weapons to leftist forces in El Salvador for a "final offensive" before Reagan took office. In response the Carter administration laid the groundwork for a more assertive course against Nicaragua as it planned to stop economic assistance.

MEDIATING BETWEEN ISRAEL AND EGYPT

Carter's most surprising and enduring accomplishment occurred at Camp David, the presidential retreat in the Maryland mountains, in September 1978, where he brokered a settlement between two old adversaries, Egypt and Israel. The summit meeting between Egyptian president Anwar Sadat and Israeli prime minister Menachem Begin climaxed a remarkable reversal of alignments begun the year before. The United States assisted the process, but not necessarily because of the shrewdness in its diplomacy. In fact, fear that American efforts to arrange a "comprehensive settlement of the Palestinian problem" might backfire encouraged Sadat to take an unprecedented trip to Jerusalem to address the Knesset, or parliament, on November 19, 1977.

Both Israelis and Egyptians had been alarmed when Carter publicly called for a "homeland" for the displaced Palestinians in the summer of 1977. Despite Carter's denial that a homeland implied the creation of a Palestinian state, Israel's newly elected conservative government headed by Begin feared that the United States might deal directly with the Palestine Liberation Organization (PLO). Neither did Sadat care for the PLO, considering it a radical organization committed to the overthrow of conservative Arab governments. Accordingly, he sent feelers to the Israelis through King Hassan of Morocco and President Nicolai Ceauçescu of Romania. Israel's one-eyed foreign minister, Moshe Dayan, one of the most recognizable men in the world, grabbed a wig and false moustache and slipped into Fez, Morocco, to prepare the ground. Then, in response to a November 14 question by CBS news correspondent Walter Cronkite, Sadat stunned the world by expressing willingness to go to Israel.

Sadat did not receive the enthusiastic reception he hoped for in Jerusalem. His hosts liked to call for "no more war," but they refused to make a grand gesture of their own by relinquishing all territory seized in the 1967 war. Instead, Begin and Dayan proposed a series of ministerial talks with the Egyptians leading to a bilateral peace treaty.

At this point the United States entered as mediator. Sadat got his hero's welcome from Congress, press, and president when he came to Washington in February 1978. Cronkite called him the "man of the century," and Carter described him as a "great statesman." For the remainder of the spring and summer, Secretary of State Vance arranged a series of encounters between Dayan and Egyptian foreign minister Ibrahim Khalil. Eventually, the diplomats agreed to a meeting of their heads of government hosted by Carter at Camp David.

For two weeks Sadat, Begin, Carter, and a small army of aides argued over a "framework" for a peace treaty. The suspicious Israelis tried to separate the Egyptian and Palestinian questions. They insisted that any agreement with Egypt should void commitments Cairo had with Arab states to join a war against Israel. Sadat became impatient with the Israelis' legalistic quibbles. Carter and his advisers, eager for any sort of agreement to bolster their prestige, sided with the Egyptians. The president, who mastered every detail of the geography of the Sinai Desert, had been fed up with Begin's hectoring before the conference began. Nothing happened over the next two weeks to soften his opinion. The three leaders met together only once, and that encounter proved so tense that Carter decided to shuttle between the Egyptians and the Israelis. His chats with Sadat were music to his ears, while meetings with Begin were filled with charges of bad faith. Finally, on Friday, September 15, Carter announced that he would dissolve the summit on Sunday night whether there was a framework or not. Fearful of being labeled an obstacle to peace, Begin put forward ambiguous language suspending for a time new Jewish settlements on the West Bank of the Jordan River. He explicitly agreed to total Israeli withdrawal from the Sinai Peninsula and the dismantlement of Jewish settlements there. Sadat, for his part, accepted the separate peace. The treaty between Israel and Egypt would be linked only to continued negotiations over the future of the West Bank.

When Carter, Begin, and Sadat smiled for the camera at the White House on that Sunday evening, they thought that a peace treaty was within easy reach. In fact, it took another six months of presidential Mideast travel, cajolery, and badgering to bring the two men to the White House lawn for a signing ceremony on March 26, 1979. The president guaranteed a pact committing Israel to withdraw from the Sinai in return for peace and diplomatic recognition from Egypt. The United States promised $2 billion to underwrite the cost of moving Israel's advanced airfield from the Sinai to Israel proper. America would organize an international peacekeeping force after the Israelis completed their departure in 1982. In an additional document Egypt and Israel left open the issue of sovereignty on the West Bank, promising continued talks leading to "full autonomy" for the Palestinian

President Jimmy Carter hosts Prime Minister Menachem Begin of Israel (left) and
President Anwar Sadat of Egypt (right) at Camp David, September 1978.
(*Jimmy Carter Library*)

Arabs living there. The final status of the West Bank and East Jerusalem
would be decided after a five-year interim period of autonomy.

Much to the surprise of the United States, Egypt, and Israel, no other Arab
state joined the peace process. The PLO denounced it as a betrayal of the
Palestinians and threatened any West Bank Arabs who might want to join the autonomy talks. Egypt found itself ostracized by other Arab states. Neither Jordan
nor Saudi Arabia, two states with which Washington had good relations, joined
the Camp David peace process. By May 1980, the date set for an agreement
on West Bank autonomy, Sol Linowitz, the American delegate to the talks,
glumly announced that a final arrangement eluded his grasp.

PLAYING THE CHINA CARD

The Carter administration completed the opening to China begun by President Nixon when it exchanged ambassadors with the People's Republic
in January 1979. Recognition of Beijing served to heighten tensions with

the Soviet Union while consolidating the power of National Security Adviser Brzezinski. He went to Beijing in May 1977. On an outing to the Great Wall of China, he challenged his hosts to race up the stairs with the words "Last one to the top gets to fight the Russians."

By December 1978 Carter was ready to play the "China card" against the Soviet Union by restoring full diplomatic relations with Beijing. On January 1, 1979, the American embassy in Taiwan changed into a "foundation," while the United States upgraded its Beijing office to a regular embassy. In late January and early February Deng Xiaoping, vice chairman of the Chinese Communist Party and the guiding force behind the movement away from Maoist revolutionary orthodoxy, visited the United States. Not since Nikita Khrushchev peeled an ear of corn in an Iowa cornfield in 1959 had Americans taken such notice of a foreign leader. At stops in Washington, Houston, and Seattle Deng pointed fingers at the "hegemonists" of the Kremlin and warned of a new war unless the West woke up. He donned a ten-gallon hat, accepted "honorary membership" in NATO, and was roundly cheered by workers in a defense plant. Two weeks after his return to China, Deng put his anti-Soviet rhetoric into practice by ordering the People's Liberation Army to attack Vietnam. That friend of the Soviet Union had recently invaded Cambodia, an ally of China.

THE FAILURE OF ARMS CONTROL

The opening to China helped poison relations with the Soviet Union, and the signing of a new Strategic Arms Limitation Treaty (SALT II) in June 1979 could not stop further deteriorations. The new administration came to Washington with high hopes of actually reducing the nuclear arsenals of both super-powers. In March 1977 Secretary of State Vance went to Moscow to present a plan for across-the-board reductions to Soviet president Leonid Brezhnev. The Soviet leadership reacted coolly to suggestions that ignored the careful provisions for future arms control laid down in the SALT I agreement (1972) and the Vladivostok agreement of 1975. Rebuffed in Moscow, Vance returned to Washington and instructed the Arms Control and Disarmament Agency to continue along the path blazed by Henry Kissinger.

Vance and Paul Warnke, the delegate to the SALT talks, considered any agreement setting upper limits on armaments superior to an untrammeled arms race. In two years of bargaining, Soviet and American negotiators in Vienna, Washington, and Moscow hammered out a treaty acknowledging essential "parity" in the nuclear forces of both sides. They produced a design to lessen the dangers posed by "destabilizing" weapons systems, that is, those that raised fears that the other side planned a first strike. Each agreed to stop construction of new fixed ICBMs and pledged not to relocate fixed ICBMs, not to convert light ICBMs into heavy ones, and not to increase the "throw weight," or warhead destructive power, of their missiles. Each would limit the number of its MIRVs and cruise missiles (small, virtually unde-tectable flying bombs) to 1,320. Under this provision the Soviet Union would dismantle 200 MIRV'd ICBMs, while the United States foreswore testing of cruise missiles with a range greater than 600 kilometers. The treaty would expire in 1985. Negotiators also arrived at a Joint Statement of Principles for SALT III, maintaining parity while reducing overall levels of armaments.

Jimmy Carter immersed himself in the welter of numbers in the weeks before the signing ceremony scheduled for Vienna the third week of June. He knew that the arms control process had aroused suspicious Cold War-riors who considered the Soviet Union ahead in the arms race and doubted if it would keep its end of the bargain. On the eve of his departure, he learned that Sen. Henry Jackson (D., Wash.), a longtime hawk, had decided that the treaty "favors the Soviets" and to sign it would be "appeasement in its purest form." Stung by Jackson's allusion to Neville Chamberlain's toting an umbrella home from his capitulation to Adolf Hitler at Munich, Carter stood bareheaded in a rainstorm when he disembarked from the plane at Vienna. "I'd rather drown than carry an umbrella," he growled.

Carter kissed Brezhnev on both cheeks before each put his name to the treaty on June 24. The document encountered a buzzsaw when it reached the Senate. The Joint Chiefs of Staff endorsed the treaty as reducing the likelihood of a first strike, but their representative on the negotiating team, Air Force General Edward Rowny, resigned and testified against the treaty. Outside Congress a louder chorus rose against SALT and accommodation with the Soviet Union. The Committee on the Present Danger, a pressure group formed in 1975 to lobby against détente, opposed "world order rhetoric" with the observation that "the principal threat to our nation, to world peace, and to the cause of human freedom is the Soviet drive for dom-inance based on unprecedented military buildup." Norman Podhoretz, editor of *Commentary* magazine and a leading "neoconservative" (former lib-erals who focused on the dangers of communism) blamed "isolationism" and "the culture of appeasement" for producing SALT II. Faced with such charges, the Carter administration hesitated about asking for a vote on SALT II in the fall of 1979 and then withdrew the treaty in January 1980.

ECONOMIC TRIALS AND A GOVERNMENT SHAKE-UP

The world and American economies never really recovered from the four-fold rise in energy costs following the Arab oil embargo of 1973. Carter addressed the energy crisis in March 1977, soon after taking office, when he called for the "moral equivalent of war" to reduce dependence on foreign petroleum. He wore a sweater before a roaring fireplace when he delivered a folksy homily to the public on the virtues of energy conservation and substitution. After two years of debate Congress passed a modified energy program taxing "windfall" oil company profits, allowing the eventual decontrol of oil and gas prices, and establishing a new Department of Energy. James Schlesinger, a brilliant economist who had served earlier Republican administrations as head of the CIA and the Defense Department, took over at Energy and warned that unless the United States imported less foreign oil "this society may not make it." By 1979 American consumers paid more than $50 billion yearly for the 8 million barrels of oil they imported each day. Things got worse in June as gasoline seemed unavailable at any price. (The official cost doubled, from $18 to $36 a barrel.) The Iranian revolution that erupted early in the year cut that country's oil production by 90 percent. Four-hour-long gasoline lines formed at filling stations as angry motorists punched each other, pulled guns on line jumpers, and cursed President Carter.

This second oil shock helped produce worldwide recession even sharper than the 1974–1975 downturn. Many nations turned in desperation to Western banks, awash in petrodollars. In late June 1979 Carter went to Tokyo for the annual meeting of the heads of the seven largest economies in the noncommunist world (the United States, Great Britain, France, West Germany, Italy, and Japan). He heard complaints from each of his fellow summiteers, who hated the sinking dollar, wondered when the United States would reduce its inflation rate of 13 percent, and pressed Carter to halve American oil imports. Upon returning Carter's advisers gave him the grim word that the country blamed him for gas lines and economic stagnation. Carter then went to Camp David, where he brooded for ten days. Returning to Washington on July 19, he delivered a public excoriation and apology to his countrymen. He noted "our people are losing that faith, not only in government itself but in the ability as citizens to serve as the ultimate rulers and shapers of our democracy." He quoted a governor who told him "Mr. President, you are not leading this nation—you're just managing the government." Four days later he dropped four cabinet secretaries, including Schlesinger and Blumenthal, and requested expressions of loyalty from those who remained.

One cabinet-level appointee who survived temporarily was UN ambassador Andrew Young. His days were numbered, though, in July 1979. He had been prone from the start to offhand comments about foreign affairs— calling the British "the most racist society in history," welcoming a Cuban brigade in Ethiopia as a "stabilizing force," and describing Ayatollah Ruhallah

Khomeini, leader of Iran's religious fundamentalists, as "something of a saint." When Carter called his principal advisers to Camp David in July, he dressed Young down as an "embarrassment to this administration." Nevertheless, he decided to keep him because of his appeal to black Americans. Not only did Young occupy a highly visible position in the administration, he had helped change American policy toward Africa. At his urging the United States joined Great Britain in arranging majority rule in Rhodesia, renamed Zimbabwe after 1979. He made friends for the United States in Nigeria, a major oil supplier, by his criticism of the system of racial segregation, apartheid, practiced in South Africa. At the UN he sped negotiations for an end to South African occupation of Southwest Africa (Namibia) and the creation of a black majority government there. In August, however, Young resigned under pressure when reports appeared that he had secretly conferred with Zehdi Terzi, the Palestine Liberation Organization's permanent observer to the UN. Israel's supporters expressed outrage at this apparent violation of a five-year-old U.S. pledge to have nothing to do with the PLO. Angry black leaders for their part accused American Jews and Israeli diplomats of forcing Young's exit. Carter said nothing to reduce inflamed passions over the Young affair.

AMERICA'S IRANIAN BONDAGE

Journalists wrote of a "failed presidency" in the summer of 1979. None of Carter's problems matched those created by the encounter with revolutionary nationalism in Iran. Opposition to the rule of Shah Mohammed Reza Pahlevi built in early 1978, soon after Carter raised his glass to the "respect, admiration and love" in which the Iranian people held their monarch. Widespread street demonstrations broke out in January and February. The mullahs and ayatollahs (religious leaders of the Shi'ite Muslims, who made up 90 percent of the population) joined bazaar merchants, students, and opposition politicians in objecting to the quality of the shah's rule. They could not agree on what they disliked most, but none had good words for the presence of 50,000 Americans training the military, building industrial plants, and operating the oil fields that provided some $20 billion in annual revenue. Opposition coalesced behind Ruhallah Khomeini, an eighty-year-old ayatollah who had lived in exile, first in Iraq and then in France, for the previous fourteen years. Cassette tapes circulated of Khomeini's calls to rid the country of the shah, his family, SAVAK (the secret police), and the Americans and create an Islamic republic committed to traditional Muslim virtues.

Throughout the upheavals the shah dismissed his opponents as "people who are easily instigated. They hear a few words and immediately they are electrified and stop thinking." Yet he responded slowly to the challenges to his rule. In February French doctors diagnosed a fatal cancer that affected his judgment, so he relied on guidance from confused officials in faraway Washington. While National Security Adviser Brzezinski urged firmness, Secretary of State Vance decided that the monarch had to step aside for a civilian government. In late August a theater fire killed 377 Iranians, and the opposition blamed SAVAK agents for setting the blaze and blocking the exits. Hundreds of thousands took to the streets. On September 6 the shah, acting on advice from Brzezinski in Washington, proclaimed martial law. The next day troops fired on a demonstration, killing between 700 and 2,000 protestors.

Carter sided with Vance over Christmas, and on December 30 the shah named Shapour Bahktiar as prime minister. In mid-January the monarch left the country for Egypt. Bahktiar lasted two more weeks before Khomeini returned in triumph from Paris and ordered his arrest. The prime minister fled in fear for his life, and the ayatollah appointed as premier Mehdi Bazargan, a veteran of the nationalist party of Mohammed Mossadeq, overthrown by the CIA in 1953.

From February to October 1979, Ambassador William Sullivan in Iran and officials in Washington urged an accommodation to the new Islamic republic. American civilians quietly left the country, but the embassy continued to operate. The staff received a temporary fright in late February when demonstrators entered the forty-acre compound, but the Iranian police evicted them. Marches on the compound took place weekly as hundreds of thousands chanted "death to the United States, death to Carter!"

The United States had not offered asylum to the deposed shah, who spent the first ten months of 1979 wandering from Egypt to Morocco to the Bahamas to Mexico. His friends Henry Kissinger and David Rockefeller pressed the Carter administration to permit him to come to New York for an operation on his cancerous spleen. Convinced that relations with Iran had stabilized, Carter authorized the admission of the deposed ruler on humanitarian grounds on October 22.

In Tehran Khomeini greeted the news with "America expects to take the shah there, engage in plots, and our young people are expected to simply remain idle." He encouraged his followers to take to the streets once more. The largest demonstrations in history convulsed the capital as 3 million people marched on the embassy on November 1. On November 4 hundreds of the most militant revolutionaries stormed the fence, but this time the police did not evict them. Instead, Khomeini called the compound a "nest of spies." Praising the militants as "ten thousand martyrs," he called on the "Great Satan Carter" to return the shah for trial and hand back his fortune, estimated at a preposterous $40 billion, to pay for his crimes. Unless these conditions were met, the militants at the embassy would keep sixty-nine diplomats, marine guards, and private American citizens imprisoned. Parading their blindfolded hostages, they threatened to try and execute them as spies.

The seizure of the hostages became the news story of the year in the United States. The number of captives fell to fifty-three after the militants released some of the black and female prisoners in December, but those who remained became the focal point of national shame. CBS began introducing its evening news as "day #4... 5...6..." for the prisoners. ABC started a special evening edition at 11:30 P.M. called simply "America Held Hostage." Pop singer Pat Boone released a song entitled "The Hostage Prayer." He wrote to hotstage families "I believe this crisis has really made us one family, in concern and love, in anguish, and in prayer."

Carter announced that he would not leave the White House until he secured the hostages' release. In December the president froze $8 billion in Iranian assets, doused the lights on the national Christmas tree, and told a visiting group of congressmen that American "national honor" would not be assuaged even after the return of the hostages. Later in the month Brzezinski and Jordan encouraged the shah to leave for Panama. Carter told visiting Democratic members of Congress "I don't give a damn whether you like or dislike the shah.... The issue is that American hostages, 50 of them, are being held by kidnappers, radical and irresponsible kidnappers, with the encouragement ansd support of the Iranian government." The president grew increasingly pessimistic about negotiating with Khomeni. He wrote in his diary "it's almost impossible to deal with a crazy man."

Carter's obvious anguish over the hostages did not secure their return, but it did offer a temporary boost to his popularity. In December 66 percent of those polled favored his handling of the crisis versus 32 percent who opposed it. Carter also overtook the challenge from Massachusetts senator Edward M. Kennedy, who decided in November to make a try for the Democratic presidential nomination. At one time Kennedy led Carter by two to one in the polls, but the incumbent's "Rose Garden strategy" of looking presidential to resolve the hostage problem wounded the challenger's chances in early 1980. By March, however, Kennedy seemed to have recovered with a victory in the New York primary. New polls showed that only 31 percent of the public thought Carter's strategy was successful in dealing with Iran, while 47 percent perceived that it had failed.

Having successfully avoided the stump as he bargained for the hostages, Carter now felt a prisoner himself in the White House. If the militants held the Americans through November, he might never campaign against the Republican nominee, and the continued humiliation would remind voters of presidential failure. He therefore approved a military rescue mission despite

Secretary of State Vance's assurances to Europeans that the United States would not use force. On April 24 eight air force helicopters took off in a dust storm from the carrier *Nimitz* for a rendezvous at Tabriz in the Iranian desert, a staging area for an assault on the embassy. The rescue mission got no farther. Two of the machines choked on the dust and started to turn back when they collided with one another and a transport plane that crashed, killing eight servicemen. Carter canceled the project. The militants dispersed the fifty-three hostages, thereby making future rescues impossible.

The mission prompted Vance's resignation, as he had opposed the use of force and seen his world order viewpoint gradually lose ground to Brzezinski's proposals over the previous year. Carter appointed Maine senator Edmund Muskie as the new secretary of state. The rescue attempt did liberate the chief executive from the White House. Saying he "had never dreamed" the crisis would last so long and that it now was "manageable," he departed the Rose Garden for the campaign trail. Public interest in the hostages diminished, too, as any mention of the captives was painful. As the summer wore on, a new government took power in Iran headed by Abdul Hassan Bani-Sadr. Since the shah died in Egypt in late July, the United States no longer could return him even if it wanted to. Negotiations opened in August on exchanging the remaining hostages for Iran's

Blindfolded American hostages being paraded before Iranian revolutionaries at the
captured U.S. embassy, November 1979
(Corbis)

frozen assets. The talks made headway through the fall but stalled the week before the American presidential election. After Ronald Reagan won Carter worked incessantly in the last months of his term to arrange the hostages' release. His patience paid off in the final hours of his administration, when Algeria helped broker the return of the captives in exchange for the unfreezing of Iran's assets. Tehran let the Americans fly out of Iran as soon as Carter left office and Reagan was sworn in as president.

THE REVIVAL OF THE COLD WAR AND THE ELECTION OF 1980

Another more important foreign policy issue, renewed conflict with Moscow, appeared in early 1980. On December 27, 1979, some 80,000 Soviet troops poured into the neighboring country of Afghanistan to prop up the shaky government of leftist Babrak Karmal. Carter responded with typical hyperbole. He regretted that the Soviets had "lied" to him and called their move "the gravest threat to peace since the Second World War." In early January he withdrew the SALT II Treaty from the Senate, where it was doomed anyway. He forbade Americans to participate in the Moscow Olympic Games the following July, slapped an embargo on American grain and sophisticated electronic equipment bound for the Soviet Union, promised to raise defense spending by 5 percent in real terms for each of the next five years, ordered young men to register for a potential draft, and proclaimed a Carter Doctrine under which the United States would fight for its "national interests" should the Soviet Union threaten the oil of the Persian Gulf.

Yet Carter's new anti-Soviet line did not stop the erosion of public support. The Committee on the Present Danger endorsed the candidacy of Republican Ronald Reagan with the charge that the president's change of heart had come too late. Reagan on the right, Kennedy on the left, and John Anderson, an Illinois Republican congressman running an independent presidential campaign from the center of the political spectrum, all questioned the incumbent's "competence."

Once nominated by the Republicans, former California governor Reagan promised a "strong America." Telling the Veterans of Foreign Wars that the war in Vietnam had been a "noble cause," he implied that a "Vietnam syndrome"—fear of intervention—had paralyzed Carter. He denigrated the emphasis on human rights for having undermined the shah and led to the hostage crisis. He did not indicate what he would do to secure the captives' release but hinted that had he been president they would not have been imprisoned in the first place. The Republican promised to rearm America at a faster rate, kill SALT II, and, most of all, "speak with a single voice" in foreign affairs.

Carter's pollsters told him that the voters finally turned against him the last weekend of the campaign, when it appeared that no deal would be reached with Iran to free the captives. On November 4, exactly one year after the seizure of the Tehran embassy, Reagan won the election with 51 percent of the vote. Carter received 42 percent, and Anderson captured 6 percent. As significant as Reagan's victory was the election of a Republican Senate majority for the first time since 1952.

Jimmy Carter's efforts to shift the focus of American diplomacy away from competition with the Soviet Union to the management of interdependence failed. Bad luck plagued Carter. He was elected in 1976, at a time when Americans responded to moral appeals. Two years later a sour world economy and domestic inflation cancelled voters' enthusiasm for helping poorer nations in the southern Hemisphere. Soviet behavior also contributed to Carter's downfall. Moscow's assertiveness in the Third World made it harder for Carter to declare the end of the Cold War. The Iranian revolution and the seizure of hostages at the American embassy in Tehran virtually ensured Carter's defeat at the polls.

Even if fortune had been kinder, though, the Carter administration's foreign policy would have experienced troubles. Cyrus Vance and Zbigniew Brzezinski, his two principal international lieutenants, clashed repeatedly. As historian Gaddis Smith writes, "only a President with deep experience in foreign affairs and a grasp of the issues equal or superior to that of such contending advisers could have prevented crippling contradictions. Carter lacked such experience and grasp." He appeared to vacillate before finally siding with the anti-Soviet positions of Brzezinski. At that point his rhetoric sounded harsh and unsophisticated. An outsider who distrusted Washington, Carter warred with Congress. When he needed lawmakers' help in 1980, they rejected him. The public did, too, in 1980, replacing him with an administration that tried to restore American preeminence.

CHAPTER THIRTEEN

The End of the Cold War, 1981–1992

U.S.–Soviet relations underwent a remarkable transformation in the twelve years of the administrations of Ronald Reagan and George H. W. Bush. Reagan's was the most anti-Soviet administration in decades, but it eventually presided over a new era of détente. At his first news conference the president denounced the Soviet leaders as scoundrels who reserved the right to "lie, cheat, and steal" to advance the communist cause. In June 1982 he told the British Parliament that Soviet-style communism would one day be consigned to the "ash heap of history." He identified the Soviet Union as "the focus of evil" in the modern world, as he told a convention of religious broadcasters that the Kremlin had amassed an "evil empire."

Throughout Reagan's first term he and Secretary of Defense Caspar Weinberger pushed forward with the largest peacetime military buildup since 1940. "We do not know how much time we have left," the secretary warned the Senate in 1982. Fear of a super-power war rose further when, in March 1983, the president promised a defensive shield against incoming ballistic missiles. Called the Strategic Defense Initiative (SDI) by its supporters and derided by critics as "Star Wars," a science fiction fantasy, this twenty-year research and development project carried a price tag that could not be estimated. Guesses ranged from $100 billion to $1 trillion. More concretely, the Reagan administration and the NATO allies went forward with plans, created at the end of the Carter administration, to deploy medium-range ballistic and cruise missiles in Western Europe. The Soviets responded in late 1983 by walking out of all arms control talks with the United States. At the beginning of the election year of 1984, therefore, there had been no progress on either Strategic Arms Reduction Talks (START), the Reagan administration's new name for Strategic Arms Limitation Talks (SALT), or a treaty reducing intermediate nuclear forces (INF) of the sort both the Soviets and the United States had installed in Europe.

To domestic critics the Reagan administration's harsh anti-Soviet rhetoric and military buildup raised the specter of nuclear war. A grassroots movement favoring a "nuclear freeze" spread quickly in 1982 and 1983. One of its proponents, Sen. Edward M. Kennedy (D., Mass.), brought cheers from the delegates to the Democratic National Convention in 1984 when he assailed the refusal of the president to meet with the leaders of the Soviet Communist Party. Every president since Herbert Hoover had done so, Kennedy thundered, "but not Ronald Reagan." Democratic presidential candidate Walter Mondale recommended that the leaders of the Soviet Union and the United States agree to meet yearly at the summit. The president and his campaign managers scoffed in turn that this represented the sort of woolly minded idealism their assertive foreign policy was designed to combat.

FROM CONFRONTAION TO DÉTENTE WITH THE SOVIET UNION

Reagan put Mondale's suggestion that he meet with Soviet leaders into practice over the course of his next term. In the next four years Reagan had more meetings with the leader of the Soviet Union than any of his predecessors. He and Mikhail Gorbachev had summits lasting from two and a half hours to four days in Geneva in November 1985; in Reykjavik, Iceland, in October 1986; in Washington in December 1987; in Moscow in June 1988; and in New York in December 1988.

Gorbachev became party chairman in early 1985 after two dizzying years of changes at the top. Leonid Brezhnev died in November 1982, replaced by Yuri Andropov, former head of the KGB, who became ill within the year. The problem remained throughout 1984 when Konstantine Chernenko, also ill, took over. He died in March 1985, succeeded by Mikhail Gorbachev.

The new chairman was far different from his predecessors. Fifty-four years old, young by the standards of recent Soviet leaders, and well educated, Gorbachev plunged into a major reform of the Soviet system. Denouncing the eighteen-year Brezhnev era as "the period of stagnation," he promised perestroika, liberalization of the stagnant economy, and glasnost, greater openness in politics. He worried that his country might not be able to bear the weight of the military buildup created since the Cuban missile crisis of 1962. He vowed to reach an agreement with the United States to free resources for his economic program.

Over the next four years Gorbachev was everywhere: at home, in Europe, in Latin America, and in the United States. Old anticommunists such as Conservative prime minister Margaret Thatcher of Britain found him charming and called him "a friend." He presented more of a challenge to the Reagan administration than the slow, unimaginative men who had led the Kremlin in recent years.

In the five meetings between Gorbachev and Reagan, the two gradually revived détente, even if Reagan resisted using the word. Their first two summits, at Geneva in November 1985 and at Reykjavik in October 1986, were tentative, even stormy affairs. The two men's wives did not get along at first. "Who does this dame think she is?" Nancy Reagan complained about Raisa Gorbachev.

Worse followed at Reykjavik. Neither President Reagan nor Secretary of State Shultz nor Secretary of Defense Weinberger was prepared for the far-reaching proposals that Gorbachev sprang on them. The Soviet leader offered 50-percent cuts in strategic ballistic missiles, leading to their elimination. In return he demanded that the United States stop work on Star Wars, or SDI. Reagan refused, and Shultz looked miserable as he announced the collapse of the meeting to a press conference on a cold Sunday afternoon. The secretary could not even predict when, or if, there would be another meeting of the heads of government.

Events proved that the momentum of better relations between the superpowers was too strong to be derailed by the failure in Iceland. A summit did take place in Washington in December 1987, which bore concrete results in a secondary field of arms control. On December 6 Reagan and Gorbachev signed a treaty on intermediate nuclear forces. The two powers agreed to withdraw and destroy all of the intermediate-range missiles they had stationed in Europe over the past decade. The treaty had been drafted over the previous several months, so there was no repetition of the frantic negotiations between Henry Kissinger, Richard Nixon, and Leonid Brezhnev that had occurred at the Moscow summit in May 1972. Unlike Nixon, Reagan was not hailed as a master geopolitician, and his deputies were not lauded as geniuses, as Kissinger had been. But Reagan did win praise for a general improvement of relations with his main rival. "The atmospherics at the December summit in Washington was positive," admitted Marshall D. Shulman of Columbia University, who had earlier served as President Carter's special adviser on the Soviet Union. The INF treaty went forward despite the lack of progress on the thornier issue of strategic weapons. Only Nancy Reagan and Raisa Gorbachev continued to get in each other's way, as the American First Lady believed that her Soviet counterpart tried to upstage her on their tours of art galleries.

The last year of the Reagan administration saw further improvements in superpower relations. In April representatives of the two governments concluded an agreement in Geneva calling for the phased withdrawal of Soviet forces from Afghanistan. When President Reagan went to Moscow for another summit with Gorbachev in June, he explained that the new Soviet leader had not been responsible for sending the troops to Afghanistan in the first place. "They've changed," he added when asked whether he believed that the Soviet Union still represented the "focus of evil in the modern world." He received an enthusiastic welcome from students at Moscow State University. The presence of an old foe such as Reagan in the heart of the Soviet Union was the most important symbolic result of the Moscow meeting. He seemed to get along famously with Gorbachev, whom he now referred to as a "friend."

Relations between the two superpowers continued to get better for the remainder of the Reagan administration. By the fall Prime Minister Thatcher asserted that "the cold war is over." Gorbachev and Reagan met once more, before the expiration of the American president's term, when the Soviet leader, now president as well as party chairman, addressed the United Nations General Assembly in New York on December 7, 1988. He announced that his country would unilaterally reduce its military forces by 500,000 men and 10,000 tanks over the next two years. This was a very different performance from that of the last Soviet leader to address the UN, Nikita Khrushchev's pounding the table with his shoe in 1960. The usually sober *New York Times* exulted "perhaps not since Woodrow Wilson presented his Fourteen Points in 1918 or since Franklin Roosevelt and Winston Churchill promulgated the Atlantic Charter in 1941 has a world figure demonstrated the vision Mikhail Gorbachev displayed yesterday at the United Nations." President Reagan said "I heartily approve" of the proposal to reduce Soviet conventional forces before lunching with the Soviet president after his UN speech. The warmth between the two powers seemed genuine as the wives of the presidents dropped their earlier frostiness. The *New York Times* headlined this sort of détente "ANOTHER OBSTACLE FALLS: NANCY REAGAN AND RAISA GORBACHEV GET CHUMMY." By the end of the Reagan administration, the détente promised in the early 1970s had revived, and serious people contemplated the end of the Cold War.

CRISES IN CENTRAL AMERICA AND THE CARIBBEAN

The Reagan administration returned to an earlier era of attempted U.S. domination over the political destiny of Central America and the Caribbean. Official Washington sought to erase the memory of Vietnam and the supposed weakness of the Carter years by confronting leftists in Central America. It helped keep the revolutionaries from power in El Salvador, militarily overthrew the Marxists on the Caribbean island of Grenada, but failed in its principal objective—making the Sandinista government in Nicaragua "cry uncle," as the president once put it. Support for the contras strained relations with friendly states in the hemisphere, provoked public protests at home, angered Congress, and led to the greatest foreign policy scandal of the Reagan administration.

"Let's win one in El Salvador," urged columnist William Safire early in 1981. For conservatives such as Safire and Secretary of State Alexander Haig, the growing tension in Central America reminded them of Vietnam. This time, they believed the outcome for the United States would be different. The administration quickly sent fifty-five American military advisers to El Salvador to assist the army in its war against a combined front of Marxist and Social Democratic guerrillas. Washington also underwrote the cost of an ambitious land reform program undertaken by the moderate Christian Democratic government of José Napoleon Duarte.

The Christian Democrats held on in El Salvador throughout the Reagan administration, but their tenure was never secure. Duarte faced challenges from the right as well as the left. Death squads associated with the Salvadoran armed forces roamed the country killing tens of thousands of civilians, including teachers, physicians, common farmers, and church workers. Haig alienated many Catholics when he speculated that four American churchwomen—three nuns and a lay worker—who had been murdered in December 1980 may have "run a blockade" or been "caught in a crossfire." Campuses erupted as demonstrators carried signs demanding "NO MORE VIETNAMS. U.S. OUT OF EL SALVADOR." Congress passed legislation requiring presidential certification of "improvement" in human rights before additional aid could be granted. Duarte tried to comply, but rightists in the army and legislature dogged his tracks. In 1982 and 1988 the extreme right won control of the national assembly, severely restricting Duarte and the Christian Democrats.

As in Vietnam, American military advisers were frustrated as they helped the Salvadoran army fight a "nine-to-five war" against well-motivated guerrillas. This time, however, the war was closer to the United States, and the guerrillas lacked the material support the Vietnamese had enjoyed from China and the Soviet Union. Reagan went on a public relations offensive in 1983 to shore up public and congressional support for military aid to El Salvador. He urged critics to set aside "passivity, resignation and defeatism" in the face of a "challenge to freedom and security in our hemisphere." Doubters would not be stilled. Sen. Christopher Dodd offered the official Democratic Party response immediately after Reagan spoke.

Labeling the search for military solutions a "formula for failure," he recollected the disillusionment of Vietnam.

The public seemed bewildered and frustrated. A *New York Times*–CBS
News poll revealed that only 25 percent knew that the United States supported the government of El Salvador, 12 percent knew that it backed the
contras in Nicaragua, and a meager 8 percent understood both alignments;
57 percent opposed sending troops to El Salvador, while 32 percent would
back such a move if it would avert a communist takeover. Philip Converse,
a public opinion specialist at the University of Michigan, noticed a "sort of
Vietnam pall across these numbers. People have less of a support reflex than
they would have, pre-Vietnam."

From the administration's point of view something had to be done to
arrest the downward slide in public support for the assertive policy in Central America. In June 1983 Reagan reached out to Henry Kissinger, an old
target of scorn, to head a Bipartisan Presidential Commission on Central
America. The Kissinger Commission spent six months studying the complex
issues and published their findings in early 1984. It tried to satisfy everyone,
explaining that the roots of the problems in Central America were social,
not the result of communist plots. It noted that Soviet policy in the region
had been "gradualist and ambiguous," not reckless. It urged a major increase
in U.S. involvement in all aspects of Central America's problem. It called for
an additional $8 billion in American economic assistance to the region over
the next five years. Congress provided less than half that amount. It also recommended that Washington continue to support the military in El Salvador
and the contras in Nicaragua. The effort at balance only sounded weak.

As the Kissinger Commission went about its work, the focus of attention
shifted to the Caribbean, where the United States sent troops to overthrow
the revolutionary government of Grenada. The Reagan administration had
objected to the Marxist government of Prime Minister Maurice Bishop, which
had ruled since 1979. The United States had suspended all foreign aid and
sought to isolate Grenada. By 1983 the only U.S. presence on the island was
at the St. George's University School of Medicine, where 500 aspiring young
American doctors were studying. Bishop had good relations with Fidel Castro, and his New Jewel movement galvanized anti-American nationalism in
other Caribbean states. In the summer of 1983, however, Bishop seemed to
draw away from Cuba, softened his anti-Yankee rhetoric, and signaled a readi-
ness for a rapprochement with Washington. On October 12 a more militant
faction of the New Jewel movement, led by Gen. Hudson Austin, staged a
coup, murdered Bishop, declared martial law, and imposed a strict curfew
on the island.

The Reagan administration perceived a challenge. If the new government
flourished, Washington's brave talk about turning back revolution in the

U.S. troops hold prisoners at gunpoint during the invasion and occupation of
Grenada, October 1983.
(Corbis)

hemisphere would ring hollow. Direct military intervention, on the other
hand, promised value for the billions invested in the military since 1981. On
Sunday, October 23, the American public was stunned when commandos
bombed a marine barracks in Beirut, Lebanon. The shock of this raid could
further erode public support for the use of force. Before dawn on Tuesday
morning, October 25, a force of 1,900 U.S. marines and army airborne forces
landed on the island. After three days of fighting with the Grenada army and
600 Cuban construction workers, the Americans arrested the new government and proclaimed the island liberated. Reagan announced that he had
acted against "a brutal gang of leftist thugs" to save the lives of the American medical students and at the request of a little-known five-member Organization of Eastern Caribbean States.

Initially, some members of Congress were outraged. "We do not have the
right" to invade a sovereign state, said New York Democratic senator Daniel
Patrick Moynihan. Speaker of the House Thomas P. O'Neill (D., Mass.), upset
that he had not been consulted as provided for by the 1973 War Powers Act,
called it "gunboat diplomacy" and grumbled that the president "is going
down the wrong road." Seven members of the House drafted a resolution of
impeachment against the president.

Yet public support for the military action soared. Recruitment offices
were briefly swamped. Nothing did more to generate public enthusiasm than

pictures of medical students falling to their knees and kissing American soil upon their return home. Such scenes and remarks such as "I don't think there's any more beautiful sight than the United States and the rangers who arrived to save us" erased earlier declarations by the director of the school that the students had never been in danger. Within two weeks Speaker O'Neill exercised a strategic retreat, led a fourteen-member congressional delegation to the island, and announced that the invasion had been "justified." During the presidential election campaign of 1984, Republican ads featured footage of the grateful medical students with devastating effect against former vice president Walter Mondale, the Democratic nominee, who had initially condemned the military action.

Memories of Grenada faded, though. Of greater significance were the unsuccessful attempts by the Reagan administration to evict the Sandinista government of Nicaragua led by President Daniel Ortega. In March 1981 Reagan signed a "Presidential Finding" authorizing the CIA to pay, train, and arm disaffected Nicaraguans to overthrow the Sandinistas. The CIA recruited between 5,000 and 10,000 of these contras in the first two years, rising to nearly 20,000 in 1985. Many of the fighters and commanders were former Somoza national guardsmen; a few of the top political leaders had originally been part of an alliance against the Somoza dictatorship.

Within a year this "secret war" became common knowledge. Congress passed a resolution sponsored by Rep. Edward Boland (D., Mass.), chairman of the House Committee on Intelligence, expressly forbidding the use of American funds to overthrow the government of Nicaragua. Other Latin American states warned Washington that it was pursuing a dangerous course. In January 1983 the foreign ministers of Colombia, Mexico, Panama, and Venezuela met on Contadora, an island off the Panama coast, to forge a diplomatic solution to the impasse between Washington and Managua. Over the next two years "the Contadora process" became a shorthand code for a negotiated settlement of the U.S.-sponsored contra war against Nicaragua.

Washington displayed little interest in negotiations, however. In September 1983 President Reagan signed another finding authorizing support to the contras for the vague purpose of "putting pressure on the Sandinistas" to stop sending arms to the leftist guerrillas in El Salvador. Since this finding did not promise the overthrow of the government, it circumvented the first Boland amendment. In a nationally televised speech Reagan urged the public to pressure Congress to provide $24 million for the contras. "Communist subversion is not an irreversible tide," he said. "We have seen it rolled back in Grenada."

Congress could not be moved, though, after the news broke in April 1983 that the CIA had mined Nicaragua's harbors and bombed the oil storage facilities at Corinto. Aid for the contras, appropriated by Congress, expired on October 1, 1984. Lawmakers thereupon passed another version of the Boland resolution, banning government funds for the contras. This prohibition remained in effect until mid-1986, when Congress once more provided money for the contras.

In 1987 and 1988 the contras did poorly in their war against the Sandinistas, as the United States backed away from its earlier support. The growing scandal of the diversion of funds from Iran arms sales to the contras undermined always tenuous congressional support. The Nicaraguan forces fought better than the contras. The long-dormant Contadora process revived after President Oscar Arias of Costa Rica urged a cease-fire and an amnesty in 1987. He won a Nobel Peace Prize for his efforts. In March 1988 the contras signed a cease-fire with the Sandinistas, agreeing to lay down their arms in return for negotiations leading to an opening of the political system.

MUDDLING IN THE MIDDLE EAST

The Reagan administration wrestled with the problems of the Middle East for eight years but had little success in resolving them. A public opinion poll taken in April 1985 revealed that Americans regarded the Camp David accords, brokered by Jimmy Carter in 1978 and 1979, the greatest achievement of recent foreign policy, while they considered the Reagan administration's involvement in Lebanon in 1982–1984 its greatest failure.

In September 1982 the United States landed troops in the eastern Mediterranean for the first time since 1958. This unplanned and poorly executed effort to mediate a war between Israel and the Palestine Liberation Organization quickly bogged down in the complicated civil war of scores of religious and political factions in Lebanon. Originally, the Reagan administration had hoped to change the subject of Mideast disputes from the Arab-Israeli conflict to the new Cold War between East and West. Secretary of State Alexander Haig sought to forge what he called a "strategic consensus" between Jerusalem and anticommunist Arab states. Neither side was interested, and Washington pulled away from the effort to further the mediation between Israel and the Arabs as envisioned in the Camp David formula.

In June 1982 Israel, perceiving a "green light" from Haig, attacked the PLO in Lebanon. Instead of a brief, successful campaign, the war dragged on. Haig resigned on June 25, angry that National Security Adviser William P. Clark had opened his own channels of communications with the PLO. Haig left with the admonition that Reagan had shunned the path of "consistency, clarity and steadiness" he had promised. The president immediately named George P. Shultz as his new secretary of state.

Shultz's first test came later that summer as the Israelis had blasted their way to the outskirts of Beirut. The PLO remained intact. Shultz and special envoy Philip Habib worked out a plan for the PLO to evacuate Beirut under the protection of a multinational force made up of American, French, and Italian marines. A smiling PLO leader, Yassir Arafat, led his fighters from the bombed-out city in late August, and the multinational force withdrew. The new secretary of state thereupon persuaded President Reagan to announce a "fresh start" in Mideast peace negotiations. On September 1 he proposed a formula of "peace in exchange for territory." Israel would yield the West Bank to a Palestinian "homeland in confederation with Jordan" in return for security and normal relations with its neighbors. Neither Israel nor the Arab states accepted the plan.

All hell broke loose less than three weeks later following the September 14 assassination of Bashir Gemayal, leader of the Christian Phalange Party who had just been elected president of Lebanon. Israel's army occupied Muslim West Beirut on the 15th; two days later Gemayal's Christian militia entered two Palestinian refugee camps and went on a bloody rampage. They slaughtered between 200 and 800 Palestinian men, women, and children. Immediately afterward the multinational force of American, French, and Italian marines returned for an indefinite stay.

Originally, the marines were welcomed by most factions in Lebanon as peacekeepers, but soon they provoked resentment from Shi'ite Muslims and Syrians, who also had troops in Lebanon. Washington never made clear the precise purpose of the force or how long it would remain in the midst of an ever more dangerous civil war. On April 18, 1983, a suicide squad bombed the American embassy in Beirut, killing sixty-three, including seventeen Americans. By the fall the marines were siding openly with some Christian factions, shelling Muslim and radical positions. Early on Sunday morning, October 23, suicide terrorists driving trucks loaded with TNT blew up the American marine headquarters near the Beirut airport, killing 241 marines and navy personnel as they slept.

American policy lay in ruins along with the barracks. For a while Reagan put on a brave face, insisting that the U.S. force would remain in Beirut. "If others feel confident they can intimidate us and our allies in Lebanon, they will become more bold elsewhere." In his January 25, 1984, State of the Union message, Reagan reiterated that the marines would stay in Beirut. This was just talk. Two weeks later Lebanon's fragile government collapsed, and chaos reigned in the capital. Restless House Democrats prepared a resolution demanding the marines' withdrawal. The president removed them to ships offshore but still said he had not "bugged out" under fire.

The United States lowered its public profile in the Arab-Israeli dispute over the next five years. A new coalition between the more moderate Labor Party and the nationalist Likud bloc took power in Israel in September 1984 and began the process of removing Israel's army from southern Lebanon. Washington watched and hoped that the issue would recede from public view. It did, but in the meantime peace between Israel and the Arabs remained only a dream.

The unreal calm was shattered on December 9, 1987, when Palestinians in the West Bank and Gaza Strip, dominated by Israel and ignored by other Arabs, began an uprising, or intifada, against the twenty-year-old occupation. Over the next year Palestinians demonstrated, scrawled slogans on walls, struck, threw rocks, hurled gasoline bombs, and stabbed Israelis. The Israelis responded with tear gas, rubber bullets, clubs, and live ammunition. In the first year of the intifada Israeli soldiers and settlers killed more than 330 Arabs, while thirteen Israelis lost their lives to the insurgents. Caught by surprise, the United States tried once more to breathe life into the moribund peace process. In March Secretary Shultz called for the revival of the land-for-peace formula and the interim autonomy arrangement of the Camp David agreement. Israel, however, rejected Shultz's proposal of an international conference to formulate a framework for resolving the Palestinian issue. Shultz's initiative died.

Nine months later, after the presidential elections, the United States abruptly reversed a thirteen-year ban on official contact with the PLO when Shultz announced on December 14 that Washington was willing to open a "dialogue" with Yassir Arafat. The PLO chairman recognized Israel's right to exist, observed that two UN Security Council resolutions adopted after the 1967 and 1973 Arab-Israeli wars provided a framework for negotiations, and "renounced" terrorism. Shultz made it easier for his successors in the Bush administration to act as a broker between Israel and the Palestinians.

Farther west in the Mediterranean the United States engaged in small-scale warfare with Libya. This radical Islamic state, ruled since 1969 by a charismatic and demogogic strongman, Col. Muammar Khaddafy, used its oil wealth to bankroll some of the more violent terrorists operating in Europe and the Middle East. Hoping to put Khaddafy "back in his box," as Secretary of State Shultz once observed, American ships and planes patrolled the Gulf of Sidra, north of Libya's coast, throughout the Reagan administration. The Libyans rose to the bait twice. In August 1981 and December 1988 American navy jets downed Libyan warplanes approaching for an attack. A far more serious episode took place on the night of April 14–15, 1986, when American jets from carriers in the Mediterranean and bases in Britain bombed five targets in Libya. The raid was ordered in retaliation for a series of terrorist episodes in Europe linked to Libya, the most recent of which was the bombing of a Berlin nightclub frequented by GIs. One of the aims of the raid was the death of Khaddafy. He escaped, but his daughter was killed and two of his sons were injured. A total of 77 percent of the American public polled immediately after the bombing approved of it.

The United States also reacted to events, rather than planned carefully, as the war between Iran and Iraq dragged on for nearly nine years, from 1980 to 1988. With bad relations with both Baghdad and Tehran, the United States watched from the sidelines, supporting neither for six years. As many as 2 million soldiers and civilians lost their lives in the bloodiest fighting since the Second World War. In 1985–1986 the White House became more directly involved, secretly arming Iran. When news of the clandestine shipments fanned an outraged backlash at home, the administration reversed course and sided with Iraq. In May 1987 the U.S. navy began escorting Kuwaiti oil tankers, reflagged as American vessels, through the Persian Gulf. In May 1987 an Iraqi fighter mistook the destroyer *Stark* for an Iranian vessel, fired a French Exocet missile at it, and killed thirty-seven sailors. The navy continued its patrols, still siding with Iraq against Iran. In August one of the reflagged tankers, sailing in front of warships supposed to protect it, hit an Iranian mine. The following July 3 the crew of the USS *Vincennes* became as confused as the Iraqi pilots, mistook an Iranian civilian airliner for a hostile jet, and blasted it out of the sky, killing 290. Washington compensated the victims, an act of generosity hardly welcomed by an American public that still detested all things Iranian. A month later, in August, Iran and Iraq, exhausted by their losses, signed a cease-fire.

THE IRAN-CONTRA CONNECTION

On November 3, 1986, an obscure Lebanese weekly, *Al Shiraa*, with close ties to the revolutionary government of Iran, reported that former U.S. National Security Adviser Robert McFarlane had secretly visited Tehran in May. He carried a Bible and a cake in the shape of a key with a mission to negotiate the release of American hostages in Lebanon in return for a supply of spare parts for Iran's military. This article opened a window on a hitherto secret American foreign policy, staffed by White House operatives, former CIA agents, and shadowy arms dealers beyond the control of the State or Defense departments or the knowledge of Congress.

As the story unfolded over the next eight months it engulfed the White House and seriously undermined public support for Reagan's foreign policy. On November 25 Attorney General Edwin Meese revealed that Lt. Col. Oliver North of the National Security Council staff had arranged for the transfer of $10 million to $30 million in payments Iran had made for arms in 1985 and 1986 to rebels fighting the Nicaraguan government. During that time the Boland amendment had prohibited any U.S. government funds for the contras. David Durenberger (R., Minn.), chairman of the Senate Intelligence Committee, threatened, "It will be a cold day in Washington before any more money goes into Nicaragua." At the same time Reagan fired North and his superior, Adm. John Poindexter, who had succeeded McFarlane as national security adviser in December 1985. Even as the president dropped North, he described him as a "national hero" and telephoned to say that "your work will make a great movie some day."

Before the filmmakers went to work, though, a presidential commission and Congress exposed North's network. Reagan appointed a special review board chaired by former senator John Tower (R., Tex.) working with former national security adviser Brent Scowcroft and former secretary of state Edmund Muskie. They investigated from December 1986 to February 1987 and found that the initiative to Iran was the brainchild of McFarlane, CIA director William Casey, North, several Israelis, and an Iranian go-between. Throughout 1985 and 1986 the United States had helped Israel and private arms merchants ship hundreds of tons of missiles and spare aircraft parts to Iran. The objective had always been to encourage Iran to release American

President Ronald Reagan confers with National Security Adviser Robert McFarlane (left) and Secretary of State George Shultz (right) aboard Air Force One. McFarlane was a principal architect of the arms-for-hostages transfer, but Shultz opposed it.
(Ronald Reagan Library)

hostages held in Lebanon. The Tower Commission concluded that the scheme "was handled almost casually ... with an expectation that the process would end with the next arms-for-hostage exchange." They portrayed Reagan as remote, unaware of what subordinates did in his name, and ignorant of the implications of their actions. They decided that the president had "a concept of the initiative that was not accurately reflected in the reality of the operation." They faulted Chief of Staff Donald Regan, Secretary of Defense Weinberger, and Secretary of State Shultz for not forcefully stopping dealing arms for hostages, even though they thought it a terrible idea. "That policy was a wrong policy," said Muskie, "and it was the President's policy." The Tower board recognized that news of the Reagan White House negotiating with agents of the Ayatollah Khomeini was a public relations catastrophe. The connection "ran directly counter to the administration's own policy on terrorism," they wrote. "The result," they observed, "was a U.S. policy that worked against itself ... an unprofessional, and, in substantial part, unsatisfactory operation."

While the Tower board damned the president for managerial negligence, it did not directly connect him with the illegal decision to divert profits from the arms sales to the contras. A congressional investigation followed the money trail to discover who knew of the diversion. The committees, chaired by Daniel Inouye (D., Hawaii) in the Senate and Lee Hamilton (D., Ind.) in the House, held joint hearings to determine, as Sen. David Boren (D., Okla.) asked, "Did the president faithfully carry out the spirit of the law, or was he ignoring it? Did he subvert the process himself by trying to raise funds to get money to the contras?"

From May until July the committees heard secondary figures explain how North had solicited money for the contras from wealthy Texas widows, rightwing brewers, the Sultan of Brunei, and the governments of Taiwan and Saudi Arabia. By July a picture of North had emerged as a driven, ambitious young man who, one colleague described, "came into the NSC as an easel carrier and ended up the world's most powerful lieutenant colonel."

Media excitement boiled over as North himself began four days of televised testimony on July 7. North revealed that he held a "shredding party," destroying the written record of his activities as Justice Department officials entered his office in November. He explained, "I thought I had received authority from the president," even though he never heard from Reagan directly. He explained that CIA Director Casey and he arranged for him to be the "fall guy" should the scheme be revealed. "I was supposed to be dropped like a hot rock," he said, but "I wasn't willing to become the victim of a criminal prosecution." That was why, he explained, he was now implicating his superiors in the plan to divert money from the arms sales to the contras. Two weeks later John Poindexter told the committee "the buck stops with me" when lawmakers pressed him to explain if Reagan had been involved in the diversion. Poindexter also revealed that he "tore up" a presidential finding on the arms sales. Frustrated committee members knew that with the record destroyed they never would learn for certain about Reagan's role.

North's testimony temporarily altered public opinion about the diversion to the contras and the colonel himself. He offered a more spirited defense of the Nicaragua rebels than Reagan had, and opinion polls briefly showed that a majority of the public now backed aiding them. That majority melted within a month.

Just as short-lived was the "Ollie mania" that swept the country after he testified. *U.S. News and World Report* explained that his blue eyes and boyish grin "erased the impression that he was a man with Walter Mitty's grip on reality." One Minnesota woman remarked, "He turned my whole mind around. He's fabulous." Bumper stickers reading "THANK YOU, OLLIE" popped up. Congress was deluged with letters and telegrams running twenty to one in favor of North. Friends raised hundreds of thousands of dollars that they promised to his legal defense fund.

Passions quickly faded. Much about North encouraged manipulators and confidence operators. The telegram wave had been orchestrated by local Republican parties and abetted by Western Union, which profited from the business. More than 75 percent of the money raised for his defense remained with the fund-raisers and never reached his legal team. In March 1988 a special prosecutor indicted North, Poindexter, and two of the arms dealers for violating the ban on aiding the contras, defrauding the government, and obstruction of justice. Now needing millions, North resigned from the Marine Corps and toured the country, speaking on behalf of conservative politicians and raising money for his own defense. His supporters urged President Reagan to issue a preemptive pardon before North went to trial.

While the public sobered up about North, his testimony deflated the congressional effort to attach responsibility for Iran-contra to the president. Reagan declined to damage his own standing with the public by pardoning his subordinates for their roles in the Iran-contra affair. North, Poindexter, and several lesser arms dealers and go-betweens were tried and convicted of perjury and the misuse of government funds. A federal appeals court later overturned the convictions of North and Poindexter on the ground that they had been promised immunity from prosecution in return for their testimony before the congressional committee investigating Iran-contra. In 1992 the special prosecutor handling the case brought charges of perjury against former secretary of defense Caspar Weinberger. Although Weinberger had opposed the sale of weapons to Iran, he had denied to Congress that he had kept notes of his activities during crucial meetings in early 1985.

Discovery of Weinberger's handwritten diary led the prosecutor to bring the indictment.

FOREIGN POLICY IN THE ELECTION OF 1988

When candidates addressed foreign affairs during the election campaign of 1988, they concentrated on the past. Like nearly all of their fellow citizens, the men seeking the Democratic and Republican presidential nominations could not anticipate the earthquake about to topple the communist world. Instead of preparing for the end of the Cold War, both the winner of the November election, Republican vice president George H. W. Bush, and the loser, Massachusetts Democratic governor Michael Dukakis, remained frozen in a traditional debate over how to confront the Soviets and project American military power around the world. The credentials and experience each man might bring to the job counted for more than specific proposals each made for the future direction of American foreign relations. The vice president presented an impressive résumé in foreign affairs—ambassador to the United Nations, representative to the People's Republic of China, and director of Central Intelligence in the Nixon and Ford administrations. Dukakis, on the other hand, had little overseas experience, having devoted himself to public service and politics in Massachusetts after returning from two years of duty as an army private in 1954.

The discussion of foreign affairs in the 1988 election became a referendum on the Reagan administration's accomplishments and failures. Dukakis tried to use Bush's service in the Reagan administration against him by tying the vice president to the Iran-contra scandal. The governor noted that the vice president claimed to regard Oliver North as a "national hero" and had invited him to his 1987 Christmas party. But the issue faded as Reagan refused to offer preemptive pardons to North and Poindexter. Furthermore, Bush refused to answer specific questions about his participation in the arms-for-hostage swap, other than to affirm that he had been "out of the loop" when top Reagan officials contemplated supplying weapons to Iran.

Bush had more success than Dukakis in deriding his opponent's foreign affairs positions. Bush pointed to the genuine warmth developed between Reagan and Gorbachev to demonstrate that the military buildup of the Reagan administration had not led to war, as some critics had predicted. Bush assailed Dukakis for advocating deep cuts in overall defense spending and a halt to the development of the Strategic Defense Initiative.

Dukakis had little success raising other foreign policy disappointments of the Reagan years. Dukakis concentrated his criticism on the failed effort by the Reagan administration to evict General Manuel Noriega from power in Panama. A federal grand jury in south Florida indicted Noriega in February 1988 for running cocaine into the United States. Soon after his indictment, news leaked that the Panamanian strongman had been on the CIA's payroll for more than a decade. Dukakis raised the specter that Bush, director of Central Intelligence in 1976, had overlooked Noriega's unsavory behavior. Noriega's ability to stay in power despite Washington's economic pressure allowed Dukakis to cast doubt on the foreign affairs competence of the Reagan-Bush administration. Dukakis promised that his administration would not "do business with a drug running Central American dictator." Dukakis's charges did not strike a deep chord with the general public, but they did irritate Bush. What to do about Noriega became an immediate problem for the new Bush administration.

Dukakis's intermittent discussion of foreign affairs had little effect on the outcome of the election, which Bush won comfortably. In the end voters appreciated Reagan's accomplishments with the Soviets and felt comfortable with the continuity promised by Bush.

THE REAGAN RECORD

The foreign policy record of the Reagan administration was one of the most surprising of the twentieth century. The president and his principal advisers came to office with a narrowly ideological view of the world. Harshly antagonistic toward Soviet-style communism, they appeared to consider compromise with Moscow a sign of weakness or folly in their predecessors. Yet the Reagan administration proved to be exceptionally skillful in its negotiations with the Soviets after the advent of Mikhail Gorbachev. Throughout his presidency Reagan held a series of simple ideas about foreign policy. He believed in strength—especially of the military sort—the moral virtues of the United States, and the evils of communism. His critics derided him for the lack of sophistication of these opinions. Indeed, in Reagan's first term such ideas threatened to bring the nuclear super-powers to the brink of war. By 1987, however, Reagan had adapted to the new face of the Soviet Union. Despite his intellectual limitations, Reagan exercised real political leadership in his dealings with the Soviets.

It was to Reagan's credit that he understood the changes in Soviet policy undertaken by Mikhail Gorbachev, and he thereupon dropped his hostile anti-Soviet rhetoric, allowing the Cold War to end. Yet more of the credit for ending the Cold War probably goes to Gorbachev than to any other single individual. Gorbachev acknowledged the deep structural flaws in the Soviet system, and he believed that only an end to the Cold War would allow his country to survive into the twenty-first century. He was only half right, as events were to prove that the Soviet Union was doomed. Reagan and supporters of his hostile policies argue that the American toughness eventually convinced Gorbachev to change. The reality is somewhat different. As Raymond Garthoff, the foremost analyst of the end of the Cold War, writes, "the crusading spirit evidenced by American leaders and their indictment of the Soviet system were largely irrelevant to the outcome." Indeed, the adversarial attacks coming from Washington before 1988 probably "made it harder for Gorbachev to liberalize Soviet internal and international behavior because the powerful domestic conservative forces with which he was in constant struggle objected that he was giving in to American pressures, sacrificing Soviet interests and kowtowing to the West."

American diplomacy descended into illegality during the Iran-contra scandal; the disregard for congressional constraints on the executive intensified the already high level of public distrust of government officials. By reversing the Carter administration's emphasis on the protection of human rights, already weakened in 1980, the Reagan administration diminished affection for the United States abroad. The United States was often too quick to use force in the 1980s, and the military buildup of the Reagan years contributed to a crushing burden of debt. Nevertheless, the ability of Ronald Reagan to seize the moment contributed to lifting the fear of nuclear annihilation that had made the Cold War a nightmare.

GEORGE H. W. BUSH AND THE END OF THE COLD WAR

Soviet-style communism collapsed with astonishing speed between 1989 and 1991. On November 9, 1989, the Berlin Wall tumbled. Less than a year later Germany was reunited as a capitalist, democratic country. Revolutions swept away communist governments across Eastern Europe. Most spectacularly of all, the Soviet Union ceased to exist on December 31, 1991. President George H. W. Bush characterized the end of the Soviet system as "one of the most important developments of this century—the revolutionary transformation of a totalitarian dictatorship and the liberation of its people from its smothering embrace."

For a brief moment, from 1989 to 1991, Bush and his principal foreign policy advisers spoke optimistically about the creation of a "new world order." They believed that the United States would work with partners directly and within the framework of the United Nations to promote international harmony. Reality confounded this promise of international cooperation. The Bush administration successfully organized a multinational military coalition to compel Iraq to withdraw its military occupation from the oil-rich emirate of Kuwait, but in the aftermath of the six-week Persian Gulf War of 1991, the Bush administration could not deliver the international stability many people hoped would follow the Cold War. In 1992 Bush dropped references to American sponsorship of a new world order. Americans turned inward in the aftermath of the Cold War. Bush's emphasis on his stewardship of international affairs became a disadvantage with a public that perceived him as being out of touch with concerns of ordinary people.

With the end of the Cold War, U.S. foreign policy confronted a variety of smaller problems it had not had during the forty-year confrontation with the Soviet Union and its allies. The Soviet Union did not exist after 1991, and U.S. policy makers no longer had to manage relations with another superpower. The danger of nuclear annihilation no longer hung over the world. Ordinary Americans paid less attention to international affairs in the 1990s than they had at any time since 1945.

Bill Clinton, the successful Democratic Party candidate in 1992, won the White House by emphasizing the problems of the middle class. As soon as he was elected he promised to "focus on the economy like a laser. Foreign policy will come into play as it affects the economy." Like many of his predecessors, however, he found that foreign affairs took on increasing prominence. The Clinton administration embraced the growing economic interdependence of the world, a process called globalization. From 1993 to 2000 the United States also engaged in several high-profile humanitarian interventions during the Clinton administration. At century's end U.S. foreign policy no longer displayed the sharp clarity of purpose it had shown at the height of the Cold War. The very complexity of America's attempts to come to grips with the post–Cold War world reflected reality.

THE BUSH FOREIGN AFFAIRS TEAM

George H. W. Bush came to the presidency with long experience in foreign affairs. He had acquired a wide circle of political acquaintances around the world in his years of government service. He selected an unusually close-knit circle of foreign policy advisers. His friend James A. Baker III served as secretary of state until July 1992, when he stepped down to manage Bush's unsuccessful campaign for reelection. Lawrence A. Eagleburger, a veteran diplomat with experience at the highest level of the State Department going back to the Nixon administration, was secretary of state for the last seven months of the Bush administration. Bush went back to his associates in the Ford administration for other high officials. Brent Scowcroft, national security adviser under Ford, took up those duties in the Bush administration. Dick Cheney, Ford's chief of staff when Bush had been director of central intelligence, served as secretary of defense in the Bush administration. To round out his set of foreign policy advisers, Bush elevated Gen. Colin Powell, Reagan's last national security adviser, to become the first African-American chairman of the Joint Chiefs of Staff.

This unusually tight foreign policy team worked well with the president. Their partnership ended the bickering among the president's top foreign policy advisers that had bedeviled the Reagan administration. While they were united and mostly comfortable with one another, Bush's foreign policy team held a narrow vision of U.S. interests. Their approach suited Bush, who continuously stressed his "obligation to temper optimism with prudence" in foreign affairs. All veterans of the Cold War, the Bush foreign policy team focused on state-to-state relations, felt uncomfortable stressing the advancement of human rights, and slowly realized that the confrontation with the Soviet Union had ended. Their caution served them well, however, in managing the transition from communism to capitalism.

THE END OF COMMUNISM

The Bush administration moved with painstaking caution in its early months toward a new relationship with the communist states. Bush's moves scarcely anticipated the earthquake in the communist world in 1989. Popular revolutions broke out in Eastern Europe. Hundreds of thousands of East Germans fled their country to the West in the summer of 1989. Thousands of their countrymen who remained behind in the German Democratic Republic took to the streets in protest against the communist regime. The GDR leaders considered using police or troops against their own people, but Soviet president Mikhail Gorbachev discouraged them. Instead of resisting, the GDR government ordered the wall to be opened on November 9, allowing anyone who wanted to leave to do so. That night thousands of jubilant East Berliners clambered atop the wall. Wrecking balls tore down the wall over the next several months. On October 2, 1990, the GDR ceased to exist, and its constituent states became part of the Federal Republic of Germany. Similar revolutions occurred in all the communist nations of Eastern Europe. Everywhere governments came to power promising the end of communism, the creation of free markets, democratic institutions, and the rule of law.

The U.S. government did not become publicly involved in the drama unfolding behind what used to be called the Iron Curtain. Bush resisted calls for him to rush to Berlin and triumphantly proclaim victory in the Cold War. He won high praise from analysts for the quiet confidence with which he supported Chancellor Helmut Kohl's efforts to unify Germany. As Philip Zelikow and Condoleeza Rice, two national security council staff members,

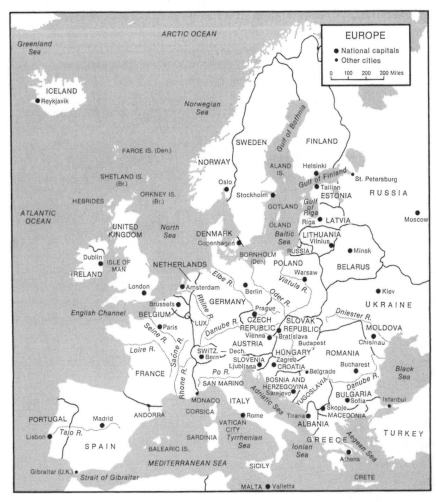

observed in *Germany Unified and Europe Transformed* (1995), Bush "could not imagine an end to the Cold War that did not leave Europe whole and free. It fell to him to deliver on that promise. And he did." Bush developed a personal relationship with Soviet president Gorbachev. He met often with the Soviet leader and hoped to enlist him as a partner in the new world order.

Gorbachev's hold on power weakened in 1991. The Soviet economy approached collapse in the summer. Soviet politics were tumultuous. Boris Yeltsin, the elected president of the Russian Federation, became the leader of the democratic opposition. Gorbachev became more embattled when opponents in the military, the Communist Party, and the secret police tried to depose him in a coup d'état on August 19. The plot collapsed within days after Yeltsin led thousands of Muscovites into the streets in protest.

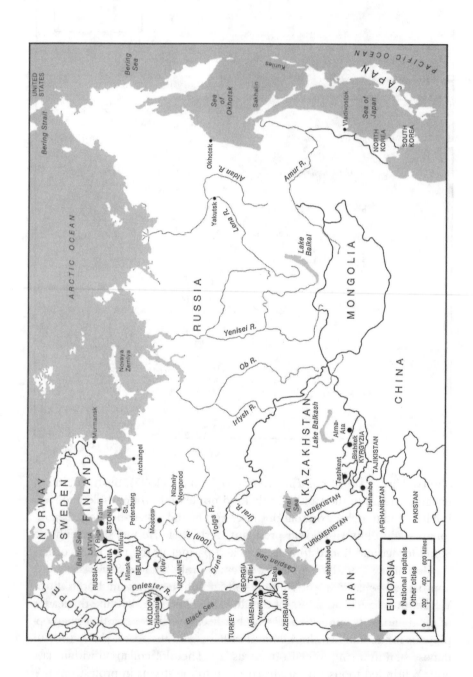

The coup hastened the death of the Soviet empire and transformed East–West relations. During the height of the coup crisis, Bush offered Yeltsin his unqualified support. After Yeltsin faced down the plotters, he held unchallenged power. He moved quickly to shed the remnants of communist power. Throughout the country crowds tore down statues of communist heroes and restored the prerevolutionary names to streets, squares, towns, and cities. In the fall Leningrad became St. Petersburg once more. On December 25 Gorbachev resigned as the last president of the Soviet Union, and a week later the country ceased to exist. Yeltsin remained president of the Russian Federation, the most powerful of the successor nations. Bush tried to establish a personal relationship with Yeltsin, but for the remainder of the Bush administration American officials remained concerned that the Russian president was a highly emotional and unsteady partner.

THE UNITED STATES AND DISORDER IN THE THIRD WORLD

The end of the Cold War highlighted the disorders of the developing world. The Bush administration reformulated U.S. policy toward the Western Hemisphere to follow a pragmatic rather than ideological course. It minimized the zealous anticommunism of the Reagan administration's approach to the conflicts in Central America. The nations of that region themselves moved toward reducing their civil and international wars. The guerrilla war in El Salvador wound down in 1989. In February 1990 voters in Nicaragua ousted the Sandinista government. The Bush administration jubilantly proclaimed a new era of democracy in the hemisphere.

In one country, Panama, the rule of law came at the point of U.S. guns. In December 1989 the Bush administration sent U.S. troops into Panama City to arrest Manuel Noriega, the country's dictator. Fifty-five Panamanian National Guard troops and twenty-three U.S. soldiers lost their lives in seventy-two hours of fighting. Approximately 500 civilian bystanders were killed in the cross fire. The United States captured Noriega and returned him to Miami for trial on drug charges. In April 1992 a federal jury convicted him of smuggling cocaine. Elections took place in Panama, and civilian rule resumed. But Panama's economy remained mired throughout the 1990s.

About a year after the U.S. invasion of Panama, a few poor residents of that country who had welcomed the arrival of the Americans as saviors now cursed them and shouted the name of Saddam Hussein, the dictator of Iraq, Washington's latest nemesis. On August 2, 1990, Iraq invaded and annexed its neighbor Kuwait, seizing that country's vast oil reserves. Within days President Bush began organizing an international coalition to roll back the conquest. Asserting that "this is naked aggression; it will not stand," Bush

*Iraq/
Hussein*

personally encouraged world leaders to oppose Iraq. The United States led the UN Security Council to issue a series of resolutions demanding that Iraq quit Kuwait. The United States also assembled a military force of 700,000 from twenty-eight countries. This air, land, and sea coalition was stationed in Saudi Arabia and in the Persian Gulf near Kuwait and Iraq.

After the expiration of twelve UN resolutions demanding that Iraq withdraw, on January 16 the coalition began ferocious bombing of Iraq and Iraqi positions in Kuwait. Bush's management of the coalition against Iraq won high praise. He constantly worked the telephones, speaking to dozens of foreign leaders. He kept such disparate Arab countries as Egypt, Morocco, the Gulf states, and Syria aligned against Iraq. He maintained the support of NATO allies. He also maintained the benevolent neutrality of the Soviet Union.

After six weeks of relentless bombardment of Iraq, the UN forces launched a ground assault. The battered Iraqi forces retreated in disarray. On February 27, exactly 100 hours after the ground war began, Bush announced the liberation of Kuwait and the end of the war. His personal popularity hit a stratospheric 89 percent in March of 1991, but the aftermath of the war was messy. Saddam Hussein remained in power in Iraq, and minority Shi'ites in the south and Kurds in the north suffered extreme hardship. The UN continued an arms and economic embargo on Iraq. The United States and Britain sent planes to patrol "no-fly zones" in the north and south to protect Shi'ites and Kurds. The unsettled conditions in postwar Iraq tarnished the victory in the Gulf War, and Bush's public approval began to fade in the fall of 1991.

CHAPTER FOURTEEN

The Mixed Blessings of Globalization, 1993–2000

The Democratic Party nominated Arkansas governor Bill Clinton to challenge President George H. W. Bush in the election of 1992. Clinton believed that the end of the Cold War and Bush's apparent successes might work to his advantage. The contrast between Bush's apparent mastery of diplomacy and his befuddlement with the nation's economic problems sapped the public's confidence in his leadership. During the campaign Clinton asserted that Bush and his foreign policy lieutenants lacked a broad vision of what American foreign policy should be in the post–Cold War era. The world had changed, Clinton said, but the Bush administration wanted to conduct "business as usual." He attacked Bush for coddling the Communist regime in China. The administration, he said, played the China card even after "our opponents had thrown in their hand." He criticized Bush for having been slow to support the democratic forces in Russia led by President Boris Yeltsin. He also accused Bush of standing idly by while a humanitarian catastrophe occurred in the Balkans. Vice presidential candidate Al Gore even challenged the Bush administration's claims of a victory in the Gulf War with Iraq. "If they're such whizzes at foreign policy," he complained, "then why was Iraqi president Saddam Hussein still in power?" President Bush dismissed Clinton and Gore as rank amateurs. "My dog Millie knows more about foreign policy than those two bozos," he insisted.

The public thought Clinton and Gore knew enough, and they elected Clinton president. Immediately after the election Clinton promised to use foreign policy to expand American trade. He also insisted that U.S. foreign policy had to be based on "the moral principles most Americans share." The end of the Cold War figured prominently in Clinton's inaugural address, when he proudly pointed to a "world warmed by the sunshine of freedom." "Our hopes, our hearts, and our hands," he said, "are with those on every continent who are building democracy and freedom."

The collapse of Soviet-style communism and the end of the four-decades-long Cold War seemed to diminish the importance of foreign affairs for Americans. Bill Clinton won the presidency in 1992 by emphasizing the problems of the middle class. Immediately after his election he promised to "focus on the economy like a laser. Foreign affairs will come into play as it affects the economy." Clinton and his principal foreign policy advisers enthusiastically embraced the growing economic interdependence of the world, a process called globalization. Clinton sought to manage the transition of the Soviet Union from a Cold War rival into an American partner. He engaged in several high-profile humanitarian interventions around the globe. He devoted countless hours and thousands of miles of travel to mediating peace between Israel and the Palestinians, only to have the prize of a comprehensive peace elude him in the last months of his administration.

CLINTON'S APPROACH TO FOREIGN POLICY

Clinton administration officials believed the United States had to remain deeply engaged in foreign affairs. For eight years they pressed an ambitious agenda. Politically, they advocated the expansion of democratic values and human rights abroad. The administration often deployed armed forces to dampen ethnic tensions. The United States tried to mediate apparently intractable conflicts. It supported the increasing economic interdependence of the world and sought to channel this globalization in ways that spread prosperity.

The administration compiled a mixed record. Supporters of the Clinton administration applauded its efforts to make sense of the complexities of the post–Cold War world. The Clinton administration took domestic and international risks to make the world more peaceful and prosperous. Critics painted a darker picture, however. They charged the Clinton administration with inability to formulate a clear set of principles to apply after the Cold War. They complained that Clinton officials acted inconsistently, overextended U.S. power, and mismanaged crises.

The truth reflected neither of these stereotypes. The Clinton administration deserved credit for acknowledging that the post–Cold War world was far more complex than the world had been during the height of East–West tension. The United States did try to apply imaginative solutions to these complicated issues. At the same time, the Clinton administration often exaggerated the ability of the United States to shape the contours of the post–Cold War world. By the time Clinton left office in January 2001, the world was not nearly as harmonious as he and his principal foreign policy advisers had hoped or expected when they began their stewardship.

THE CLINTON FOREIGN POLICY TEAM

Clinton selected veterans of earlier Democratic administrations to fill the top foreign policy positions in his administration. Most of them advocated centrist foreign policy positions. All believed that the world had changed significantly after the Cold War. They thought the United States had a predominant role to play as the world's only super-power and that globalization and trade expansion held enormous promise for people everywhere. They also believed in the use of military force to advance humanitarian aims.

In the eight years of the Clinton administration, there were two secretaries of state. Warren Christopher (1993–1997), a careful, soft-spoken Los Angeles lawyer, had served as deputy secretary of state during the Carter administration. He saw his role more as solving problems as they arose than constructing a grand design for American foreign policy. Madeleine Albright, secretary of state in Clinton's second term (1997–2001), cast a longer shadow. The Czech-born Albright's family had fled twice from their homeland—first from the Nazis and then from the Communists. Memories of the brutality of totalitarian regimes made Albright willing to use military force to advance human rights. She was U.S. ambassador to the United Nations in the first Clinton administration. In that position she pressed for international humanitarian intervention in the Balkans. She continued to advocate a forceful international and U.S. intervention to promote human rights while she served as secretary of state.

Clinton's other foreign policy advisers also blended the use of military force and moral suasion. He had two national security advisers, Anthony Lake (1993–1997) and Samuel R. "Sandy" Berger (1997–2001). Lake remembered the trauma of the Vietnam War, and he was reluctant to deploy American forces unilaterally. He also believed that the post–Cold War environment made multilateral actions to advance human rights more feasible. Berger came to the post of national security adviser after a career as a trade lawyer. He thought globalization helped ordinary people at home and abroad. He also favored strong action to promote human rights.

Clinton had an uneasy relationship with the American military throughout his administration. During the campaign of 1992, critics assailed him for having avoided military service during the Vietnam War. As soon as he took office, he suffered additional complaints for ordering the military to include gay men and women in its ranks. Chairman of the Joint Chiefs of Staff Colin Powell objected so strenuously that Clinton told Secretary of Defense Les Aspin to review the issue of including gays in the military. Six months later the Defense Department issued regulations forbidding the military to inquire into the sexual orientation of service personnel. At the same time, military men and women were forbidden to disclose that they were gay. This "don't ask, don't tell" policy hardly satisfied either advocates or opponents of including gays in the military.

Clinton's secretaries of defense and directors of central intelligence struggled to develop clear policies on the use of force in the post–Cold War era. Secretary of Defense Les Aspin (1993–1994) began his career as one of the "whiz kids" in Robert McNamara's Pentagon during the Johnson administration. He had acquired a reputation as one of the most thoughtful military reformers as chair of the House Committee on Armed Services in the 1980s. He wanted to deploy a smaller, quicker, smarter armed force in the 1990s. But Aspin never developed a rapport with the heads of the uniformed services, who dismissed him as a naive idealist. He was fired in late 1993 after eighteen American marines lost their lives during a firefight while on a humanitarian mission in Somalia.

Clinton then turned to William Perry (1994–1997), a weapons expert, as his next secretary of defense. Perry cared more about nuts and bolts issues of military procurement than strategy. He established closer relations with the uniformed services, and he moved the military toward adopting a new generation of lighter weapons and more maneuverable ships, planes, and armored vehicles. In Clinton's second term the president appointed former Maine Republican senator William Cohen (1997–2001) in an effort to create bipartisan support. Cohen presided over the Defense Department during the bombing of Kosovo in the spring of 1999.

Three directors of central intelligence served during the Clinton administration. The first, James Woolsey (1993–1994), had a bad personal relationship with the president. Woolsey believed Clinton lacked interest in foreign policy generally and in intelligence specifically. After he resigned Woolsey harshly criticized Clinton's foreign policy for intellectual laziness. John Deutch (1994–1997), a civilian defense and intelligence analyst, helped restore CIA morale, which had been battered by the discovery that a high-ranking official had spied for years for the Soviet Union. George Tenet (1997–2001), a former staff member of the Senate Intelligence Committee and deputy director under Deutch, directed the CIA during Clinton's second term. Tenet became deeply involved in foreign policy. The CIA gave information to the military during the bombing of Kosovo. Tenet provided technical assistance to the American effort to mediate a peace agreement between Israel and the Palestinians.

In 1999 and 2000 intelligence and the security of classified government information became contentious political issues. Republican critics of the-Clinton administration accused it of mishandling sensitive information about American nuclear weapons. The charges proved to be highly exaggerated. While they circulated officials in the State Department, the CIA, and government weapons laboratories lost their security clearances. Among them were John Deutch, whose practice of working on classified material on his unclassified home computer ran afoul of the new, intense scrutiny of officials' security clearances.

THE PROMISE AND PERILS OF GLOBALIZATION

Clinton ran for president in 1992 as a "New Democrat," someone who recognized the profound changes in the domestic and international economy. He stressed the need to educate American workers to compete in a changing international economy dominated by high technology. Expanding U.S. commerce played a central role in the Clinton administration's foreign policy. The Commerce and Treasury departments and the U.S. special trade representative worked to open foreign markets to American products and services and the U.S. market to overseas enterprises.

The Clinton administration succeeded in having Congress ratify the North American Free Trade Agreement (NAFTA), a common market for the United States, Canada, and Mexico, in 1993. NAFTA had been negotiated by the Bush administration over the opposition of important elements in the Democratic Party. Labor unions and environmentalists opposed NAFTA. The former feared the loss of jobs to lower-wage workers in Mexico. The latter worried that Mexico would not enforce strict environmental standards. Independent presidential candidate Ross Perot assailed NAFTA. He predicted a "giant sucking sound" as U.S. jobs went south of the border. Clinton submitted NAFTA to both houses of Congress for their approval in 1993. In the midst of the congressional consideration, vice President Al Gore debated Ross Perot on CNN's *Larry King Live* program. Gore made Perot look fearful and pessimistic. The vice president handed Perot a photograph of Senator Reed Smoot and Representative Charles Hawley, the sponsors of the notorious 1930 tariff thought to have worsened the Great Depression. "Perot Gored" ran the headlines, and NAFTA passed both the House and the Senate.

The practical results of NAFTA fulfilled neither the high hopes of its advocates nor the worst fears of its detractors. Clinton told a meeting of Western Hemisphere leaders in early 1994 that he hoped to conclude a free trade agreement for the entire hemisphere by 2005, but almost immediately conditions deteriorated in Mexico. The presidential election campaign in

Mexico took an ugly turn in March 1994, when Donaldo Colasio, the candidate of the long-ruling Institutional Revolutionary party (PRI) was murdered. His replacement, Ernesto Zedillo, a Yale University–trained economist, supported NAFTA, stronger ties with the United States, and reform of Mexico's notoriously corrupt political system. Zedillo confronted an economic and political crisis within weeks of taking office on December 1, 1994. Wealthy Mexicans sent their money out of the country. Zedillo devalued the Mexican peso, but it continued to fall. In early 1995 Mexico neared default on its foreign debt. The U.S. Treasury provided an emergency credit of $20 billion to stabilize the Mexican economy. At the same time, a peasant revolt erupted in the southern Mexican state of Chiapas. The Mexican armed forces responded harshly. These events combined to send Mexico into a sharp year-long recession.

The Mexican turmoil cast a pall over NAFTA in the United States. Congress refused to give Clinton the authority to reach quick agreements with other Latin American states. Gradually, though, NAFTA seemed to be working. The dire predictions of lost jobs did not come to pass. Studies indicated a slight net gain in employment due to the new common market; more benefits would be realized over the next decade. Mexico's economy revived in 1998. In 2000 Mexico held its freest presidential election. President Zedillo allowed an open contest within the PRI to select that party's presidential nominee, Francisco Labastida. Vicente Fox, the eventual winner of the presidential election, came from the opposition National Action Party (PAN). For the first time in seventy-one years, a candidate other than the nominee of the PRI took power in Mexico.

Clinton went forward with globalization despite the doubts expressed by many members of his own Democratic Party. Labor unions and their supporters in Congress believed that the United States had helped transform the fifty-year-old General Agreement on Tariffs and Trade (GATT) into the World Trade Organization (WTO). More than 160 nations joined this international organization. They committed themselves to lowering trade barriers and taking commercial disputes to the WTO for resolution. The WTO met in Seattle from November 30 to December 2, 1999. Clinton, Washington state officials, and American business leaders expected a triumphal celebration of the worldwide benefits of globalization. But what they got was an ugly upheaval—part demonstration, part riot, and part street theater. More than 10,000 demonstrators converged on Seattle determined to stop the WTO delegates from meeting. They represented a vast array of interests, people, and causes—human rights advocates, supporters of labor unions, environmentalists, supporters of indigenous peoples, religious activists, opponents of bankers, critics of fast food, opponents of genetic engineering, and anarchists. The demonstrators succeeded in cutting the meeting short.

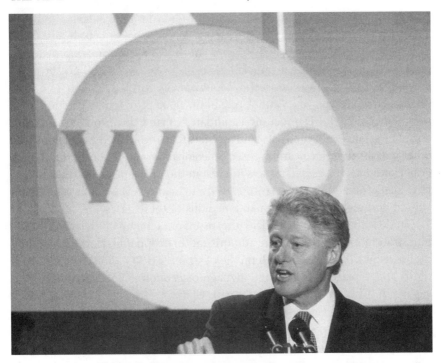

President Bill Clinton addressing the World Trade Organization,
a major forum of globalization
(Clinton Presidential Library)

Four months later a similar coalition demonstrated against the annual meeting of the World Bank and the International Monetary Fund in Washington. The capital's police force was better prepared than had been the Seattle police, and the meetings went forward. The demonstrations alerted the Clinton administration and World Bank and IMF officials to the costs of globalization. The international financial organizations vowed to pay more attention to the needs of the poor.

During the Clinton administration the United States went further than it ever had before in taking international action to protect the environment. The Bush administration had opposed many provisions of the 1992 Rio de Janeiro Treaty protecting the diversity of plant and animal species. The Bush administration also resisted international efforts to halt global warming caused by the emission of gases that cause a "greenhouse effect" and that deplete the atmosphere's ozone layer. During the 1992 presidential campaign Bush mocked Democratic vice presidential candidate Al Gore as "ozone man," a reference to Gore's ardent environmentalism.

The Clinton administration signed the 1997 Kyoto Protocol, in which 150 nations worldwide agreed to reduce the release of carbon-based gases (the ones scientists hold responsible for global warming) to 5.2 percent below 1990 levels. Europe pledged to cut its level 8 percent below 1990 levels, Japan 6 percent, and the United States 7 percent. But the Clinton administration faced strong congressional opposition to the Kyoto Protocol, and it never submitted it for ratification to the Republican-controlled Senate. The issue of global warming played a minor role in the 2000 presidential election. Vice president Gore, the Democratic candidate, treated the problem of global warming as an established fact and insisted that the United States join with other nations to reduce carbon-based emissions. George W. Bush, the Republican candidate, expressed far less interest in the problem of global warming. He called for additional scientific study to make certain that a problem existed and was caused by human emissions of these gases.

Trade expansion emerged as the primary element of the Clinton administration's Asian policy. The administration dropped its hostile campaign rhetoric toward the People's Republic of China's (PRC) violation of human rights and replaced it with the language of economic and commercial engagement. Clinton met eight times with China's leaders at the annual Asia-Pacific Economic Cooperation conference. For seven years the Clinton administration annually requested that Congress grant China trade equality commensurate with that of other nations. Lawmakers complied despite objections from a coalition made up of supporters of human rights, labor union activists, and conservatives who revived fears of China as a military threat. Granting China "permanent normal trade relations" (PNTR) also became embroiled in presidential politics. Vice president Al Gore desperately wanted the support of several of the labor unions most opposed to reducing trade barriers with China. He soft-pedaled his earlier ardent backing of free trade. Finally, though, in 2000 Congress granted China PNTR, paving the way for the PRC to join the WTO.

Expanding commerce helped the United States take the fateful step toward restoring diplomatic relations with Vietnam. By 1993 large U.S.-based multinational corporations—including Coca Cola, Chase Manhattan Bank, Citigroup, General Motors, and United Airlines—felt shut out of their fair share of trade with Vietnam because the United States maintained an economic embargo on its old adversary. In addition, the nearly 1 million Americans of Vietnamese ancestry wanted an end to travel restrictions so they could visit relatives in their former homeland. In 1994 the United States ended the nineteen-year-old embargo. The next year Washington and Hanoi restored diplomatic relations. Douglas "Pete" Peterson, who served six years as a prisoner of war in North Vietnam, became the first U.S. ambassador to the Socialist Republic of Vietnam. While serving in Hanoi after 1995 he married a woman of Vietnamese origin who had become an Australian citizen. Peterson worked tirelessly to heal the wounds of war and promote commerce with and travel to and from Vietnam. The Vietnamese people greeted Peterson with enthusiasm. American businesses also found Peterson an ally. By 1997, however, some of the early bloom had worn off the rose of U.S.–Vietnamese trade. Peterson spent more and more of his time fighting the stifling Communist bureaucracy on behalf of American investors.

In November 2000 Clinton paid a triumphal visit to Vietnam. Thousands of Vietnamese lined the streets of Hanoi at midnight to catch a glimpse of the president's motorcade from the airport. Enormous, enthusiastic crowds of Vietnamese greeted Clinton wherever he went. "I love him," shouted a saleswoman in Ho Chi Minh City, still called by most people by its old name, Saigon, "He is so handsome." Clinton encouraged America's former adversary to embrace the global marketplace of goods and ideas. He told young Vietnamese to embrace a world of "entrepreneurship, innovation and competition."

HUMANITARIAN INTERVENTION

The Clinton administration actively intervened to promote human rights abroad. Most high-level officials shared a desire to use the influence and military strength of the world's only super-power to contain hatreds around the world. They expressed differences, though, on how deeply the United States should commit itself. They wanted to avoid endangering American service personnel. They also feared getting too far in front of public opinion. In some situations, for example, Africa, the United States made only half-hearted efforts, and conditions there deteriorated. Closer to home, in Haiti, intervention helped restore a semblance of order to a deeply troubled land. The most complex U.S. intervention came in provinces of the former Yugoslavia in the Balkans. There the Clinton administration slowly projected a more robust presence than had its predecessors in the Bush administration. In 1995 the United States helped arrange a cease-fire in the brutal civil war between Serbs and Muslims in Bosnia. It also joined allies in NATO in a two-month-long bombing campaign in 1999 to stop Serb repression of ethnic Albanians in Kosovo.

Clinton inherited from Bush a major U.S. military humanitarian intervention in the East African country of Somalia. Heart-breaking television pictures of mass starvation in Somalia prompted Bush in December 1992 to dispatch 28,000 U.S. ground troops to create what the president called a "secure environment" in which food could be distributed. The American force separated the warring factions in the civil war, and they protected the international relief agencies distributing the food. The television news showed food reaching desperately hungry people. Clinton supported the humanitarian mission, and the new administration turned the relief effort over to a UN force in May. By June only 4,000 U.S. troops remained in Somalia. Madeleine Albright, the U.S. ambassador to the UN, explained the mission of the new UN force as "the restoration of an entire country as a proud, functioning and viable member of the community of nations." The UN force identified Mohammed Farah Aideed, the head of one of the warring clans, as the principal obstacle to the ambitious program of nation building.

Over the summer with American assistance the UN troops attacked Aideed's forces and tried to capture him. On October 3 Aideed's forces shot down an American Black Hawk assault helicopter in Mogadishu, Somalia's capital city. In the ensuing fire fight U.S. Marines killed more than 200 of Aideed's fighters. Eighteen Marines were killed, and one was captured. A jubilant crowd of Somalis dragged the body of one dead Marine through the streets. Back in the United States horrified viewers saw the grisly scene unfold on television. Public support for the Somalia relief effort evaporated immediately. Clinton withdrew the remainder of the U.S. military force by the end of 1993. Secretary of Defense Les Aspin, another casualty of the catastrophe in the streets of Mogadishu, resigned.

The policy of humanitarian intervention in Africa also suffered a nearly fatal blow with the sad end of the mission to Somalia. Badly burned by the loss of American lives in Mogadishu, the Clinton administration did not respond effectively to a humanitarian calamity in the East African country of Rwanda. Centuries-old ethnic conflict between the majority Hutu and minority Tutsi peoples reached a climax in the spring of 1994. A new Hutu-dominated government came to power and embarked on a genocide of the Tutsis. Armed gangs roamed the streets of every hamlet, village, and city in the country, slaughtering Tutsis and Hutus friendly to them. Tens of thousands of bodies were thrown into rivers, which literally ran dark with blood. This time, though, the United States refused to send its own armed forces to stop the carnage. The United States said the UN and Europe should take the lead. They did, but only to evacuate European aid workers. Finally, in the summer of 1994, after more than 750,000 people were killed, the United States sent a contingent of fewer than 1,000 troops to transport other nations' soldiers to restore order in Rwanda. One of the great humanitarian catastrophes of the twentieth century could have been averted had the United States and its European allies responded more quickly and with greater courage.

Closer to home in the Western Hemisphere, the Clinton administration intervened to restore a democratically elected government in Haiti. The miserable conditions in Haiti became an issue in the presidential election of 1992. Clinton assailed the Bush administration for standing idly by when the democratically elected government of Jean-Bertrand Aristide was overthrown by a military junta led by Gen. Raoul Çedras in 1991. The Arkansas governor characterized as inhumane the Bush administration's policy of turning away thousands of Haitian boat people trying to enter the United States. Clinton deplored the inconsistency of U.S. policy. The Bush administration returned Haitians to their homes on the ground that they were only looking for better economic opportunity. In contrast, the Immigration and Naturalization Service admitted Cuban refugees, identified as fleeing political persecution. Clinton said the United States should show more sympathy to the Haitians while at the same time trying to improve conditions in Haiti.

In office Clinton found the Haitian boat people a significant problem. He remembered the high political cost he had paid for admitting Cuban refugees in 1980. As governor of Arkansas he had permitted the Carter administration to send thousands of Cubans to Fort Chafee, Arkansas. Disturbances in the refugee camps had contributed to his defeat for reelection that fall. In 1993 the Coast Guard continued the Bush administration's practice of returning Haitians to their homeland. This apparent reversal of Clinton's campaign promise to welcome the Haitians alarmed some of Clinton's staunchest supporters in the African-American community.

In 1994 the Clinton administration moved against the Haitian military junta of Gen. Çedras. In August the United States sponsored a UN resolution authorizing the use of force to restore Aristide to power. Conservatives in the U.S. Senate, led by Republican Jesse Helms of North Carolina, succeeded in passing a resolution opposing deployment of the U.S. military to oust Çedras and restore Aristide. Nevertheless, in September the Pentagon went forward with plans to invade Haiti. Former President Jimmy Carter, a supporter of human rights but an opponent of military intervention, asked Clinton's permission to make a personal appeal for Çedras to leave office peacefully. Clinton reluctantly agreed, and Carter led a team made up of former chairman of the Joint Chiefs of Staff Colin Powell and Sen. Sam Nunn (D., Ga.) to Haiti on September 17. On the evening of September 19, as U.S. planes laden with an invasion force were about to take off, Çedras agreed to step down peacefully.

The United States then sent a 20,000-member peacekeeping force to supervise Aristide's return to power. He served the remainder of his term and peacefully transferred power to a newly elected president, Rene Préval, in 1996. The United States gradually withdrew its forces, and then conditions deteriorated in Haiti. The economy never revived, Aristide continued to wield power behind the scenes, and the Préval government shut down the opposition-controlled parliament for more than a year. In 1999 the United States suspended direct economic aid to Haiti, channeling assistance through nongovernmental organizations. In June 2000 Haiti conducted rigged legislative elections. In November Aristide won another term as president in an election boycotted by the opposition. A weary Clinton administration barely acknowledged his victory. The United States and the UN continued to press Haiti to establish the rule of law.

The program of humanitarian intervention faced its most severe test in the former Yugoslavia. Once again the Clinton administration faced problems left over from its predecessor. The Bush administration had avoided taking a stand on conflict in the Balkans. Secretary of State James A. Baker considered the breakup of Yugoslavia to be a problem for the Europeans. In 1991 civil war broke out in Bosnia, a province of Yugoslavia, and the United States supported an embargo on exporting arms to the warring parties. The combatants were the Orthodox Christian Serbs, the Catholic Croats, and the Muslim Bosnians. The Serbs controlled the bulk of the Yugoslav army in Bosnia. They imposed a siege of the province's capital, Sarajevo, inhabited largely by Muslim Bosnians. Serb artillery rained shells on this beautiful, modern city. Reports emerged from Bosnia of mass killings of Bosnians by Serbs.

During the 1992 campaign Clinton assailed the Bush administration for its indifference to the greatest loss of life in Europe since 1945. Clinton supported a policy of "lift and strike": lift the arms embargo to help the Muslims and order air strikes to break the siege of Sarajevo. But the Clinton administration moved at a glacial pace to stop the slaughter. Soon after Clinton took office he became worried that the ethnic hatreds between Serbs and Muslims ran so deep that outside intervention would not solve the problem. Many members of Congress also warned against U.S. intervention in the Bosnia civil war. Within the administration UN ambassador Madeleine Albright urged the use of force against the Serbs. Republican Senate leader Bob Dole of Kansas also favored the lift and strike policy, but most prominent officials feared stepping into a quagmire.

The conflict intensified in the summer of 1995. A Serb attack on the Muslim town of Srebrenica culminated in the massacre of up to 4,000 Bosnian men and boys whose bodies were found in shallow graves. Bosnian Serb soldiers raped thousands of Muslim women and girls. American leaders were sickened by the massacre. Deputy Secretary of State Strobe Talbott characterized it as "another European holocaust." In the wake of Srebrenica the Clinton administration finally overcame its resistance to using air power.

In August the United States and its NATO allies, especially Britain and France, launched air strikes against Serb artillery, tanks, and ammunition depots. The Croats, who previously had maintained an uneasy alliance with the Serbs, now turned on them and launched a military offensive of their own. The Serb armed forces fell back toward what remained of Yugoslavia. In Yugoslavia's capital, Belgrade, Slobodan Milosevic worried about the complete collapse of Serb power. He agreed to attend a peace conference.

The Balkans after the breakup of Yugoslavia

On November 1 representatives of Yugoslavia, Croatia, and Bosnia met at a U.S. Air Force base in the southwestern Ohio city of Dayton. For three weeks U.S. special ambassador for the Balkans Richard Holbrooke shuttled among the delegations. On November 21 Holbrooke presided over the initialing of the Dayton Accords. The agreements called for an immediate cease-fire and the lifting of the siege of Sarajevo. The parties agreed to share political power in an independent state of Bosnia. Representatives of the three groups would share a rotating presidency. The United States agreed to lead an International Implementation Force (IFOR) of about 60,000 soldiers to maintain the peace in Bosnia. The United States provided 20,000 of the troops, and NATO allies contributed the remaining 40,000. Clinton characterized the U.S. participation in IFOR as a moral imperative. U.S. troops would not fight in Bosnia but help "the people of Bosnia to secure their own peace agreement." He said that in Bosnia "America and America alone can and should make the difference for peace."

The public and congressional reactions to the Dayton Accords and the U.S. contribution to IFOR were lukewarm at best. Opinion polls showed the public almost evenly divided on whether the United States should deploy armed forces in Bosnia. Congress reflected these misgivings. In 1995 Republicans controlled both houses of Congress for the first time in forty years. Conservative Republicans in the House of Representatives disdained Clinton. Sue Myrick, a new Republican representative, dismissed the Dayton document as "not worth the paper it is written on. If it were, there would be no need to send American troops over there. There is nothing that President Clinton can say that will change my mind." The House nearly passed legislation cutting off funds for U.S. troops in Bosnia. The Dayton Accords and IFOR proved to be more successful than critics anticipated. The shooting stopped, normal life returned to Bosnia, and the economy revived. But deep division and bitterness remained. IFOR did little to capture dozens of indicted war criminals and bring them to trial at the International Criminal Tribunal for the Former Yugoslavia set up at The Hague.

Clinton responded by agreeing to remove all U.S. military from IFOR by the end of 1996, but conditions remained so tense in Bosnia that Clinton later decided only to gradually withdraw part of the U.S. contingent from IFOR. In 2000 about 8,000 of the original U.S. force remained keeping the peace in Bosnia. The Dayton Accords and IFOR proved to be more successful than critics anticipated. The shooting stopped, normal life returned to Bosnia, and the economy revived. But deep division and bitterness remained. IFOR did little to capture dozens of indicted war criminals and bring them to trial at the International Criminal Tribunal for the Former Yugoslavia setup at The Hague.

The U.S. deployment in Bosnia set the stage; NATO forces went to war for the first time since the founding of the alliance in 1949. For seven weeks in the spring of 1999, NATO aircraft bombed Serbia, one of the remaining provinces of Yugoslavia. U.S. warplanes carried out more than 80 percent of the bombing in an operation designed to force Yugoslav president Slobodan Milosevic to remove his armed forces from the southern province of Kosovo. The crisis in Kosovo arose from the animosities between Albanian Muslims, or Kosovars, who made up 90 percent of the province's population, and minority Serbs, who dominated Kosovo's public institutions. Milosevic suspended Kosovo's autonomy in 1989, giving Serbs the upper hand in the province. A movement for Kosovo independence or annexation by Muslim Albania arose after 1991. The United States and its NATO allies maintained that Kosovo should remain a part of Yugoslavia, but they pressed Milosevic to restore autonomy and cease the oppression of the Albanian Muslims.

Conditions worsened for Muslims in Kosovo in 1998. Local Serbs and the Yugoslav army arrested thousands of Kosovars suspected of sympathizing with the Kosovo Liberation Army (KLA), guerrillas fighting for an independent Kosovo. More than 300,000 Albanians fled their homes. In October Clinton sent Richard Holbrooke to Belgrade to warn Milosevic that NATO would bomb Yugoslavia unless the Yugoslav army stopped the attacks on the Albanians. Milosevic relented and permitted international humanitarian aid agencies access to Kosovo. The relief effort averted a humanitarian disaster in the winter of 1998–1999, but by February 1999 Kosovars feared another Yugoslav offensive. A peace conference opened at Rambouillet outside Paris on February 6. The United States, the European NATO members, Yugoslavia, and several delegations from Kosovo worked to restore autonomy to Kosovo and force Milosevic to accept a NATO peacekeeping force in the province. Neither Milosevic nor the Albanian Kosovars would sign an agreement.

With the collapse of the Rambouillet conference, the United States and the other NATO countries decided to bomb Yugoslavia into accepting an international peacekeeping force in Kosovo. On March 24, 1999, NATO planes bombed Serbia. At the very beginning of operation Allied Force, Secretary of State Albright, National Security Adviser Berger, and President Clinton all believed that Milosevic would surrender in a matter of days.

President Bill Clinton and Secretary of State Madeleine Albright confer during the
Kosovo war, April 1999.
(Clinton Presidential Library)

Albright considered him to be a bully who "understands only the language of force." Clinton ruled out a ground war, saying that that he "did not intend to put our troops in Kosovo to fight a war."

Hopes evaporated within days that Milosevic would succumb to the NATO bombing. Instead, he sent the Yugoslav army on a rampage inside Kosovo. Serbs burned Albanian crops and villages. Thousand upon thousands of Albanians fled their homes in cars, buses, trains, and on foot. Within a month more than 1 million Muslim refugees had left Kosovo for camps in neighboring countries. NATO stepped up its bombing in response to the humanitarian disaster, but the bombing seemed only to unite the Serb population behind Milosevic's defiance of NATO. Clinton continued to resist calls to send ground troops into the war, a move he feared would destroy public support for the campaign against Yugoslavia. Fear of suffering allied casualties or prisoners of war also made NATO commanders insist that the warplanes fly higher than 15,000 feet to release their bombs. Flying so high made it harder to hit Yugoslav tanks and guns in Kosovo. The NATO planes also hit civilians by mistake. More than 200 civilian Serbs lost their lives. One target hit by mistake caused a near rupture in U.S.–Chinese relations. On May 7 a U.S. B-2 bomber mistakenly hit the People's Republic of China embassy in Belgrade. Three Chinese lost their lives, setting off furious anti–U.S. protests in Beijing. The United States apologized to the PRC and paid $20 million in compensation. Relations between the United States and the PRC remained strained for another year.

The U.S. and NATO stepped up the war in mid-May. Warplanes knocked out much of Serbia's electricity grid and destroyed major bridges and rail lines in Kosovo and Yugoslavia. The Clinton administration no longer ruled out the use of ground troops. The International Criminal Tribunal for the Former Yugoslavia indicted Milosevic as a war criminal. Russia, a long-time supporter of Milosevic, now cooperated with NATO and told Milosevic he had to accept the alliance's demands. Facing defeat, Milosevic agreed; on June 10 NATO stopped the bombing. In mid-June a Kosovo Force (KFOR) consisting of 60,000 troops from the United States and European NATO countries entered Kosovo to supervise the return of the refugees and keep the peace. Within three months more than 1 million Albanian Kosovars had returned to their homes, but deep hatreds remained between Muslims and Serbs. Over the next eighteen months KFOR maintained an uneasy peace in the province. Milosevic remained in power until October 2000, when he left office after being defeated in a presidential election. The new president, Vojislav Koštunica, restored diplomatic ties to the United States.

The end of the Kosovo war brought little celebration in the United States. The war lasted far longer than anyone predicted. Clinton seemed shocked by the endurance of Yugoslavia's resistance. Michael Mandelbaum, a former supporter of Clinton's who became one of his sharpest critics, characterized the Kosovo war as a "perfect failure." He claimed that the attacks made conditions worse in Kosovo and weakened the alliance. This harsh judgment seemed exaggerated. As Ivo H. Daalder and Michael E. O'Hanlon wrote in *Winning Ugly: NATO's War to Save Kosovo* (2000), NATO "badly mishandled the war's early going," but "Kosovo is a much better place today than it would have been absent NATO intervention."

The value of humanitarian intervention became an issue during the 2000 presidential election campaign. Vice president Al Gore, the Democratic candidate, took an expansive view of America's role in the post–Cold War world. He supported the Clinton administration's commitment to using U.S. power to promote human rights around the globe. He reminded Americans that the United States had successfully engaged in nation building after the Second World War, when it had brought democratic institutions to Germany and Japan and helped restore the economies of Europe through the Marshall Plan. George W. Bush, the Republican candidate, adopted a much narrower conception of American interests. The purpose of the U.S. military "is to fight and win wars," he said. He belittled the Clinton administration's approach to nation building. He suggested that he would withdraw the remaining U.S. forces from Bosnia and Kosovo. Yet when Bush was asked during one of his debates with Gore to identify a recent U.S. humanitarian intervention he opposed, he listed only the 1994 peacekeeping mission to Haiti.

MEDIATING DEADLY CONFLICTS

The Clinton administration made extensive efforts at mediating two centuries-old conflicts: the strife between Catholics and Protestants in Northern Ireland and the hostility among Israel, the Palestinians, and the Arab states. In each case the disputes came closer to resolution than ever before. In each case progress alternated with despair, as extremists on all sides of the issues opposed compromises.

The problems in Northern Ireland, or Ulster, originated in the unresolved status of the six northern provinces of Ireland, which had remained part of the United Kingdom after the independence of the Irish Republic in 1922. Ulster had a dominant Protestant majority and a Catholic minority of approximately 40 percent of the population. After 1922 Protestants controlled the political and economic life of Northern Ireland. In 1969 violence broke out between fighters of the Irish Republican Army (IRA), a militant Catholic group seeking union with the Irish Republic, and Protestants. After waves of bombings, kidnappings, and killings, the British government suspended Northern Ireland's local parliament and sent troops to impose peace in Ulster. The violence continued, however, and life became dreary, dangerous, and deadly in Northern Ireland for decades.

Irish-Americans followed events in Northern Ireland closely after the troubles began in 1969. Many sympathized with the plight of Catholics in Northern Ireland. Some sent money to the IRA. Other leading Irish-American Catholics, such as Democratic senators Edward M. Kennedy of Massachusetts and Daniel Patrick Moynihan of New York, considered the violent tactics of the IRA too extreme and encouraged a dialogue between Catholics and Protestants throughout Ireland. For most of the 1970s and 1980s, the U.S. government avoided commenting on Northern Ireland. American officials considered the problems there to be a matter for the British and Irish governments and the warring factions in Ulster to resolve.

Clinton took a much more active interest in Northern Ireland than had any of his predecessors. During the campaign of 1992, he appealed to Irish-Americans with the pledge that the United States should promote human rights and a peaceful resolution of the dispute in Northern Ireland. In 1994 the Clinton administration lifted the ban on the admission to the United States of officials of the Sinn Fein party, the political arm of the IRA. Clinton hosted Sinn Fein leader Gerry Adams after Adams promised to renounce violence. In 1997 the United States became even more deeply involved in brokering a political compromise in Northern Ireland. In May of that year, Tony Blair of the British Labor Party won a landslide election victory over John Major of the Conservative Party and became prime minister of Great Britain. Blair's relations with Clinton were as friendly as Major's had been frosty. Blair welcomed Clinton's appointment of former Democratic Senate majority leader George Mitchell as a mediator in the Northern Ireland conflict.

Mitchell, a Catholic, won the trust of various factions in Northern Ireland, officials of the Irish Republic, and the British government. He worked doggedly in late 1997 and early 1998 to bring the parties together. His efforts bore fruit on April 10, 1998. This Good Friday Agreement between the Irish and British governments and eight of Northern Ireland's ten political parties created a power-sharing arrangement. All parties agreed to an end to the violence and to decommission their stocks of weapons. Protestants and Catholics agreed to govern jointly in a reconstituted national assembly. The Irish Republic dropped its constitutional claim to Northern Ireland. A majority of Protestants and Catholics in Northern Ireland lauded the Good Friday Agreement as the best chance to restore a functioning society. In both Northern Ireland and the Irish Republic Clinton became the most popular American president since John F. Kennedy. But extremists within the IRA carried out some of the most deadly bombings of the twenty-nine-year-old conflict in the summer of 1998. Protestants retaliated with murders of their

On September 13, 1993, President Bill Clinton encouraged Israel's prime minister
Yitzhak Rabin and Palestine Liberation Organization president Yasser Arafat to shake
hands on the White House lawn.
(Clinton Presidential Library)

own. The Ulster Unionist Party, the main Protestant political group, also
objected to continuing the power-sharing government unless the IRA turned
in all of its weapons. At the end of 2000, the U.S.-brokered peace in Northern Ireland hung by a thread.

The Clinton administration experienced its moments of greatest exhila-
ration and deepest despair as it continued the American mediation of the
Israel-Palestinian-Arab dispute. In the summer of 1993, the Israeli government led by Labor Party Prime minister Yitzhak Rabin opened secret talks
with the Palestine Liberation Organization (PLO) in Oslo, Norway. In late
August the two sides agreed to a phased withdrawal of Israeli troops from
the Gaza Strip and much of the West Bank over the next five years. PLO
chairman Yasser Arafat would rule over a Palestine National Authority (PNA)
in the areas to be evacuated by Israel. Israel and the PLO promised to reach
a final agreement to settle the status of Jerusalem and the political standing
of the Palestine National Authority within five years.

Although Israel and the PLO fashioned their agreement without direct
American involvement, they wanted U.S. endorsement of their efforts. On
September 13, 1993, Arafat and Rabin, two former bitter enemies, met on
the White House lawn to sign the agreement. A moment later Clinton took
each leader in an arm and nudged them into a handshake that was cheered
by hundreds of assembled dignitaries and millions watching on TV.

A new era of Middle Eastern cooperation seemed to open in the heady atmosphere of the Arafat–Rabin handshake. Arab states throughout the Middle East opened diplomatic relations with Israel. In October 1994 Clinton flew to the border between Israel and Jordan to witness another historic treaty establishing full peace between the two countries.

But the road to peace became much rockier. A significant minority of Israelis and Palestinians opposed compromise, and extremists killed scores of Israelis and Palestinians in the two years after the signing ceremony on the White House lawn. A Jewish extremist opposed to making peace with the Palestinians assassinated Rabin in November 1995. Six months later Benjamin Netanyahu, leader of the nationalist Likud Party, was elected Israel's prime minister. Netanyahu's relations with Clinton were as bitter as Rabin's had been sweet. The United States continued to mediate between Israel and the PNA, but the original deadline for reaching a final status agreement, September 1998, passed. In July 1999 the Labor Party returned to power in Israel under the leadership of Prime Minister Ehud Barak, a protégé and admirer of Yitzhak Rabin. Barak promised to negotiate a settlement with Arafat within eighteen months. Clinton threw himself into the negotiations, hosting Barak and Arafat at a sixteen-day marathon meeting at Camp David in July 2000. But Camp David II, as it was called in reference to the 1977 meeting hosted by President Jimmy Carter, failed. Barak offered far-reaching concessions to Arafat. The Palestinian leader declined to engage in give-and-take bargaining. He demanded sovereignty over East Jerusalem as the capital of an independent state of Palestine. Barak refused. Two months later the worst violence in a decade broke out between Israel and the Palestinians.

In December 2000 and January 2001 Clinton continued to press Barak and Arafat to accept a compromise that would give both Israel and a new state of Palestine control over parts of Jerusalem. Barak accepted, but Arafat did not. Clinton concluded in his memoirs that "Arafat's rejection of my proposal after Barak had accepted it was an error of historic proportions." Clinton left office on Janaury 20, and a few weeks later Barak was defeated in an election for prime minister by Ariel Sharon, a hardliner who opposed the concessions Barak was willing to make. The violence between Israel and the Palestinians got worse.

RELATIONS WITH THE FORMER SOVIET UNION
AND EASTERN EUROPE

The Clinton administration tried to help the states of the former Soviet Union and communist Eastern Europe peacefully complete their transition to democracy and market economies. Following the advice of his friend

Deputy Secretary of State Strobe Talbott, Clinton maintained support for Russian president Boris Yeltsin. Russia's economy continued to deteriorate from 1993 to 1995, and Yeltsin's popularity plunged with the falling ruble. The United States sympathized with the Russian leader's difficulties when ultranationalists and Communists in parliament tried to oust him in the fall of 1993. Yeltsin responded by sending the army to bombard the parliament building. Washington expressed understanding and said that Yeltsin was the real democrat in Russia. The United States also expressed only the mildest disapproval when Yeltsin ordered Russian troops into a brutal war to suppress the secession of the Republic of Chechnya in the Caucasus. The United States openly backed Yeltsin when he ran for reelection in 1996. Most observers believed that Yeltsin, suffering from heart disease and alcoholism, would lose to the candidate of the newly revived Communist Party, but Yeltsin roused himself for one last campaign in favor of reform. The new Russian billionaires rallied to his cause. Whatever misgivings most Russians had about Yeltsin's erratic behavior, they did not want to return to the bad old days of a Communist police state. Yeltsin easily won reelection, and the Clinton administration heaved a sigh of relief.

Yeltsin's obvious infirmities became undeniable immediately after he won. He was rarely seen in public, and he went to the hospital every few weeks. He hired and fired prime ministers every few months. The economy had revived in time for the 1996 election, but it nearly collapsed in the late summer of 1998, when Russia defaulted on its foreign debt. This debt crisis set off a plunge in world financial markets. Only quick intervention by the U.S. Federal Reserve Board prevented an international financial meltdown. When Yeltsin recovered sufficiently to work, he engaged in another war in Chechnya, even bloodier than the last. Once more the United States did not strongly criticize the Russian tactic used to defeat the Chechens. Russia sympathized with its traditional ally Yugoslavia during the initial stage of NATO's 1999 bombing campaign to relieve Yugoslavia's grip on Kosovo. Russian public opinion became increasingly hostile to the West in general and the United States in particular during the Kosovo war. Yet Clinton's friendship with Yeltsin paid dividends when Russia persuaded Yugoslavia's president, Slobodan Milosevic, to accept NATO's terms in June 1999.

Yeltsin had one more surprise in store. On December 31, 1999, he announced his immediate resignation as Russia's president. His successor, Vladimir Putin, a former secret service operative, won election in his own right in March 2000. Putin pursued a more nationalist foreign policy than Yeltsin. Putin met more regularly with leaders of Britain, France, and Germany than with Clinton. When Clinton traveled to Moscow in June 2000, he held businesslike but not warm meetings with Putin. By contrast, Clinton's courtesy call on Yeltsin had had the genuine bonhomie of two old friends.

In 1999 Hungary, Poland, and the Czech Republic joined the NATO alliance. The Clinton administration advocated NATO expansion as a way of firmly anchoring the former communist states of Eastern Europe in the West. The three new members had gone further than any of the former communist states of Eastern Europe toward establishing democratic institutions. For these countries NATO membership validated the progress they had made since the end of the Cold War. But Russia's military resented the eastern expansion of NATO as a sign of American efforts to dominate the post–Cold War world.

THE CLINTON FOREIGN POLICY RECORD

When Bill Clinton left office in January 2001, Americans were generally satisfied with their preeminent place in the world. The global economy was booming, and people and governments everywhere seemed to embrace the values trumpeted by the United States of transparency, the rule of law, and open markets. The apparently widespread acceptance that the United States had properly won the Cold War made questions of foreign affairs seem less important than at any time since 1945. At the end of the Clinton administration the president and his foreign policies were widely popular. Few people foresaw the extraordinary difficulties looming.

CHAPTER FIFTEEN

Global Disorders in the Twenty-First Century

When the twenty-first century opened in 2000, Americans had many reasons to be satisfied with the state of the world. The post–Cold War era seemed to have vindicated the four-decades-long policy of containment, which had been the bedrock of U.S. foreign policy. The American economy was enjoying an unprecedented boom, with productivity and stock prices soaring and American products dominating world markets. The new prosperity was all the more welcome because it was unexpected. American political and legal standards were the world norm. Globalization, the knitting together of the world economically, socially, and culturally, had a few critics. For the most part, however, opinion leaders in the United States embraced globalization as both inevitable and beneficial. Secretary of State Madeleine Albright called the United States the "indispensable nation." She meant both that American power was required to solve humanitarian problems around the world and also that American economic, political, cultural, and social values were admired everywhere.

Twenty months later, in September 2001, the world was seen as a much more dangerous place. Universal progress no longer seemed inevitable. Faith in the acceptance of the bounty of globalization and American standards seemed misplaced. The United States gained deep international sympathy in the immediate aftermath of the al-Qaeda terrorist attacks on New York City and the Pentagon of September 11, 2001, but this support proved short lived. The administration of President George W. Bush declared war on international terrorism. It pursued a unilateral foreign policy that demanded that nations either cooperate with the United States or be perceived as supporting terrorism. In 2003 the United States began a war in

Iraq designed to force Saddam Hussein from power and create a stable, democratic government that would serve as a model for other states in the Middle East. The war confounded these optimistic hopes, and public support for continuing American involvement in Iraq dissipated at home. Internationally, the United States lost all the support it had enjoyed in the days after September 11. The Bush administration seemed committed, however, to a Wilsonian vision of a world organized to follow an American political, economic, and cultural model.

FOREIGN AFFAIRS AND THE ELECTION OF 2000

Foreign affairs played a small but significant role in the 2000 presidential election campaign between Democratic candidate Al Gore and Republican governor George W. Bush of Texas. Gore promised to continue the Clinton administration's policies of engagement across a wide front of issues. The vice president wanted the United States to continue to make globalization work. He supported earlier humanitarian interventions and indicated he would do more of them. The United States would also continue multinational efforts at environmental protection. As the challenger, Bush took a more critical approach to recent American foreign policy. He had little experience in or knowledge of foreign affairs, so he relied on veterans of previous Republican administrations to provide him an agenda. In 1999 George P. Shultz, who served as secretary of state under President Ronald Reagan, introduced him to Condoleezza Rice, a Stanford professor of international relations who had worked on the national security council staff in his father's administration. Rice met regularly with Bush in 1999 and 2000, and she explained to him that the world remained a dangerous place despite the end of the Cold War and the apparent universal acceptance of the benefits of globalization.

During the campaign Bush accused the Clinton administration of lacking consistency and ignoring military threats from China, North Korea, and Iran. He decried what he characterized as a sharp decline in the morale of U.S. armed forces. "Help is on the way," he told cheering crowds near military bases. He indicated that a Bush administration would provide more resources to the military but deploy them less often than had the Clinton administration. He opposed the Clinton administration's policy of nation building, and he insisted that the purpose of the American military "is to fight and win wars." Bush believed that foreign affairs consisted primarily of maintaining national security, and he promised construction of a missile defense system. Gore favored a more expansive approach, combining support for nation building, further U.S. efforts to mediate between Israel and the

Palestinians, and deepening the U.S. commitment to globalization. Neither candidate addressed dangers posed by international terrorism, nor did either suggest that the post–Cold War era was about to come to an end and the world become suddenly a more dangerous place. Bush prevailed in the closest election in a century. Gore actually received 500,000 more popular votes, and only a controversial U.S. Supreme Court decision that stopped a recount in Florida gave that state's electoral votes and the presidency to Bush.

BUSH'S FOREIGN POLICY APPROACH BEFORE SEPTEMBER 11

Bush went back to his father's and earlier Republican administrations to staff high foreign policy positions. Vice President Dick Cheney, who had served in the Ford and first Bush administrations, became Bush's key adviser on domestic and foreign affairs. Colin L. Powell, national security adviser under President Ronald Reagan and chairman of the Joint Chiefs of Staff in the first Bush administration, became the first African American secretary of state. Bush chose Condoleezza Rice, also African American, to be his national security adviser. Powell resigned at the beginning of Bush's second administration in 2005, and Rice replaced him as secretary of state. Stephen P. Hadley, Rice's deputy national security adviser, stepped up to the national security adviser's position. Donald Rumsfeld, an old friend of Cheney's from the Ford administration, where he had been secretary of defense, took up that post again in 2001. He remained in that position into Bush's second term.

At first it appeared as if Bush's foreign policy advisers were remarkably unified. Bush favored secrecy and a top-down management style. He had little interest in debating options, and he deplored leaks to the press. This tight discipline over the government's message prevailed in Bush's first term, especially in the year after the terrorist attacks on New York City and the Pentagon on September 11, 2001. As time went on, however, cracks opened. Secretary of State Powell was at odds with Vice President Cheney and Secretary of Defense Rumsfeld as the United States moved toward war with Iraq in 2002 and 2003. Rumsfeld, an accomplished bureaucratic infighter, had poor relations with the uniformed military leaders. He believed they resisted calls to modernize the armed forces into leaner, more mobile, and more lethal units. Many high-ranking military officers had grave reservations about Rumsfeld's and his civilian advisers' plan of attack on Iraq. They kept these misgivings mostly quiet before the war and in the months after the United States toppled Saddam Hussein's government in 2003, but as the war went badly for the United States from the middle of 2003 onward, military complaints about Rumsfeld's high-handedness grew louder.

In its first six months the new Bush administration pursued a much more unilateral foreign policy than had its predecessor. Bush announced to the dismay of environmentalists at home and abroad that the United States would not support the Kyoto Protocol limiting the emission of greenhouse gases. The new administration characterized the People's Republic of China as a strategic rival rather than as a partner. In April 2001 Chinese warplanes forced an American reconnaissance jet flying inside China's twelve-mile coastal territorial limits to land in China. The United States was forced to offer an apology to receive the return of the crew. The Bush administration tried to press forward with a missile defense system, the deployment of which would require abrogation of the 1972 Anti-Ballistic Missile (ABM) treaty. Both European allies and the government of Russia voiced objection to dropping the ABM Treaty.

The Bush administration also hoped to avoid the Clinton administration's deep daily involvement in the Israeli–Palestinian-Arab dispute as the violence in Israel and the Palestinian Authority's territories, begun in September 2000, continued. In February 2001 Israel elected Ariel Sharon of the nationalist Likud Party prime minister. He formed a national unity government with the defeated Labor Party. By mid-2001 more than 700 people had lost their lives in almost daily fighting. In the summer of 2001, CIA Director George Tenet and Secretary of State Powell tried but failed to arrange a cease-fire between Israelis and the Palestinians. The high hopes of the Camp David summit of July 2000 for a comprehensive settlement seemed very remote.

AL-QAEDA AND INTERNATIONAL TERRORISM

Fear of international terrorism sponsored by Islamic radicals was a significant but not preeminent concern of American policy makers in the 1990s. On February 26, 1993, a little more than a month after Bill Clinton became president, several supporters of Osama bin Laden, the Muslim extremist leader of al-Qaeda, drove an explosives laden Ryder rental truck into the parking garage of the World Trade Center in lower Manhattan. Although the bomb failed to bring down the Twin Towers and kill tens of thousands, as the plotters had hoped, the blast killed six people and injured more than 1,000. Clinton ordered the National Security Council to coordinate a search for the bombers. In Janaury 1995 the FBI arrested one of the bombers, Ramzi Youssef, who said that he hoped to demolish the World Trade Center and kill 250,000. He also revealed that Khaled Sheik Mohammed, one of Osama bin Laden's top lieutenants, had helped plot the bombing.

Bin Laden moved his headquarters from Sudan to Afghanistan in 1996, where he continued to plan attacks on American interests around the world.

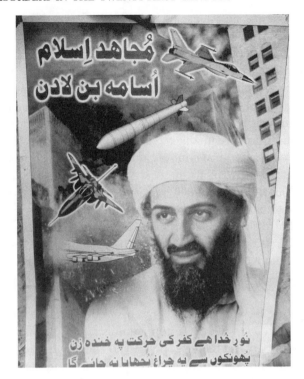

Osama bin Laden, the leader of al-Qaeda, organized the attacks on the World Trade
Center and the Pentagon on September 11, 2001.
(U.S. Department of Defense)

In 1998 he issued a fatwa, or interpretation of Islamic law, in which he said
that the United States had proclaimed war against God and his prophet,
Mohammed, and it was the duty of every Muslim to kill Americans anywhere
in the world. His anger against the United States had been kindled by the
presence of American troops in his homeland of Saudi Arabia during and
after the Gulf War of 1991, U.S. support for Israel, and a general sense that
the United States and the West denigrated, mocked, and expressed contempt for Muslim civilization. In August 1998 al-Qaeda teams detonated
truck bombs outside the U.S. embassies in Nairobi, Kenya, and Dar es
Salaam, Tanzania. Twelve Americans and more than 200 embassy workers
and visitors of other nationalities were killed, and more than 5,000 people
were injured.

Clinton ordered air strikes against bin Laden's Afghanistan headquarters
and a Sudanese factory the CIA believed was producing nerve gas. The attacks
killed dozens but failed in their objective of disrupting al-Qaeda. Bin Laden
had left the Afghan camp a few hours before the attack and was not hurt,
and the factory turned out to be an innocent pharmaceutical plant. Clinton's

domestic opponents and even some of his supporters suspected that he had ordered the air strikes less out of a desire to retaliate against terrorism, than to distract public attention from his testimony in a sex scandal involving his relations with Monica Lewinsky, a twenty-one-year-old intern.

The Lewinsky affair and the generally good economic times were of far greater interest to the public than the whereabouts of Osama bin Laden. The CIA continued to track him for the remainder of Clinton's term, but American operatives were unable to kill or capture him. Border agents captured an al-Qaeda operative entering the United States from Canada with a bomb designed to explode in Los Angeles International Airport on January 1, 2000. In October 2000 in the midst of the presidential election campaign, al-Qaeda commandos blew a hole in the hull of the navy destroyer *Cole* in a harbor off the coast of Yemen, killing seventeen sailors, disabling the ship, and causing more than $100 million in damage. Clinton ordered stepped-up diplomatic efforts to force the government of Afghanistan, ruled by the Islamic Taliban movement, to expel bin Laden into American custody.

Once George W. Bush's election was assured by a Supreme Court decision in early December 2000, Clinton administration officials briefed their successors on the problems they were likely to encounter. Clinton told Bush that he regretted not killing or capturing bin Laden and that "you will find that by far your greatest threat is bin Laden and al-Qaeda." Clinton's national security adviser, Samuel R. Berger, told his successor, Condoleezza Rice, that the new administration would spend more time on al-Qaeda and terrorism than on any other issue. Neither Bush nor Rice recall being warned in such stark terms, and both believed that terrorism was a secondary issue compared to the collapse of the Mideast peace negotiations between Israel and the Palestinians, the threat from China, and the possibility that North Korea might develop a nuclear bomb.

In the first months of 2001 National Security Adviser Rice downgraded the status of the Counterterrorism Security Group despite warnings from its director, Richard Clarke, that the threat from bin Laden was growing. Intelligence agencies intercepted so much "chatter" from al-Qaeda operatives around the world about the potential for a major strike against the United States that CIA Director George Tenet proclaimed that "the system was flashing red" in mid-summer. In July the CIA briefed Rice about the imminent danger of a terrorist assault inside the United States. On August 6 the CIA delivered to Bush the president's daily brief entitled "Bin Laden determined to strike in U.S." The paper explained that bin Laden planned his operations carefully for many years "and is not deterred by setbacks." Neither Rice nor Bush indicated to the briefers that they believed these warning portended an immediate or looming threat.

SEPTEMBER 11 AND THE WAR IN AFGHANISTAN

Catastrophe struck on the brilliantly clear late summer morning of September 11, 2001, when nineteen al-Qaeda hijackers seized four commercial airliners. They crashed two of them into the 110-story north and south towers of the World Trade Center in New York's lower Manhattan. Within ninety minutes of the initial impact the buildings collapsed in flames, smoke, and dust. More than 2,750 people were killed. Another plane slammed into the Pentagon, killing 184 people. A fourth jet was hijacked after taking off from Newark International Airport bound for Los Angeles. The terrorists wanted to fly it into either the U.S. Capitol or the White House, but passengers stormed the cockpit. The hijackers then crashed the airliner into a field near Pittsburgh, Pennsylvania.

The attacks and the collapse of the Twin Towers were seen live on television in the United States and throughout the world. Members of Congress gathered on the Capitol steps and spontaneously began to sing "God Bless America." Demonstrations of support for the United States took place in cities across Europe, Canada, Australia, and Japan. The French newspaper *Le Monde*, often highly critical of U.S. culture, politics, and foreign policy, ran a front page editorial under the headline, in French, "We Are All Americans." In the days and weeks after the attacks, Americans of all political persuasions flew American flags in front of their homes and wore American flag pins on their clothing.

President Bush's response to the attacks on the day they occurred seemed confused and possibly frightened, but he quickly recovered his balance. He visited the site of the World Trade Center, quickly labeled Ground Zero, grabbed a bullhorn, and shouted to the firefighters and rescue workers "I can hear you, and so the whole world will hear you." In the days after September 11, the Bush administration turned away from the rhetoric of the 2000 campaign, in which he promised that the United States would pursue a "humble foreign policy." Bush now pursued a war on terror. He adopted the foreign policy prescriptions of prominent neoconservatives, who had been advocating muscular American foreign policy that would sweep away dictatorial regimes around the globe. Their replacements would be democratic governments committed to free markets and friendly to the United States.

On September 20 he delivered a well-received speech to Congress in which he promised that "whether we bring our enemies to justice, or bring justice to our enemies, justice will be done." He demanded that the Taliban in Afghanistan arrest Osama bin Laden and turn him over to the United States or face an American attack. He proclaimed war on terrorism, but he denied that the United States was at war with Islam. Directly addressing the world's 1 billion Muslims, he said, "We respect your faith.... Its teachings

A U.S. Army helicopter off-loads American soldiers in Afghanistan in the war against the Taliban.
(U.S. Department of Defense)

are good and peaceful, and those who commit evil in the name of Allah blaspheme the name of Allah."

In the days after his remarks, Bush's popularity exceeded 90 percent. Congress passed the PATRIOT Act, which expanded the Justice Department's powers to conduct surveillance on terror suspects. Congress also authorized an American attack against the Taliban, with only one dissenting vote. NATO allies agreed to join the United States in waging war on the Taliban. Air strikes began in early October. The U.S. military used mostly Special Forces and Army Ranger units to bolster Afghan rebel forces that had been fighting the Taliban for years. In December these rebels captured Kabul, the capital of the country, and the other major cities of Afghanistan. The Taliban government melted away. Ominously, however, the United States failed to capture or kill Osama bin Laden.

The United States installed a new government in Afghanistan led by Hamid Karzai, a pro-Western former exile. The United States encouraged the Afghans to draft an enlightened constitution promising democratic elections and granting full equality to women. Karzai won election to the presidency in October 2004, and the United States poured billions of dollars into reconstruction and the building of schools and hospitals. But the Taliban were not completely eliminated, and they gathered strength in 2005 and 2006. In the summer of 2006 the United States turned the defense of Afghanistan over to NATO, and fighting intensified. Taliban fighters returned from havens in neighboring Pakistan to attack the Karzai government, which did not fulfill its initial promise to improve life or provide security.

PLANNING THE IRAQ WAR

Even before the Taliban were ousted in December 2001, a far bigger and more dangerous war loomed. The Bush administration put in motion a plan to attack Iraq and drive Saddam Hussein from power on September 12, when the president told his top aides to look for evidence that Saddam had been behind the September 11 attacks. CIA Director Tenet explained that the agency had no evidence of Iraqi involvement and that Saddam's secular government was at odds with the Islamic fundamentalism of al-Qaeda. Nevertheless, Deputy Defense Secretary Paul Wolfowitz insisted that the attacks were too sophisticated to have been planned by a tiny band of terrorists operating from caves in Afghanistan. He was certain that Iraq was involved.

Over the next few months Wolfowitz, Rumsfeld, and Cheney prodded the Pentagon to draw up plans for an American attack on Iraq. In December 2001 the *New York Times* printed a story by reporter Judith Miller asserting that Saddam Hussein was working on facilities to manufacture chemical, biological, and even nuclear weapons, in violation of numerous UN resolutions following the Gulf War of 1991 demanding that Iraq dismantle its weapons of mass destruction (WMD).

In January 2002 Bush identified Iraq, Iran, and North Korea as an "axis of evil arming to threaten the peace of the world." He warned ominously that "time is not on our side" and that "the United States of America will not permit the world's most dangerous regimes to threaten us with the world's most dangerous weapons." In June Bush announced a new American strategy in a speech at West Point. He said "we must take the battle to the enemy, disrupt his plans, and confront the worst threats before they emerge." Commentators quickly labeled this plan for preemptive war the "Bush Doctrine."

Secretary of State Colin Powell watched the administration's threats to Iraq with growing concern because he believed that President Bush was not carefully constructing an alliance the way his father, George H. W. Bush, had done before the Gulf War of 1990–1991. Under the Bush Doctrine the United States would act unilaterally if necessary, not feel bound by

Vice President Dick Cheney was one of the most ardent advocates of
the war with Iraq.
(U.S. Department of Defense)

UN procedures, and require that its traditional allies choose either to join
with it or be labeled a supporter of terrorism. Powell urged Bush to seek
international and congressional support before attacking Iraq. Bush did so,
but only grudgingly. He told the United Nations on September 12, 2002,
that the world body was in danger of sinking into irrelevance if it did not
authorize military action to enforce its resolutions demanding that Saddam
Hussein abandon his weapons of mass destruction. In October Congress
voted by a two-thirds majority to authorize the president to attack Iraq to
compel its disarmament. Many Democrats who had opposed the legislation
authorizing war against Iraq in 1991 changed their minds and voted in favor
this time. The Gulf War of 1991 had proven to be militarily much easier than
skeptics had expected. In the fall of 2002 the public was persuaded that Saddam Hussein had ties to al-Qaeda, so a vote in favor of war seemed expe-
dient and popular. Opposition to the war risked having a member of Congress
labeled weak on the fight against terrorism.

Throughout the winter of 2002–2003 Bush built a case for war and tried
to gather allied support. In December CIA Director Tenet assured Bush that

the evidence that Saddam maintained chemical, biological, and nuclear weapons was a "slam dunk." He later expressed regret for the remark and for not acknowledging that the evidence of Iraq's possession of WMD was tenuous. Vice President Cheney and Defense Secretary Rumsfeld pressured the CIA for concrete examples that the United States could use to persuade the world. Many analysts were skeptical of evidence that came from Iraqi exiles with obvious axes to grind against Saddam Hussein's murderous regime, but they complied with the requests. Journalists also reported as fact the reports that Saddam had reconstituted his weapons. In February 2003 Powell went before the UN Security Council with pictures and intercepted telephone calls that, he assured the world body, proved that Saddam was hiding WMD. He later admitted that this speech, which proved to be based on false information, was the low point of his professional life.

Powell was unable to persuade the United Nations to adopt a resolution authorizing force. British prime minister Tony Blair was a staunch supporter of the case for war, as were the prime ministers of Italy and Spain, but other allies from the Gulf War such as Germany and France this time opposed attacking Iraq. UN weapons inspector Hans Blix also counseled against a resolution authorizing force, since he said that Saddam was allowing his units some access to sites where banned weapons were suspected. He advised patience at least until the end of the summer of 2003, when his inspections would verify whether Saddam actually had WMD. Facing vetoes by France, Russia, and China, the UN Security Council declined to pass a resolution authorizing the United States to use force against Iraq. French foreign minister Dominique de Villepin addressed the UN Security Council and warned the United States of the dangers: "To those who think that the scourge of terrorism will be eradicated through the case of Iraq, we say they run the risk of failing in their objective. The outbreak of force in this area which is so unstable can only exacerbate the tensions and fractures on which the terrorists feed." The council chamber erupted in cheers and applause at these words, much to the disgust of U.S. ambassador John Negroponte. Turkey, a NATO ally of the United States that borders Iraq, stunned the Bush administration in March when it refused permission to launch an attack from its territory.

International opposition to an early attack on Iraq provoked ridicule in the United States. Conservative radio talk show hosts labeled Blix a fool or an outright agent of Saddam. French concerns that another war with Iraq would not be as easy as the Gulf War and would be likely to inflame Arab sentiments against the United States ignited a wave of anti-French anger. The House of Representatives renamed french fries "freedom fries" in its cafeterias, and calls went out to boycott French wine and cheese. Kenneth Adelman, a prominent neoconservative advocate of attacking Iraq, wrote in the *Washington Post* in February 2003 that he believed "demolishing Hussein's

Colin Powell, secretary of state 2001–2005, was a reluctant
supporter of war with Iraq.
(U.S. Department of Defense)

military power and liberating Iraq would be a cakewalk." Vice President
Cheney predicted the American forces would be "greeted as liberators in the
streets of Baghdad." For advocates of war, an Iraq rid of WMD and free of Hussein's tyranny would prove to be a beacon of democracy in the Middle East.

Senior officials also dismissed concerns expressed within the administration about the potential difficulties that lay ahead in Iraq. Gen. Erik Shinseki,
the chief of staff of the army, told Congress that it would require a force of
300,000 to 400,000 Americans. Secretary of Defense Donald Rumsfeld, who
wanted a mobile lethal force of no more than 140,000, angrily derided Shinseki and declined to extend his term. Glenn Hubbard, the chairman of the
President's Council of Economic Advisers, told Congress that war with Iraq
would cost between $200 billion and $400 billion. Bush dismissed him from
the government. Senior officials ignored concerns that war against Saddam
would be expensive. They recalled how the Gulf War of 1991 had cost the
United States very little because of allied contributions. Deputy Secretary of Defense Wolfowitz said that after the United States succeeded in toppling Saddam, Iraq would be able to pay for its reconstruction out of its vast oil wealth.

WAR AND INSURGENCY IN IRAQ

On March 17 Bush delivered an ultimatum to Saddam Hussein to leave Iraq or face war. Two days later, on March 19, the United States attacked by air and on land. The first Gulf War of 1991 lasted six weeks, and it appeared that the war to oust Saddam would be over even faster and with fewer American casualties. On April 9 American forces completed their race to Baghdad, occupied the capital, and helped a small but clearly jubilant crowd of Iraqis tear down one of the hundreds of statues of the dictator. It appeared that the swift victory and the regime change Rumsfeld anticipated had been achieved.

Disturbing signs appeared even as anti-Saddam Baghdad residents fired guns in the air to celebrate Saddam's end. The United States had no plans to preserve order or get Iraq's economy up and running. Mobs poured into government offices, electrical power stations, schools, and hospitals, stripping them bare of everything valuable. Looters even attacked the Iraqi National Museum, stealing thousands of priceless antiquities. Even more ominously, the weapons of mass destruction that Iraqi exiles assured the United States Saddam had stockpiled were nowhere to be found. The American armed forces searched the sites where the exiles told them the weapons were hidden, and much to Americans' shock and dismay, they discovered that the UN weapons inspectors had done a thorough job. By mid-May some analysts were considering an unthinkable idea—maybe Saddam did not have chemical, biological, or nuclear weapons.

In May 2003 these doubts and reports of disorder in Iraq barely registered in the United States. Bush's approval ratings remained at historically high levels. On May 2 Bush donned a navy flight suit and sat in the copilot's seat as an antisubmarine jet landed on the aircraft carrier *Abraham Lincoln.* He stood before a sign reading "Mission Accomplished" and told the 5,000 cheering members of the crew that "major combat operations in Iraq have ended.... And now our coalition is engaged in securing and reconstructing that country."

Security and reconstruction never happened. The Defense Department made no plans before the invasion for an occupation, but it resisted efforts by the State Department to implement its own more robust blueprint. Between 2003 and 2004 the United States directly ran Iraq's affairs through a Coalition Provisional Authority (CPA). The CPA's first administrator, Gen. Jay Garner, had bad relations with Defense Secretary Donald Rumsfeld, and he lasted only until June 2003. His replacement was Paul "Jerry" Bremer, who never seemed up to the job. He had a utopian vision of a free market Iraq modeled on Western democracies. He wanted to rid the country of the influence of Saddam Hussein's Ba'ath Party, and he disbanded the 500,000-strong Iraqi army. Unemployment soared to 50 percent in some areas of the country, but the CPA relied on American contractors more than local Iraqis to work on reconstruction projects. By the summer of 2003, hopes were fading among Iraqis that the United States would bring them a better life. In December 2003 spirits revived temporarily when American forces captured Saddam Hussein and turned him over to Iraqi authorities for prosecution. Six months later the United States officially ended its occupation and handed power to a provisional Iraqi government. Over the next eighteen months Iraq drafted a constitution with American help and elected a permanent government. At each of these milestones there was a brief flicker of hope that Iraq was on the road to stability, but these hopes never turned into facts.

An insurgency against the Americans and Iraqis who cooperated with them began in the summer of 2003 and gained in ferocity over the next three years. Initially, the United States dismissed the insurgents, who planted bombs and sniped at American forces as they walked through the streets of Baghdad, as a few remnants of Saddam's regime, "dead enders" as Rumsfeld and Cheney called them. When a reporter asked Bush about the rising number of American deaths in July 2003, the president snapped "There are some who feel … that they can attack us. My answer is 'Bring 'em on.' We've got the force necessary to deal with the security situation." His boast seemed only to inflame the insurgents, who attacked with greater ferocity.

Bush was wrong, and the attacks got worse. In 2006 Bush, who was loath to admit having made mistakes, acknowledged that "'bring it on' kind of tough talk … sent the wrong signal to people. I learned some lessons about expressing myself maybe in a little more sophisticated manner." The Pentagon, which had expected to draw down the American commitment from 140,000 to 50,000 by the end of 2003, could not do so. Instead, it rotated forces in and out of Iraq. By 2006 some American military personnel had served three six-month tours of duty in Iraq. As the insurgency continued the American death toll mounted. It passed 1,000 in 2004 and climbed beyond 2,750 in 2006. Approximately 20,000 American forces suffered wounds. The death toll among Iraqis was far higher, with estimates ranging from 50,000 to 900,000 in the three and a half years after the war began.

With the mounting casualties and questions about the rationale for the war, American support for fighting in Iraq began to decline. Doubts rose in the summer of 2003, when it became clear that Saddam Hussein did not possess WMD. Some intelligence analysts began to complain that the administration had distorted the evidence to convince a skeptical Congress that Iraq had WMD. When the Iraq Survey Group, the joint CIA-Defense Department team that scrutinized Iraq for WMD, issued its final report concluding that Saddam had dismantled his WMD programs in the aftermath of the first

President George W. Bush with Secretary of Defense Donald Rumsfeld, whose brusque
advocacy of the war in Iraq alienated many people and led to his resignation in
November 2006
(U.S. Department of Defense)

Gulf War, the initial justification for the war, ridding Iraq of WMD, had now
proven false.

In July 2003 the Commission on September 11 issued its report, which
was highly critical of both the Clinton and Bush administrations' handling
of terrorism before the attacks. The commission's report also denied that
Saddam Hussein had played any role in the attacks. Bush administration officials had previously insisted that Saddam had close ties with al-Qaeda, and
many Americans continued to believe he had some involvement in September 11 through the election campaign of 2004.

The war's cost also mounted. In September 2003 Bush asked Congress
for an additional $87 billion for the wars in Afghanistan and Iraq. The ex-
pectation that Iraq's oil money would pay for the war and reconstruction was
proving false. In the debate over the $87 billion members began likening
the growing American involvement in Iraq to the debacle in Vietnam more
than thirty years before. Iowa Democratic senator Thomas Harkin, a Vietnam era veteran, said "this may not be Vietnam, but it sure smells like it."

Most of the candidates who ran for the Democratic nomination to challenge Bush in 2004 were senators who had voted in favor of authorizing war against Iraq in 2002. In the fall of 2003 they faced Democratic primary voters who had grown disillusioned with the war, and they distanced themselves from the war. The eventual Democratic Party nominee was Massachusetts senator John Kerry, a decorated Vietnam War veteran who had first come to national prominence at the age of 26 when he spoke out against the Vietnam War. Throughout the campaign Kerry criticized the Bush administration's poor diplomacy and lack of planning for the postwar period. He never disavowed his vote for the war, however, and Bush was able to portray him as a waffler on Iraq specifically and the war on terror more generally. Bush defeated Kerry by approximately 3 million votes.

Although Kerry lost the election, domestic opposition to America's role in Iraq grew. Massachusetts Democratic senator Edward Kennedy, who, unlike Kerry, had voted against the authorization for war in October 2002, declared that "Iraq is George Bush's Vietnam." Echoes of the atrocities of the Vietnam War resounded in April 2004 when Seymour Hersh, the reporter who had broken the story of the 1968 My Lai massacre, reported in the *New Yorker* magazine that U.S. service members and CIA operatives had tortured and degraded Iraqi prisoners. The story came with nauseating pictures of naked Iraqi prisoners, some with bags over their heads, being led to mock executions, threatened with snarling dogs, and forced to wear women's underwear over their faces.

Other stories surfaced over the next two years about the more than 500 al-Qaeda prisoners being held in a prison on the navy base at Guantánamo Bay, Cuba, being subjected to degradation and torture. Reports also were made public that the CIA transferred terror suspects from American custody to other countries that tortured them. The Supreme Court ruled in 2006 that the government had to bring the Guantánamo detainees to trial. Many members of Congress demanded that the administration renounce the use of torture in interrogating terrorism suspects, but the White House forced a compromise that gave it wide latitude to abuse captives.

By late 2005 57 percent of the American public believed that it had been a mistake for the United States to have gone to war in Iraq. The cost of the war passed $300 billion, a figure that administration officials had insisted was ludicrously high in 2003. As the war went on in 2006 with the situation in Iraq deteriorating into sectarian violence that claimed the lives of 100 people a day, a plurality of Americans thought the United States should leave Iraq. Bush's approval also declined in 2006 to less than 40 percent.

In 2006 many of the early backers of the Iraq war publicly denounced the Bush administration's conduct of the war. They said if they had known how badly Cheney, Rumsfeld, and Rice would bungle the war they would not have advocated invading Iraq. Kenneth Adelman, the former Reagan administration official who had predicted that toppling Saddam Hussein would be "a cake walk," expressed his remorse. He said that Bush's national security team "turned out to be among the most incompetent teams in the post-war era." Adelman believed that the war had been so badly botched by the Bush administration that it invalidated the entire neoconservative foreign policy agenda. He defined neoconservatism in foreign affairs as "the idea of a tough foreign policy on behalf of morality, the idea of using our power for moral good in the world" and proclaimed it "dead, at least for a generation." Richard Perle, another prominent neoconservative who as head of the Defense Policy Board had been one of the loudest voices calling for war in Iraq, said had he "seen where we are today, and people had said, 'Should we go into Iraq?' I think now I probably would have said, 'No.'"

Journalists published books harshly critical of the Bush administration's handling of Iraq and the war on terror. Thomas Ricks, a military correspondent of the *Washington Post*, entitled his book on the Iraq war *Fiasco*. He condemned Rumsfeld and the civilian leadership of the Pentagon and the White House for going to war in Iraq without a plan for the occupation or for reconstruction. Michael Isikoff and David Corn wrote in *Hubris* that the Bush administration purposely misled the United States into war with Iraq on the false premise that Saddam possessed WMD. Ron Susskind wrote in *The One Percent Doctrine* that the Bush administration so exaggerated threats from terrorists that they took military action even if there was only a 1 percent chance that a threat was real. Journalist Bob Woodward's three books on Bush's foreign policy revealed the most about the public's changing attitude toward the president's conduct of the war on terror and the war in Iraq. The first, *Bush At War* (2002), lauded Bush and his principal advisers for their decisiveness in the aftermath of the September 11 attacks. The second, *Plan of Attack* (2004), subtly criticized Bush, Cheney, and Rumsfeld for focusing on a threat from Iraq in the immediate aftermath of the September 11 attacks. The book also, however, praised them for their toughness and verve. The third book in the series, *State of Denial: Bush at War, Part III* (2006), presented a far more critical assessment, and it forthrightly denounced Bush as a foreign policy failure. He and his principal aides refused to see the catastrophe looming in Iraq and lacked the ability to adjust to it.

THE PERILS OF UNILATERALISM

President Bush devoted his second inaugural address in January 2005 to the promotion of freedom worldwide. He echoed themes raised by President Woodrow Wilson at the time of World War I, saying "it is the policy of the

United States to seek and support the growth of democratic movements and institutions in every nation and culture, with the ultimate goal of ending tyranny in our world." Unlike Wilson, however, who advocated collective security and working with other countries multilaterally through his brainchild, the League of Nations, the Bush administration often disdained international cooperation and insisted that others follow American leadership. The predictable result was that many traditional friends of the United States felt bullied. When things went badly for the United States in Iraq, allies were hard to find.

In his September 20, 2001, speech proclaiming war on terrorism, Bush explained that "Every nation, in every region, now has a decision to make. Either you are with us, or you are with the terrorists." These calls resonated in 2001, but they alienated other nations after the United States invaded Iraq in 2003. Instead of responding to calls to cooperate more with other governments through the United Nations, the Bush administration continued to pursue a unilateral foreign policy that alienated traditional allies.

In 2005 Bush nominated John Bolton as ambassador to the United Nations. Bolton was a highly divisive neoconservative who had offended many State

National Security Adviser (2001–2005) and later Secretary of State Condoleezza Rice
(2005–) was Bush's closest foreign policy adviser.
(U.S. Department of Defense)

Department officials when he had been in charge of nuclear nonproliferation issues. One colleague called him a "kiss up, kick down kind of guy." He seemed to disdain the very organization to which he was appointed, saying it might be a good thing if the top ten stories of the UN Secretariat building were blown up. The Senate declined to confirm him, but Bush sent him to the UN anyway with a recess appointment that ran through 2006. Bolton tempered his abrasiveness somewhat when he came to New York, but other countries and UN Secretary General Kofi Annan viewed his presence as an irritant. In 2006 the United States had only limited success in crafting a UN response to Iran's and North Korea's development of nuclear weapons. The UN Security Council adopted a resolution demanding that Iran permit the International Atomic Energy Agency to inspect its nuclear reactors or face possible sanctions. Iran refused, but the United States was unable to persuade China and Russia to adopt sanctions against Iran. North Korea exploded an atomic weapon in October 2006. Bolton was able to secure a UN resolution deploring the detonation and imposing sanctions. Although China and Russia voted for the resolution, they were reluctant to impose the sanctions. After the Democrats regained control of Congress in the 2006 election, Bolton resigned, and Bush nominated Zalmay Khalilzhad, the U.S. ambassador to Iraq, to replace him at the UN.

The Bush administration's unilateralism also put it at odds with other nations in its handling of the Israeli-Palestinian-Arab dispute. The Bush administration believed that Bill Clinton had made a mistake by becoming so deeply involved in seeking a settlement between Israel and the Palestinians. With the collapse of Clinton's initiative at the end of his term, the situation deteriorated into great violence and recrimination. Bush called for the creation of a Palestinian state alongside Israel, but he did not become personally involved. He sent a succession of mediators to the regions, but none had the high profile of earlier envoys. The United States believed that the parties' attitudes had hardened so much that any new effort would fail. Bush formed a close relationship with Israel's hard-line prime minister, Ariel Sharon, who wanted to crush the Palestinian uprising before engaging in peace negotiations.

A glimmer of hope appeared after the death of Yasser Arafat in November 2004. His successor, Mahmoud Abbas, was a moderate leader who believed the violent Palestinian uprising was self-defeating. He favored resuming negotiations with Israel. Sharon seemed to abandon his support for Jewish settlements in territory captured in 1967 when he completed a unilateral withdrawal from Gaza and a small portion of the West Bank in the summer of 2005. He indicated that he would withdraw unilaterally from more of the West Bank over the next several years.

But these hopes proved illusory. Sharon suffered a stroke in early 2006. His replacement, Ehud Olmert, won an election with a promise of further

West Bank withdrawals. There was new leadership among the Palestinians, who elected Hamas, a Muslim organization that vowed to eliminate Israel. The United States and the European Union declared Hamas a terrorist organization and refused it aid.

In the summer of 2006 war broke out between Israel and Hezbollah, a Muslim militia in Lebanon also committed to Israel's destruction, after Hezbollah fighters captured two Israeli soldiers inside Israel. The United States and Great Britain backed Israel, expecting it quickly to vanquish Hezbollah and deal a blow to its backer, Iran. A few days after the war began Bush attended a meeting of the Group of Eight industrialized nations in St. Petersburg, Russia. Viewers around the world saw and heard him put a roll in his mouth, chew it, and shout to the British prime minister "Yo, Blair, we've got to make Syria [a backer of Hezbollah] stop this shit." Bush's boorishness and his cavalier treatment of Blair, the one friend the United States could count on among the major powers, seemed to encapsulate the American president's lack of understanding of how to conduct foreign affairs.

Instead of the quick Israeli victory the Americans expected, the war went on for thirty-four days. UN Secretary General Annan criticized Israel and the United States for an unnecessary war. Eventually, the United States and France sponsored a UN Security Council resolution calling for the return of the Israeli prisoners, a cease-fire, the disarmament of Hezbollah, and the sending of an international force to southern Lebanon. The cease-fire held, a force was deployed, but Hezbollah refused to disarm and did not return the prisoners. Hezbollah won praise throughout the Arab world for having withstood Israel's armed forces for more than a month. In the aftermath of its unsuccessful war in Lebanon, Israel dropped its plan for additional withdrawals from the West Bank. The situation between Israel and the Palestinians seemed direr than it had been in decades. The United States was perceived as giving unqualified support to Israel and uninterested in and unable to bring the parties together.

The Iraq war, Bush's divisive rhetoric, and the U.S. insistence on unquestioned obedience took a heavy toll on world opinion of the United States. The United States was greatly admired around the world at the end of the Clinton administration. In 2002, in the months after the terrorist attacks of September 11, 2001, great sympathy existed for the United States. But world views of the United States declined from 2003 to 2006. Attitudes in the Muslim world were especially hostile to the United States. Only 15 percent of those polled in Jordan, an Arab state traditionally friendly to the United States, had a favorable opinion. In Turkey favorable opinion of the United States declined from 52 percent in 1999–2000 to 12 percent in 2006. In Pakistan, a country whose leader, Pervez Musharraf, had become an ally

Favorable Opinions of the U.S.

	1999/2000 %	2002 %	2003 %	2004 %	2005 %	2006 %
Great Britain	83	75	70	58	55	56
France	62	63	43	37	43	39
Germany	78	61	45	38	41	37
Spain	50	–	38	–	41	23
Russia	37	61	36	47	52	43
Indonesia	75	61	15	–	38	30
Egypt	–	–	–	–	–	30
Pakistan	23	10	13	21	23	27
Jordan	–	25	1	5	21	15
Turkey	52	30	15	30	23	12
Nigeria	46	–	61	–	–	62
Japan	77	72	–	–	–	63
India	–	54	–	–	71	56
China	–	–	–	–	42	47

1999/2000 survey trends provided by the Office of Research, U.S. Department of State

Source: Pew Global Attitude Project, June 26, 2006

of the United States in the war on terror, barely a quarter of the population had a favorable opinion of the United States.

Attitudes toward President George W. Bush were harsh among allies. A poll conducted by leading newspapers in Great Britain, Canada, and Mexico in the fall of 2006 revealed that 69 percent of the British public believed U.S. policy has made the world less safe since 2001. Only 7 percent believed American actions in Iraq and Afghanistan made the world more secure. Some 62 percent of Canadians and 57 percent of Mexicans believed that the United States had made the world more dangerous. When people in Great Britain were asked who posed a threat to world peace, 87 percent said Osama bin Laden, and 69 percent said North Korea's Kim Jong Il; 75 percent indicated that Bush threatened the security of the world.

The American public signaled its strong desire for a changed course in Iraq in the 2006 midterm elections when it gave majorities in both the House and the Senate to Democrats. The day after the election Bush announced that he was replacing Secretary of Defense Donald Rumsfeld with Robert Gates, who had served as director of Central Intelligence during the administration of George H. W. Bush. Gates was a member of the Iraq Study Group chaired by James A. Baker III, secretary of state in the administration of the first president Bush. Both Gates and Baker had expressed skepticism about the grandiose hopes to remake Iraq.

Richard Armitage, deputy secretary of state under Colin L. Powell from 2001 to 2005, who had clashed bitterly with Rumsfeld and Vice President

Cheney in the months before the Iraq war, also suggested that the United States needed to change course, cooperate more with traditional friends, and appeal to the world's hope for prosperity and harmony. In early November 2006 Armitage told an audience in Australia that "After 9/11 we were exporting ... our anger and our fear. It's time to turn another face to the world, a more traditional face such as the export of hope and opportunity and inspiration."

Yet at the beginning of 2007 it remained to be seen whether U.S. foreign policy would become more cooperative with traditional allies and replace appeals to fear of terrorism with concrete expressions of hope, opportunity, and inspiration. President Bush rejected the advice of the Iraq Study Group that the United States engage all of Iraq's neighbors in negotiations to end the violence and stabilize the region. The Bush administration considered two of these neighbors, Iran and Syria, to be terrorist organizations responsible for much of the strength of the insurgency in Iraq.

Instead, Bush advocated a "surge" of 21,500 additional American troops to stop the daily killings in Baghdad. More than 60 percent of the American public disapproved of the plan to increase American troop strength in Iraq. The Bush administration also took an increasingly bellicose stand toward Iran, which it charged was developing nuclear weapons. As had been the case in the months before the United States attacked Iraq in 2003, many traditional European allies agreed with the American assessment of a threat, but they differed sharply with Washington's apparent quickness to use military might against Iran. There was widespread acknowledgment that a nuclear-armed Iran led by a militant Shi'ite government could prove to be a grave danger to the stability of the Middle East. It stood to become the dominant power in the Persian Gulf, a chilling prospect to oil-rich Sunni Muslim countries such as Saudi Arabia, the Gulf states, and Kuwait, each allied with the United States. But most American allies believed that a military attack on Iran would provoke a backlash against American power even more severe than the insurgency that had torn Iraq apart after 2003. In 2007 Americans at home and traditional friends internationally were deeply concerned that the United States was not using its power wisely.

Selected Bibliography

The field of diplomatic history has undergone a transformation in the last twenty years, drawing heavily on the insights and theoretical rigor of other social science disciplines. The best introduction to this new work is Michael Hogan and Thomas Paterson, eds., *Explaining the History of American Foreign Policy* (2004). There are several recent bibliographies of twentieth-century American diplomatic history. The comprehensive work is Robert Beisner, ed., *American Foreign Relations Since 1600: A Guide to the Literature* (2002); an electronic updated version is also available, Thomas W. Zeiler, ed., *American Foreign Relations: A Guide to the Literature since 1600* (2007). http://ebooks.abc-clio.com.

Four academic or quasi-scholarly journals that commenced publication at various times after the First World War include current information and historical research on America's international relations. They are *Foreign Affairs* (1922–), *World Politics* (1947–), *Foreign Policy* (1971–), and *Diplomatic History* (1977–). *Diplomatic History*, the journal of the Society for Historians of American Foreign Relations, regularly publishes excellent historiographical essays on chronological and topical subjects of interest to students of American diplomacy. It also carries important articles on the new theoretical approaches to the field. See also *American Historical Review, Journal of American History, International History Review*, and *American Political Science Review*.

GENERAL INTERPRETATIONS

General interpretations of American diplomatic history and foreign policy fall into three broad categories: nationalist, realist, and radical or revisionist.

The first "dean" of American diplomatic historians, Samuel Flagg Bemis, set forth the nationalist interpretation in the 1920s and expressed it most force-fully in *American Foreign Policy and the Blessings of Liberty* (1962). The major expressions of the realist critique of American foreign policy are George F. Kennan, *American Diplomacy* (1951) and *Realities of American Foreign Policy* (1954); Robert E. Osgood, *Ideals and Self-Interest in America's Foreign Relations* (1953); Hans J. Morgenthau, *In Defense of the National Interest: A Critical Ex-amination of American Foreign Policy* (1951); and Reinhold Niebuhr, *The Children of Light and the Children of Darkness* (1948). Recent restatements of realism are two works by Frank Ninkovich, *Modernity and Power: A History of the Domino Theory in the Twentieth Century* (1994), and *The Wilsonian Century: United States Foreign Policy Since 1900* (1999). Revisionist writing owes much to two works by Charles Beard: *The Idea of National Interest* (1934) and *The Open Door at Home* (1935). Modern revisionist, radical, or "left-liberal" writing on foreign policy follows the path set by William Appleman Williams in *The Tragedy of American Diplomacy* (1972), *The Contours of American History* (1961), *America Confronts a Revolutionary World* (1978), and *Empire as a Way of Life* (1980). The readings of Jerald A. Combs, ed., *Nationalist, Realist and Radical: Three Views of American Diplomacy* (1972), offer a good debate.

Several sophisticated interpretations are H. W. Brands, *What America Owes the World: The Struggle for the Soul of Foreign Policy* (1998); Michael H. Hunt, *Ideology and United States Foreign Policy* (1987); Walter Russell Mead, *Special Providence: American Foreign Policy and How It Changed the World* (2001); and Emily S. Rosenberg, *Spreading the American Dream: American Economic and Cul-tural Expansion, 1890–1945* (1982).

Beyond the general accounts listed above, several detailed accounts re-veal the competitive world in which the United States has operated. The best history of the imperial rivalries at the end of the nineteenth century remains William Langer, *The Diplomacy of Imperialism,* 2 vols. (1935). Frank Ninkovich, *The United States and Imperialism* (2001) is an imaginative inquiry that makes great use of the most up-to-date scholarship on U.S. and European imperi-alism. Amy Kaplan and Donald Pease, eds., *Cultures of U.S. Imperialism* (1993) explains the cultural dimension of U.S. expansion.

Two British liberals, John Hobson, *Imperialism* (1902), and Norman Angell, *The Great Illusion* (1911), note the growing interdependence of the world's economies and the effects this had upon international relations. Discussions of modern interest in themes of interdependence appear in John Mickelth-wait and Adrian Wooldrige, *A Future Perfect: The Esssentials of Globalization* (2000), and David Mosler and Bob Catley, *Global America: Imposing Liberalism on a Recalcitrant World* (2000).

Among general works dealing with the process of creating foreign pol-icy, the best are Marie T. Henehan, *Foreign Policy and Congress* (2000); Barry

Rubin, *Secrets of State* (1984); Burton M. Sapin, *The Making of United States Foreign Policy* (1966); I. M. Destler, *Presidents, Bureaucrats and Foreign Policy* (1972); Francis O. Wilcox, *Congress, the Executive and Foreign Policy* (1971); and Thomas Franck and Edward Weisband, *Foreign Policy by Congress* (1979). Richard Neustadt and Ernest May, *Thinking in Time: The Uses of History for Decisionmakers* (1986), explains the uses and abuses of historical thought by officials.

The effects on foreign policy of nongovernmental actors appear in Barry Hughes, *The Domestic Context of Foreign Policy* (1978); Edward Crapol, ed., *Women and American Foreign Policy*, 2d ed. (1992); Robert D. Schulzinger, *The Wise Men of Foreign Affairs: The History of the Council on Foreign Relations* (1984); Charles Chatfield, *For Peace and Justice: Pacifism in America, 1914–1941*, and *Peace Movements in America* (1973); Charles De Benedetti, *The Peace Reform in American History* (1980); De Benedetti's edited work *Peace Heroes in Twentieth Century America* (1986); and John W. Chambers II, *The Eagle and the Dove: The American Peace Movement and United States Foreign Policy, 1900–1922* (1992).

FROM THE SPANISH-AMERICAN WAR TO WORLD WAR I, 1898–1914

Good general surveys of the causes, conduct, effects, and historiography of the Spanish-American-Philippine War appear in Max Boot, *The Savage Wars of Peace: Small Wars and the Rise of American Power* (2002); Thomas Schoonover, *Uncle Sam's War of 1898 and the Origins of Globalization* (2003); Mark Gilderhus, *The Secondary Century: U.S.–Latin American Relations Since 1889* (2000); Ernest May's well-documented *Imperial Democracy* (1961); and David Trask's massive military history, *The War with Spain* (1981). Frank Ninkovich, *The United States and Imperialism*, is indispensable. Samuel Flagg Bemis claims that the seizure of colonial territory after the war represented a "great aberration" in *The Latin American Policy of the United States* (1943). The strategic importance of the war with Spain receives full treatment in John A. S. Grenville and George Berkeley Young, *Politics, Strategy and American Diplomacy, 1873–1917* (1966). Walter Millis mocks American participation in the war with *The Martial Spirit* (1931). Kristin Hoganson, *Fighting for American Manhood: How Gender Politics Provoked the Spanish-American and Philippine-American Wars* (1998) explores the gender aspects of the war.

The movement against taking colonial territory is treated in Robert Beisner, *Twelve Against Empire* (1968); and Paolo Coletta, *William Jennings Bryan*, 3 vols. (1964–1969).

A good interpretive overview of the period after 1900 appears in Lloyd C. Gardner's "American Foreign Policy, 1900–1921: A Second Look at the Realist Critique of American Diplomacy," in Barton Bernstein, ed., *Towards a New Past* (1968).

The realist critique of the Open Door policy appears in A. Whitney Griswold's *The Far Eastern Policy of the United States* (1938), which argues that John Hay was naive and moralistic in proposing the Open Door policy. George F. Kennan concurs in *American Diplomacy* (1951). William Appleman Williams suggests that the Open Door policy stood at the center of American foreign policy in his *Tragedy of American Diplomacy*, (1972). Thomas McCormick's *China Market: America's Quest for Informal Empire* (1967), an expert revisionist account, explains that Hay played a weak hand as well as he could. Michael Hunt's subtle *Frontier Defense and the Open Door* (1973) argues that the Chinese had as much to do with writing the notes as the Americans. More general accounts of United States–Chinese relations are Warren Cohen, *America's Response to China* (2000), and Michael Schaller, *The United States and China: Into the Twenty-First Century* (2002).

The American war in the Philippines is covered in Stanely Karnow, *In Our Image: America's Empire in the Philippines* (1989); Peter Stanley, *A Nation in the Making: The Philippines, 1898–1935* (1977); and Paul A. Kramer, *The Blood of Government: Race, Empire, the United States, and the Philippines* (2006).

The growth of the Anglo-American rapprochement after the Spanish-American War receives full discussion in Charles S. Campbell, *Anglo-American Understanding, 1898–1903* (1957); Lionel Gelber, *The Rise of Anglo-American Friendship: A Study in World Politics, 1898–1906* (1938); and Bradford Perkins, *The Great Rapprochement: England and the United States* (1968).

The best study of TR's diplomacy remains Howard K. Beale, *Theodore Roosevelt and the Rise of America to World Power* (1956). A highly readable biography of Roosevelt, based on the most recent scholarship, is H.W. Brands, *T.R.: The Last Romantic* (1997). See also Gilderhus, *The Second Century: U.S.–Latin American Relations Since 1887*, and Ninkovich, *The United States and Imperialism.*

Specialized studies of Roosevelt's actions during the Panama crisis are Walter LaFeber's masterly *The Panama Canal: The Issue in Historical Perspective* (1979) and David McCullough's *The Path Between the Seas: The Building of the Panama Canal* (1976). The standard account of the Monroe Doctrine and the Roosevelt Corollary is Dexter Perkins, *A History of the Monroe Doctrine* (1955). Dana Munro's *Intervention and Dollar Diplomacy in the Caribbean, 1900–1921* (1964) is comprehensive.

Discussions of Roosevelt's relations with Russia and Japan appear in Arthur Thompson and Robert Hart, *The Uncertain Crusade: America and the Russian Revolution of 1905* (1970); Walter LaFeber, *The Clash: A History of U.S.–Japanese Relations* (1997); and Akira Iriye, *Pacific Estrangement: Japanese and American Expansion, 1897–1911* (1972).

The movement for international law and international organization is covered well by Francis Anthony Boyle, *Foundations of World Order: The Legalist Approach to International Relations, 1898–1922* (2000). Emily S. Rosenberg,

Financial Missionaries to the World: The Politics and Culture of Dollar Diplomacy, 1900–1930 (1999), is a splendid cultural study. The standard account of Taft's foreign policy is Walter Scholes and Marie Scholes, *Foreign Policies of the Taft Administration* (1970).

Arthur Link is the foremost biographer of Woodrow Wilson. See his *Wilson*, 5 vols. (1947–1986), *Wilson the Diplomatist* (1956), *Woodrow Wilson and the Progressive Era, 1910–1917* (1959), and *War, Revolution and Peace* (1980). Thomas J. Knock, *To End All Wars: Woodrow Wilson and the Quest for a New World Order* (1992), places Wilson's diplomacy in the context of progressive thought, although it concentrates on World War I. Paolo Coletta's *William Jennings Bryan* (1964–1969) is a sympathetic three-volume work. William C. Widenor's *Henry Cabot Lodge and the Search for American Foreign Policy* (1980) has something on this period.

Far Eastern developments in the Taft-Wilson years receive treatment in Michael Hunt, *Frontier Defense and the Open Door* (1973); Jerry Israel, *Progressivism and the Open Door: America and China, 1905–1921* (1971); Charles Vevier, *The United States and China* (1955); and Edward H. Zabriskie, *American-Russian Rivalry in the Far East, 1895–1914* (1946).

Intervention in Central America and the Caribbean receives coverage in Thomas Schoonover, *The United States in Central America, 1860–1911* (1991); Lester Langley, *The Banana Wars: An Inner History of the American Empire, 1900–1934* (1983); and Mary Renda, *Taking Haiti: Military Occupation and the Culture of U.S. Imperialism, 1915-1940* (1998), which explores the cultural dimensions.

Good studies exist on American meddling in Mexico. P. Edward Haley's *Revolution and Intervention: The Diplomacy of Taft and Wilson with Mexico* (1970) discusses 1910–1917. Lloyd C. Gardner's *Safe for Democracy: The Anglo-American Response to Revolution, 1913–1923* (1984) contains useful material on Mexico. Volumes two through five of Arthur Link's massive *Wilson* (1947–) contain many chapters on U.S.–Mexican relations. Peter Calvert's *The Mexican Revolution, 1910–1914* (1968) explains the international environment of the revolution. Kenneth Grieb's *The United States and Huerta* (1969) covers 1913–1914. Robert E. Quirk's *An Affair of Honor: Woodrow Wilson and the Occupation of Vera Cruz* (1962) explains the April 1914 embroglio. Robert Freeman Smith's *The United States and Revolutionary Nationalism in Mexico* (1972) is comprehensive. Friedrich Katz's *The Secret War in Mexico* (1981) has a good international perspective. John Womack's *Zapata* (1972) presents excellent social history of the roots of revolution.

THE FIRST WORLD WAR AND THE VERSAILLES PEACE, 1914–1920

The question of American entry into the First World War inspires bibliographies. See Richard Leopold, "The Problem of American Intervention,

1917: An Historical Retrospect," *World Politics* (1950); and Ernest May, *American Intervention: 1917 and 1941* (1960). Warren Cohen's *The American Revisionists* (1966) is a historiographical record of what dissenters said about American entry into the First World War from 1917 to the late 1940s.

Arno Mayer's "World War I," in C. Vann Woodward, ed., *The Comparative Approach to American History* (1968), is indispensable for understanding the meaning of the First World War. William A. Williams, *Tragedy of American Diplomacy* (1972), presents a revisionist account.

Several works trace the development of Wilson's ideas of diplomacy. See Knock's *To End All Wars*; Lloyd E. Ambrosius, *Woodrow Wilson and the American Diplomatic Tradition* (1987) and his *Wilsonian Statecraft* (1991); and N. Gordon Levin, *Woodrow Wilson and World Politics* (1968).

Other figures appear in Daniel Smith's *Robert Lansing and American Neutrality* (1958). There is as yet no good biography of Edward M. House, but see Charles Seymour, *The Intimate Papers of Colonel House* (1926–1928). John Garry Clifford's *The Citizen Soldiers: The Plattsburgh Training Camp Movement, 1913–1920* (1972) discusses preparedness. William Widenor's *Henry Cabot Lodge* (1980) and John Garraty's *Henry Cabot Lodge* (1953) treat a major opposition figure. Merlo J. Pusey's biography *Charles Evans Hughes*, 2 vols. (1951), discusses the election of 1916.

The standard accounts of the diplomacy of neutrality are Ernest May, *The World War and American Isolation* (1959); Lord Patrick Devlin, *Too Proud to Fight: Woodrow Wilson's Neutrality* (1975); and Arthur S. Link, *Wilson*, III, *The Struggle for Neutrality, 1914–1915*; IV, *Confusions and Crises, 1915–1916*; and V, *Campaigns for Progressivism and Peace, 1916–1917*. John Milton Cooper's *The Vanity of Power: American Isolation and the First World War* (1969) is a quicker survey.

The American mood on the eve of the Great War is discussed in Henry May, *The End of American Innocence* (1959); Charles Forcey, *The Crossroads of Liberalism* (1961); Ronald Steel, *Walter Lippmann and the American Century* (1980); David Noble, *The Progressive Mind* (1980); and Richard Hofstadter, *The American Political Tradition and the Men Who Made It* (1948). Radical dissent appears in Theodore Roszak, ed., *War and the Intellectuals: Writings of Randolph Bourne* (1961).

The American approach during the war consciously differed from that of other belligerents. The best assessment of Wilson's outlook is in Arno J. Mayer, *Political Origins of the New Diplomacy* (1959). N. Gordon Levin's *Woodrow Wilson and World Politics* (1968) expands Mayer's analysis.

The origins of Wilson's Fourteen Points receive attention as well in books dealing with wider subjects. Ronald Steel's *Walter Lippmann and the American Century* (1980) and Lawrence Gelfand's *The Inquiry: American Preparations for Peace, 1917–1919* (1963) examine the role of outside experts in advising the government.

Developments at home are explained best in David Kennedy's *Over Here: The Home Front in the First World War* (1980). What happened to dissenters is discussed in Nick Salvatore, *Eugene V. Debs: Citizen and Socialist* (1982); Melvin Dubofsky, *We Shall Be All: A History of the Industrial Workers of the World* (1968); and Carl Bode, *Mencken* (1969). Propaganda efforts are treated in George Blakey, *Historians on the Homefront: American Propagandists and the Great War* (1970); James R. Mock and Cedric Larson, *Words That Won the War: The Story of the Committee on Public Information* (1938); and Carol S. Gruber, *Mars and Minerva: World War I and the Uses of Higher Learning in America* (1976). Mobilization practices appear in Daniel R. Beaver, *Newton D. Baker and the American War Effort, 1917–1919* (1966). Economic mobilization for total war is well covered in Jordan A. Schwarz, *The Speculator: Bernard M. Baruch in Washington, 1917–1965* (1981). Washington politics are covered in Seward W. Livermore, *Politics Is Adjourned: Woodrow Wilson and the War Congress, 1916–1918* (1966).

The story of intervention in the Russian civil war appears in George F. Kennan, *Soviet-American Relations, 1917–1920,* 2 vols. (1956–1958), and *Russia and the West Under Lenin and Stalin* (1961); Richard H. Ullman, *Anglo-Soviet Relations, 1917–1921,* 3 vols. (1961–1971); and William A. Williams, *American-Russian Relations, 1781–1947* (1952), *The Tragedy of American Diplomacy* (1962), and *America Confronts a Revolutionary World* (1978). Lloyd Gardner's *Safe for Democracy,* mentioned above, is a sophisticated account of intervention in Russia.

Negotiations leading toward the armistice appear in Harry Rudin, *Armistice 1918* (1938); and a newer work, Arthur Walworth, *America's Moment: 1918* (1978).

The best work on the social, economic, and political context of the peace conference is Arno J. Mayer's *Politics and Diplomacy of Peacemaking* (1967). The most recent scholarship appears in Margaret MacMillan, *Paris 1919: Six Months that Changed the World* (2002). Harold Nicolson's memoir of the conference, *Peacemaking, 1919* (1931), is enjoyable. John Maynard Keynes's *Economic Consequences of the Peace* (1920) is bitter, while James T. Shotwell's *At the Paris Peace Conference* (1937) expresses the undimmed faith of an old Wilsonian. Thomas A. Bailey's *Woodrow Wilson and the Lost Peace* (1944) is sympathetic to the president without ignoring his faults. A physician, Edwin A. Weinstein, has written *Woodrow Wilson: A Medical and Psychological Biography* (1981) to explain some of the president's behavioral quirks.

The following describe the reception of the treaty in the United States: Lloyd Ambrosius's *Woodrow Wilson and the American Diplomatic Tradition,* previously noted; John Milton Cooper, Jr., *Breaking the Heart of the World: Woodrow Wilson and the Fight for the League of Nations* (2001); and William C. Widenor, *Henry Cabot Lodge and the Search for American Foreign Policy* (1980).

Wilson's economic diplomacy in the period after the armistice is described by Carl Parrini in *Heir to Empire: United States Economic Diplomacy, 1916–1923* (1969).

THE INTERWAR PERIOD, 1921–1939

Two works place the interwar period into proper context: E. H. Carr, *The Twenty Years' Crisis, 1919–1938: An Introduction to the Study of International Relations* (1939); and Gordon Craig and Felix Gilbert, eds., *The Diplomats, 1919–1939* (1993). Warren Cohen, *Empire Without Tears: America's Foreign Relations, 1921–1933* (1987), contains an excellent factual overview of the period.

Economic issues and relations with Europe are discussed in Carl Parrini, *Heir to Empire* (1969); Herbert Feis, *The Diplomacy of the Dollar: The First Era, 1919–1933* (1950); Marc Trachtenberg, *Reparations in World Politics* (1980); Melvyn Leffler, *The Elusive Quest: America's Pursuit of French Security and European Stability, 1919–1933* (1979); Joan Hoff Wilson, *American Business and Foreign Policy, 1920–1933* (1971); and Henry Blumenthal, *Illusion and Reality in Franco-American Diplomacy* (1986).

The secretaries of state in the twenties are treated in Merlo J. Pusey, *Charles Evans Hughes* (1951); and L. Ethan Ellis, *Frank B. Kellogg and American Foreign Relations* (1961).

The Middle East in the twenties is covered well in Michael B. Oren, *Power, Faith, and Fantasy: America in the Middle East, 1776 to the Present* (2007).

Cultural and political relations with Asia appear in Akira Iriye's *After Imperialism: The Search for a New Order in the Far East, 1921–1931* (1965). Rodman Paul's *The Abrogation of the Gentlemen's Agreement* (1936) explains the connection between immigration and foreign policy in the early twenties.

Many of the works listed for the earlier period deal with U.S. policy in Latin America in the twenties. Others are David Schmitz, *Thank God, They're on Our Side: The United States and Rightwing Dictatorships, 1921–1965* (1999); Dana G. Munro, *The United States and the Caribbean Republics in the 1920s* (1972); Joseph S. Tulchin, *Aftermath of War: World War I and U.S. Policy Toward Latin America* (1971); Arthur C. Millspaugh, *Haiti Under American Control* (1930); William Kamman, *A Search for Stability: United States Diplomacy Toward Nicaragua, 1925–1933* (1968); and Neill McCauley, *The Sandino Affair* (1967).

The Washington Conference and naval rivalries are discussed by Thomas H. Buckley, *The Washington Conference, 1921–1922* (1970); Roger Dingman, *Power in the Pacific: The Evolution of Japanese and American Naval Policies* (1975); Stephen Roskill, *Naval Policies Between the Wars, I, The Period of Anglo-American Antagonism, 1919–1929* (1968); and John Chalmers Vinson, *The Parchment Peace: The United States Senate and the Washington Conference, 1921–1922* (1955).

Plans for peace and the maintenance of the old Wilsonian flame are discussed with sympathy by Denna Fleming in *The United States and World Organization, 1920–1933* (1938), disdain by Robert Ferrell in *Peace in Their Time: The Origins of the Kellogg-Briand Pact* (1952), and optimism by James T. Shotwell in *War as an Instrument of National Policy and Its Renunciation* (1929). Hamilton Fish Armstrong's memoirs, *Peace and Counterpeace: From Wilson to Hitler* (1971), provide the observations of a chastened Wilsonian.

The international effects of the economic collapse receive a whimsical discussion in John Kenneth Galbraith's *The Great Crash* (1955, 1966). Charles Kindleberger's *The World in Depression* (1974) is the standard account.

The diplomatic distress of the Hoover administration is well told in Robert Ferrell's *American Diplomacy in the Great Depression: Hoover-Stimson Foreign Policy, 1921–1933* (1957). Richard Current's *Secretary Stimson: A Study in Statecraft* (1954) is a biting assessment of Hoover's principal adviser.

The best general account of FDR's foreign policy is Robert Dallek, *Franklin D. Roosevelt and American Foreign Policy, 1932–1945* (1979). Robert Divine's *The Reluctant Belligerent* (1979) and *The Illusion of Neutrality* (1962), both good, provide a less detailed overview. William Leuchtenburg, *Franklin D. Roosevelt and the New Deal* (1962); James MacGregor Burns, *Roosevelt: The Lion and the Fox* (1960); Frank Friedel, *Roosevelt*, 2 vols. (1952–1956); and Arthur M. Schlesinger, Jr., The Age of Roosevelt, 3 vols. (1957–1960), all have good foreign policy material.

Far Eastern affairs received attention under both Hoover and Roosevelt. The best accounts of the Manchurian crisis are Walter LaFeber, *The Clash: A History of U.S.–Japanese Relations* (1997), and Christopher Thorne's *The Limits of Foreign Policy: The West, The League and the Far Eastern Crisis of 1931–1933* (1973). Dorothy Borg's *The United States and the Far Eastern Crisis of 1933–1938* (1964) and Dorothy Borg and Shumpei Okamoto, eds., *Pearl Harbor as History, Japanese-American Relations, 1931–1941* (1973), extend the story to 1941. Stephen Pelz, *Race to Pearl Harbor* (1974), covers naval competition in the Pacific; and James R. Leutze, *Bargaining for Supremacy* (1977), adds British naval policy to the Far Eastern arms race.

The New Deal's flawed attempts to reach international monetary accord are covered by Herbert Feis, *1933: Characters in Crisis* (1966); and Alfred E. Eckes, *A Search for Solvency* (1977). Lloyd C. Gardner's fine *Economic Aspects of New Deal Diplomacy* (1964) is comprehensive, while Frederick C. Adams's *Economic Diplomacy: The Export Import Bank and American Foreign Policy, 1933–1941* (1976) is a good special study.

Recognition of the Soviet Union and subsequent U.S.–Soviet relations are covered by Edward Bennett, *Recognition of Russia* (1970); Beatrice Farnsworth, *William C. Bullitt and the Soviet Union* (1967); William A. Williams, *American-Russian Relations, 1781–1947* (1952); and Joan Hoff Wilson, *Ideology and Economics: U.S. Relations with the Soviet Union, 1918–1933* (1974). For what happened to the foreign service officers who went to the Soviet Union, see George F. Kennan, *Memoirs, 1925–1950* (1967); and Hugh De Santis, *The Diplomacy of Silence: The American Foreign Service, the Soviet Union and the Origins of the Cold War, 1933–1947* (1980).

The movement for neutrality legislation and nonintervention is treated by Selig Adler, *The Isolationist Impulse* (1957); Warren Cohen, *The American Revisionists* (1966); Jordan A. Schwarz, *The Speculator: Bernard M. Baruch in Washington, 1917–1965* (1981); and John E. Wiltz, *In Search of Peace: The Senate Munitions Inquiry, 1934* (1963). Betty Glad's *Key Pittman: The Tragedy of a Senate Insider* (1986) uses insights from social psychology to trace a colorful career.

The growth of FDR's Good Neighbor policy is covered by Mark Gilderhus, *The Second Century*; David Schmitz, *Thank God, They're on Our Side: The United States and Rightwing Dictatorships, 1921–1965* (1999); and Bryce Wood, *The Making of the Good Neighbor Policy* (1961).

The domestic and diplomatic reaction to the Spanish Civil War is covered by three books: Allen Guttmann, *The Wound in the Heart: America and the Spanish Civil War* (1962); F. Jay Taylor, *The United States and the Spanish Civil War, 1936–1939* (1956); and Richard P. Traina, *American Diplomacy and the Spanish Civil War* (1968).

The minimal response to the plight of refugees from Hitler first received attention in Arthur Morse's inflammatory *While Six Million Died* (1968). More scholarly but equally damning treatments are Henry Feingold, *The Politics of Rescue: The Roosevelt Administration and the Holocaust, 1938–1945* (1970); David S. Wyman, *Paper Walls: America and the Refugee Crisis, 1938–1941* (1968), and Samantha Power, *"A Problem from Hell": America and the Age of Genocide* (2002).

Arnold A. Offner's *American Appeasement: United States Foreign Policy and Germany, 1933–1938* (1968) charges the Roosevelt administration with blindness to the dangers of Germany.

THE SECOND WORLD WAR, 1940–1945

Many of the general works on FDR listed above apply to the Second World War. Mark A. Stoler, *Allies in War: Britain and America Against the Axis Powers, 1940–1945* (2005) is a good introduction. Robert Dallek's *Franklin D. Roosevelt and United States Foreign Policy, 1933–1945* (1979) is superb. Warren Kimball's *The Juggler: Franklin Roosevelt as World Statesman* (1991) and *Forged in War: Roosevelt, Churchill and the Second World War* (1997) are highly sophisticated works. Gerhard L. Weinberg, *A World at Arms: A Global History of World War II* (1994) is massive.

Special studies of domestic politics during the neutrality period are Wayne S. Cole, *America First: The Battle Against Intervention, 1940–1941* (1953); Geoffrey Smith, *To Save a Nation: American Counter-Subversives, the New Deal and the Coming of World War II* (1973); and Manfred Jonas, *Isolationism in America, 1935–1941* (1967).

The general diplomatic history of the years immediately before Pearl Harbor is covered in two controversial volumes by William Langer and S. Everett Gleason, *The Challenge to Isolation, 1937–1940* (1952) and *The Undeclared War, 1940–1941* (1953). The writers, both former State Department officials, received access to papers denied to other researchers. An account based on declassified intelligence documents is Waldo Heinrichs, *Threshold of War: Franklin Delano Roosevelt and American Entry into World War II* (1988).

For relations with Germany, see James V. Compton, *The Swastika and the Eagle: Hitler, the United States and the Origins of World War II* (1967); and Saul Friedlander, *Prelude to Downfall: Hitler and the United States, 1939–1941* (1967). The Atlantic Conference between Churchill and Roosevelt is explained best by Theodore Wilson's *The First Summit: Roosevelt and Churchill at Placentia Bay, 1941* (1971).

Relations with Japan before Pearl Harbor are discussed in Dorothy Borg and Shumpei Okamoto, eds., *Pearl Harbor as History: Japanese-American Relations, 1931–1941* (1973), a series of essays by specialists on the military, economic, and diplomatic background of war between the United States and Japan. See also the previously mentioned work by LaFeber, *The Clash.* Gordon Prange, *At Dawn We Slept: The Untold Story of Pearl Harbor* (1981), over twenty years in the writing, supersedes all previous accounts. Roberta Wohlstetter's *Pearl Harbor: Warning and Decision* (1962) explains what Americans knew and when they knew it about the impending attack. Herbert Feis's *The Road to Pearl Harbor* (1950) represents a conventional interpretation by a former State Department official.

Roosevelt's leadership of the anti-Axis coalition is covered in Eric Larrabee's *Commander in Chief: Franklin Delano Roosevelt, His Lieutenants and Their War* (1986). The president's complicated relationship with Winston Churchill emerges best in Warren Kimball, ed., *Churchill and Roosevelt: The Complete Correspondence*, 3 vols. (1984), and his *Forged in War: Roosevelt, Churchill and the Second World War* (1997). See also Randall B. Woods, *A Changing of the Guard: Anglo-American Relations, 1941–1946* (1990); and Mark A. Stoler, *Allies and Adversaries: The Joint Chiefs of Staff, the Grand Alliance and U.S. Strategy in World War II* (2000). Planning for the postwar period is covered by Diana Shaver Clemens, *Yalta* (1970); Russell Buhite's *Decision at Yalta* (1986); John Lewis Gaddis, *The United States and the Origins of the Cold War, 1941–1947* (1972); Lloyd Gardner's subtle *Architects of Illusion: Men and Ideas in American Foreign Policy, 1941–1949* (1970); Richard Gardner,

Sterling-Dollar Diplomacy (1956); Robert Hathaway, *Ambiguous Partnership: Britain and America, 1944–1947* (1981); George C. Herring, *Aid to Russia, 1941–1946* (1976); Godfrey Hodgson, *The Colonel: The Life and Wars of Henry Stimson, 1867–1950* (1990); Gabriel Kolko, *The Politics of War, 1943–1945* (1968); and Michael Sherry, *Preparing for the Next War* (1977), a major departure.

The war in the Far East and American attitudes toward colonialism and Asia are covered by John Dower, *War Without Mercy: Race and Power in the Pacific War* (1986); Akira Iriye, *Power and Culture* (1980); William Roger Louis, *Imperialism at Bay: The United States and the Decolonization of the British Empire* (1978); Michael Schaller, *The U.S. Crusade in China, 1938–1945* (1979); Kenneth Shewmaker, *Americans and the Chinese Communists, 1927–1945: A Persuading Encounter* (1971); and Christopher Thorne, *Allies of a Kind: The United States, Great Britain and the War Against Japan, 1939–1945* (1979), a brilliant book.

Petroleum politics and the Middle East are discussed in the previously mentioned Michael Oren, *Power, Faith, and Fantasy: America in the Middle East, 1776 to the Present;* Irvine H. Anderson, *Aramco, the United States and Saudi Arabia* (1981); Aaron David Miller, *Saudi Arabian Oil and American Security, 1939–1948* (1980); and Michael Stoff, *Oil, War and American Security: The Search for a National Policy on Foreign Oil, 1941–1947* (1980).

Special studies on the war in Europe include David S. Wyman, *The Abandonment of the Jews: America and the Holocaust, 1941–1945* (1984); Herbert Feis, *The Spanish Story* (1948); William Langer, *Our Vichy Gamble* (1947); Robert Murphy, *Diplomat Among Warriors* (1964) (Murphy was Eisenhower's representative in North Africa); Milton Viorst, *Hostile Allies: FDR and Charles de Gaulle* (1965); Dorothy Shipley White, *Seeds of Discord: de Gaulle, Free France and the Allies* (1964); and Julian Hurstfield, *America and the French Nation, 1939–1945* (1986). James E. Miller's *The United States and Italy, 1940–1950* (1987) bridges the Second World War and the Cold War.

Intelligence gathering and covert operations attract enormous attention from authors. The literature is of generally low quality, but some of the better are Allen Dulles, *The Secret Surrender* (1966); Bradley F. Smith, *The Shadow Warriors: The OSS and the Origins of the CIA* (1983); R. Harris Smith, *OSS: The Secret History of America's First Central Intelligence Agency* (1972); and Anthony Cave-Brown, *The Last Hero: Wild Bill Donovan* (1983).

The development of strategic bombing, the surrender of Japan, and the use of atomic diplomacy are covered in several works. Start with Michael J. Hogan, ed., *Hiroshima in History and Memory* (1996). Michael Sherry's *The Rise of American Airpower* (1987) is superb. Gar Alperovitz, *Atomic Diplomacy: Hiroshima and Potsdam* (1965), is a revisionist work that argues that an inept Truman used the bomb to frighten the Russians and mask his own inadequate grasp of international relations. Herbert Feis, *The Atomic Bomb and the*

End of World War II (1966), challenges Alperovitz. Martin J. Sherwin's *A World Destroyed: Hiroshima and Its Legacies* (2003) elegantly weaves diplomatic and scientific history and supersedes earlier accounts. Kai Bird and Martin J. Sherwin, *American Prometheus: The Triumph and Tragedy of J. Robert Oppenheimer* (2005) explains the connections of science and poltiics from the 1930s through the 1960s by concentrating on the career of Oppenheimer, the "father of the atomic bomb."

POST–WORLD WAR II AMERICA: GENERAL STUDIES

Several works are useful for treating the post–Second World War period as a coherent whole. Start with James T. Patterson, *Grand Expectations: The United States, 1945–1974* (1996) and his *Restless Giant: The United States from Watergate to Bush v. Gore* (2005). For foreign affairs see Walter LaFeber, *America, Russia, and the Cold War, 1945–2006*, 10th ed. (2006); and John Lewis Gaddis, *The Cold War: A New History* (2006), *The Long Peace* (1987), and *Strategies of Containment* (2005).

Useful recollections and recommendations by participants are George W. Ball, *The Past Has a Different Pattern* (1982), which covers forty years; George F. Kennan, *Memoirs*, 2 vols. (1967, 1972); and J. William Fulbright, *Old Myths and New Realities* (1964) and *The Arrogance of Power* (1966).

The revolutionary effects of nuclear weapons are discussed by Marc Trachtenberg, *History and Strategy* (1991); Alexander George and Richard Smoke, *Deterrence in American Foreign Policy* (1974), a definitive study; Henry A. Kissinger, *Nuclear Weapons and Foreign Policy* (1957), a dated account by an important man; and two splendid surveys by Michael Mandelbaum, *The Nuclear Revolution* (1980) and *The Nuclear Question* (1979).

For the changing international economic environment, see John Mickelthwait and Adrian Wooldrige, *A Future Perfect: The Esssentials of Globalization* (2000); C. Fred Bergsten, *The Dilemmas of the Dollar* (1975); Diane B. Kunz, *Butter and Guns: America's Cold War Economic Diplomacy* (1997); Robert Solomon, *The International Monetary System, 1945–1976* (1976); and Thomas W. Zeiler, *Free Trade Free World: The Advent of GATT* (1999).

THE EARLY COLD WAR, 1945–1952

Detailed works offering contrasting accounts of the origins of the Cold War are, among others, Lloyd C. Gardner, *Architects of Illusion: Men and Ideas in American Foreign Policy, 1941–1949* (1970); John Lewis Gaddis, *The United States and the Origins of the Cold War, 1941–1947* (1972) and his *We Now Know:*

Rethinking Cold War History (1997); Fraser Harburtt's *The Iron Curtain: Churchill, America and the Origins of the Cold War* (1986), which is good on the transatlantic context; Deborah Larsen's *Origins of Containment: A Psychological Explanation* (1985), which breaks new ground; Melvyn P. Leffler, *A Preponderance of Power: National Security, the Truman Administration and the Cold War* (1992) and his *The Specter of Communism: The United States and the Origins of the Cold War, 1917–1953* (1994); Thomas J. McCormick, America's *Half-Century* (1989); Thomas G. Paterson, *Soviet-American Confrontation* (1974); Hugh Thomas, *Armed Truce: The Beginnings of the Cold War, 1945–1947* (1987); and Daniel Yergin, *Shattered Peace: The Cold War and the Origins of the National Security State, 1943–1949* (1978). See also works on World War II.

For the policies and personalities of the Truman administration, see Robert L. Beisner, *Dean Acheson: A Life in the Cold War* (2006); Bruce Kuklick, *Blind Oracles: Intellectuals and War from Kennan to Kissinger* (2006); Aaron Friedberg, *In the Shadow of the Garrison State: America's Anti-Statism and Its Cold War Grand Strategy* (2000); Alonzo Hamby, *Man of the People: A Life of Harry Truman* (1995); Michael J. Hogan, *A Cross of Iron: Harry S Truman and the Origins of the National Security State* (1998); David Mayers, *George Kennan and the Dilemmas of U.S. Foreign Policy* (1988); Wilson D. Miscamble, *George F. Kennan and the Making of American Foreign Policy, 1947–1950* (1991); and Anders Stephenson, *Kennan and the Art of Foreign Policy* (1989).

Accounts of domestic politics, the search for subversives, and the origins of the Cold War are Richard M. Nixon, *Six Crises* (1963); David Oshinsky, *A Conspiracy So Immense: The World of Joe McCarthy* (1983); Ellen Schrecker, *No Ivory Tower: McCarthyism and the Universities* (1986); and Geoffrey Stone, *Perilous Times, Free Speech in Wartime, 1798–2001* (2003).

Atomic issues are treated by Paul Boyer, *By the Bomb's Early Light: American Thought and Culture at the Dawn of the Atomic Age* (1985); Kai Bird and Martin J. Sherwin, *American Prometheus: The Triumph and Tragedy of J. Robert Oppenheimer*; Michael J. Hogan, ed., *Hiroshima in History and Memory* (1996); and Gregg Herkin, *The Winning Weapon: The Atomic Bomb in the Cold War, 1945–1950* (1980).

Studies on U.S. relations with Europe in the Truman administration include Leonard Dinnerstein, *America and the Survivors of the Holocaust* (1982); John Lewis Gaddis, *Strategies of Containment* (2005), a sympathetic exposition of Kennan's thought; Michael J. Hogan, *The Marshall Plan: America, Britain and the Reconstruction of Western Europe, 1947–1952* (1987), which is richly detailed; Robert A. Pollard, *Economic Security and the Origins of the Cold War* (1985), which also treats the Marshall Plan; Jessica C. E. Gienow Hecht, *Transmission Impossible: American Journalism as Cultural Diplomacy in Postwar Germany, 1945–1955* (1999); Lawrence Kaplan, *The United States and NATO: The*

Formative Years (1984); George F. Kennan, *Memoirs*, 2 vols. (1967, 1972); Bruce Kuklick, *American Policy and the Divison of Germany* (1972); Walter Lippmann, *The Cold War* (1947, rev. 1973); Thomas A. Schwartz, *America's Germany: John J. McCloy and the Federal Republic of Germany* (1991); Ronald Steel, *Walter Lippmann and the American Century* (1980); and Lawrence Wittner, *American Intervention in Greece, 1943–1949* (1982).

On the Middle East see the works by Michael Oren, *Power, Faith, and Fantasy* (2007); Michael Cohen, *Truman and Israel* (1990); Bruce Kuniholm, *The Origins of the Cold War in the Near East* (1980); Steven L. Spiegel, *The Other Arab-Israeli Conflict: Making America's Middle East Policy from Truman to Reagan* (1985); and Robert Stookey, *The United States and the Arab States* (1975).

Asian relations from 1945 to 1953 are treated by Nick Cullather, *Illusions of Influence: The Political Economy of United States–Philippines Relations, 1942–1960* (1994); Mark Philip Bradley, *Imagining Vietnam and America: The Making of Postcolonial Vietnam, 1919–1950* (2000); William Border, *The Pacific Alliance: United States Foreign Economic Policy and Japanese Trade Recovery, 1947–1955* (1984); Bruce Cumings, *The Origins of the Korean War*, 2 vols. (1981–1991), which places the conflict in its international setting; Rosemary Foot, *The Wrong War: American Policy and the Dimensions of the Korean Conflict, 1950–1953* (1985), and her *A Substitute for Victory* (1991), based on recently opened archives; Marc S. Gallicchio, *The Cold War Begins in Asia* (1988); Lloyd C. Gardner, *Approaching Vietnam: From World War II Through Dienbienphu, 1941–1954* (1988), a good place to start studying the Vietnam War; Robert J. McMahon, *The Cold War on the Periphery: The United States, India and Pakistan* (1994) and his *The Limits of Empire: The United States and Southeast Asia Since World War II* (1999); Andrew Rotter, *The Path to Vietnam: Origins of American Commitment to Southeast Asia* (1988); John W. Dower, *Embracing Defeat: Japan in the Wake of World War II* (1999), a brilliant work of cultural history; Michael Schaller, *The American Occupation of Japan* (1985) and his *Douglas MacArthur: The Far Eastern General* (1989); and William Stueck, *The Korean War: An International History* (1995).

FROM EISENHOWER'S NEW LOOK TO ESCALATION IN VIETNAM, 1953–1968

The cultural milieu of the Cold War is captured in Elaine Tyler May's *Homeward Bound: American Families in the Cold War Era* (1988). Intellectual aspects of the Cold War appear in Nils Gilman, *Mandarins of the Future: Modernization Theory in Cold War America* (2003), and David Engerman, *Modernization from the Other Shore: American Intellectuals and the Romance of Russian Development* (2003).

Policies and personalities of the Eisenhower era are covered by Stephen E. Ambrose, *Eisenhower*, 2 vols. (1983, 1984); and H. W. Brands, *Cold Warriors: Eisenhower's Generation and American Foreign Policy* (1988) and his *The Specter of Neutralism: The United States and the Emergence of the Third World, 1947–1960* (1989). Richard H. Immerman, *John Foster Dulles: Piety, Pragmatism and Power in U.S. Foreign Policy* (1999) is based on the most recent research. For an analytical discussion of the relationship between strategy and domestic politics, see Aaron Friedberg, *In the Shadow of the Garrison State* (2000), and Robert Bowie and Richard Immerman, *Waging Peace: How Eisenhower Shaped an Enduring Cold War Strategy* (1999). Stephen E. Ambrose's *Nixon*, 3 vols. (1987–1991) contains much material on foreign affairs. John Lewis Gaddis's *The Long Peace* and *Strategies of Containment* contain penetrating essays on Eisenhower's foreign policies.

Defense, nuclear weapons, and scientific policies of the Eisenhower administration appear in Robert Divine, *Blowing on the Wind: The Nuclear Test Ban Debate, 1954–1960* (1979); Samuel Huntington, *The Soldier and the State* (1957) and *The Common Defense* (1961); Edward Kolodziej, *The Uncommon Defense and Congress, 1945–1963* (1966), a response to Huntington; James R. Killian, *Sputnik, Scientists and Eisenhower* (1977); and Warner Schilling, Paul Hammond, and Glenn Snyder, *Strategy, Politics and Defense Budgets* (1962). Michael Beschloss, *Mayday: Eisenhower, Khrushchev and the U-2 Affair* (1986), is a fast-paced account weaving espionage, science, and diplomacy.

Covert operations in Guatemala and Iran are discussed by Odd Arne Westad, *The Global Cold War: Third World Interventions and the Making of Our Times* (2005); Richard H. Immerman, *The CIA in Guatemala: The Foreign Policy of Intervention* (1982); Stephen G. Rabe, *Eisenhower and Latin America: The Foreign Policy of Anticommunism* (1987), discussing the entire hemisphere; Stephen Kinzer, *All the Shah's Men: An American Coup and the Roots of Middle East Terror* (2003), which analyzes the coup in Iran and its larger implications; and Barry Rubin, *Paved with Good Intention: The United States and Iran* (1980).

Relations with the Middle East during Ike's term are explained in Michael B Oren's *Power, Faith, and Fantasy: America in the Middle East* (2007); Peter L. Hahn, *The United States, Great Britain and Egypt, 1945–1956* (1991), and *Caught in the Middle East: U.S. Policy Toward the Arab-Israel Conflict, 1945–1961* (2004); Diane B. Kunz, *The Economic Diplomacy of the Suez Crisis* (1991); Richard E. Neustadt, *Alliance Politics* (1970), a comparison of the Suez affair and the 1962 Skybolt missile controversy; and Hugh Thomas, *The Suez Affair* (1966).

Relations with Asia are discussed in Gordon H. Chang, *Friends and Enemies: The United States, China and the Soviet Union, 1948–1972* (1990); Dennis Merrill, *The United States and India's Economic Development, 1947–1963* (1990); and William O. Walker III, *Opium and Foreign Policy* (1991). On Indochina, see George C. Herring, *America's Longest War: The United States and*

Vietnam, 1950–1975 (1996); Stanley Karnow, *Vietnam: A History* (1991); and Robert D. Schulzinger, *A Time for War: The United States and Vietnam, 1941–1975* (1997).

Detailed works on the first Indochina war include Melanie Billings-Yun, *Decision Against War: Eisenhower and Dienbienphu, 1954* (1988); Bernard Fall, *Street Without Joy* (1972), a vivid description of the fighting, and *Hell in a Very Small Place* (1966), the classic account of Dienbienphu; Melvin Gurtov, *The First Vietnam Crisis, 1953–1954* (1967); and Mark Atwood Lawrence, *Assuming the Burden: Europe and the American Commitment to Vietnam* (2005). Robert F. Randle, *Geneva, 1954* (1969), is the best discussion of the peace conference. The most comprehensive accounts of U.S. policy after Geneva appear in David L. Anderson, *Trapped by Success: The Eisenhower Administration and Vietnam, 1953–1961* (1991), and Seth Jacobs, *America's Miracle Man in South Vietnam: Ngo Diem, Religion, Race, and U.S. Intervention in Southeast Asia* (2004). See also the works listed below on American escalation in Vietnam.

Major figures in the Kennedy and Johnson administrations receive attention from Michael Beschloss, *Kennedy and Khrushchev: The Crisis Years* (1991); James N. Giglio, *The Presidency of John F. Kennedy* (1992); Diane B. Kunz, ed., *The Diplomacy of the Crucial Decade: American Foreign Relations During the 1960s* (1994); Herbert Parmet, *JFK: The Presidency of John F. Kennedy* (1984), based on the documentary record; Thomas Paterson, ed., *Kennedy's Quest for Victory, American Foreign Policy, 1961–1963* (1989); Thomas Schoenbaum, *Waging Peace and War: Dean Rusk in the Truman, Kennedy and Johnson Years* (1988); and Thomas W. Zeiler, *Dean Rusk: Defending the American Mission Abroad* (2000), which places Rusk in the context of Wilsonianism. Kai Bird, *The Color of Truth: McGeorge Bundy and William Bundy, Brothers in Arms* (1998), and Deborah Shapley, *Promise and Power: The Life and Times of Robert McNamara* (1993), are good biographies of important figures. Elizabeth Cobbs Hoffman, *All You Need Is Love: The Peace Corps and the Spirit of the 1960s* (1999), has excellent descriptions. See also David Halberstam, *The Best and the Brightest* (1972), filled with remarkable anecdotes; Roger Hilsman, *To Move a Nation: The Politics of Foreign Policy in the Kennedy Administration* (1964); Theodore Sorensen, Kennedy (1965), by the president's principal speechwriter; Arthur M. Schlesinger, Jr., *A Thousand Days* (1966) and *Robert F. Kennedy and His Times* (1978); Robert Dallek, *An Unfinished Life: John F. Kennedy, 1917–1963* (2004), and *Flawed Giant: Lyndon Johnson and His Times, 1961–1973* (1998); and Randall Bennett Woods, *Fulbright: A Biography* (1995), and *LBJ: Architect of American Ambition* (2006). Thomas W. Zeiler, *American Trade and Power in the 1960s* (1992), subtly discusses economic diplomacy.

For relations with Latin America, see Odd Arne Westad, *The Global Cold War,* (2003); Gilderhus, *The Second Century* Mark T. (2000); Gaddis Smith, *The Last Years of the Monroe Doctrine* (1994); and Bavid F. Schmitz, *Thank God They're on Our Side* (1999). For Cuba, see Thomas G. Paterson, *Contesting Castro: The United States and the Triumph of the Cuban Revolution* (1994); Trumbull Higgins, *The Perfect Failure: Kennedy, Eisenhower and the Bay of Pigs* (1987); Wayne S. Smith, *The Closest of Enemies: A Personal and Diplomatic History of the Castro Years* (1987); Richard E. Welch, *Response to Revolution: The United States and the Cuban Revolution, 1959–1961* (1985); and Peter Wyden, *Bay of Pigs* (1979). On the intervention in the Dominican Republic, see Piero Gleijeses's brilliant *The Dominican Crisis* (1978); Abraham Lowenthal, *The Dominican Intervention* (1972); and Jerome Slater, *Intervention and Negotiation: The United States and the Dominican Revolution* (1970).

On the Cuban missile crisis and its effects on relations with the Soviet Union and the NATO allies, see Graham Allison and Philip Zelikow, *Essence of Decision: Explaining the Cuban Missile Crisis* (1997), which applies theories of bureaucratic politics; Ernest R. May and Philip Zelikow, *The Kennedy Tapes: Inside the White House During the Cuban Missile Crisis* (1997) shows the president's command of the process. Irving Janis, *Victims of Groupthink* (1972), awards Kennedy high marks; and John Newhouse, *De Gaulle and the Anglo Saxons* (1971), explains the French leader's distress at his exclusion from great events. Edward Kolodziej's *The Politics of Grandeur* (1975) is the best account of French foreign policy under de Gaulle and Pompidou. On the Middle East see Warren Bass, *Support Any Friend: Kennedy's Middle East and the Making of the U.S.-Israel Alliance* (2003), and Michael B. Oren, *Six Days of War: June 1967 and the Making of the Modern Middle East* (2002).

The Americanization of the War in Vietnam from 1961 to 1968 has generated a large and growing literature. Start with the books by George Herring, Stanley Karnow, and Robert D. Schulzinger already mentioned. See George McT. Kahin, *Intervention: How America Became Involved in Vietnam* (1986), and contrast it with Larry Berman, *Planning a Tragedy: The Americanization of the War in Vietnam* (1983), and Fredrik Logevall, *Choosing War: The Last Chance for Peace and the Escalation of the Vietnam War* (1999). R. B. Smith, *An International History of the Vietnam War*, 3 vols. (1983–1991), treats the subject from an international perspective. Gabriel Kolko, *Anatomy of a War: Vietnam, the United States and the Modern Historical Experience* (1986), places the war in a revolutionary context. Other good general accounts are by James P. Harrison, *The Endless War: Vietnam's Struggle for Independence* (1989), and Marilyn B. Young, *The Vietnam Wars* (1990).

Significant episodes and personalities in the war are covered by Andrew Preston, *The War Council: McGeorge Bundy, the NSC, and Vietnam* (2006), and Ellen J. Hammer, *A Death in November: America in Vietnam, 1963* (1987), which discusses the overthrow of Diem. An American soldier's story appears in Neil Sheehan, *A Bright Shining Lie: John Paul Vann and America in Vietnam* (1988). William C. Berman describes how a senator came to oppose the war in *William*

Fulbright and the Vietnam War (1988). David L. DiLeo's *George Ball, Vietnam and the Rethinking of Containment* (1991) analyzes the activities of a dissenter. Seymour Hersh, *My Lai 4* (1970), describes the massacre. Don Oberdorfer's *Tet* (1971) is an eyewitness report.

For domestic consequences of the war, look at Lawrence Baskir and Peter Strauss, *Chance and Circumstance: The War, the Draft and the Vietnam Generation* (1978). Charles DeBendedetti with Charles Chatfield, *An American Ordeal: The Antiwar Movement of the Vietnam Era* (1990), is encyclopedic. See also Tom Wells, *The War Within: America's Battle over Vietnam* (1994).

FROM DÉTENTE TO THE POST–COLD WAR WORLD, 1969–2001

The best overviews of the years since 1969 appear in John Lewis Gaddis, *The United States and the End of the Cold War* (1992), and Raymond L. Garthoff, *Detente and Confrontation: American-Soviet Relations from Nixon to Reagan* (1994). Melvin Small, *The Presidency of Richard Nixon* (1999); William Bundy, *A Tangled Web: The Making of Foreign Policy in the Nixon Presidency* (1998); and Jeremi Suri, *Power and Protest: Global Revolution and the Rise of Détente* (2003) are based on the widest range of sources. For memoirs of the Nixon and Ford administrations, consult Richard Nixon, *RN: The Memoirs of Richard Nixon* (1977), and Gerald R. Ford, *A Time to Heal: The Autobiography of Gerald R. Ford* (1978). On Henry Kissinger consult his own story in his memoirs, *White House Years* (1979), *Years of Upheaval* (1982), and *Years of Renewal* (1999). Studies of Kissinger include Robert Dallek, *Nixon and Kissinger: Partners in Power* (2007); Jussi Hahnimaki, *The Flawed Architect: Henry Kissinger and American Foreign Policy* (2004); and Jeremi Suri, *Henry Kissinger and the American Century* (2007).

For changes in the international economic environment, see works listed at the beginning of the section on the post–World War II period. See also Paul Kennedy, *The Rise and Fall of the Great Powers* (1987), and Clyde V. Prestowitz, Jr., *Trading Places: How We Allowed Japan To Take the Lead* (1988).

On strategic arms negotiations and conventional arms sales, see Raymond Garthoff, *Detente and Confrontation* (1992); Gerard Smith, *Doubletalk: The Story of the First Strategic Arms Limitation Talks* (1980); and Andrew Pierre, *The Global Politics of Arms Sales* (1982).

On covert activities in the Nixon and Ford administrations, see Odd Arne Westad, *The Global Cold War* (2005); Thomas Powers, *The Man Who Kept the Secrets: Richard Helms and the CIA* (1979); and J. Anthony Lukas, *Nightmare: The Underside of the Nixon Administration* (1976). John Stockwell, *In Search of Enemies* (1979), explains CIA actions in Angola. John Dinges and Saul Landau, *Assassination on Embassy Row* (1980), reveals covert activities by Chileans in the United States.

The end of the war in Vietnam is discussed by the general works on the Nixon and Ford administrations. Consult the bibliography in George Herring's *America's Longest War* and Robert D. Schulzinger's *A Time for War*. See also William Shawcross, *Sideshow: Kissinger, Nixon and the Destruction of Cambodia* (1979); Arnold R. Isaacs, *Without Honor: Defeat in Vietnam and Cambodia* (1983); Nguyen Tien Hung and Jerrold Schechter, *The Palace File* (1986), which argues that the United States betrayed Saigon after 1973; and Robert Shaplen, *Bitter Victory* (1986), an incisive journalist's account of the postwar world. The Nixon administration's treatment of the antiwar movement receives good coverage in Melvin Small, *Johnson, Nixon and the Doves* (1988). Read Robert D. Schulzinger, *A Time for Peace: The Legacy of the Vietnam War* (2006) for the effect of the war on subsequent U.S. foreign policy, politics, and culture.

For China read Evelyn Goh, *Constructing the U.S. Rapprochement with China, 1961–1974: From "Red Menace" to Tacit Ally* (2005), and Margaret MacMillan, *Nixon and Mao: The Week That Changed the World* (2007).

For the Middle East after 1977, see Michael Oren, *Power, Faith and Fantasy: America in the Middle East (2007)*; William Quandt's *Decade of Decision* (1978); and Steven L. Spiegel, *The Other Arab-Israeli Conflict: The Making of America's Middle East Policy from Truman to Reagan* (1985), both of which discuss the Arab-Israeli conflict. James Bill, *The Eagle and the Lion* (1988), has useful information on the growth of Washington's commitment to the shah of Iran.

For foreign policy in the Carter administration, start with Burton I. Kaufman, *The Presidency of James E. Carter, Jr.* (1993), and Gaddis Smith, *Morality, Reason and Power: American Diplomacy in the Carter Years* (1986). Consult the memoirs by the principals: Jimmy Carter, *Keeping Faith* (1982); Zbigniew Brzezinski, *Power and Principle* (1983); and Cyrus Vance, *Hard Choices* (1983). Human rights are covered by Sandra Vogelsgesang, *American Dream, Global Nightmare* (1980). Immigration and refugee issues are covered in Gil Loescher and John Scanlan, *Calculated Kindness* (1986), and David Reimers, *Still the Golden Door: The Third World Comes to America* (1992).

For relations with Central America, consult William M. LeoGrande, *Our Own Backyard: The United States in Central America, 1977–1992* (1999). On Nicaragua, see Robert Pastor, *Condemned to Repetition: The United States and Nicaragua* (1987), and Anthony Lake, *Samoza Falling* (1989).

Arms control and defense policies are covered in Raymond Garthoff, *Detente and Confrontation*, previously mentioned; and Michael Krepon, *Strategic Stalemate: Nuclear Weapons and Arms Control in American Politics* (1984).

For the Camp David accords, look at William B. Quandt, *Camp David: Peacemaking and Politics* (1986), and memoirs by participants: Ezer Weizman, *The Road to Peace* (1980); Moshe Dayan, *Breakthrough* (1981); and Anwar Sadat, *In Search of Identity* (1980).

For Iran consult David Farber, *Taken Hostage: The Iran Hostage Crisis and America's First Encounter with Radical Islam* (2006); Barry Rubin, *Paved with Good Intentions: The United States and Iran* (1980); and Gary Sick, *All Fall Down: America's Tragic Encounter with Iran* (1986), the story as seen by the Carter administration's expert on Iran at the National Security Council.

On the conservative counterattack in the 1980 election, consult Michael Schaller, *Right Turn: America in the Reagan-Bush Years, 1980-1992* (2007).

The literature on the Reagan administration already is large. Start with Lou Cannon, *President Reagan: The Role of a Lifetime* (1991); Frances Fitzgerald, *Way Out There in the Blue: Reagan, Star Wars and the End of the Cold War* (2000); and Raymond Garthoff, *The Great Transition: American–Russian Relations and the End of the Cold War* (1994).

The memoirs of the Reagan years contain useful information on foreign affairs. See Alexander Haig, *Caveat: Reagan, Realism and Foreign Policy* (1984); Constantine Menges, *Inside the National Security Council* (1988); Donald Regan, *For the Record* (1988); George P. Shultz, *Turmoil and Triumph* (1993); Larry Speakes, *Speaking Out* (1988); and Caspar Weinberger, *Fighting for Peace: Seven Critical Years at the Pentagon* (1991).

Covert operations and the Iran-contra affair receive treatment in Theodore Draper, *A Very Thin Line: The Iran-Contra Affairs* (1991); John Tower et al., *The Tower Commission Report* (1987); and Bob Woodward, *Veil* (1987).

On the Reagan administration's Central American policy, see William LeoGrande, *Our Own Backyard*, previously mentioned, and Robert Pastor, *Condemned to Repetition*, previously mentioned.

On the Middle East, refer to Spiegel's *The Other Arab-Israeli Conflict*, noted above; Wolf Blitzer, *Between Washington and Jerusalem* (1985); Itamar Rabinovich, *The War for Lebanon, 1970–1983* (1984); and Avner Yaniv, *Dilemmas of Security: Politics, Strategy and the Israeli Experience in Lebanon* (1987).

The profound changes in world politics since 1989 are covered in Michael Beschloss and Strobe Talbott, *At the Highest Levels* (1993), and Michael Hogan, ed., *The End of the Cold War* (1992). Discussions of post–Cold War issues appear in Richard Benedick, *Ozone Diplomacy: New Directions for Saving the Planet* (1991); Paul Kennedy, *Preparing for the Next Century* (1993); and Misha Glenny, *The Fall of Yugoslavia* (1992). For information on the first Bush administration, see Raymond Garthoff's *The Great Transition*, cited above. The principals have written useful memoirs. See George Bush and Brent Scowcroft, *A World Transformed* (1998), and James A. Baker, *The Politics of Diplomacy: Revolution, War and Peace, 1989–1992* (1995). Philip Zelikow and Condoleezza Rice, *Germany Unified and Europe Transformed* (1995), is an insiders' account of the end of the Cold War in Europe based on documentary evidence. Bruce Jentleson, *With Friends Like These: Reagan, Bush and Saddam* (1994), and Bob Woodward *The Commanders* (1991), discuss the wars in the Persian Gulf and Panama.

A substantial body of literature on the Clinton administration has appeared. Consult Madeleine Albright, *Madame Secretary* (2003); Bill Clinton, *My Life* (2004); John F. Harris, *The Survivor: Bill Clinton in the White House* (2005); William Hyland, *Clinton's World: Remaking American Foreign Policy* (1999); and Thomas Lippman, *Madeleine Albright and the New American Diplomacy* (2000). Case studies are Lester H. Brune, *The United States and Post–Cold War Interventions: Bush and Clinton in Somalia, Haiti and Bosnia, 1992–1998* (1998); Stephen Cohen, *Failed Crusade: America and the Tragedy of Post Communist Russia* (2000); Ivo H. Daalder, *Getting to Dayton: The Making of America's Bosnia Policy* (2000); Ivo H. Daalder and Michael E. O'Hanlon, *Winning Ugly: NATO's War to Save Kosovo* (2000); Richard Holbrooke, *To End a War* (1998), his memoir of the Dayton process; Michael Ignatieff, *Virtual War: Kosovo and Beyond* (2000); Robert S. Litwak, *Rogue States and U.S. Foreign Policy: Containment After the Cold War* (2000); Samantha Power, *"A Problem from Hell": America and the Age of Genocide* (2002); and Dennis Ross, *The Missing Peace: The Inside Story of the Search for Middle East Peace* (2004).

For U.S. foreign policy after September 11, 2001, consult *The 9/11 Commission Report* (2003); Richard A. Clarke, *Against All Enemies: Inside America's War on Terror* (2004); James Mann, *The Rise of the Vulcans: The History of Bush's War Cabinet* (2004); Lawrence Wright, *Al Qaeda and the Road to 9/11* (2006); Thomas Ricks, *Fiasco: The American Military Adventure in Iraq* (2006); Ron Suskind, *The One Percent Doctrine: Deep Inside America's Pursuit of Its Enemies since 9/11* (2006); Bob Woodward, *Bush at War* (2002), *Plan of Attack* (2004), and *State of Denial: Bush at War, Part III* (2006); Michael Isikoff and David Corn, *Hubris: The Inside Story of Spin, Scandal, and the Selling of the Iraq War* (2006); and Rajiv Chandrasekaran, *Imperial Life in the Emerald City: Inside Iraq's Green Zone* (2006).

Index

Page numbers in **bold** refer to maps, photographs, and tables.